Critical Multiculturalism:
Rethinking Multicultural and Antiracist Education

Edited by

Stephen May

UK Falmer Press, 1 Gunpowder Square, London, EC4A 3DE
USA Falmer Press, 325 Chestnut Street, 8th Floor, Philadelphia, PA 19106

First published in 1999

**A catalogue record for this book is available from the British
Library**

ISBN 0 7507 0768 2 cased
ISBN 0 7507 0767 4 paper

**Library of Congress Cataloging-in-Publication Data are available
on request**

Jacket design by Caroline Archer

Typeset in 10/12pt Mono Bembo by
Graphicraft Limited, Hong Kong

*Printed in Great Britain by Biddles Ltd., Guildford and King's Lynn on paper
which has a specified pH value on final paper manufacture of not less than 7.5
and is therefore 'acid free'.*

Contents

Contents

FOR PROFESSOR BARRY TROYNA
1951–1996

List of Tables and Figures

Preface

The catalyst for this volume was a 1993 book review in *New Community* by Barry Troyna. In that review, he compared two recent edited collections on multicultural education — one from Britain and one from the US — and made the comment that, given their differing national concerns and trajectories, each would have benefited considerably from knowledge of the other. As he concluded, 'the need for dialogue between the two is plain for all to see' (1993, p. 372).

As it happened, this was something which I had actually been thinking about for some time. I had already attempted to reconcile debates on multiculturalism on both sides of the Atlantic in my own work on multicultural education in New Zealand. This view was reinforced on my subsequent arrival in Britain in 1993. It was clear to me then, as now, that the unhelpful dichotomization of multicultural and antiracist education throughout the 1980s in Britain still lingered on. It was equally clear to me that a necessary and long overdue *rapprochement* between British multiculturalists and antiracists could be facilitated by a greater understanding of North American debates around multiculturalism and critical pedagogy. Barry Troyna's review prompted me to action, and this, some five years later, is the result.

Fittingly then, this collection is dedicated to Barry. I am only sorry that he is not here to see it. His untimely death from cancer in February 1996 was a personal and professional loss to many, myself included. As a committed antiracist in the British tradition, there is no doubt much in here with which he would have disagreed. He was sceptical to the end about the value of multiculturalism and its potential reconcilement with antiracism. However, he also shared a great deal of common ground with the particular interests and concerns of this volume. His work (and his life) was characterized by a passionate and unshakeable commitment to social justice in general and to antiracism in particular — a commitment that was grounded in the experiences of his own working-class Jewish childhood in North London. He was especially concerned that the academic pursuit of antiracism was always linked to, and outworked in educational policy and practice — that it actually made a difference for students. And, as his many collaborators over the years will attest, he demonstrated in his own work the merits of an inclusive and democratic approach to research practice. The absence of his eloquent, impassioned, and often good humoured perspective remains a significant and still tangible loss.

In addition, thanks are due to the many who helped me to see this project to its eventual (and belated) conclusion. To my fellow contributors for agreeing to participate, for putting up with my harrying, and for getting there in the end. To first Malcolm Clarkson, and then (upon Malcolm's retirement) Anna Clarkson at Falmer Press for their encouragement and, most of all, patience with regard to the inevitable delays and crises that accompany an edited collection. To my colleagues in the sociology department at Bristol who provide such an enjoyable environment in which to work. And finally, to the two real loves of my life — Janet, my wife, and Ella, our baby daughter — without whom this project, and many more things besides, would not have been possible.

Reference

TROYNA, B. (1993) Leicester, M. and Taylor, M. (eds) *Ethics, Ethnicity and Education* (London: Kogan Page, 1992) and Grant, C. (ed.) *Research and Multicultural Education: From the Margins to the Mainstream* (Basingstoke, England; Falmer Press, 1992), *New Community*, **19**, pp. 372–3.

Stephen May
University of Bristol
August, 1998

Introduction: Towards Critical Multiculturalism

Stephen May

Over the years, multicultural education has promised much and delivered little. Since its popularization in the late 1960s and early 1970s, proponents have argued that multicultural education, and the associated notion of cultural pluralism, can accomplish all manner of things. A central claim has been that multicultural education can foster greater cultural interaction, interchange and harmony, both in schools and beyond. It has also regularly been touted as the best educational means of addressing and redressing long-standing patterns of differential achievement for minority students. The result has been a proliferating academic debate on multiculturalism over the last 30 years and a burgeoning multicultural education industry in curricular and resource development (although, as we shall see, the two have seldom actually informed each other).

However, these debates about multicultural education, and the industry it has spawned, have also been characterized by a depressing disjuncture between their vaulting, high minded ambitions and the ongoing reality of school life for minority (and majority) students. In short, multicultural education has had a largely negligible impact to date on the life *chances* of minority students, the racialized attitudes of majority students, the inherent monoculturalism of school practice, and the wider processes of power relations and inequality which underpin all these. So much for that then — or, at least, so it would seem.

But recent trends suggest that we may be turning a corner. Multicultural education may finally be about to realize its potential and, along with it, fulfil the hopes and expectations of its many proponents. And not before time. Necessarily, much has changed — and has had to change — for this long-held possibility to regain any credibility after so many decades of disappointment. In the process, the very focus and parameters of the debate have been recast, and many of the perceived weaknesses of past approaches to multicultural education have been, or are now being addressed.

I do not want to rehearse at length here an already voluminous literature on the merits and demerits of past multicultural education theory and practice (see May, 1994a). Nonetheless, it is important to point out, however briefly, the key issues which the theory and practice of multicultural education are currently facing. This is necessary not only because these issues feature so prominently in what follows but also, and perhaps more importantly, because in the light of them we need to consider and articulate how we might move forward — how we might realize the possibilities of multiculturalism more effectively. This latter end is the central aim of this present volume.

Racism

A key weakness historically of multicultural education theory and practice has been an overemphasis on the significance of curricular change and an underemphasis, and at times disavowal, of the impact of structural racism on students' lives. In effect, multiculturalists have been charged with an overoptimistic view of the impact of the multicultural curriculum on the social and economic futures of minority students. Concomitantly, multicultural education has been criticized for a simplistic and naive view of wider social and cultural power relations. Principal among its critics in this regard have been British antiracist educators. Such critics, notably the late Barry Troyna, have argued that multiculturalism is an irredeemably 'deracialized' discourse of schooling; an educational approach which reifies culture and cultural difference, and which fails to address the central issue of racism within society. Little wonder, antiracists have argued, that multicultural education has failed to ameliorate, let alone contest, the wider patterns of racial discrimination and disadvantage faced by minority students.

Antiracists, in contrast, have made this their central concern. In a series of provocative and thoughtful publications, proponents have developed a critical perspective of schooling within the broader framework of contemporary 'race relations' and have advocated a form of political education which directly addresses the impact of racism on students' lives (see, for example, Brandt, 1986; Gillborn, 1990, 1995; Troyna, 1987, 1993; Troyna and Hatcher, 1992). While this movement has been dominated by British commentators — a result of its origins as a neo-Marxist critique of British multiculturalism — it has also been articulated in the United States by the likes of Michael Apple, David Theo Goldberg and Cameron McCarthy (see Apple, 1986, 1996; Goldberg, 1994; McCarthy, 1990; McCarthy and Crichlow, 1993), in Canada by George Dei (1996) and Roxana Ng (1993, 1995), and in Australia by Fazal Rizvi (1991, 1993).

Notwithstanding the particularly vituperative nature of the multicultural/antiracist debates in Britain — a feature to which I will return below — the antiracist critique has led to the development of a more critical conception of multicultural education theory and practice. In so doing, attention has shifted away in more critical multiculturalist accounts from the earlier — and implicitly pathological — preoccupation with ethnic minority educational achievement. Instead, broader structural questions of racism and disadvantage have come to be directly addressed, as well as questions concerning how to include majority as well as minority students in educating for a multicultural society (see, for example, May, 1994a; Nieto, 1996).

Identities

But antiracism has also had particular problems of its own. Leaving aside the inevitable antipathy of the Right to antiracist principles, the privileging of racism over other forms of inequality in early articulations of antiracist education has resulted in a preoccupation with 'colour racism' and the black–white dichotomy. This has led critics on the Left to suggest that antiracism adopts a 'grand theory' approach which, in attributing racism as the primary modality in intercultural relations, is both reductive and essentialist (see Donald and Rattansi 1992; MacDonald *et al.*, 1989: Modood, 1992, 1998). Such an approach subsumes other factors such as class, religion and gender, and fails to address adequately postmodern accounts of identity as multiple, contingent, and subject to rapid change (Gilroy, 1992; Hall, 1992; Rattansi, 1992, this volume).

The unwillingness of antiracists to incorporate a culturalist approach — a legacy of their rejection of all things multicultural — has also meant that they have been unable to address the impact of 'new racist' discourses and their largely culturalist and nationalist emphases (Barker, 1981; Small, 1994; Wetherell and Potter, 1992). In effect, the monistic conception of black–white relations adopted by many antiracists has proved inadequate in addressing new, multiple racisms and the particular historical and contextual dimensions which underpin them (cf. May; McLaren and Torres; Rattansi; Short and Carrington, this volume).

In many ways, this has been a peculiarly British problem; a product of the initial dichotomization of multicultural and antiracist education there — principally, by antiracist proponents — and the entrenched positions which resulted. Indeed, it has only been recently that British antiracists have sought some accommodation with multiculturalism, albeit still somewhat cautiously, in order to adopt a more contingent, situational account of racism, ethnicity and culture (see Gillborn, 1995). In the United States, the significant influence of critical pedagogy — articulated most prominently through the writings of Paolo Freire, and adherents like Henry Giroux and Peter McLaren — has provided a radical, antiracist conception of multiculturalism which has largely avoided the reductionisms and oversimplifications apparent in British antiracism. Moreover, multiculturalism in the US, as elsewhere, has faced criticism principally from reactionary commentators, thus facilitating the development of a broad radical democratic alliance of antiracist/multicultural educators (see Sleeter, 1995). Again, this is only just beginning to occur in Britain.

That said, the historical significance of slavery in the US has meant that the racialization of black–white relations has remained a prominent, perhaps defining feature of discussions around racism, disadvantage and minority rights there (Kymlicka, 1989). Consequently, the actual notion of 'race' has an ongoing valency in the US — both in public policy and within academic debates — which tends to undermine the problematic and contested nature of the concept. 'Race' is also, as a consequence, frequently elided with ethnicity and culture in US debates. This has created difficulties of translation between debates on 'race' and racism in the US and elsewhere; a point highlighted by Caddick (1996) in her searing critique of McCarthy and Crichlow (1993). It also has important implications for terminology which I will discuss further below.

Capitalism, Globalization and the Nation-state

The influence of critical pedagogy is also prominent in recent developments linking multicultural education with wider issues of socio-economic and political inequality. The ongoing ravages of late capitalism — particularly on the poor and the marginalized

— are increasingly being addressed and contested by critical multicultural educators, again most notably in the US (see Giroux, 1997; Kincheloe and Steinberg, 1997; Kozol, 1991; McLaren, 1995, 1997; McLaren and Torres, this volume). In the process, the inexorable globalization of capital, its effects on the economies of nation-states, its links with historical and contemporary forms of racism and colonialism, and its impact on the changing nature of work and patterns of employment are also being critically examined (see also Kalantzis and Cope, this volume).

In a parallel development, political issues surrounding the current organization of modern nation-states have likewise been brought into question (see May, 1999, this volume). This includes a critique of the differential apportionment of social and political access and power among different ethnic, cultural and social groups within the nation-state, and the reflection of these disparities, at least in part, in the cultural and linguistic hegemonies which underpin its public sphere. This critique links multicultural/antiracist education to debates in sociology and political theory concerning the historical constructedness of modern nation-states, the central roles of language and education in establishing and maintaining a 'common' civic culture, and the more pluralized alternatives that a politics of multiculturalism implies. Central here are questions to do with the *public* representation of minorities within the civic realm, and related arguments surrounding the balance between the need to maintain a common culture and language on the one hand, and to recognize and accommodate for cultural and linguistic pluralism on the other.

These broader debates — both with respect to the reach and effects of capitalism, and to questions surrounding the pluralization of the public sphere of the nation-state — have also highlighted the processes by which dominant forms of ethnicity are made 'invisible' in discussions of multiculturalism. The growing analysis of 'whiteness' — which explores the political, social, and historical *situatedness* of white ethnicities, and the hegemonic processes which lead to their universalization and normalization — is a recent and welcome product of these discussions (see, for example, Bonnett, 1993, 1996; Frankenberg, 1993; McLaren, 1997; McLaren and Torres, this volume; Roediger, 1992, 1994).

Theory, Policy and Practice

A further long-standing criticism of multicultural and antiracist education has been an inability to link effectively theory, policy and practice. Moreover, this criticism has particular purchase for more critical multicultural/antiracist conceptions. While rightly highlighting the theoretical naivety of early forms of multicultural education, critical educators have in turn been pilloried for an inability to relate the critical theory they espouse to actual multicultural policy and practice. Multicultural education may historically have been under-theorized, and at times simply wrongly theorized, but at least it could be applied programmatically in schools. Too often, the concerns of critical educators have been largely ignored because they have presented as theory divorced from practice; a concern of radical academics with little immediate relevance to either policy makers or practitioners.

In this respect, Barry Troyna has conceded that early conceptions of British antiracism ended up being 'little more than an exercise in left-wing gesture politics' (1993, p. 42). Likewise, critical educators in the US have themselves been criticized for pointing out at length the travails of a racist, undemocratic education system without offering much in the way of viable, implementable alternatives at the level of the school. After all, it is one thing to proclaim that the world needs to be changed, it is quite another to provide concrete ways by which we might begin the process (Caddick, 1996; cf. Moodley; Rattansi, this volume).

National Limits

Another issue currently being addressed is the extent to which debates around multicultural/antiracist education have been hermetically sealed within national boundaries. The majority of published material in the field is directed almost solely to national markets with their own particular historical and ideological emphases. Little, if any, reference is made to developments elsewhere and attempts to build a cross-national perspective have been extremely rare (for some notable exceptions, see Banks and Lynch, 1986; May, 1994a; Modgil *et al.*, 1986; Moodley, 1992).

This tendency to national insularity, while understandable, has had a number of unfortunate consequences. Most notable among them, perhaps, has been the disparate and uneven development of multicultural/antiracist theory. For example, I have argued elsewhere (see May, 1994a, b) that the parochial and oppositional nature of the UK debate between multiculturalists and antiracists could have benefited much earlier from an awareness of developments in the US around critical pedagogy. Likewise, the British antiracist critique has, until recently (cf. Sleeter, 1995), seldom been acknowledged or addressed in US debates on multiculturalism.

Similarly, debates in Britain and continental Europe on 'race' and racism (see, for example, Balibar and Wallerstein, 1991; Fenton, 1999; Miles, 1989, 1993; Rattansi and Westwood, 1994) provide a useful means by which to deconstruct the continued unproblematic use of 'race' as an ontological category in academic and policy discussions in the US. Again, this is only just beginning to occur (see McLaren and Torres, this volume; Miles and Torres, 1996).

Outline

Given the various issues highlighted above, this volume aims to bring together, for the first time, leading exponents of critical multicultural education from around the world. While much of this introduction has focused on the British/US nexus, the volume also includes contributors from Australia (Kalantzis and Cope), Canada (Hodson, Moodley), New Zealand (May) and South Africa (Carrim and Soudien). Their contributions provide an understanding of the national contexts in which they work but also add significantly to the broader theoretical, policy and pedagogical debates outlined above. Contributions are by no means monological. Some contributions are avowedly more postmodern than others, and one contribution (Carrim and

Soudien) continues to work within a reconstructed antiracist tradition rather than a critical multicultural one. Instead, the aim has been to provide a cross-national *dialectic* between critical multicultural and antiracist educators that critically engages with, and to some extent summarizes the latest thinking on critical multiculturalism.

A problem that quickly emerges though with any cross-national volume is the widely differing use of terminology from one context to the next. Where I can, I have regularized this as much as possible — particularly, with regard to consistently highlighting the problematic nature of the term 'race'. However, I have retained terms which have a clear salience in particular national contexts — notably, 'people of colour' in North American discourse — so as not to perpetuate a hegemonic discourse of my own.

More seriously, any volume which lays claim to international(ist) pretensions faces the key questions of representation and coverage. In this respect, I acknowledge that contributors to this volume are still principally drawn from the so called 'First World'. Indeed, academic debates about multicultural education continue to be preoccupied principally with its implications for 'developed', western nation-states. Thus, while this volume does attempt a more internationalist perspective, it must also be seen as only a limited beginning in this direction.

A related criticism here is a tendency to ignore in debates on multiculturalism the voices and concerns of indigenous peoples. Seldom in US and Canadian literature on multicultural education, for example, are Native Americans and/or Inuit acknowledged, let alone discussed (although see Moodley, this volume). Likewise, multicultural educational initiatives in New Zealand and Australia are often criticized by Maori and Aboriginal peoples respectively for failing to acknowledge their *bicultural* rights as indigenous peoples and the specificities of their historical subjugation, colonization and even, at times, genocide, *within their own country* (see Caddick, 1996; Hodson, this volume; May, 1998a, b). These omissions have to do with the elision in much social, political and educational discourse between polyethnic rights and multinational rights (see Kymlicka, 1995a, 1995b; May, 1999; Shapiro and Kymlicka, 1997).[1] There is neither the space nor the opportunity to discuss this distinction further here. However, the hope is that some day soon discussions of multicultural/antiracist education will do so as a matter of course.

As for the integration of theory, policy and practice, I have dispensed with the practice — almost *de rigueur* these days — of compartmentalizing what follows into 'theoretical', 'policy' and 'pedagogical' sections. *All* chapters in the volume explore these concerns — and, more importantly, their interconnections — although, inevitably, the emphases and foci of particular chapters will differ.

The first three chapters (May; McLaren and Torres; Rattansi) concentrate on broader theoretical concerns arising from recent developments in critical multiculturalism, particularly with respect to the various challenges that postmodernism presents. Stephen May examines the question of cultural differences in multiculturalism and the central problematic of how to recognize such differences without essentializing them. In so doing, he critically evaluates both conservative and postmodern critiques of multiculturalism. Peter McLaren and Rodolfo Torres examine the problematic nature of 'race' as a concept, the relative absence of discussions of capitalism and class in much multicultural literature, and the issues and implications that surround the nascent academic analysis of whiteness. Ali Rattansi explores the implications for antiracist initiatives — both within education and beyond it — of postmodern conceptions of identity and difference. For Rattansi, antiracism must centrally include an understanding of the multiplicity of racisms, and its complex and, at times, contradictory articulation with other forms of identity, discrimination and inequality. All three contributors conclude with discussion of how their conceptions of critical multiculturalism can be applied to pedagogy and practice.

Chapters 4–8 (Sleeter and Montecinos; Moodley; Carrim and Soudien; Short and Carrington; Nieto) explore the possibilities and limitations of multicultural/ antiracist educational theory and practice in different national contexts, while also drawing on empirical data. Christine Sleeter and Carmen Montecinos examine differing approaches to multicultural teacher education in the US, with a specific emphasis on the link between teacher training and community involvement, thus highlighting an important area of educational activity that is often overlooked in the preoccupation with schools. Kogila Moodley assesses the impact of racism, and the efficacy of various approaches to antiracism in Canadian schools, with particular reference to the responses of students and teachers. Nazir Carrim and Crain Soudien outline the limitations of multicultural education initiatives in post-apartheid South Africa, particularly in formerly racially segregated schools, and instead advocate the development of a critical antiracism. Geoffrey Short and Bruce Carrington compare and contrast perceptions of national identity among primary (elementary) school children in Britain and the USA, and examine these responses in light of the articulation of new, cultural forms of racism. The emphasis on students — a surprising omission in much multicultural education literature — is furthered by Sonia Nieto's chapter. She discusses the implications for critical multiculturalism of the educational experiences of two US minority students — one African-American, one Chicano. The voices of these students provide a powerful reminder of just what is at stake personally in educational debates on multiculturalism.

The final two chapters (Hodson; Kalantzis and Cope) explore specific pedagogical implications with respect to critical multiculturalism. Derek Hodson outlines what a critical multiculturalist conception of science and technology teaching and learning might entail; a conception that includes deconstructing the hegemonic imperatives underlying common articulations of science and (re)politicizing science and science education to more socially just ends. Mary Kalantzis and Bill Cope explore pedagogical debates surrounding traditional, progressive and critical approaches to educating for diversity. Returning to some of the themes in the second chapter by McLaren and Torres, they argue that in these times of fast capitalism and the rapid reconfiguration of nation-states, a reconceived multiculturalism is, or at least should be, critical to the education of majorities as well as minorities — that is, that it should be central to *all* educational activity. They illustrate how such an enterprise might be operationalized with respect to the teaching of literacy.

To conclude, the following contributions represent the cutting edge of the theory and practice of multicultural education. Critical multiculturalism, as it is broadly articulated here, incorporates postmodern conceptions and analyses of culture and identity, while holding onto the possibility of an emancipatory politics. It specifically combines multicultural/antiracist theoretical streams which have, for too long, 'talked past each other'. It emphasizes the crucial links between theory, policy and practice, providing a critical and practical account of culturally pluralist forms of schooling. And finally, it lends itself to the possibilities of a cross-national dialogue in which the differing theoretical and practical concerns of a variety of national contexts can be reflectively and reflexively explored.

In developing this critical multiculturalist position, contributors to the volume also clearly acknowledge the limits of education — in the end, education cannot compensate for society, nor should it be asked to. However, the critical multicultural/ antiracist endeavours outlined here offer a crucial doorway of hope. This hope is a simple one — that in these increasingly dyspeptic times of fast capitalism, proliferating racisms, political, social and cultural oppressions, and the continued evisceration of the poor and disenfranchised, a radical educational politics of social justice, antiracism, and democracy can still somehow, and against the odds, make a difference.

Note

1 'Polyethnicity' refers to the fact that modern nation-states increasingly comprise a variety of minority ethnic groups, usually as a result of migration. The USA is perhaps the clearest example of a polyethnic state in this regard. However, the concept of polyethnicity, while recognizing ethnic heterogeneity, ignores the historical status and rights of national minority groups (including indigenous peoples) who are currently a minority, not because of voluntary migration, but because of historical colonization, conquest, or confederation (Kymlicka, 1995a). Thus, the USA, for example, is also a *multinational* state, comprising Native Americans and some Hispanic communities (notably, Puerto Ricans and Chicanos) who have through colonization, become minorities in their own land. What has tended to happen up until now is that both these types of minority group have been treated *in the same way* by the dominant ethnic group. In other words, indigenous peoples and other national minorities have been treated as merely one of a number of competing 'ethnic groups' laying claim to the nation-state's limited social, economic and political resources. The discourses of multiculturalism, and multicultural education, tend to perpetuate this process of elision and are thus treated with considerable caution by indigenous peoples (see May, 1999).

References

APPLE, M. (1986) *Teachers as Text: A Political Economy of Class and Gender Relations in Education*, New York: Routledge and Kegan Paul.

APPLE, M. (1996) *Cultural Politics and Education*, Buckingham: Open University Press.

BALIBAR, E., WALLERSTEIN, I. (eds) (1991) *Race, Nation, Class: Ambiguous Identities*, London: Verso.

BANKS, J. and LYNCH, J. (eds) (1986) *Multicultural Education in Western Societies*, Eastbourne, England: Holt, Rinehart and Winston Ltd.

BARKER, M. (1981) *The New Racism: Conservatives and the Ideology of the Tribe*, London: Junction.

BONNETT, A. (1993) *Radicalism, Antiracism and Representation*, London: Routledge.

BONNETT, A. (1996) 'Antiracism and the critique of white identities', *New Community*, **22**, pp. 97–110.

BRANDT, G. (1986) *The Realisation of Anti-racist Teaching*, Lewes: Falmer Press.

CADDICK, A. (1996) 'Review of C. McCarthy and W. Crichlow (eds), *Race, Identity and Representation in Education* (New York: Routledge, 1993)', *Curriculum Inquiry*, **26**, pp. 331–40.

DEI, G. (1996) *Anti-racism Education: Theory and Practice*, Halifax, Canada: Fernwood.

DONALD, J. and RATTANSI, A. (eds) (1992) *'Race', Culture and Difference*, London: Sage.

FENTON, S. (1999) *Ethnicity: Social Structure, Culture and Identity in the Modern World*, London: Macmillan.

FRANKENBERG, R. (1993) *The Social Construction of Whiteness: White Women, Race Matters*, Minneapolis: The University of Minnesota Press.

GILLBORN, D. (1990) *'Race', Ethnicity and Education: Teaching and Learning in Multiethnic Schools*, London: Unwin Hyman/Routledge.

GILLBORN, D. (1995) *Racism and Antiracism in Real Schools*, Buckingham: Open University Press.

GILROY, P. (1992) 'The end of antiracism', in DONALD, J. and RATTANSI, A. (eds), *'Race', Culture, and Difference*, London: Sage, pp. 49–61.

GIROUX, H. (1997) *Pedagogy and the Politics of Hope: Theory, Culture and Schooling*, Boulder, CO: Westview Press.

GOLDBERG, D. (ed.) (1994) *Multiculturalism: A Critical Reader*, Oxford: Basil Blackwell.

HALL, S. (1992) 'New ethnicities', in DONALD, J. and RATTANSI, A. (eds) *'Race', Culture and Difference*, London: Sage, pp. 252–9.

KINCHELOE, J. and STEINBERG, S. (1997) *Changing Multiculturalism*, Buckingham: Open University Press.

KOZOL, J. (1991) *Savage Inequalities: Children in America's Schools*, New York: Harper Perennial.

KYMLICKA, W. (1989) *Liberalism, Community and Culture*, Oxford: Clarendon Press.

KYMLICKA, W. (1995a) *Multicultural Citizenship: A Liberal Theory of Minority Rights*, Oxford: Clarendon Press.

KYMLICKA, W. (1995b) 'Introduction', in KYMLICKA, W. (ed.) *The Rights of Minority Cultures*, Oxford: Oxford University Press, pp. 1–27.

MacDONALD, I., BHAVNANI, R., KHAN, L. and JOHN, G. (1989) *Murder in the Playground: The Report of the MacDonald Inquiry into Racism and Racial Violence in Manchester Schools*, London: Longsight Press.

MAY, S. (1994a) *Making Multicultural Education Work*, Clevedon, England: Multilingual Matters.

MAY, S. (1994b) 'The case for antiracist education', *British Journal of Sociology of Education*, **15**, pp. 421–8.

MAY, S. (1998a) 'Language and education rights for indigenous peoples: Maori in Aotearoa/ New Zealand', *Language, Culture and Curriculum*, **11**, 3.

MAY, S. (ed.) (1998b) 'Indigenous community-based education, Special issue', *Language, Culture and Curriculum*, **11**, 3.

MAY, S. (1999) *Language, Education and Minority Rights*, London: Longman, forthcoming.

McCARTHY, C. (1990) *Race and Curriculum: Social Inequality and the Theory and Politics of Difference in Contemporary Research on Schooling*, Bristol, PA: Falmer Press.

McCARTHY, C. and CRICHLOW, W. (eds) (1993) *'Race', Identity and Representation in Education*, New York: Routledge.

McLAREN, P. (1995) *Critical Pedagogy and Predatory Culture*, New York: Routledge.

McLAREN, P. (1997) *Revolutionary Multiculturalism: Pedagogies of Dissent for the New Millennium*, Boulder, CO: Westview Press.

MILES, R. (1989) *Racism*, London: Routledge.

MILES, R. (1993) *Racism after 'Race Relations'*, London: Routledge.

MILES, R. and TORRES, R. (1996) 'Does "race" matter? Transatlantic perspectives on racism after "race relations"', in AMIT-TALAI, V. and KNOWLES, C. (eds) *Resituating Identities: The Politics of Race, Ethnicity and Culture*, Peterborough, Ontario, Canada: Broadview Press, pp. 26–46.

MODGIL, S., VERMA, G., MALLICK, K. and MODGIL, C. (eds) (1986) *Multicultural Education: The Interminable Debate*, Lewes, England: Falmer Press.

MODOOD, T. (1992) *Not Easy Being British: Colour, Culture and Citizenship*, Stoke-on-Trent: Runnymede Trust and Trentham Books.

MODOOD, T. (1998) 'Anti-essentialism, multiculturalism and the "recognition" of religious groups', *Journal of Political Philosophy*, **6**.

MOODLEY, K. (1992) *Beyond Multicultural Education: International Perspectives*, Calgary, Canada: Detselig.

NG, R. (1993) 'Racism, sexism and nation building in Canada', in MCCARTHY, C. and CRICHLOW, W. (eds) *Race, Identity and Representation in Education*, New York: Routledge, pp. 50–9.

NG, R. (1995) 'Teaching against the grain: Contradictions and possibilities', in NG, R., STATON, P. and SCANE, J. (eds) *Anti-racism, Feminism and Critical Approaches to Education*, Westport: Bergin and Garvey, pp. 129–52.

NIETO, S. (1996) *Affirming Diversity: The Sociopolitical Context of Multicultural Education* (2nd ed.), New York: Longman.

RATTANSI, A. (1992) 'Changing the subject? Racism, culture, and education', in DONALD, J. and RATTANSI, A. (eds) *'Race', Culture, and Difference*, London: Sage, pp. 11–48.

RATTANSI, A. and WESTWOOD, S. (eds) (1994) *Racism, Modernity, and Identity*, Cambridge: Polity Press.

RIZVI, F. (1991) 'The idea of ethnicity and the politics of multicultural education', in DAWKINS, D. (ed.) *Power and Politics in Education*, London: Falmer Press, pp. 161–96.

RIZVI, F. (1993) 'Children and the grammar of popular racism', in MCCARTHY, C. and CRICHLOW, W. (eds) *Race, Identity and Representation in Education*, New York: Routledge, pp. 126–39.

ROEDIGER, D. (1992) *The Wages of Whiteness: Race and the Making of the American Working Class*, London: Verso.

ROEDIGER, D. (1994) *Towards the Abolition of Whiteness: Essays on Race, Politics, and Working Class History*, London: Verso.

SHAPIRO, I. and KYMLICKA, W. (eds) (1997) *Ethnicity and Group Rights*, New York: New York University Press.

SLEETER, C. (1995) 'An analysis of the critiques of multicultural education', in BANKS, J. and BANKS, C. (eds) *Handbook of Research on Multicultural Education*, New York: Macmillan, pp. 81–94.

SMALL, S. (1994) *Racialised Barriers: The Black Experience in the United States and England in the 1980s*, London: Routledge.

TROYNA, B. (ed.) (1987) *Racial Inequality in Education*, London: Tavistock.

TROYNA, B. (1993) *Racism and Education*, Buckingham: Open University Press.

TROYNA, B. and HATCHER, R. (1992) *Racism in Children's Lives: A Study of Mainly-white Primary Schools*, London: Routledge.

WETHERELL, M. and POTTER, J. (1992) *Mapping the Language of Racism: Discourse and the Legitimation of Exploitation*, London: Harvester Wheatleaf.

1 Critical Multiculturalism and Cultural Difference: Avoiding Essentialism

Stephen May

The theory and practice of multiculturalism, of which multicultural and antiracist education form a central part, currently faces opposition on two key fronts. The first constitutes an alliance of conservative and some liberal commentators whose principal aim is to defend orthodox liberalism against a politics of difference represented by multiculturalism (see, for example, Bullivant, 1981; Hughes, 1993; Ravitch, 1992; Schlesinger, 1991, 1992). Building on a post second world war consensus of orthodox liberalism in social and political theory (see Claude, 1955; Glazer, 1975; Porter, 1965, 1975), these commentators argue that only the current organization of nation-states — represented most clearly by the neutrality of the civic realm — can ensure personal autonomy, equality, and common citizenship (at least in theory). In contrast, they argue that the politics of multiculturalism — which they equate directly with the increasing *public* recognition of various minority ethnic, cultural and/or religious identities — is inherently destabilizing and destructive of the common bonds of nationhood. In their view, multiculturalism is an approach which replaces universalism with particularism and which introduces ethnicity unnecessarily and unhelpfully into the civic realm — that is, 'civil society' in Gramsci's (1971) sense of the term.[1] Indeed, at their most apocalyptic, these critics suggest that the accommodation of multiculturalism may result in the immolation and/or 'balkanization' of previously quiescent, harmonious nation-states. And all because the 'cult of ethnicity', to use Schlesinger's (1992) pejorative phrase, unnecessarily hardens ethnic group boundaries; bringing difference and division where once was unity and common purpose. The spectres of Rwanda and the former Yugoslavia provide convenient and seemingly salutary examples here of where multiculturalism might eventually take us.

Opposition to multiculturalism also comes from the Left, however. In relation to education, this has centred historically on the inability of multicultural education initiatives to address adequately the structural inequalities faced by minority students, most notably racism. The British antiracist movement, in particular, adopted a neo-Marxist critique of multiculturalism along these lines, arguing that a preoccupation with superficial culturalism left the life chances of minority students unchanged and the hegemony of majority students, their values and their forms of knowledge, unchallenged. This was most notable in the work of early antiracist proponents in Britain such as Chris Mullard (1982) and Godfrey Brandt (1986), and most consistently represented throughout the 1980s and early 1990s by the work of Barry

Troyna and his collaborators (Troyna, 1982, 1987, 1993; Troyna and Hatcher, 1992; Troyna and Williams, 1986). Michael Apple, David Theo Goldberg and Cameron McCarthy have echoed these debates to some extent in the United States (Apple, 1996; Goldberg, 1994; McCarthy, 1990; McCarthy and Crichlow, 1993). However, the often vituperative and entrenched nature of British multicultural and antiracist (op)positions, particularly in the latter's heyday in the 1980s, has not been replicated to the same extent in the US or elsewhere (see May, 1994; Sleeter, 1995).

Proponents of multiculturalism have responded to this broad antiracist left critique, not least in this volume, by acknowledging more directly the role of unequal power relations and the inequalities and differential effects that ensue from them. However, in so doing, they have also more recently come to face another, perhaps more intractable problem — a problem brought on to some extent by this very process of accommodation with antiracist theory. For example, the privileging of racism over other forms of discrimination in early conceptions of antiracism resulted in an increasing preoccupation with 'colour racism' and the black–white dichotomy. These emphases in antiracist theory considerably understate both the multiplicity of racisms and their complex interconnections with other forms of inequality (Gilroy, 1992; Modood, 1992; McLaren and Torres, this volume). Relatedly, they fail adequately to conceptualize and address the increasing articulation of new 'cultural racisms' where 'race' as a signifier is transmuted into the seemingly more acceptable discourse of 'cultural differences' (cf. Rattansi, 1992, this volume; Short and Carrington, this volume). In effect, essentialist racialized discourses are 'disguised' by describing group differences principally in cultural and/or historical terms — ethnic terms, in effect — without specifically mentioning 'race' or overtly racial criteria (Barker, 1981; Small, 1994; Wetherell and Potter, 1992). New racisms, in this sense, can be described as a form of *ethnicism* which, as Avtar Brah describes it:

> defines the experience of racialized groups primarily in 'culturalist' terms: that is, it posits 'ethnic difference' as the primary modality around which social life is constituted and experienced. . . . This means that a group identified as culturally different is assumed to be internally homogeneous. . . . ethnicist discourses seek to impose stereotypic notions of common cultural need upon heterogeneous groups with diverse social aspirations and interests. (1992, p. 129)

But the problems of cultural essentialism and the reification of group-based identities highlighted by Brah, and mobilized so effectively by racist proponents, also continue ironically to haunt much multicultural theory and practice. This is particularly evident within multicultural education where the regular invocation of 'cultural difference' often presents culture as *sui generis* (Hoffman, 1996). In the process, ethnicity is elided with culture and both come to be treated as 'bounded cultural objects', to borrow a phrase from Richard Handler (1988), which are seen to attach unproblematically to (most usually) ethnic minority students. This naive, static and undifferentiated conception of cultural identity, and the allied notion of the incommensurability of cultures, end up being not that dissimilar from the new racisms of the Right. Both appear to abandon universalist notions of individual choice, rights and responsibility in order to revalorize closed cultures, roots and traditions (Lloyd, 1994; Werbner, 1997a).

Multiculturalism in this conception also stands in direct contrast to much postmodern theorizing on identi*ties* which — with its related concepts of hybridity, syncretism, creolization, and new ethnicities — highlights the 'undecidability' and fluidity of much identity formation. Indeed, it is now almost *de rigueur* in this post-modern age to dismiss *any* articulation of group-based identity as essentialist[2] — a totalizing discourse that excludes and silences as much as it includes and empowers (see, for example, Anthias and Yuval-Davis, 1992; Bhabha, 1994; Gilroy, 1993; Giroux, 1992; Hall, 1992; Yuval-Davis, 1997a). Viewed in this way, multiculturalism's advocacy of group-based identities, and any educational recognition attached to them, appears to be brought into serious question.

It is here then that critiques from the Left ally with those from the Right in highlighting the potential of multiculturalism unhelpfully to essentialize and reify ethnic and cultural difference(s). In what follows, I want to examine the veracity of these charges, from both quarters. In so doing, I will concentrate principally on the wider social and political issues surrounding the politics of multiculturalism. How-ever, I will conclude by outlining some tentative thoughts on how these wider debates might lead to a theory of multicultural/antiracist education which incorp-orates both a *critical* and *non-essentialist* approach to cultural difference.

Defending Liberal Democracy:
Mobilizing against Multiculturalism

Conservative and (some) liberal opponents[3] of multiculturalism are particularly exer-cised by the implications that a group-based politics of difference might have on the current organization and legitimacy of modern nation-states. And they are right to be worried. The nation-state may still remain the bedrock of the political world order, exercising internal political and legal jurisdiction over its citizens, and claim-ing external rights to sovereignty and self-government in the present inter-state system. But the nation-state is also under increasing pressure — both from above and below. From above, the inexorable rise of globalization, along with the bur-geoning influence of multinational corporations and supranational political organiza-tions, have required modern nation-states to re-evaluate the limits of their own political and economic sovereignty (cf. Kalantzis and Cope; McLaren and Torres, this volume). From below, and this is where the politics of multiculturalism plays an important part, minority groups are increasingly exerting the right to both greater private and, crucially, *public* recognition of their various ethnic, cultural and/or religious identities. In the process, the public discourse on national identity, its parameters, and its constituent elements, are opened up for debate. In short, the nation-state is being asked, even forced to *reimagine* itself along more plural and inclusive lines. And not before time.

But if opponents of multiculturalism are dismayed by its pluralizing implica-tions, they are far from silent about them. In recent years, a vigorous counter-attack has been launched advocating the benefits of unity, universalism and nationhood over the fissiparous politics of difference and dissent that is multiculturalism. Or so the story goes. This counter-attack builds on a long tradition of orthodox liberalism and has come to be couched in terms of what Brian Bullivant (1981) has termed 'the pluralist dilemma'.

The pluralist dilemma, for Bullivant, is 'the problem of reconciling the diverse political claims of constituent groups and individuals in a pluralist society *with the claims of the nation-state as a whole*' (1981: x; my emphasis); what he elsewhere describes as the competing aims of 'civism' and 'pluralism'. Other commentators have suggested similar distinctions: 'roots' and 'options' (Rokkan and Urwin, 1983); 'state' and 'community' (Smith, 1981); and, drawing on Saussure, 'parochialism' and 'intercourse' (Edwards, 1994). All these distinctions emphasize, like Bullivant's, the apparent polarities involved in the task of national integration; the difficulties of reconciling social cohesion on the one hand with, on the other, a recognition and incorporation of ethnic, linguistic and cultural diversity within the nation-state. In an earlier analysis, Schermerhorn has described these countervailing social and cultural forces as *centripetal* and *centrifugal* tendencies. As he observes:

> Centripetal tendencies refer both to cultural trends such as acceptance of common values, styles of life, etc, as well as structural features like increased participation in a common set of groups, associations, and institutions. . . . Conversely, centrifugal tendencies among subordinate groups are those that foster separation from the dominant group or from societal bonds in one way or another. Culturally this most frequently means retention and presentation of the group's distinctive tradition in spheres like language, religion, recreation etc. (1970, p. 81)

Historically, two contrasting approaches have been adopted in response to the pluralist dilemma which Gordon (1978, 1981) has described as 'liberal pluralism' and 'corporate pluralism'. Liberal pluralism is characterized by the absence, even prohibition, of any ethnic, religious, or linguistic minority group possessing separate standing before the law or government. Its central tenets can be traced back to Rousseau's conception of the modern polity as comprising three inseparable features: freedom (non-domination), the absence of differentiated roles, and a very tight common purpose. On this view, the margin for recognizing difference within the modern nation-state is very small (Taylor, 1992). Corporate pluralism, in contrast, involves the recognition of minority groups as legally constituted entities, on the basis of which, and depending on their size and influence, economic, social and political awards are allocated. Glazer (1975) and Walzer (1992a, 1992b) draw similar distinctions between an approach based on 'non-discrimination' — which involves, in Glazer's memorable phrase, the 'salutary neglect' of the State towards ethnic minorities — and a 'corporatist' (Walzer) or 'group rights' (Glazer) model.

It is clear, however, that for conservative commentators (and many liberal ones also) only liberal pluralism will do.[4] In the end, civism *must* be favoured over pluralism while the corporatist intentions of multiculturalism must be specifically disavowed. As such, the 'claims of the nation-state as a whole' — emphasizing the apparently inextricable interconnections between social cohesion and national homogeneity — are invariably invoked against more pluralist conceptions of the nation-state where ethnic, linguistic and cultural differences *between different groups* are accorded some degree of formal recognition. In this construction, individual and universal 'citizenship' rights are mobilized in opposition to collective and particularist 'ethnic' rights. As such, formal differentiation within the nation-state on the grounds of (ethnic) group association is rejected as inimical to the individualistic and meritocratic tenets of liberal democracy. Where countenanced at all, alternative ethnic affiliations should be restricted solely to the private domain since the formal recognition of collective (ethnic) identity is viewed as undermining personal and political autonomy, and fostering social and political fragmentation. As Will Kymlicka observes, 'the near-universal response of [conservatives and] liberals has been one of active hostility to minority rights. . . . schemes which single out minority cultures for special measures . . . appear irremediably unjust, a disguise for creating or maintaining . . . ethnic privilege' (1989, p. 4). Any deviation from the strict principles of universal political citizenship and individual rights is seen as the first step down the road to apartheid. Or so it seems. The resulting consensus is well illustrated by Brian Bullivant:

> Certain common institutions essential for the well-being and smooth functioning of the nation-state as *a whole* must be maintained: common language, common political system, common economic market system and so on. Cultural pluralism can operate at the level of the *private*, rather than public, concerns such as use of ethnic [sic] language in the home. . . . But, the idea that maintaining these aspects of ethnic life and encouraging the maintenance of ethnic groups almost in the sense of ethnic enclaves will assist their ability to cope with the political realities of the nation-state is manifestly absurd. (1981, p. 232)

The Cult of Ethnicity

These themes have been prominently displayed in the often vituperative debates surrounding multiculturalism, bilingualism and 'Afrocentrism' in the United States, particularly in relation to education (see, for example, Bloom, 1987; D'Souza, 1992; Hirsch, 1987; Hughes, 1993; Ravitch 1992; Schlesinger, 1991, 1992). Arthur Schlesinger's Jr's book, *The Disuniting of America* (1992), provides us with an influential and representative example here of the conservative critique of corporate pluralism. While his views are by now well known, it is worth rehearsing them again briefly here.

As his title suggests, Schlesinger, a noted liberal historian, has argued to much public acclaim against the 'disuniting' of America by the 'cult of ethnicity':

> A cult of ethnicity has arisen both among non-Anglo Whites and among non-white minorities to denounce the idea of the melting pot, to challenge the concept of 'one people', and to protect, promote, and perpetuate separate [ethnic] communities. . . . The new ethnic gospel rejects the unifying vision of individuals from all nations melted into a new race [sic]. Its underlying philosophy is that America is

not a nation of individuals at all but a nation of groups, that ethnicity is the defining experience for most Americans, that ethnic ties are permanent and indelible. . . . The ethnic interpretation, moreover, reverses the historic theory of America as one people — the theory that has thus far managed to keep American society whole. (1992, pp. 15–16)

For Schlesinger, this 'ethnic cheerleading' is preservationist rather than transformative and results in a view of America which, instead of being 'composed of individuals making their own unhampered choices', is increasingly 'composed of groups more or less ineradicable in their ethnic character'. The result is a 'multiethnic dogma [which] abandons historic purposes, replacing assimilation by fragmentation, integration by separatism' (1992, pp. 16–17).

Schlesinger directs particular opprobrium here at the emergence among African-Americans of an 'Afrocentric' view of American (and world) history, along with its formal promotion in schools under the rubric of multiculturalism. For Schlesinger, these developments are simply nationalist myth making, along the lines of Hobsbawm's (1990; see also Hobsbawm and Ranger, 1983) 'invention of tradition', and lead inevitably to cultural reification and essentialism. The rise of Afrocentrism may be understandable — given the consistent exclusion of black voices in previous historical accounts — but it is still *bad* history, albeit of a manifestly different kind from that which preceded it. On this view, Afrocentrism is not the answer to the problems of racism and marginalization faced by African-Americans since it simply replaces one form of ethnic and/or cultural exclusiveness (and exclusion) with another.[5] Indeed, Schlesinger asserts that the end game of this 'filiopietistic commemoration' (1992, p. 99) — or, more prosaically, the worship of ancestors — will actually confirm rather than ameliorate self-pity and self-ghettoization among African-Americans. Rather, he avers:

would it not be more appropriate for [ethnic minority] students to be . . . encouraged to understand the American culture in which they are growing up and to prepare for an active role in shaping that culture? . . . . As for self-esteem, is this really the product of ethnic role models and fantasies of a glorious past? Or does it not result from a belief in oneself that springs from achievement, from personal rather than [ethnic] pride? (1992, pp. 90, 92)

Schlesinger also extends his trenchant and apocalyptic critique of Afrocentrism to include an attack on bilingualism and the bilingual movement in the USA, along with its strong links to Hispanic communities. In similar vein to the 'English Only' movement in the USA,[6] Schlesinger rejects out of hand the official recognition of minority languages in the public sphere:

The separatist movement is by no means confined to the black community. Another salient expression is the bilingualism movement. . . . In recent years the combination of the ethnicity cult with a *flood* of immigration from Spanish-speaking countries has given bilingualism new emphasis. The presumed purpose is transitional. . . . Alas, bilingualism has not worked out as planned: rather the contrary. . . .

indications are that bilingual education retards rather than expedites the movement of Hispanic children *into the English-speaking world* and that it promotes segregation more than it does integration. Bilingualism shuts doors. It nourishes self-ghettoization, and ghettoization nourishes racial antagonism. . . . using some language other than English *dooms* people to second class citizenship in American society. (1992, pp. 107–8; my emphases)

In attributing bilingualism with the same fractious and regressive characteristics as Afrocentrism, Schlesinger invokes, once again, the rhetoric of national cohesion. 'A common language is a necessary bond of national cohesion in so heterogeneous a nation as America . . . institutionalized bilingualism remains another source of the fragmentation of America, another threat to the dream of "one people" ' (1992, pp. 109–110; see also Hirsch, 1987). His parting comments echo this conclusion when he returns directly to the question of the pluralist dilemma: 'The question America confronts as a pluralistic society is how to vindicate cherished cultures and traditions without breaking the bonds of cohesion — common ideals, common political institutions, common language, common fate — that hold the republic together?' (1992, p. 138). His answer, by now, should come as no surprise: 'the bonds of social cohesion in our society are sufficiently fragile, or so it seems to me, that it makes no sense to strain them by encouraging and exalting cultural and linguistic apartheid. The American identity will never be fixed and final; it will always be in the making' (1992, p. 138). *Quod erat demonstrandum*, or so it seems.

Critiquing Liberal Democracy: A Case of Vested Interests

Such is the current orthodoxy among conservatives and liberals as to the question of the pluralist dilemma. When in doubt, the historical and political imperatives of civism should prevail, as should (for conservative commentators like Schlesinger at least) the related prerogative of the dominant ethnic group to determine what that civism should comprise. But how satisfactory is this broadly articulated position and what viable alternatives are there, if any? We can begin to unravel these questions by first highlighting some of the key inconsistencies that are evident in Schlesinger's conservative polemic.

Like most defences of orthodox liberalism, Schlesinger's account constructs the person *solely* as a political being with rights and duties attached to their status as *citizens*. Such a position does not countenance private identity, including a person's communal membership, as something warranting similar recognition. These latter dimensions are excluded from the public realm because their inevitable diversity would lead to the complicated business of the State mediating between different conceptions of 'the good life' (Dworkin, 1978; Rawls, 1985). On this basis, personal *autonomy* — based on the political rights attributable to citizenship — always takes precedence over personal (and collective) *identity* and the widely differing ways of life which constitute the latter. In effect, personal and political participation in liberal democracies, as it has come to be constructed, ends up denying group difference and posits all persons as interchangeable from a moral and political point of view (Young, 1993).

However, this strict separation of citizenship and identity in the modern polity is problematic on two key counts. First, it understates, and at times disavows, the significance of wider communal affiliations, including ethnicity, to the construction of individual identity. As Michael Sandel (1982) observes, in a communitarian critique of liberalism, there is no such thing as the 'unencumbered self' — we are all, to some extent, *situated* within wider communities which shape and influence who we are.[7] Likewise, Charles Taylor argues that identity 'is who we are, "where we're coming from". As such, it is the background against which our tastes and desires and opinions and aspirations make sense' (1992, pp. 33–4). These critics also highlight the obvious point that certain goods such as language, culture and sovereignty, cannot be experienced alone; they are, by definition, *communally shared* goods. A failure to account for these communal goods, however, has led to a view of rights within liberal democracy which is inherently individualistic and which cannot appreciate the pursuit of such goods other than derivatively (Coulombe, 1995; Taylor, 1992; Van Dyke, 1977). In short, individualistic conceptions of the good life may preclude shared community values that are central to one's identity (Kymlicka, 1989, 1995a). This approach can be regarded as even more problematic when one considers, for example, that indigenous and other non-western groups tend to place greater emphasis on shared communal values *as ends in themselves* than does the more individualistically oriented West (Corson, 1993, 1998; May, 1994).

Second, and relatedly, there is no such thing as the neutral state. Despite what Schlesinger and other like-minded commentators would have us believe, ethnicity has never been absent from the civic realm. Rather, the civic realm represents the particular (although not necessarily exclusive) *communal* interests and values of the dominant ethnic group *as if* these values were held by all. In Charles Taylor's succinct analysis, the 'supposedly neutral set of difference-blind principles [that constitute the liberal] politics of equal dignity is in fact a reflection of one hegemonic culture. . . . [it is] a particularism masquerading as the universal' (1992, pp. 43–4). In a similar vein, Iris Marion Young argues that if particular groups 'have greater economic, political or social power, their group related experiences, points of view, or cultural assumptions will tend to become the norm, biasing the standards or procedures of achievement and inclusion that govern social, political and economic institutions' (1993, p. 133).

This hegemonic process is clearly illustrated in Schlesinger's valorization of homogeneity as simply the proper application of Reason (Goldberg, 1994); a valorization most starkly apparent in his advocacy of a common American culture. While acknowledging, albeit grudgingly, the possibilities of heterogeneity, Schlesinger's argument is unequivocal about homogeneity as the historically prevalent condition of social life and, as such, an ideal to be pursued and recaptured at all cost. This conclusion is encapsulated in his bold assertion of American history as 'the dream of one people' (1992, p. 110); a far from unproblematic assertion, as it turns out, since it can be accused of the very same features of 'bad history' and 'history as therapy' which Schlesinger had levelled at Afrocentrism. As Robert Hughes, another liberal commentator, candidly concedes, America 'has always been a heterogeneous country and its cohesion, whatever cohesion it has, can only be based on mutual respect. There never was a core America in which everyone looked the same, spoke the same language, worshipped the same gods and believed the same things' (1993, p. 12).

The idea of an homogeneous common culture is thus simply another variant of the nationalist myth-making that Schlesinger accuses his opponents of promoting. Indeed, *all* nationalist histories are therapeutic to some extent and contain inevitable elisions and absences. As Ernest Renan has famously observed, 'forgetting, I would even go so far as to say historical error, is a crucial factor in the creation of a nation' (1990, p. 11). Benedict Anderson's (1991) notion of the nation as an 'imagined community' also highlights this point. All nations, he argues, are imagined; it is only the nature of that imagining which remains in question.[8] If one recognizes this, then the key question becomes not so much the teaching of bad or therapeutic history but *whose* history one wants to teach; a question which, in turn, highlights the central issue of hegemonic power relations. As Peter McLaren asserts of Schlesinger and other conservative critics in the USA:

> conservative attacks on multiculturalism as separatist and ethnocentric carry with them the erroneous assumption by White Anglo constituencies that North American society fundamentally constitutes social relations of uninterrupted accord. The liberal view is seen to underscore the idea that North American society is largely a forum of consensus with different minority viewpoints accretively added on. We are faced here with the politics of pluralism which largely ignores the workings of power and privilege. (1995, pp. 126–7)

McLaren's analysis allows us to question the very notion of a commonly shared (American) culture and the supposedly unified and consensual history underpinning it. Common to whom, one might ask, and on whose terms? Who determines its central values and/or sets its parameters? Who is subsequently included and/or excluded from full participation in its 'benefits' and, crucially, at what cost since the 'price' minorities usually have to pay for full participation is the disavowal of their cultural, linguistic and religious practices (cf. Howe, 1992)?

Suffice it to say that Schlesinger does not address these questions. Like other conservative commentators, he assumes an homogeneous common culture as an historical and political given and, following from this, that the choice in the pluralist dilemma is one of either/or. Ethnic minorities must *either* give up their cultural and linguistic identities *or* prejudice both the social cohesion of the nation-state and the possibilities of their own individual social and economic success. As McLaren observes, this approach wants to assimilate ethnic minorities 'to an unjust social order by arguing that every member of every ethnic group can reap the benefits of neocolonialist ideologies and corresponding social and economic practices. But a prerequisite of joining the club is to become denuded, [de-ethnicized] and culturally stripped' (1995, p. 122). Indeed, even those minority members who plead the conservative line — and who are, accordingly, much trumpeted as a result — generally do so from a position of personal ethnic and/or cultural dislocation (see

D'Souza, 1992; Rodriguez, 1983, 1993). The result leaves little or no room for *negotiation*; little or no opportunity for changing 'the rules of the game'. And why is this? Because 'our' common bonds are too fragile, too easily dismembered or dismantled by the demands of particularism. One wonders what should be so fragile about western civilization and, conversely, what is so radical about multiculturalism that this should be the case (Hughes, 1993). But this, conservatives like Schlesinger insist, is what is centrally at stake.

This brings me to two related inconsistencies in conservative accounts of liberal pluralism, of which Schlesinger's polemic is an exemplar. On the one hand, Schlesinger derisively describes group-based affiliations as mere 'ethnic cheerleading' and argues that these are essentially preservationist rather than transformative. And yet, on the other hand, he ends up, as we have seen, invoking a majoritarian version of the same process — a *prior*, and *preeminent* civic or 'national' identity to which all should subscribe. While deploring the nationalistic jargon of Afrocentrism, Schlesinger thus asks us to make the same kind of nationalistic choice — to choose an homogeneous *national* identity over an *ethnic* one. It must be one or the other — a prior nationalism that trumps all other identities (Calhoun, 1993a). Such a position not only considerably understates the possibilities of holding dual or multiple identities, except oppositionally, it also allows no room for a dynamic and multifarious conception of nationhood. The end result is not too dissimilar to the preservationist and group-based conceptions that conservatives like Schlesinger have purportedly set themselves against. As Sonia Nieto (1995) observes, the charge of ethnic cheerleading by conservatives may stem more from the fear that *their* ethnic cheerleading is being challenged than from any notion of wanting to retain a common national identity 'for the good of all'.

In this light, the racism underlying much of the conservative critique of multiculturalism also becomes more readily apparent, despite protestations to the contrary. For example, it is hard to imagine Schlesinger defending his view of bilingualism as self-ghettoization in relation to speaking French or some other 'prestigious' language variety (Dicker, 1996); indeed, one might well expect the reverse to be the case. Rather, in directing his critique of bilingualism towards Hispanic communities in the USA, it is clear that the central issues for Schlesinger have more to do with 'race', immigration and class than with bilingualism per se (see Wildavsky, 1992).

Furthermore, the inevitable connections that are drawn by Schlesinger and other conservatives between ethnic differentiation, conflict, and fragmentation, remain open to question. While conflict and fragmentation have undoubtedly occurred from ethnic differentiation, *they need not always do so*. Likewise, the national integration envisaged by conservatives has not always resulted in — indeed has seldom actually achieved — inclusion, consensus and cohesion for all ethnic groups within nation-states. (Nor, one might venture, would some necessarily want it to). Rather, as Iris Marion Young asserts, 'when oppressed or disadvantaged social groups are different from the dominant groups, then an allegedly group-neutral assimilationist strategy of inclusion only tends to perpetuate inequality' (1993, p. 133).

Indeed, it is a significant irony that conservative and liberal commentators fail to recognize that ethnic conflict and fragmentation arise most often *not* when compromises are made between ethnic groups or when formal ethnic, linguistic and/or religious rights are accorded some degree of recognition, *but when these have been historically avoided, suppressed or ignored.* This is true, for example, of Canada, Belgium, Northern Ireland and Sri Lanka. If this contra-indicated position is actually the case, then far from ensuring national unity, the denial of ethnicity may well be a principal catalyst of *disunity.* In short, attempting to enforce ethnic, linguistic and/or religious homogeneity is far more likely to foster disunity than to ameliorate it (see May, 1999).

Be that as it may, Schlesinger's central charge against the romantic historical revisionism associated with Afrocentrism retains some purchase. And this is where criticism from the Left also enters the picture. Kincheloe and Steinberg (1997), for example, describe Afrocentrism as a form of 'left-essentialist multiculturalism' (see also McLaren, 1995) which links cultural difference and identity ineluctably to an historical past of cultural authenticity. Such a conception may well be motivated by a principal concern to acknowledge positively cultural difference, to address historical and current patterns of disadvantage, racism and marginalization, and, from that, to effect the greater pluralization of the nation-state, particularly in its public sphere. However, for a broad alliance of liberal/left/postmodernist critics, it does so at the cost of *overstating* the importance of ethnicity and culture, and *understating* the fluid and dialogic nature of inter- and intra-group relations. In effect, communitarian conceptions of multiculturalism like Afrocentrism are charged with operating a model of group membership which is at odds with the complexities of identity in the modern world (Burtonwood, 1996). As Edward Said argues, 'no one today is purely one thing. Labels like Indian, or woman, or Muslim, or American are no more than starting points' (1994, p. 407).

Interestingly, a similar charge of monism has been directed at early conceptions of British antiracism which, in their almost exclusive preoccupation with racism, resulted in 'a grand theory totally at odds with the fractured, rapidly changing identity politics of contemporary society' (Gillborn, 1995, p. 66). In response, more recent conceptions of antiracism, of which Gillborn's 'critical antiracism' is an exemplar (cf. Carrim and Soudien, this volume), advocate an approach in which ethnicity and culture are recognized as being continually negotiated and recreated. Gillborn argues that this should lead to 'a more sophisticated recognition of the diversity within and between groups that are the subject of racism' (1995, p. 85; see also Donald and Rattansi, 1992). This broad critique of 'left-essentialist multiculturalism' and early forms of antiracism is illustrated by two allied, although theoretically quite distinct conceptions — cultural hybridity and the cosmopolitan alternative. Both celebrate the notion of cultural mixture and, concomitantly, disavow the validity of so called 'rooted' identities like ethnicity.

Cultural Hybridity: The Postmodern Critique

The articulation of cultural hybridity — and related concepts such as mestizaje and creolization — is a prominent feature of the work of British theorists Stuart Hall,

Homi Bhabha and Paul Gilroy, among others. Hall's (1992) discussion of 'new ethnicities' (cf. Rattansi, this volume), Bhabha's (1994) celebration of creolization and subaltern voices from the margin, and Gilroy's (1993) discussion of a Black Atlantic — a hybridized, diasporic black counter-culture — all foreground the transgressive potential of cultural hybridity. Hybridity is viewed as being able to subvert categorical oppositions and essentialist ideological movements — particularly, ethnicity and nationalism — and to provide, in so doing, a basis for cultural reflexivity and change (Werbner, 1997a). Out with the old singular, in with the new plurality — a plurality of cultures, of knowledges, and their continuous interspersion, where 'ethnic absolutism' has no place and 'where "race" will no longer be a meaningful device for the categorization of human beings' (Gilroy, 1993, p. 218).

Within the discourses of hybridity, and of postmodernism more broadly, the new social agents are plural — multiple agents forged and engaged in a variety of struggles and social movements (Giroux, 1997). Conversely, hybridity theory is entirely opposed to universalism, traditionalism and any idea of ethnic or cultural rootedness. In line with postmodernism's rejection of totalizing, meta-narratives, exponents of hybridity emphasize the contingent, the complex, and the contested aspects of identity formation. Multiple, shifting and, at times, nonsynchronous identities are the norm for individuals. This position highlights the social and historical constructedness of culture and its associated fluidity and malleability. It also posits contingent, local narratives — what Lyotard (1984) has described as *petits récits* — in opposition to the totalizing narratives of ethnicity and nationalism. The rejection of totality and foundationalism in hybridity theory, and its replacement by a plethora of local identities, thus lends itself to a politics of difference which is commensurable with multiculturalism. Like multiculturalism, the end result is the deconstruction and ultimate rejection of the idea of a 'universal', neutral civic realm. Accordingly, hybridity theorists, like multiculturalists, are fundamentally opposed to the conservative and orthodox liberal defence of the nation-state discussed above and argue, instead, for a *differentiated* politics of representation.

However, where hybridity theorists differ from multiculturalism is in sharing with conservative commentators a view of ethnicity and nationalism as misconceived 'rooted' identities. Similarly, these identities are ascribed with the negative characteristics of essentialism, closure and conflict. Postmodernists, like multiculturalists, may thus argue for the pluralization of the nation-state via a differentiated local politics, but they do so via a *rejection*, not a defence of singular ethnic and cultural identities. Rather, as Homi Bhabha (1994) argues, it is the 'inter' and 'in-between', the liminal 'third space' of translation, which carries the burden of the meaning(s) of culture in this postmodern, postcolonial world. Others have described this process as one of 'border crossing' (see Anzaldúa, 1987; Di Leonardo, 1994; Giroux, 1992; Rosaldo, 1989).

Hybridity theory, as part of the wider postmodern critique, appears to offer us, among other things, a more contingent, situational account of identity and culture — a process which involves *decentring* the subject (cf. Rattansi, this volume) and contesting essentialism wherever it is found. But there are also limits to hybridity. First, in arguing for the inter and in-between, hybridity is still predicated on the notion of (previous) cultures as complex wholes (Friedman, 1997; Wicker, 1997). In juxtaposing the merits of the heterogeneous hybrid against the homogeneous ethnicist or nationalist, hybridity assumes that the liminal 'third space' is replacing the bounded, closed ones that preceded it. Border crossing, in effect, assumes that (closed) borders were there to begin with. However, as Jonathan Friedman (1997) points out, this simply perpetuates an essentialist conception of culture rather than subverting it since, as Lévi Strauss (1994) has argued, all cultures are heterogeneous, arising out of cultural mixture. The juxtaposition of purity/hybridity, authenticity/mixture — so central to hybridity theory — is thus fundamentally misconceived. In the end, hybridity is meaningless as a description of 'culture' because it museumizes culture as 'a thing' (Werbner, 1997a; see also Caglar, 1997; Modood, 1998).

Second, an advocacy of hybridity carries with it the imputation that all group-based identities are essentialist. This is most clearly demonstrated in the conflation of ethnicity and nationalism with racism which, as so called 'rooted' identities, are all treated with equal disparagement (see Anthias and Yuval-Davis, 1992; Chambers, 1994; Gilroy, 1987). This is simply wrong. There are many examples of ethnic and national categorization which do involve the imputation of essentialized notions of racial and/or cultural difference, leading in turn to social and/or political closure, hierarchization, exclusion and/or violence. The cultural racism of the New Right is an obvious example here, as indeed is Schlesinger's account of American national identity discussed earlier. But while ethnic and national categories *may* be essentialized in the same way as 'race' categories have been historically, *they need not always be.* Nor are ethnic relations necessarily hierarchical, exploitative and conflictual in the same way that 'race relations' invariably are (Jenkins, 1994, 1997; Rex, 1973). Indeed, it has often been the case that the global impact of racism has overridden previously non-hierarchized ethnic categories (Balibar, 1991; Fenton, 1999).

This distinction is further highlighted by Lévi-Strauss' (1985) attempt to differentiate between ethnocentrism and racism. Here he argues that strong cultural identities might just as well lead to cultural creativity and constructive interchange as to racism. In order to distinguish which is which, Werbner (1997a, b) asserts that we need to make a crucial distinction that is not made in discussions of hybridity — that between 'objectification' and 'reification'. The former is a necessary requirement for any representation of collective identity and may be regarded as broadly comparable to Anderson's (1991) conception of the 'imagined community' discussed above. The latter is particular only to those representations of identity, like racism, which exclude, silence or violate. This allows for the possibility of *non-essentialist* ethnic and national identities which can be compared and contrasted with racisms by their *performative* effects (cf. Rattansi, this volume). As Werbner observes, 'whether nationalism or ethnicity are "good" or "evil" depends on the ability (and right) of members of ethnic or national collectivities to engage in reflexive self-critical distancing from their own cultural discourses, and hence also to recognize the potential validity of other discourses/communities of language' (1997a, p. 14).

In reality, of course, ethnic (and national) identifications are likely to shift continuously between both poles (Werbner, 1997b) and examples which tend to the essentialist end of the spectrum are still clearly dominant (see below; Kalantzis and

Cope, this volume). Nonetheless, the possibility of a non–essentialist, critically-reflective conception of ethnic and/or national identity remains, as does the ability to distinguish between various forms of collective action. In this last respect, Werbner (1997b) concludes that the politics of ethnicity, which objectifies communities situationally and pragmatically with regard to questions of redistributive justice in the public sphere, can be clearly distinguished from the violent essentializing of racism.

The failure to make these crucial distinctions points to a third weakness of hybridity theory — the considerable disparity between the intellectual celebration of hybridity and the *reality* of the postmodern world. This world *is* increasingly one of fractured, and fracturing identities. But these identities are generally *not* hybrid; just the opposite, in fact. Nation-states, as conservatives and liberals will be the first to tell you, are facing a plethora of ethnic, regional and other social and cultural minority demands, many of which are couched in singular, collectivist terms. The tendency to rootedness and to boundary maintenance thus militates against ecumenism, and these tendencies are generated and reinforced by the real fragmentation occurring within and between nation-states in a global era (Friedman, 1997). Given this, Friedman proceeds to observe, the valorization of hybridization is largely self-referential and self-congratulatory:

> hybrids, and hybridization theorists are products of a group that self-identifies and/or identifies the world in such terms, not as a result of ethnographic understanding, but as an act of self-definition — indeed, of self-essentializing — which becomes definition for others via the forces of socialization inherent in the structures of power that such groups occupy: intellectuals close to the media; the media intelligentsia itself; in a sense, all those [and, one might add, *only* those] who can afford a cosmopolitan identity. (1997, p. 81)

Ahmad (1995), in a similarly scathing critique, argues that articulations of hybridity fail to address adequately the social and political continuities and transformations that underpin individual and collective action in the real world. In that world, he argues, political agency is 'constituted not in flux or displacement but in given historical locations'. Moreover, it is sustained by a coherent 'sense of place, of belonging, of some stable commitment to one's class or gender or nation' (1995, pp. 16, 14).

Friedman's and Ahmad's critiques of hybridity accord here with two wider criticisms often levelled at postmodern discourses. First, postmodernism is criticized for an overemphasis on aesthetics at the expense of politics — a preoccupation which, as Berman (1992; see also 1983) acerbically observes, has seen postmodernists appropriate the modernist language of radical breakthrough, wrench it out of its moral and political context, and transform it into a purely aesthetic language game. Second, and relatedly, postmodernism is attributed both with failing to describe accurately, and with retreating from the (post)modern world as it actually is. In so doing, postmodernism abdicates the possibility of social criticism — preferring, in Habermas' (1979) memorable riposte, an ethics and politics of exhaustion to one that holds on to the possibility of radical, emancipatory democratic change. In short, postmodernism prefers the language of critique to the language of transformation and hope (Giroux, 1997).

The Cosmopolitan Alternative

These arguments and counter-arguments with regard to hybridity theory are strongly echoed in debates within liberal political theory around the closely allied notion of the 'cosmopolitan alternative' (Waldron, 1993, 1995; see also Hannerz, 1992). Jeremy Waldron, in a trenchant critique of group-based rights, objects to the idea that our choices and self-identity are defined by our ethnicity and asserts, instead, the need for a 'cosmopolitan alternative'. As he dismissively observes, 'though we may drape ourselves in the distinctive costumes of our ethnic heritage and immure ourselves in an environment designed to minimize our sense of relation with the outside world, no honest account of our being will be complete without an account of our dependence on larger social and political structures that goes far beyond the particular community with which we pretend to identify' (1995, p. 104). On this view, people can pick and choose 'cultural fragments' from various ethnocultural sources, without feeling an allegiance to any one in particular. Thus, Waldron argues, an Irish-American who eats Chinese food, reads Grimm's Fairy Tales to their child, and listens to Italian opera actually lives in a 'a kaleidoscope of cultures'. While Waldron concedes that we need cultural meanings of some kind, he argues that we do not need *specific* cultural frameworks: 'we need to understand our choices in the contexts in which they make sense, but we do not need any single context to structure our choices. To put it crudely, we need culture, but we do not need cultural integrity' (1995, p. 108).

Like hybridity theory, Waldron proceeds on this basis to argue that any advocacy of group-based identities, and specific rights which may be seen to attach to these, necessarily assumes an homogeneous conception of ethnic groups (see Waldron, 1995, pp. 103–5). Likewise, he is particularly critical of notions of cultural 'purity' and 'authenticity' which, he asserts, are regularly employed by ethnic minority groups in support of differential treatment in the public sphere. These attempts at cultural delineation are manifestly artificial in his view and can only result in cultural stasis and isolationism.

However, as Will Kymlicka (1995a) has countered, also from within liberal theory, the assertion of minority recognition and difference, and particular rights associated with this, is most often *not* based on some simplistic desire for cultural 'purity'. Defenders of minority rights are rarely seeking to preserve their 'authentic' culture if that means returning to cultural practices long past. If it was, it would soon meet widespread opposition from individual members. Rather, it is the right 'to maintain one's membership in a distinct culture, and to continue developing that culture in the same (impure) way that the members of majority cultures are able to develop theirs' (1995a, p. 105). Cultural change, adaptation and interaction are entirely consistent with such a position. As Kymlicka argues elsewhere (1995b, pp. 8–9), minority cultures wish to be both cosmopolitan and to embrace the cultural interchange that Waldron emphasizes. However, this does not necessarily entail Waldron's own 'cosmopolitan alternative' which denies that people have any deep bond to their own historical cultural and linguistic communities.

In similar vein, Kymlicka asserts that minority rights 'help to ensure that the members of minority cultures have access to a secure cultural structure *from which to make choices for themselves*, and thereby promote liberal equality' (1989, p. 192; my emphasis). On this view, minorities continue to exercise their individual (citizenship) rights within their particular cultural (and linguistic) milieux and, of course, contextually, in relation to other cultural groups within a given nation-state. The crucial element, however, is that members of the minority are themselves able to retain a significant degree of control over the process — something which until now has largely been the preserve of majority group members. The key issue thus becomes one of cultural *autonomy* rather than one of retrenchment, isolationism, or stasis.

In a related critique of Waldron's position, Margalit and Raz (1995) argue that people today may well adopt (and adapt) a varied range of cultural and social practices but that this does not necessarily diminish their allegiance to an 'encompassing group' with which they most closely identify (see also Taylor, 1992). As they observe:

> membership of such groups is of great importance to individual well-being, for it greatly affects one's opportunities, one's ability to engage in the relationships and pursuits marked by culture. Secondly . . . the prosperity of the culture is important to the well-being of its members. . . . people's sense of their own identity is bound up with their sense of belonging to encompassing groups and . . . their self-respect is affected by the esteem in which these groups are held. (1995, pp. 86–7)

Moreover, if members of dominant ethnic groups typically value their own cultural membership, it is clearly unfair to prevent minority groups from continuing to value theirs. As Kymlicka again observes, 'leaving one's culture, while possible, is best seen as renouncing something to which one is reasonably entitled' (1995a, p. 90). Relatedly, he argues:

> The freedom which liberals demand for individuals is not primarily the freedom to go beyond one's language and history, but rather the freedom to move within one's societal culture, to distance oneself from particular cultural roles, to choose which features of the culture are most worth developing, and which are without value. (1995a, pp. 90–1)

Kymlicka's and Margalit and Raz's critiques of Waldron's position, as with the critiques around hybridity theory, point to the urgent need to *understand* and *theorize* adequately the ongoing collective purchase of ethnicity and the social and cultural practices which may be associated with it. We may well demonstrate, as individuals, a considerable degree of latitude in our attachment to and choice of particular social and political identities. As such, ethnic choices and identifications may vary in their salience — both in themselves, and in relation to other social identities — at any given time and place. Yet, at the same time, we need to acknowledge, and explain why 'at the collective as opposed to the individual level, ethnicity remains a powerful, explosive and durable force' (Smith, 1995, p. 34).

In addition, we need to incorporate a recognition of power relations in the process of ethnic ascription, since it is clear that when it comes to ethnicity — or any other identity for that matter — some have more choices than others. In this respect, individual and collective choices are circumscribed by the ethnic categories available at any given time and place. These categories are, in turn, socially and politically defined and have varying degrees of advantage or stigma attached to them (Nagel, 1994). Moreover, the range of choices available to particular individuals and groups varies widely. A white American may have a wide range of ethnic options from which to choose, both hyphenated and/or hybrid. An African-American, in contrast, is confronted with essentially one ethnic choice — black; irrespective of any preferred ethnic (or other) alternatives they might wish to employ. This example highlights the different ethnic choices available to majority and minority group members; the result, in turn, of their differing access to the civic realm of the nation-state. In short, identity choices are not available to all individuals or groups in the same way. They are structured by class, ethnic and gender stratification, objective constraints, and historical determinations (Hicks, 1991; McLaren, 1997). Both hybridity theory and the cosmopolitan alternative fail to recognize this.

But what is the alternative? How can we acknowledge group-based cultural differences — which clearly exist — while at the same time holding on to a non-essentialist conception of culture? Or, to put it another way, how can we take ethnicity seriously in a way that does not entail its reification as a set of fixed cultural properties? How too can we incorporate a recognition of power relations in the structuring of ethnic and cultural identities and the choices that ensue from them? Not easily, is the short answer. However, one way to do so, I want to suggest, is via Bourdieu's notion of habitus.

Ethnicity as Habitus

Bourdieu's analysis of habitus is principally concerned with social class (see Bourdieu, 1984, 1990a, 1990b; Bourdieu and Passeron, 1990; Bourdieu and Wacquant, 1992). However, since Bourdieu describes habitus as 'a system of dispositions common to all products of the same conditionings' (1990b, p. 59), the application of habitus to ethnicity and ethnic identity formation is equally applicable (see Bentley, 1987; May, 1994; Smaje, 1997; Wicker, 1997). For Bourdieu, habitus comprises *all* the social and cultural experiences that shape us as a person; his use of the term 'dispositions' is an attempt to capture fully this meaning. Specifically, there are four key aspects of habitus highlighted in Bourdieu's work which are useful to our discussion here: embodiment; agency; the interplay between past and present, and; the inter-relationship between collective and individual trajectories (see Reay, 1995a, 1995b). I will look at each of these elements in turn.

First, habitus is not simply about ideology, attitude or perception, it is a *material* form of life which is 'embodied and turned into second nature' (1990a, p. 63). It is, in effect, an orientation to social action (Bourdieu, 1990b). Thus, via the concept of habitus, Bourdieu explores how members of a social group come to acquire, as a result of their socialization, a set of *embodied* dispositions — or ways of viewing, and living in the world. This set of dispositions — what Bourdieu would call 'bodily hexis' — operates most often at the level of the unconscious and the mundane and might comprise in the case of ethnicity such things as attitudes to language, dress, diet and customary practices (Smaje, 1997). The key point for Bourdieu is that habitus is both shaped by, *and also shapes*, the objective social and cultural conditions which surround it. As Roy Nash observes, the habitus is 'a system of durable dispositions inculcated by objective structural conditions, but since it is embodied the habitus gains a history and generates its [own] practices [over] time even when the objective conditions which give rise to it have disappeared' (1990, pp. 433–4). Particular ethnic habitus may thus be lived out implicitly as a result of historical and customary practice. As such, they may provide the parameters of social action for many. However, in the course of those very actions they may also begin to take on a life of their own.

Second, Bourdieu's notion of habitus is concerned to explore the inter-relationship between agency and structure. While many have dismissed Bourdieu's position as structurally determinist (for a critique of this position, see Harker and May, 1993; May, 1994), his specific aim is actually to overcome the agency/structure dichotomy in sociological thought — 'to escape from structuralist objectivism without relapsing into subjectivism' (1990a, p. 61). Thus, Bourdieu argues that habitus does not *determine* individual behaviour. A range of choices, or strategic practices, is presented to individuals within the internalized framework of the habitus. Moreover, these practices, based on the intuitions of the practical sense, *orient* rather than strictly determine action. Choice is thus at the heart of habitus. However, not all choices are possible. As Bourdieu observes, 'habitus, like every "art of inventing" . . . makes it possible to produce an infinite number of practices that are relatively unpredictable (like the corresponding situations) but [which are] also limited in their diversity' (1990b, p. 55). These limits are set by the historically and socially situated conditions of the habitus' production; what Bourdieu terms both 'a conditioned and conditional freedom' (1990b, p. 55). As he proceeds to elaborate,

> being the product of a particular class of objective regularities, the habitus tends to generate all the 'reasonable' and 'commonsense' behaviours (and only those) which are possible within the limits of these regularities, and which are likely to be positively sanctioned because they are objectively adjusted to the logic characteristic of the field, whose objective future they anticipate. At the same time . . . it tends to exclude all 'extravagances' ('not for the likes of us'), that is, all the behaviours that would be negatively sanctioned because they are incompatible with the objective conditions. (1990b, pp. 55–6)

In short, improbable practices, or practices viewed as antithetical to the mores of a particular group, are rejected as unthinkable. Concomitantly, only a particular range of possible practices is considered, although this range of possibilities may evolve and change over time in relation to changing circumstances. Thus, Bourdieu posits that individuals and groups operate strategically *within the constraints* of a particular habitus, but also that they react to changing external conditions; economic, technological and political (Harker, 1984, 1990; May, 1994).

This recursive position allows Bourdieu to argue that the habitus is both a product of our early socialization, yet is also continually modified by individuals' experience of the outside world (Di Maggio, 1979). Within this complex interplay of past and present experience — the third key dimension highlighted here — habitus can be said to reflect the social and cultural position in which it was constructed, while also allowing for its transformation in current circumstances. However, the possibilities of action in most instances will tend to reproduce rather than transform the limits of possibility delineated by the social group. Hybridity and creolization are thus possible but perhaps not as common as many postmodernists would have us believe, and the process of change, if it occurs, is characteristically slow (Wicker, 1997). This is because habitus, as a product of history, ensures the active presence of past experiences which tend also to normalize particular cultural practices and their constancy over time (Harker and May, 1993). Nonetheless, this tendency towards reproduction of group mores and practices does not detract from the *potential* for transformation and change.

The fourth element of habitus — the inter-relationship between individual action and group mores — also reflects this tension. In many instances, individual practices will conform to those of the group since, as Bourdieu argues, 'the practices of the members of the same group . . . are always more and better harmonized than the agents know or wish' (1990b, p. 59). Yet Bourdieu also recognizes the potential for divergence between individual and collective trajectories. In effect, habitus within, as well as between social groups differs to the extent that the details of individuals' social trajectories diverge from one another (Reay, 1995a):

> The singular habitus of the members of the same [group] are united in a relation of homology, that is, of diversity within homogeneity reflecting the diversity within homogeneity characteristic of their social conditions of production. Each individual system of dispositions is a structural variant of the others, expressing the singularity of its position within the [group] and its trajectory. (Bourdieu, 1990b, p. 60)

There is, in all of this, a certain sense of vagueness and indeterminacy in Bourdieu's rendition of habitus and debates about its efficacy in bridging the structure/agency divide remain ongoing (see Calhoun *et al.*, 1993; Harker and May, 1993; Jenkins, 1992; Smaje, 1997). However, if the concept is employed as social *method* rather than as social *theory* — that is, as a way of thinking and a manner of asking questions, which is actually Bourdieu's preference (see Harker *et al.*, 1990) — it can be usefully applied to a discussion of ethnicity. As Gilbert summarizes it, Bourdieu's approach 'suggests an explanation of the regularities of social practice [in this case, ethnicity] as structured by the relations between, on the one hand, an objective set of historically produced material conditions, and on the other, historically produced definitions of those conditions and predispositions to act in certain ways in any historical conjuncture' (1987, pp. 40–1). This avoids the mistake of assuming a realist definition of ethnicity without diminishing the significance of ethnicity and the processes of ethnic and cultural identification. As Bourdieu observes of social class, for example — and one can clearly add ethnicity here also:

> My work consists in saying that people are located in a social space, that they aren't just anywhere, in other words, interchangeable, as those people claim who deny the existence of 'social classes' [or ethnic groups], and that according to the position they occupy in this highly complex space, you can understand the logic of their practices and determine, *inter alia*, how they will classify themselves and others and, should the case arise, think of themselves as members of a 'class' [or ethnic group]. (1990a, p. 50)

Finally, habitus is also extremely pertinent to a discussion of ethnicity — and, by extension, the politics of multiculturalism — because it is employed by Bourdieu principally in order to explore inequalities in power between dominant and subordinate groups. As Bourdieu argues, the individual and collective habitus of the former is invariably constituted as cultural capital — that is, recognized as socially valuable and normalized as such — whereas the habitus of the latter is not. This helps to explain the normalization and valorization of whiteness (cf. McLaren and Torres, this volume) and, in contrast, the prevalent perception of ethnic minority cultures and practices as regressive and 'pre-modern' in debates around multiculturalism and the nation-state (see May, 1999). It also explains why these views come to be expressed both by majority group members and by minority group members themselves — the latter usually as the end result of negative internalization. Bourdieu (1991) describes the process by which this is achieved as '*méconnaissance*' or 'misrecognition' and its inevitably deleterious consequences as 'symbolic violence'.

Implications for a Critical Multiculturalism

> . . . if we cannot engage dialectically in a committed, rigorous, humanizing manner, we cannot hope to change the world. (hooks, 1989, p. 25)

So where does this leave us in specific relation to educational responses to multiculturalism? In conclusion, I want to suggest briefly three key principles that a critical multicultural education needs to incorporate in order to develop effectively a non-essentialist politics of cultural difference (see also Nieto, this volume).

The first step in developing a non-essentialist conception of cultural difference is to unmask, and deconstruct the apparent neutrality of civism — that is, the supposedly universal, neutral set of cultural values and practices that underpin the public sphere of the nation-state. Civism, as constructed within the so called 'pluralist dilemma', is *not* neutral, and never has been. Rather, the public sphere of the nation-state represents and is reflective of the *particular* cultural and linguistic habitus of the dominant (ethnic) group. These habitus, in turn, are accorded with cultural and linguistic capital while other (minority) habitus specifically are not. The principal consequence for many minorities — at both the individual and collective level — has been the enforced loss of their own ethnic, cultural and linguistic habitus as the necessary price of entry to the civic realm (see May, 1999).

The charade of universalism and neutrality is no more apparent than within education where Bullivant describes these civic values thus: 'a minimal, common core selection of the culture transmitted to each generation of children, who will ultimately grow up as citizens' (1981, p. x). However, as should be clear by now, these values are neither 'common' to all, nor commonly available to all. While the merits of individualism, secularism, and personal autonomy with which these civic values are most commonly associated should be clearly acknowledged, so too should their historical and cultural *situatedness*, as well as, at times, their cultural *specificity*.

The latter has been highlighted with regard to specific classroom practices by a variety of ethnomethodological studies over the years (see Au and Jordan, 1981; Erickson and Mohatt, 1982; Gumperz, 1982; Heath, 1983; Jordan, 1985; Labov, 1972; Philips, 1972; Scollon and Scollon, 1981). These studies have explored the cultural and linguistic discontinuities faced by minority cultural groups within schooling. Situated principally within the linguistic traditions of discourse analysis and/or the ethnomethodology of conversation, they have highlighted how the differences between social and cultural groups at the level of conversational discourse strategies can lead to miscommunication in the educational setting. Their basic premise is that the way we speak — to whom, in what context, to what extent, and for what purpose — and our particular views of knowledge and linguistic interaction which underlie this, are culturally constrained. Discourse conventions may be considerably different even among those cultural groups who speak the same language. In contrast, most teachers assume the discourses they employ in the classroom to be culturally universal (cf. Bourdieu). The studies consistently argue that what results is miscommunication; a process which goes largely unrecognized and which, as such, offers at least a partial explanation for the poor performance of minority cultural groups who do not share the cultural and linguistic conventions of schooling. In so doing, they have argued for more 'culturally appropriate' (Au and Jordan, 1981), 'culturally compatible' (Jordan, 1985), and 'culturally responsive' (Erickson and Mohatt, 1982) pedagogies that accommodate for the different cultural discourse practices that minority children bring to the classroom.

A consequence of these pioneering studies has been the central recognition of cultural difference and, by extension, an advocacy that educational pedagogies account for the different cultural and linguistic histories, values, learning styles and practices of various minority ethnic, religious, and/or cultural *groups*. But an acknowledgment of these cultural and linguistic distinctions and their incorporation within multicultural educational practice, are not on their own enough. Indeed, there is an implicit tendency in these studies to accept the need for accommodation *to* mainstream culture — an assumption reflected in the very nomenclature employed. As Ladson-Billings (1995) observes, cultural 'compatibility', 'appropriateness' and 'congruence' all suggest a process of one way accommodation. Only cultural 'responsiveness' appears to refer to a more dynamic process of *mutual* accommodation between the cultures of home and school.

Thus, a second key move in the development of a critical multiculturalism is to *situate* these cultural differences within the wider nexus of power relations of which they form a part. It is one thing, after all, to recognize and describe cultural differences as they affect the educational performance of minority groups. It is quite another to unmask the reproductive processes which underlie these and which lead the school to prefer certain cultural values and practices (those of the dominant group) over others. In this respect, the normalization and universalization of the cultural knowledge of the majority ethnic group, and its juxtaposition with other (usually non-western) knowledges and practices, should be critically interrogated (cf. Hodson; Nieto, this volume). In particular, attention needs to be paid to the processes by which alternative cultural knowledges come to be *subjugated*, principally through the hegemonies and misrepresentations — '*méconnaissance*' or 'misrecognition' in Bourdieu's (1991) terms — which invariably accompany such comparisons (see Corson, 1993, 1998; Kincheloe and Steinberg, 1997; May, 1994; McLaren, 1995, 1997).

To this end, a critical multiculturalism needs both to recognize and incorporate the differing cultural knowledges that children bring with them to school, *while at the same time* address and contest the differential cultural capital attributed to them as a result of wider hegemonic power relations. In short, culture has to be understood as part of the discourse of power and inequality (Giroux, 1997). In the process, previously 'subjugated knowledges' (Kincheloe and Steinberg, 1997) can be revalued and simultaneously employed as counter-hegemonic critiques of dominant forms of knowledge, along with the wider social, cultural and material processes of domination to which the latter contribute. Moreover, these counter-hegemonic practices need not dispense with teaching 'necessary' educational knowledge (although they will critically evaluate, and at times contest, the construction of this necessity) — thus obviating the criticism that a multiculturalist approach to pedagogy and practice inevitably leads to the ghettoization of its students.

In my critical ethnography of Richmond Road School in New Zealand for example (see May, 1994, 1995), I have argued, again drawing on Bourdieu, that the *cultural arbitrary* in schools — that is, the particular (dominant) forms of knowledge most often recognized by schools as cultural capital — need not be confounded with what might be called the *cultural necessary* — the 'essential' or 'necessary' knowledge that schools believe they are in the business of passing on to pupils. Rather, as at Richmond Road, structural alternatives can be employed for delivering necessary school knowledge which are not only inclusive of the values and practices of both minority and majority cultures but are non-hierarchically construed. In a parallel development, Ladson-Billings (1994, 1995) advocates 'culturally relevant pedagogy' to the same end. In her examination of a number of successful teachers of African-American students (see also Nieto, 1996, this volume), she found that all these teachers adopted a culturally relevant pedagogy which comprised three key criteria: 'an ability to develop students academically, a willingness to nurture cultural competence, and the development of a sociopolitical or critical consciousness' (1995, p. 483).

However, even this is not enough. The recognition and incorporation of cultural differences within schooling, even when allied to a critique of wider power relations, still returns us to the potential problem of essentialism. In effect, an emphasis on distinctive cultural boundaries may lead in turn to a further (unhelpful) implication of cultural *boundedness*. Certainly, in much of the actual educational practice of multiculturalism, including some of its more critical variants, minority ethnic groups have often come to be represented as being *contained* within their culture and the discursive practices associated with them (see Hoffman, 1996, 1997). My discussion of habitus above does suggest that traditional cultural values and practices do exert considerable influence at both the individual and collective levels, and may accordingly be slow to change. However, habitus also accommodates for an ongoing and recursive process of cultural construction and *re*construction.

Thus, the third, and perhaps key move in developing a non-essentialist critical multiculturalism is to maintain a reflexive critique of specific cultural practices that avoids the vacuity of cultural relativism, and allows for criticism (both internal and external to the group), transformation, and change. This reflexive position on culture and ethnicity is encapsulated by a distinction drawn by Homi Bhabha (1994) between cultural *diversity* and cultural *difference*. The former, he argues, treats culture as an *object* of empirical knowledge — as static, totalized and historically bounded, as something to be valued but not necessarily *lived*. The latter is the process of the *enunciation* of culture as 'knowledg*able*', as adequate to the construction of systems of cultural identification. This involves a dynamic conception of culture — one that recognizes and incorporates the ongoing fluidity and constant change that attends its articulation in the modern world. Likewise, Stuart Hall has argued that a positive conception of ethnicity must begin with 'a recognition that all speak from a particular place, out of a particular history, out of a particular experience, a particular culture, *without being contained by that position*' (1992, p. 258; my emphasis). In other words, the recognition of our cultural and historical situatedness should not set the limits of ethnicity and culture, nor act to undermine the legitimacy of other, equally valid forms of identity.

In the end then, a critical multiculturalism must foster, above all, students who can engage critically with all ethnic and cultural backgrounds, including their own. Such an approach would allow both minority and majority students to recognize and explore the complex interconnections, gaps and dissonances that occur between their own and other ethnic and cultural identities, as well as other forms of social identity. At the same time, how ethnic and cultural identities differ in salience among individuals and across given historical and social contexts, and how these identities are situated in the wider framework of power relations, can also be highlighted. In a parallel argument drawn from feminist discourse, Nira Yuval-Davis describes this process as one of 'transversal politics' in which 'perceived unity and homogeneity are replaced by dialogues that give recognition to the specific positionings of those who participate in them, as well as to the "unfinished knowledge" . . . that each such situated positioning can offer' (1997b, p. 204). Central to this idea of transversal politics is the interrelationship between 'rooting' and 'shifting'. Each participant in the dialogue brings with them the rooting in their own grouping and identity, but tries at the same time to shift in order to put themselves in a situation of exchange with those who have different groupings and identities.

With respect to critical multiculturalism, this can involve for minority students the retention of their ethnic and cultural identities, not by a retreat into traditionalism or cultural essentialism but by a more *autonomous* construction of group identity and political deliberation (White, 1988; Kymlicka, 1995a). Kevin Robins, following Homi Bhabha, has described this as an approach that rejects 'the comforts of Tradition' in order to 'forge a new *self-interpretation* based upon the responsibilities of cultural Translation' (1991, p. 41; my emphasis; see also, Hall, 1992). For majority students, this can involve a critical interrogation of the normalization and universalization of majoritarian forms of identity — most notably, whiteness — and their subsequent 'invisibility' in discussions of ethnicity. In either instance, a non-essentialist critical multiculturalism must engage with the present and the future as well as the past, and remain open to competing conceptualizations, diverse identities, and a rich public discourse about controversial issues (Calhoun, 1993b). This reflective and reciprocal process recognizes both the *limits* and the *hybridity* of all cultures — what distinguishes and conflicts, as well as what intersects — thus avoiding the cultural essentialism that has for too long plagued articulations of multiculturalism.[9]

Notes

1 As Gramsci argues, in order to understand any nation-state as a whole, one must always distinguish between its 'State' or political and administrative structure, and its 'civil society'. The latter comprises, for example, its principal non-political organizations, its religious and other beliefs, and its specific 'customs' or ways of life. In making these distinctions, there are inevitably features which do not fit easily under either category. However, as Nairn summarizes it: 'that is relatively unimportant. What matters is that they are distinguishable, and that the singular identity of a modern society depends upon the relationship between them' (1981, p. 131).

2 Essentialism is taken to mean here the process by which particular groups come to be described in terms of fundamental, immutable characteristics. In so doing, the relational and fluid aspects of identity formation are ignored and the group itself comes to be valorized as subject, as autonomous and separate, impervious to context and to processes of internal as well as external differentiation (Werbner, 1997b).

3 While I have adopted in this chapter a broad distinction between the Left and the Right, it should be pointed out that the conservative/liberal alliance here reflects the complexities of a debate which often transcends and/or subverts these traditional political oppositions. Similarly, in the discussion of the Left critique of multiculturalism which follows, we see an equally complex alliance between postmodernist and (other) liberal commentators.

4 This is certainly the position of Gordon, Walzer and Glazer in their respective analyses of the two approaches (see also Bullivant, 1981; Edwards, 1985, 1994; Gleason 1984; Rorty, 1991; Waldron, 1993, 1995).

5 Schlesinger does acknowledge here the cumulative and ongoing effects of racism on African-Americans, although he employs this apparently magnanimous recognition in order to explain the supposedly *pathological* nature of subsequent black identities. As he states: 'black Americans, after generations of psychological and cultural evisceration, have

every right to seek affirmative action for their past. . . . For blacks the American dream has been pretty much a nightmare and, far more than white ethnics, *they are driven by a desperate need to vindicate their own identity*' (1992, p. 60; my emphasis).

6   For useful critical overviews of the 'English Only' Movement, see Baron, 1990; Crawford, 1992; Dicker, 1996; Piatt, 1990.

7   Communitarians believe that we discover our ends embedded in a social context, rather than choosing them *ex nihilo*. Their principal objection to orthodox liberalism is thus to the idea of a self divorced from, or stripped of the social features of identity.

8   Anderson is not saying here that the nation or national consciousness are *imaginary* constructs. He is merely suggesting that the idea of a collective 'national' community, like all largescale collectivities, has to be *specifically* and *consciously* cultivated since it involves conceiving of something that is beyond one's immediate day-to-day experience.

9   I would like to thank Tariq Modood for his perceptive and helpful comments on an earlier version of this chapter.

References

AHMAD, A. (1995) 'The politics of literary postcoloniality', *Race and Class*, **36**, 3, pp. 1–20.

ANDERSON, B. (1991) *Imagined Communities: Reflections on the Origin and Spread of Nationalism* (rev. ed.), London: Verso.

ANTHIAS, F. and YUVAL-DAVIS, N. (1992) *Racialized Boundaries: Race, Nation, Gender, Colour and Class and the Anti-racist Struggle*, London: Routledge.

ANZALDÚA, G. (1987) *Borderlands/La Frontera: The New Mestiza*, San Francisco: Aunt Lute Books.

APPLE, M. (1996) *Cultural Politics and Education*, Buckingham: Open University Press.

AU, K. and JORDAN, C. (1981) 'Teaching reading to Hawaiian children: Finding a culturally appropriate solution', in TRUEBA, H., GUTHRIE, G. and AU, K. (eds) *Culture and the Bilingual Classroom: Studies in Classroom Ethnography*, Rowley, MA: Newbury, pp. 139–52.

BALIBAR, E. (1991) 'The nation form: History and ideology', in BALIBAR, E. and WALLERSTEIN, I. (eds) *Race, Nation, Class: Ambiguous Identities*, London: Verso, pp. 86–106.

BARKER, M. (1981) *The New Racism: Conservatives and the Ideology of the Tribe*, London: Junction.

BARON, D. (1990) *The English-only Question: An Official Language for America?*, New Haven: Yale University Press.

BENTLEY, G. (1987) 'Ethnicity and practice', *Comparative Studies in Society and History*, **29**, pp. 24–55.

BERMAN, M. (1983) *All that Is Solid Melts into Air: The Experience of Modernity*, London: Verso.

BERMAN, M. (1992) 'Why modernism still matters', in LASH, S. and FRIEDMAN, J. (eds) *Modernity and Identity*, Oxford: Basil Blackwell, pp. 33–58.

BHABHA, H. (1994) *The Location of Culture*, London: Routledge.

BLOOM, A. (1987) *The Closing of the American Mind: How Higher Education Has Failed Democracy and Impoverished the Souls of Today's Students*, New York: Simon and Schuster.

BOURDIEU, P. (1984) *Distinction: A Social Critique of the Judgement of Taste*, Cambridge, MA: Harvard University Press.

BOURDIEU, P. (1990a) *In Other Words: Essays towards a Reflexive Sociology*, Cambridge: Polity Press.

BOURDIEU, P. (1990b) *The Logic of Practice*, Cambridge: Polity Press.

BOURDIEU, P. (1991) *Language and Symbolic Power*, Cambridge: Polity Press.

BOURDIEU, P. and PASSERON, J. (1990) *Reproduction in Education, Society and Culture* (2nd ed.), London: Sage Publications.

BOURDIEU, P. and WACQUANT, L. (1992) *An Invitation to Reflexive Sociology*, Chicago: Chicago University Press.

BRAH, A. (1992) 'Difference, diversity and differentiation', in DONALD, J. and RATTANSI, A. (eds) *'Race', Culture and Difference*, London: Sage, pp. 126–45.

BRANDT, G. (1986) *The Realisation of Anti-racist Teaching*, Lewes, England: Falmer Press.

BULLIVANT, B. (1981) *The Pluralist Dilemma in Education: Six Case Studies*, Sydney: Allen and Unwin.

BURTONWOOD, N. (1996) 'Culture, identity and the curriculum', *Educational Review*, **48**, pp. 227–35.

CAGLAR, A. (1997) 'Hyphenated identities and the limits of "culture"', in MODOOD, T. and WERBNER, P. (eds) *The Politics of Multiculturalism in the New Europe: Racism, Identity and Community*, London: Zed Books, pp. 169–85.

CALHOUN, C. (1993a) 'Nationalism and ethnicity', *Annual Review of Sociology*, **19**, pp. 211–39.

CALHOUN, C. (1993b) 'Nationalism and civil society: Democracy, diversity and self-determination', *International Sociology*, **8**, pp. 387–411.

CALHOUN, C., LIPUMA, E. and POSTONE, M. (eds) (1993) *Bourdieu: Critical Perspectives*, Cambridge: Polity Press.

CHAMBERS, I. (1994) *Migrancy, Culture and Identity*, London: Routledge.

CLAUDE, I. (1955) *National Minorities: An International Problem*, Cambridge, MA: Harvard University Press.

CORSON, D. (1993) *Language, Minority Education and Gender: Linking Social Justice and Power*, Clevedon: Multilingual Matters.

CORSON, D. (1998) *Changing Education for Diversity*, Buckingham: Open University Press.

COULOMBE, P. (1995) *Language Rights in French Canada*, New York: Peter Lang.

CRAWFORD, J. (1992) *Hold Your Tongue: Bilingualism and the Politics of 'English Only'*, Reading MA: Addison-Wesley.

DICKER, S. (1996) *Languages in America*, Clevedon, England: Multilingual Matters.

DI LEONARDO, M. (1994) 'White ethnicities, identity politics, and baby bear's chair', *Social Text*, **41**, pp. 5–33.

DI MAGGIO, P. (1979) 'Review essay on Pierre Bourdieu', *American Journal of Sociology*, **84**, pp. 1460–74.

DONALD, J. and RATTANSI, A. (eds) (1992) *'Race', Culture and Difference*, London: Sage.

D'SOUZA, D. (1992) *Illiberal Education: The Politics of Race and Sex on Campus*, New York: Vintage.

DWORKIN, R. (1978) 'Liberalism', in HAMPSHIRE, S. (ed.) *Public and Private Morality*, Cambridge: Cambridge University Press, pp. 113–43.

EDWARDS, J. (1985) *Language, Society and Identity*, Oxford: Basil Blackwell.

EDWARDS, J. (1994) *Multilingualism*, London: Routledge.

ERICKSON, F. and MOHATT, G. (1982) 'Cultural organization and participation structures in two classrooms of Indian students', in SPINDLER, G. (ed.) *Doing the Ethnography of Schooling*, Norwood, NJ: Ablex, pp. 131–74.

FENTON, S. (1999) *Ethnicity: Social Structure, Culture and Identity in the Modern World*, London: Macmillan.

FRIEDMAN, J. (1997) 'Global crises, the struggle for identity and intellectual porkbarrelling: Cosmopolitans versus locals, ethnics and nationals in an era of de-hegemonisation', in WERBNER, P. and MODOOD, T. (eds) *Debating Cultural Hybridity: Multicultural Identities and the Politics of Antiracism*, London: Zed Books, pp. 70–89.

GILBERT, R. (1987) 'The concept of social practice and modes of ideology critique in schools', *Discourse*, **7**, pp. 37–54.

GILLBORN, D. (1995) *Racism and Antiracism in Real Schools*, Buckingham: Open University Press.

GILROY, P. (1987) *There Ain't no Black in the Union Jack*, London: Hutchinson.

GILROY, P. (1992) 'The end of antiracism', in DONALD, J. and RATTANSI, A. (eds) *'Race', Culture, and Difference*, London: Sage, pp. 49–61.

GILROY, P. (1993) *Small Acts: Thoughts on the Politics of Black Cultures*, London: Serpent's Tail.

GIROUX, H. (1992) *Border Crossings*, London: Routledge.

GIROUX, H. (1997) *Pedagogy and the Politics of Hope: Theory, Culture and Schooling*, Boulder, CO: Westview Press.

GLAZER, N. (1975) *Affirmative Discrimination: Ethnic Inequality and Public Policy*, New York: Basic Books.

GLEASON, P. (1984) 'Pluralism and assimilation: A conceptual history', in EDWARDS, J. (ed.) *Linguistic Minorities, Policies and Pluralism*, London: Academic Press, pp. 221–57.

GOLDBERG, D. (1994) 'Introduction: Multicultural conditions', in GOLDBERG, D. (ed.) *Multiculturalism: A Critical Reader*, Oxford: Basil Blackwell, pp. 1–41.

GORDON, M. (1978) *Human Nature, Class and Ethnicity*, New York: Oxford University Press.

GORDON, M. (1981) 'Models of pluralism: The new American dilemma', *Annals of the American Academy of Political and Social Science*, **454**, pp. 178–88.

GRAMSCI, A. (1971) *Selections from the Prison Notebooks*, HOARE, Q. and NOWELL-SMITH, G. (eds), London: Lawrence and Wishart.

GUMPERZ, J. (1982) *Discourse Strategies*, Cambridge: Cambridge University Press.

HABERMAS, J. (1979) *Communication and the Evolution of Society*, Boston: Beacon.

HALL, S. (1992) 'New ethnicities', in DONALD, J. and RATTANSI, A. (eds) *'Race', Culture and Difference*, London: Sage, pp. 252–9.

HANDLER, R. (1988) *Nationalism and the Politics of Culture in Quebec*, Madison: Wisconsin University Press.

HANNERZ, U. (1992) *Cultural Complexity: Studies in the Organization of Meaning*, New York: Columbia University Press.

HARKER, R. (1984) 'On reproduction, habitus and education', *British Journal of Sociology of Education*, **5**, pp. 117–27.

HARKER, R. (1990) 'Bourdieu: Education and reproduction', in HARKER, R., MAHAR, C. and WILKES, C. (eds) *An Introduction to the Work of Pierre Bourdieu: The Practice of Theory*, London: Macmillan, pp. 86–108.

HARKER, R., MAHAR, C. and WILKES, C. (eds) (1990) *An Introduction to the Work of Pierre Bourdieu: The Practice of Theory*, London: Macmillan.

HARKER, R. and MAY, S. (1993) 'Code and habitus: Comparing the accounts of Bernstein and Bourdieu', *British Journal of Sociology of Education*, **14**, pp. 169–78.

HEATH, S. (1983) *Ways with Words: Ethnography of Communication in Communities and Classrooms*, Cambridge: Cambridge University Press.

HICKS, E. (1991) *Border Writing*, Minneapolis: University of Minnesota Press.

HIRSCH, E. (1987) *Cultural Literacy: What every American Needs to Know*, Boston: Houghton Mifflin.

HOBSBAWM, E. (1990) *Nations and Nationalism since 1780*, Cambridge: Cambridge University Press.

HOBSBAWM, E. and RANGER, T. (eds) (1983) *The Invention of Tradition*, Cambridge: Cambridge University Press.

HOFFMAN, D. (1996) 'Culture and self in multicultural education: Reflections on discourse, text, and practice', *American Educational Research Journal*, **33**, pp. 545–69.

HOFFMAN, D. (1997) 'Diversity in practice: Perspectives on concept, context, and policy', *Educational Policy*, **11**, pp. 375–392.

hooks, b. (1989) *Talking Back*, Boston: South End.

HOWE, K. (1992) 'Liberal democracy, equal opportunity, and the challenge of multiculturalism', *American Educational Research Journal*, **29**, pp. 455–70.

HUGHES, R. (1993) *Culture of Complaint: The Fraying of America*, New York: Oxford University Press.

JENKINS, R. (1992) *Pierre Bourdieu*, London: Routledge.

JENKINS, R. (1994) 'Rethinking ethnicity: Identity, categorization and power', *Ethnic and Racial Studies*, **17**, pp. 197–223.

JENKINS, R. (1997) *Rethinking Ethnicity*, London: Sage.

JORDAN, C. (1985) 'Translating culture: From ethnographic information to educational program', *Anthropology and Education Quarterly*, **16**, pp. 105–23.

KINCHELOE, J. and STEINBERG, S. (1997) *Changing Multiculturalism*, Buckingham: Open University Press.

KYMLICKA, W. (1989) *Liberalism, Community and Culture*, Oxford: Clarendon Press.

KYMLICKA, W. (1995a) *Multicultural Citizenship: A Liberal Theory of Minority Rights*, Oxford: Clarendon Press.

KYMLICKA, W. (1995b) 'Introduction', in KYMLICKA, W. (ed.) *The Rights of Minority Cultures*, Oxford: Oxford University Press, pp. 1–27.

LABOV, W. (1972) 'The logic of nonstandard English', in *Language in the Inner city: Studies in the Black English Vernacular*, Philadelphia: University of Pennsylvania Press, pp. 201–40.

LADSON-BILLINGS, G. (1994) *The Dreamkeepers: Successful Teachers of African American Children*, San Francisco: Jossey Bass.

LADSON-BILLINGS, G. (1995) 'Towards a theory of culturally relevant pedagogy', *American Educational Research Journal*, **32**, pp. 465–91.

LÉVI STRAUSS, C. (1985) *The View from Afar*, Oxford: Blackwell.

LÉVI STRAUSS, C. (1994) 'Anthropology, race, and politics: A conversation with Didier Eribon', in BOROFSKY, R. (ed.) *Assessing Cultural Anthropology*, New York: McGraw Hill, pp. 420–9.

LLOYD, C. (1994) 'Universalism and difference: The crisis of antiracism in France and the UK', in RATTANSI, A. and WESTWOOD, S. (eds) *Racism, Modernity, and Identity*, Cambridge: Polity Press, pp. 222–44.

LYOTARD, J. (1984) *The Postmodern Condition: A Report on Knowledge*, BENNINGTON, G. and MASSUMI, B. (Trans.), Manchester: Manchester University Press.

MARGALIT, A. and RAZ, J. (1995) 'National self-determination', in KYMLICKA, W. (ed.) *The Rights of Minority Cultures*, Oxford: Oxford University Press, pp. 79–92.

MAY, S. (1994) *Making Multicultural Education Work*, Clevedon, England: Multilingual Matters.

MAY, S. (1995) 'Deconstructing traditional discourses of schooling: An example of school reform', *Language and Education*, **9**, pp. 1–29.

MAY, S. (1999) *Language, Education and Minority Rights*, London: Longman, forthcoming.

MCCARTHY, C. (1990) *Race and Curriculum: Social Inequality and the Theory and Politics of Difference in Contemporary Research on Schooling*, Bristol, PA: Falmer Press.

MCCARTHY, C. and CRICHLOW, W. (eds) (1993) *'Race', Identity and Representation in Education*, New York: Routledge.

MCLAREN, P. (1995) *Critical Pedagogy and Predatory Culture*, New York: Routledge.

MCLAREN, P. (1997) *Revolutionary Multiculturalism: Pedagogies of Dissent for the New Millennium*, Boulder, CO: Westview Press.

MODOOD, T. (1992) *Not Easy Being British: Colour, Culture and Citizenship*, Stoke-on-Trent: Runnymede Trust and Trentham Books.

MODOOD, T. (1998) 'Anti-essentialism, multiculturalism and the "recognition" of religious groups', *Journal of Political Philosophy*, **6**.

MULLARD, C. (1982) 'Multiracial education in Britain: From assimilation to cultural pluralism', in TIERNEY, J. (ed.) *Race, Migration and Schooling*, London: Holt, pp. 120–33.

NAGEL, J. (1994) 'Constructing ethnicity: Creating and recreating ethnic identity and culture', *Social Problems*, **41**, pp. 152–76.

NAIRN, T. (1981) *The Break-up of Britain: Crisis and Neo-nationalism*, London: Verso.

NASH, R. (1990) 'Bourdieu on education and social and cultural reproduction', *British Journal of Sociology of Education*, **11**, pp. 431–47.

NIETO, S. (1995) 'From brown heroes and holidays to assimilationist agendas: Reconsidering the critiques of multicultural education', in SLEETER, C. and McLAREN, P. (eds) *Multicultural Education, Critical Pedagogy, and the Politics of Difference*, Albany: SUNY Press, pp. 191–220.

NIETO, S. (1996) *Affirming Diversity: The Sociopolitical Context of Multicultural Education* (2nd ed.), New York: Longman.

PHILIPS, S. (1972) 'Participant structures and communicative competence: Warm Spring children in community and classroom', in CAZDEN, C., JOHN, V. and HYMES, D. (eds) *Functions of Language in the Classroom*, New York: Teachers College Press, pp. 370–94.

PIATT, B. (1990) *Only English? Law and Language Policy in the United States*, Albuquerque: University of New Mexico Press.

PORTER, J. (1965) *The Vertical Mosaic*, Toronto: Toronto University Press.

PORTER, J. (1975) 'Ethnic pluralism in Canadian perspective', in GLAZER, N. and MOYNIHAN, D. (eds) *Ethnicity: Theory and Experience*, Cambridge, MA: Harvard University Press, pp. 267–304.

RATTANSI, A. (1992) 'Changing the subject? Racism, culture, and education', in DONALD, J. and RATTANSI, A. (eds) *'Race', Culture, and Difference*, London: Sage, pp. 11–48.

RAVITCH, D. (1992) 'Diversity in education', *Dialogue*, **95**, pp. 39–47.

RAWLS, J. (1985) 'Justice as fairness: Political not metaphysical', *Philosophy and Public Affairs*, **14**, pp. 223–51.

REAY, D. (1995a) '"They employ cleaners to do that": Habitus in the primary classroom', *British Journal of Sociology of Education*, **16**, pp. 353–71.

REAY, D. (1995b) 'Using habitus to look at "race" and class in primary school classrooms', in GRIFFITHS, M. and TROYNA, B. (eds) *Antiracism, Culture and Social Justice in Education*, Stoke-on Trent: Trentham Books, pp. 115–32.

RENAN, E. (1990) 'What is a nation?', in BHABHA, H. (ed.) *Nation and Narration*, London: Routledge (original, 1882), pp. 8–22.

REX, J. (1973) *Race, Colonialism and the City*, Oxford: Oxford University Press.

ROBINS, K. (1991) 'Tradition and translation: National culture in its global context', in CORNER, J. and HARVEY, S. (eds) *Enterprise and Heritage: Crosscurrents of National Culture*, London: Routledge, pp. 21–44.

RODRIGUEZ, R. (1983) *Hunger of Memory*, Bantam: New York.

RODRIGUEZ, R. (1993) *Days of Obligation: An Argument with my Mexican Father*, Penguin: London.

ROKKAN, S. and URWIN, D. (1983) *Economy, Territory, Identity*, London: Sage.

RORTY, R. (1991) *Objectivity, Relativism, and Truth: Philosophical Papers I*, Cambridge: Cambridge University Press.

ROSALDO, R. (1989) *Culture and Truth*, London: Routledge.

SAID, E. (1994) *Culture and Imperialism*, London: Vintage.

SANDEL, M. (1982) *Liberalism and the Limits of Justice*, Cambridge: Cambridge University Press.

SCHERMERHORN, R. (1970) *Comparative Ethnic Relations*, New York: Random House.

SCHLESINGER, A. (1991) 'The Disuniting of America: What we all stand to lose if multicultural education takes the wrong approach', *American Educator*, **15**, pp. 14–33.

SCHLESINGER, A. (1992) *The Disuniting of America: Reflections on a Multicultural Society*, New York: W.W. Norton and Co.

SCOLLON, R. and SCOLLON, S. (1981) *Narrative, Literacy and Face in Interethnic Communication*, Norwood, NJ: Ablex.

SLEETER, C. (1995) 'An analysis of the critiques of multicultural education', in BANKS, J. and BANKS, C. (eds) *Handbook of Research on Multicultural Education*, New York: Macmillan, pp. 81–94.

SMAJE, C. (1997) 'Not just a social construct: Theorising race and ethnicity', *Sociology*, **31**, pp. 307–27.

SMALL, S. (1994) *Racialised Barriers: The Black Experience in the United States and England in the 1980s*, London: Routledge.

SMITH, A. (1981) *The Ethnic Revival*, Cambridge: Cambridge University Press.

SMITH, A. (1995) *Nations and Nationalism in a Global Era*, London: Polity Press.

TAYLOR, C. (1992) *Multiculturalism and 'The Politics of Recognition'*, Princeton, NJ: Princeton University Press.

TROYNA, B. (1982) 'The ideological and policy response to black pupils in British schools', in HARTNETT, A. (ed.) *The Social Sciences in Educational Studies*, London: Heinemann, pp. 127–43.

TROYNA, B. (ed.) (1987) *Racial Inequality in Education*, London: Tavistock.

TROYNA, B. (1993) *Racism and Education*, Buckingham: Open University Press.

TROYNA, B. and HATCHER, R. (1992) *Racism in Children's Lives: A Study of Mainly White Primary Schools*, London: Routledge.

TROYNA, B. and WILLIAMS, J. (1986) *Racism, Education and the State: The Racialization of Educational Policy*, Beckenham: Croom Helm.

VAN DYKE, V. (1977) 'The individual, the State, and ethnic communities in political theory', *World Politics*, **29**, pp. 343–69.

WALDRON, J. (1993) *Liberal Rights*, Cambridge: Cambridge University Press.

WALDRON, J. (1995) 'Minority cultures and the cosmopolitan alternative', in KYMLICKA, W. (ed.) *The Rights of Minority Cultures*, Oxford: Oxford University Press, pp. 93–119.

WALZER, M. (1992a) *What It Means to Be an American*, New York: Marsilio.

WALZER, M. (1992b) 'Comment', in TAYLOR, C. *Multiculturalism and 'The Politics of Recognition'*, Princeton, NJ: Princeton University Press, pp. 100–1.

WERBNER, P. (1997a) 'Introduction: The dialectics of cultural hybridity', in WERBNER, P. and MODOOD, T. (eds) *Debating Cultural Hybridity: Multicultural Identities and the Politics of Antiracism*, London: Zed Books, pp. 1–26.

WERBNER, P. (1997b) 'Essentialising essentialism, essentialising silence: Ambivalence and multiplicity in the constructions of racism and ethnicity', in WERBNER, P. and MODOOD, T. (eds) *Debating Cultural Hybridity: Multicultural Identities and the Politics of Antiracism*, London: Zed Books, pp. 226–54.

WETHERELL, M. and POTTER, J. (1992) *Mapping the Language of Racism: Discourse and the Legitimation of Exploitation*, London: Harvester Wheatleaf.

WHITE, S. (1988) *The Recent Work of Jurgen Habermas*, Cambridge: Cambridge University Press.

WICKER, H-R. (1997) 'From complex culture to cultural complexity', in WERBNER, P. and MODOOD, T. (eds) *Debating Cultural Hybridity: Multicultural Identities and the Politics of Antiracism*, London: Zed Books, pp. 29–45.

WILDAVSKY, A. (1992) 'Finding universalistic solutions to particularistic problems: Bilingualism resolved through a second language requirement for elementary schools', *Journal of Policy Analysis and Management*, **11**, pp. 310–14.

YOUNG, I. (1993) 'Together in difference: Transforming the logic of group political conflict', in SQUIRES, J. (ed.) *Principled Positions: Postmodernism and the Rediscovery of Value*, London: Lawrence and Wishart, pp. 121–50.

YUVAL-DAVIS, N. (1997a) *Gender and Nation*, London: Sage.

YUVAL-DAVIS, N. (1997b) 'Ethnicity, gender relations and multiculturalism', in WERBNER, P. and MODOOD, T. (eds) *Debating Cultural Hybridity: Multicultural Identities and the Politics of Antiracism*, London: Zed Books, pp. 193–208.

2 Racism and Multicultural Education: Rethinking 'Race' and 'Whiteness' in Late Capitalism

Peter McLaren and Rodolfo Torres

There has been a remarkable tendency in current appraisals of multiculturalism to neglect or ignore profound changes in the structural dynamics and modes of capital accumulation worldwide. This is most evident in the commentaries of multiculturalist scholars whose theoretical orientations could be described as 'postmodernist' or 'post-Marxist'. The emergence of the post-Fordist socio-economic landscape and the reconfiguration of racialized social relations in cities such as Los Angeles, where we live, in our mind mandates a re-examination of contemporary perspectives on multicultural education in the United States. At this precipitous historical juncture, when an analysis of and challenge to capitalism is so urgently needed, perhaps more than in previous decades, many leftist social theorists have largely conceptualized the very idea of capitalism out of existence. In addition to promoting the strange disappearance of capitalism in the education literature on multiculturalism, contemporary responses to recent structural changes in the United States' political economy have made the issues of 'race' and racism much more complex than ever before.

The Dickensianizing of postmodern megalopolises like Los Angeles (the enhancing of the personal wealth of the few who live in places like Beverly Hills at the expense of the many who live in places like Compton or East LA) is not a natural historical event (there is nothing natural about history). It is a politically contrived dismemberment of the national conscience. And it is comfortably linked to global economic restructuring. The globalization of capital has unleashed new practices of social control and forms of internationalized class domination. This is not to suggest, however, that certain social, cultural and political institutions do not mediate the economic or that there exist relative decommodified zones.

Sustaining a meagre existence is becoming frighteningly more difficult with the passage of time for millions of 'Third World' peoples as well as 'First World' urban dwellers, including millions of inhabitants of the United States. Global capitalism is excluding large numbers from formal employment while the poor, trapped within post-Fordist arenas of global restructuring and systems of flexible specialization, appear to be less able to organize themselves into stable and homogeneous social movements.

One reason may be because labour markets are growing more segmented as full-time workers are replaced with part-time workers who have little or no access to basic benefits. The days of high-wage, high-benefit mass production manufacturing are receding into the horizon as the 'First World' bids farewell to industrialized regimes. Yet manufacturing has not completely disappeared from the United States. In Los Angeles, for example, one can witness the 'Latinization' of the working-class, as Latinos/as now make up 36 per cent of Los Angeles County's labour force in manufacturing (the nation's largest manufacturing base).

Stock options frequently increase in companies that downsize and lay off thousands of employees. It used to be a sign that a company was in trouble when it laid off large numbers of workers. Now it is very often an indication of strength, making stockholders proud. Cutting costs is everything, as business moves farther away from even a peripheral engagement with the world of ethics. In fact, capitalism has made ethics nearly obsolete. The buying and selling of labour power is currently about aesthetics, which does share a hinge with ethics, true, but the latter is subsumed by reification's terrible beauty.

The war on poverty has given way to the war on the poverty-stricken — a war that is about as mean-spirited as wars can get. The average worker has to do without the luxury of decent living standards because to improve conditions for the majority of the population would cut too deeply into the corporate profitability of the ruling elite. Rarely has such contempt for the poor and for disenfranchised people of colour been so evident as in the hate-filled politics of the last several decades.

The greed and avarice of the United States' ruling class is seemingly unparalleled in history. Yet its goals remain decidedly the same. Michael Parenti writes:

> Throughout history there has been only one thing that ruling interests have ever wanted — and that is everything: all the choice lands, forest, game, herds, harvests, mineral deposits, and precious metals of the earth; all the wealth, riches, and profitable returns; all the productive facilities, gainful inventiveness and technologies; all the control positions of the State and other major institutions; all public supports and subsidies, privileges and immunities; all the protections of the law with none of its constraints; all the services, comforts, luxuries, and advantages of civil society with none of the taxes and costs. Every ruling class has wanted only this: all the rewards and none of the burdens. The operational code is: we have a lot; we can get more; we want it all. (1996, p. 46)

As long as the small business lobby and other interests tied to capital in the United States successfully derail health care reform whenever the issue raises its disease-ravaged face, as long as the bond market continues to destroy public investment, and as long as business continues to enjoy record-high profits, acquisitions, and mergers (with the aid of corporate welfare) at the expense of wages and labour, then prosperity in the US, like its administration of social justice, will remain highly selective. And we all know who benefits from such selectivity. To remain in a state of political paralysis or inertia is to aid and abet the sickening suburbanization of the country — a suburbanization driven by a neo-liberal agenda designed to serve mainly Whites. Working under existing rules established by the National Labour Relations Act and the procedures carried out by the National Labour Relations Board, unions are being deprived of their right to organize, and this is contributing in no small way to wage decline. The situation reflects only too well what Parenti calls his 'iron law of bourgeois politics' (1996, p. 248): when change threatens to rule, then rules are changed.

Residents of the United States do not have a natural disposition to swindle the gullible, to target the poor, and to scapegoat immigrants and fashion them into *los olvidados* (the forgotten ones). The current evisceration of public protection pro- grammes, shamefully absent enforcement of environmental standards, rising health insurance premiums, and drastic declines in salaries for working people, have cata- pulted the United States onto a tragic course towards social decay and human misery — a course that is far from inevitable.

It is possible that a quarter century from now Whites might be a minority in the United States. As they continue to feel that their civil society is being despoiled and to blame immigrants for their increasing downward mobility and the disappear- ance of 'traditional' American values, Whites fall prey to the appeal of a reactionary and fascist poetics of authoritarian repression. This is especially true at a time when Whites continue to feel removed from their ethnic roots and undergo what Howard Winant has called a 'racializing pan-ethnicity as "Euro-Americans"' (1994, p. 284). Whether we decide to call our current historical context 'postmodern culture' or 'late capitalism' one cannot deny its link to the voracious exploitation of the market- place. As Cornel West writes:

> Postmodern culture is more and more a market culture dominated by gangster mentalities and self-destructive wantonness. This culture engulfs all of us yet its impact on the disadvantaged is devastating, resulting in extreme violence in every- day life. Sexual violence against women and homicidal assault by young black men on one another are only the most obvious signs of this empty quest for pleasure, property, and power. (1993, p. 258)

Rather than occupying centre stage in contemporary theoretical debates on the meaning of 'race' and 'representation' in a 'postmodern' society, current arrange- ments and configurations of the global economy serve, at most, as a barely discern- ible backdrop. This represents a significant point of contention among US leftist educators, given the dramatic changes in US class formations during the last 30 years. These changes include major shifts in perceptions of social location, prevailing attitudes, and contemporary views and representations of racialized populations.

In general, discourses in the US that deal with multiculturalism deal very little with the concept of racism and focus instead on the politics and affirmation of dif- ference. As Linda Alcoff remarks:

> As many people have pointed out, one of the persistent problems with the dis- courses in the USA around multiculturalism and cultural studies is that race, racism and racial hierarchies are relatively ignored. Explorations of culture and ethnicity can all too easily avoid any account of white supremacy and focus instead on the recognition of difference, flattening out differences in a way that makes them appear equal. Race, on the other hand, is difficult to focus on for very long without it working to discredit the imagined landscapes of pluralist difference that cultural

studies so often presupposes. And mainstream political language in both Britain and the USA codes racial talk as cultural talk, so racist claims can be cloaked as claims about cultural difference. (1996, p. 10)

Even in the case of those scholars of multiculturalism who do deal with issues of racism, racialized social practices, and racial hierarchies, few of their analyses address with sufficient analytical complexity issues of 'race' in general, and relationships among racialized social practices, gendered constructions of identity, and social class in particular. In recent years scholars in cultural studies, multicultural education, and critical pedagogy have brought new theoretical perspectives to the study of racism and education in United States society. Liberal and left liberal multiculturalists have attempted, in the main, to recast the debate over the analysis of 'race' and racism in the United States and its implications for multiculturalism and antiracist education. Although it cannot be denied that these diverse and provocative works represent a challenge to the mainstream analysis of 'race relations' and contribute significantly to our understanding of racism, they fail in our view to reconceptualize the traditional social science paradigm that relies on the reified category of 'race' to interpret racialized social relations. In the final analysis, the general conceptual framework utilized by these scholars remains buried in the conventional sociology of 'race relations' language. Further, the central dynamic of class relations is significantly absent.

Critique of Multicultural and Antiracist Education Discourse

Nowhere has this theoretical shortcoming been more evident than in contemporary discussions of multicultural education in the United States which have been fundamentally shaped by parochial notions of 'racial' identity, ethnicity, and culture. Despite an expressed commitment to social and cultural 'transformation', much of the US multicultural education literature has positioned public education within the larger context of class relations only in the most peripheral sense. Conspicuously absent from the writings of even some critical multiculturalist education scholars is a rigorous criticism of the relationship between educational practices and the changing conditions of the United States' political economy. The absence of an analysis of the capitalist wage-labour system and class relations is, in our estimation, a serious shortcoming.

A lack of political imagination in current discussions of multicultural education is evidenced by an emerging discourse on the politics of difference that continues to be anchored in a black–white binarism. For over a century, this binarism has congealed dramatically within the education literature and in doing so has considerably influenced thinking and scholarship related to social group differences. One of the most severe consequences of employing a black–white framework is the unintended practice of camouflaging the particular historical and contextual dimensions that give rise to differing forms of racism throughout the globe. Further, this conflation of racialized relations into solely a black–white paradigm has prevented scholars from engaging more fully the *specificities* of particular groups and from exploring more deeply *comparative* ethnic histories of racism and how these are linked to changing class relations in late capitalism. We argue that a continued employment of this framework will endanger the future of antiracist projects in the United States. Since one of the consequences of using this framework is the reproduction of some of the constitutive features of racism within the discourse and practice of multicultural education itself, such a conceptually impoverished framework will surely impede the development of a more critical multiculturalism. As long as a black–white dichotomy continues to be employed unproblematically, multicultural education will remain deeply invested in its own generalized incapacity to elucidate and to challenge new racialized formations.

Whilst some critics might object to our evaluation of the multicultural literature, we see our criticism born out, for example, in studies of Latino communities within the United States. Many studies of Latino populations have placed an overwhelming emphasis on linguistic questions tied to the historical production of identity and culture. This is illustrated by the growing body of education literature that focuses on issues of 'language-minority' students, and that only marginally discusses the impact of racism and class position on identity and cultural formations — as if the problems of Latino students can be resolved simply through the enactment of language policy.

'Race' as a Social Construct

We would be hard pressed to find a progressive social scientist in this day and age who would employ the construct of 'race' as a determinant of specific social phenomena associated with levels of intelligence or personality characteristics. Nevertheless, traditional arguments about 'race' dominate academic and popular discourse. What does it mean to attribute analytical status to the idea of 'race' and use it as an explanatory concept in educational discussions of theory or practice? The use of 'race' as a descriptive or analytical category has serious consequences for the way in which social life is presumed to be constituted and organized. Without first problematizing the construct 'race' in their discussions, social theorists lend credibility and legitimacy to the notion that humanity exists as genetically distinct 'racial groups' marked by a specific combination of biologically defined or imagined phenotypical characteristics and discrete cultural practices. We should not accord analytical or explanatory status to the idea of 'race' as if it corresponded to some biological or epistemological 'type', 'absolute', or monolithic social category. The use of the term 'race' has become an analytical trap precisely when it has been employed in antiseptic isolation from the messy terrain of historical and material relations. Because the term 'race' is rarely interrogated as an ideological or social construction produced within the historical and geopolitical specificity of its use, and as an artefact of the social science literature itself, it continues to be repatriated by social scientists in ways that fit their generalized models of social evolution, their systems of intelligibility, and their paradigms of cultural calculability. We say this since 'race' quite clearly articulates with power, ethnicity, gender, nation, and class. Any conceptual transition from the social category of 'race' to that of 'race relations' is sociologically illegitimate for similar reasons. For this reason the idea of 'race' should be abandoned as an analytical category within the social sciences. In addition, social scientists writing in the area of multiculturalism should not take as their object of analysis the production of 'race relations'. But we do not reject the concept of racism. Rather, we criticize the 'race relations' problematic in order to retain a concept of racism which is constructed in such a way as to recognize the existence of a plurality of historically specific *racisms*. In this sense, 'race relations' become racialized ethnic relations.

Unfortunately, the continued use of the notion of 'race' in educational research, whether intentional or not, upholds a definition of 'race' as a causal factor. In other words, significance and meaning are attributed to phenotypical features, rather than the historical, social, and discursive production of processes of racialization. Further, the use of the term 'race' often serves to conceal the fact that particular sets of social conditions experienced by racialized groups are determined by an interplay of complex social processes, one of which is premised on the articulation of racism to effect legitimate exclusion (Miles and Torres, 1996).

Yet despite the dangerous forms of distortion which arise from the use of 'race' as a central analytical category of theory-making, multiculturalist scholars — at least in the US — seem unable to break with the hegemonic tradition of its use in the social sciences. Efforts to problematize the reified nature of the term 'race' and to consider its elimination as a metaphor in our work as social scientists and antiracist activists, is quickly met with major resistance among even progressive intellectuals of all communities. Often these responses are associated with a fear of delegitimating the historical movements for liberation that have been principally defined in terms of 'race' struggles. Such responses demonstrate the tenacious and adhesive quality of socially constructed ideas and how through their historical usage these ideas become commonsense understandings that resist serious scholarly challenge. As a consequence, 'race' is frequently retained as 'an analytical category not because it corresponds to any biological or epistemological absolutes, but because it refers to investigation of the power that collective identities acquire by means of their roots in tradition' (Gilroy, 1987, p. 5).

To address this issue requires an analytical shift from 'race' to a plural conceptualization of 'racisms' and their historical articulations with other ideologies and capitalist social relations (see also Rattansi, this volume). This plural notion of 'racisms' more accurately captures the historically specific nature of racism and the variety of meanings attributed to evaluations of difference and assessments of the superiority and inferiority of various groups of people. In other words, progressive scholars should not be trying to advance a critical theory of 'race'. To persist in attributing to the idea of 'race' an analytical status can only lead us further down a theoretical and political dead-end. Instead, the task at hand is to deconstruct 'race' and detach it from the concept of racism. In our view, it is essential for scholars to understand that the construction of the idea of 'race' is embodied in racist ideology that supports the practice of racism. It is racism as an ideology that produces the notion of 'race', not the existence of 'races' that produces racisms (Guillaumin, 1995). Hence, what is needed is a clear understanding of the *plurality* of racisms and the exclusionary social processes that function to perpetuate racialized social relations. Robert Miles convincingly argues that these processes can be analysed within the framework of Marxist theory without retaining the idea of 'race' as an analytical concept:

> Using the concept of racialization, racism, and exclusionary practice to identify specific means of effecting the reproduction of the capitalist mode of production, one is able to stress consistently and rigorously the role of human agency, albeit always constrained by particular historical and material circumstances, in these processes, as well as to recognize the specificity of particular forms of oppression. (1993, p. 52)

Miles' work also supports the idea that efforts to construct a new language for examining the nature of differing racisms require an understanding of how complex relationships of exploitation and resistance — grounded in differences of class, ethnicity, and gender — give rise to a multiplicity of ideological constructions of the racialized 'other'.

The disturbing 'scientific' assertion that 'race' determines academic performance that has been made by Richard Herrnstein and Charles Murray in their (1994) book, *The Bell Curve*, illustrates the negative consequences for African-American students and other racialized groups in the US. In this case the use of the term 'race' serves to hide the truth that it is not 'race' which determines academic performance; rather, academic performance results from an interplay of complex social processes, one of which is premised on the articulation of racism to effect exclusion in the classroom and beyond.

The habitual practice of framing social relations as 'race relations' in discussions of racialized groups and schooling obfuscates the complexity of the problem. In this case, educational theorists assign a certain significance to 'racial' characteristics of students as causally implicated in school success rather than attribute student achievement to the social conditions in which practices of schooling are embedded and the ways in which these conditions are shaped by both global and local economic and political formations. The unfortunate absence of this criticism places a conceptual shroud over the real reasons why students underachieve, perform poorly on standardized tests, are over-represented in remedial programmes, and continue to drop out of high school at increasing rates. As a consequence, educational solutions are often derived from distorted perceptions of the problem.

The politics of busing in the early 1970s in the United States provides an excellent example of such distortion. Social scientists studying 'race relations' concluded that proximal contact among black and white students would decrease incidents of prejudice and that the educational conditions for black students would improve if they were bused to white (better) schools outside of their neighbourhoods. Thirty years later we are witnessing many progressive parents and educators who condemn the busing solution (a solution based on a discourse of 'race') not only as fundamentally destructive to the fabric of black and Latino communities, but also as an erroneous social experiment that failed to improve the academic performance of the children in these communities.

Thus, while we reject the term 'race' as an analytic or semantic category, we wish to emphasize that we understand 'race' to be a sociological reality with devastating effects. Racial categories continue to exist within our current social ontology (cf. Carrim and Soudien, this volume). By claiming 'race' to be to a large extent an ontological category we mean only that it has serious consequences for certain groups of people in everyday life. Linda Alcoff refers to this characteristic of 'race' as 'a visual registry operating in social relations which is socially constructed, historically evolving and culturally variegated, but nonetheless powerfully determinant over individual experiences and choices' (1996, p. 6). Alcoff claims that this visual registry needs to be described as a type of 'ontologizing difference' that operates 'at the most basic level concerning knowledge and subjectivity, being and thinking'. To say that 'race' operates as a form of social ontology means that it signifies using culturally various historical categories 'involving visual determinants marked on the body through the interplay of perceptual practices and bodily appearance' (1996, p. 7). This conception of 'race' is intended to increase the offerings of deep descriptions of reality that do not fall into essentialist categories or assume an ahistorical or transcendental status. Alcoff writes:

> My view is that the meaning of race will shift as one moves through the terrain and interplay of different discourses, where here discourses signify practices and institutions as well as systems of knowledge (a usage well exemplified in Wittgenstein's concept of a language game, which involves linguistic practices connected with and embodied in actions). The 'answer' to the question of what racial identity really is will depend on what language game we are playing, although the relativism of this situation can be mitigated by showing overlaps between language games, and by offering immanent critiques that reveal internal contradictions, such as a language game that claims to be non-racist but actually is racist. (1996, p. 8)

Like Alcoff we wish to assume a position that moves beyond simply a reliance on 'the withering away of racial categorization'. We want to do what Alcoff (1996, p. 9) rightly claims the anti-essentialist and anti-race arguments cannot do:

1 take into account the full force of 'race' as a lived experience, understanding this not as mere epiphenomenon but as constitutive of reality; and
2 acknowledge and account for the epistemological and theoretical importance that racial perspectives have had on, for example, the undermining of modernist teleologies — e.g., DuBois' use of slavery to undermine US supremacist claims, and the Frankfurt School's critique of western rationality from the perspective of the Holocaust.

'Race' and Class

According to Alex Callinicos (1993), racial differences are invented. Racism occurs when the characteristics which justify discrimination are held to be inherent in the oppressed group. This form of oppression is peculiar to capitalist societies; it arises in the circumstances surrounding industrial capitalism and the attempt to acquire a large labour force. Callinicos points out three main conditions for the existence of racism as outlined by Marx: economic competition between workers; the appeal of racist ideology to white workers; and efforts of the capitalist class to establish and maintain racial divisions among workers. Capital's constantly changing demands for different kinds of labour can only be met through immigration. Callinicos remarks that 'racism offers for workers of the oppressing "race" the imaginary compensation for the exploitation they suffer of belonging to the "*ruling* nation"' (1993, p. 39). Callinicos notes the way in which Marx grasped how 'racial' divisions between 'native' and 'immigrant' workers could weaken the working-class. United States' politicians like Pat Buchanan, Jesse Helms and Pete Wilson, to name but a few, take advantage of this division which the capitalist class understands and manipulates only too well — using racism effectively to divide the working-class.

At this point you might be asking yourselves: Doesn't racism pre-date capitalism? Here we agree with Callinicos that the heterophobia associated with pre-capitalist societies was not the same as modern racism. Pre-capitalist slave and feudal societies of classical Greece and Rome did not rely on racism to justify the use of slaves. The Greeks and Romans did not have theories of white superiority. If they did, that must have been unsettling news to Septimus Severus, Roman Emperor from Ad 193 to 211, who was, many historians claim, a black man. Racism emerged during the seventeenth and eighteenth centuries from a key development of capitalism — colonial plantations in the New World where slave labour stolen from Africa was used to produce tobacco, sugar, and cotton for the global consumer market (Callinicos, 1993). Callinicos cites Eric Williams who remarks: 'Slavery was not born of racism: rather, racism was the consequence of slavery' (cited in Callinicos, 1993, p. 24). In effect, racism emerged as the ideology of the plantocracy. It began with the class of sugar-planters and slave merchants that dominated England's Caribbean colonies. Racism developed out of the 'systemic slavery' of the New World. The 'natural inferiority' of Africans was a way that Whites justified enslaving them. According to Callinicos:

> Racism offers white workers the comfort of believing themselves part of the dominant group; it also provides, in times of crisis, a ready-made scapegoat, in the shape of the oppressed group. Racism thus gives white workers a particular identity, and one which unites them with white capitalists. We have here, then, a case of the kind of 'imagined community' discussed by Benedict Anderson in his influential analysis of nationalism. (1993, p. 38)

In short, to abolish racism in any substantive sense, we need to abolish global capitalism.

While it is certainly true that we only have access to the real through forms of signification, and that events are made indeterminate by floating signifiers, we still believe that events themselves have a similar ontological status as representations of them. In other words, we do not reject subjectivity and experience to the extent that there exists no subject capable of acting rationally and with some degree of autonomy form larger structures of power and privilege. In the act of attributing meaning to something, we need always to recognize the material and social reality of that 'something'. It is the fear of over-generalizing that 'something' that leads to the poststructuralist retreat from politics. Generally content to focus on 'domination' or microsocial structures of power, poststructuralists and postmodernists lack an effective analysis of 'exploitation' or macrostructures of power and privilege related to the international global division of labour.

Preoccupied with celebrating the undecidability and incommensurability of discourses, and uninterested in class politics, postmodernists have thus foreclosed the possibility of mounting a programme of anticapitalist struggle. While discursive undecidability is surely a feature of the textuality of everyday life, we must remember that this is a second-order feature and it is not antiseptically removed from the concrete determinations of capital. Language partakes of a second-order materiality but its features of signification — i.e., the organization, inflection and uncontainability of discourse — should not be confused with the multiple concrete determinations that make up the materiality of class struggle.

Global capitalism has a way of reshaping, reinflecting, and rearticulating postmodern discourses of dissent such that they fit securely within the manageable compass of business interests and are underwritten by safe abstract civic ideals and non-threatening constitutional-jurisprudential discourses of diversity. Despite all of the fashionable talk about the deterioration of the nation-state, the weakening patterns of cultural affiliation and social practices, and the creolization and/or hybridization of cultural identities, discourses always converge and pivot around objective labour practices. While postmodernists are correct in arguing that discourses classify, codify, commodify, and often yolk together disparate realms of signification, in their hip cleverness they are able to mount only a corporate-sponsored rebellion. The fashionable apostasy, insurgent posturing, and often sexy and always incorrigible avant-garde transgression that we have come to expect from the postmodernists haemorrhages our understanding of the relation of cultural production to the international division of labour. Through the textual supplication of the deconstructionists, modernism is given a nose-bleed and perhaps an unintended face-lift. While the postmodernists celebrate ethnic diversity and a free marketplace of ideas, their publishers mainly see green as they are able to package such post-beatnik anti-authoritarianism to a new generation of graduate students who want the thrill of rebellion without threatening their own security as future academics. Postmodernists have become capitalism's new voguish flunkies, who operate almost entirely in the officially sanctioned precincts of dissent: the sociology seminar room or bookstore.

Consequently we do not maintain, as does Jean Baudrillard for example, that labour has been transformed simply into a sign among other signs, into a structure of obedience to a code. Furthermore, we do not believe that capitalism has passed from a phase where labour is exploited to one where it is only marketed and consumed. We do not want to reduce 'being a worker' to its sign value or a practice of unequal gift exchange as Baudrillard suggests. The enemy of the worker is not the code so much as the social relations of production. Within much of the analysis by postmodernists, regimes of signification have been wrenched from their material location in narratives of human struggle. They are discovered hovering helter-skelter over the turmoil of the real. We do not believe that within postmodern cultures human needs are irrelevant. Indeed, material and symbolic needs are vitally important. The development of global postmodern cultures has done little to undermine the pervasive destructive capacities of exploitation that accompany capitalism. Consequently, as critical educators, we must never deflect our glances from the global mode of production or the dangers of internationalized class domination.

Unthinking Whiteness: Rearticulating Diasporic Praxis

The price of freedom is death.

We don't want to be around that ol'pale thing.
    Malcolm X (El Hajj Malik El Shabazz)

El deber de cada revolucionairo es hacer la revolucion.
    Che Guevara

To this end, rather than stressing the importance of diversity and inclusion, as do most multiculturalists, we think that significantly more emphasis should be placed on the social and political construction of white supremacy and the dispensation of white hegemony. The reality-distortion field known as 'whiteness' needs to be identified as a cultural disposition and ideology linked to specific political, social, and historical arrangements. As Matt Wray and Annalee Newitz, editors of *White Trash: Race and Class in America*, put it:

> It has been the invisibility (for Whites) of whiteness that has enabled white Americans to stand as unmarked, normative bodies and social selves, the standard against which all others are judged (and found wanting). As such, the invisibility of whiteness is an enabling condition for both white supremacy/privilege and race-based prejudice. Making whiteness visible to Whites — exposing the discourses, the social and cultural practices, and the material conditions that cloak whiteness and hide its dominating effects — is a necessary part of any antiracist project. (1997, pp. 3–4)

The concept of whiteness became lodged in the discursive crucible of colonial identity by the early 1860s. Whiteness at that time had become a marker for measuring inferior and superior 'races'. Interestingly, Genghis Khan, Attila the Hun, and Confucius were at this time considered as 'white'. Blackness was evaluated positively in European iconography from the twelfth to the fifteenth centuries, but after the seventeenth century and the rise of European colonialism, blackness became conveniently linked to inferiority (Cashmore, 1996). For instance, during the sixteenth and seventeenth centuries, blood purity (*limpieza de sangre*) became raised to a metaphysical — perhaps even sacerdotal — status, as it became a principle used to peripheralize Indians, Moors, and Jews. Blackness was not immediately associated with slavery. In the United States, the humanistic image of Africans created by the abolitionist movement was soon countered by new types of racial signification in which white skin was identified with racial superiority. Poor Europeans were sometimes indentured and were in some sense de facto slaves. They occupied the same economic categories as African slaves and were held in equal contempt by the lords of the plantation and legislatures. So poor Europeans were invited to align themselves with the plantocracy as 'white' in order to avoid the most severe forms of bondage. This strategy helped plantation owners form a stronger social control apparatus as hegemony was achieved by offering 'race privileges' to poor Whites as acknowledgment of their loyalty to the colonial land (Cashmore, 1996).

By the early twentieth century, European maritime empires controlled over half of the land (72 million square kilometres) and a third of the world's population (560 million people). Seventy-five million Africans died during the centuries-long transatlantic slave trade (West, 1993). The logics of empire are still with us, bound to the cultural fabric of our daily being-in-the-world; woven into our posture towards others; structured into the language of our perceptions. We cannot will our racist logics away. We need to work hard to eradicate them. We need to struggle with a formidable resolve in order to overcome that which we are afraid to confirm exists, let alone confront, in the battleground of our souls.

George Lipsitz argues that understanding the destructive quality of white identity requires what Walter Benjamin termed 'presence of mind' or 'an abstract of the future, and precise awareness of the present moment more decisive than foreknowledge of the most distant events' (1995, p. 370). Noting that 'race' is not merely a 'cultural construct' but a construct that has 'sinister structural causes and consequences', Lipsitz argues that from colonial times to the present there have existed systematic efforts 'to create a possessive investment in whiteness for European Americans'. Identifying what he calls a new form of racism embedded in 'the putatively race-neutral liberal social democratic reforms of the past five decades' (1995, p. 371), Lipsitz asserts that the possessive investment in whiteness can be seen in legacies of socialization bequeathed to United States' citizens by federal, state, and local policies toward African-Americans, Native Americans, Mexican Americans, Asian Americans, and other groups designated by Whites as 'racially other'.

In her article, 'Whiteness as property', Cheryl Harris (1993) makes the compelling case that within the legal system and within popular reasoning, there exists an assumption that whiteness is a property interest entitled to legal protection. Whiteness as property is essentially the reification in law of expectations of white privilege. Not only has this assumption been supported by systematic white supremacy through the laws of slavery and 'Jim Crow' but also by recent decisions and rationales of the US Supreme Court concerning affirmative action. Harris is correct in arguing that whiteness serves as the basis of racialized privilege in which white 'racial' identity provides the basis for allocating societal benefits in both public and private spheres. Whiteness as a property of status continues to assist in the reproduction of the existing system of racial classification and stratification in the US that protects the socially entrenched white power elite. For example, rejecting race-conscious remedial measures as unconstitutional under the Equal Protection Clause of the Fourteenth Amendment is, according to Harris, 'based on the [US Supreme] Court's chronic refusal to dismantle the institutional protection of benefits for Whites that have been based on white supremacy and maintained at the expense of Blacks' (1993, p. 1767).

Current legal definitions of 'race' embrace the norm of colourblindness and thus disconnect 'race' from social identity. Within the discourse of colourblindness, blackness and whiteness are seen as neutral and apolitical descriptions reflecting skin colour, and unrelated to social conditions of domination and subordination and to social attributes such as class, culture, language, and education. In other words, colourblindness is a concept that symmetrizes relations of power and privilege and flattens them out so that they appear equivalent. But blackness and whiteness exist symmetrically only as idealized oppositions; in the real world they exist as a dependent hierarchy, with whiteness constraining the social power of blackness. According to Harris:

> To define race reductively as simply colour, and therefore meaningless is as subordinating as defining race to be scientifically determinative of inherent deficiency. The old definition creates a false linkage between race and inferiority; the new definition denies the real linkage between race and oppression under systematic white supremacy. Distorting and denying reality, both definitions support race subordination. As Neil Gotanda has argued, colourblindness is a form of race subordination in that it denies the historical context of white domination and black subordination. (1993, p. 1768)

Likewise, Alcoff writes: 'For Whites and others who benefit in the present from a history of oppression, the appeal of universal racelessness may also lie in its ability to deface their/our race-based connections with that unpleasant past: in other words, it may entitle Whites to believe they/we don't need to acknowledge the salience of white identity and thus to avoid the moral discomfort that that identity cannot help but present' (1996, p. 10). Affirmation action (positive discrimination) thus needs to be understood not through privatizing social inequality through claims of bipolar corrective justice between black and white competitors but rather as an issue of distributive social justice and rights that focuses not on guilt or innocence but on entitlement and fairness.

Because racism and 'race' hierarchies are virtually ignored in discussions of multiculturalism in the US, the educational left has largely failed to address the issue of whiteness and the insecurities that young Whites harbour regarding their future during times of diminishing economic expectations. With their 'racially coded and divisive rhetoric', neo-conservatives may be able to enjoy tremendous success in helping insecure young white populations develop white identity along racist lines while at the same time appealing to a universal racelessness. Consider the comments by David Stowe who writes:

> The only people nowadays who profess any kind of loyalty to whiteness *qua* whiteness (as opposed to whiteness as an incidental feature of some more specific identity) are Christian Identity types and Aryan Nation diehards. Anecdotal surveys reveal that few white Americans mention whiteness as a quality that they think much about or particularly value. In their day-to-day cultural preferences — food, music, clothing, sports, hairstyles — the great majority of American Whites display no particular attachment to white things. There does seem to be a kind of emptiness at the core of whiteness. (1996, p. 74)

People don't discriminate against groups because they are different but rather the act of discrimination constructs categories of difference that hierarchically locates people as 'superior' or 'inferior' and then universalizes and naturalizes such differences. When we refer to whiteness or to the cultural logics of whiteness, we need to qualify what we mean. Here we adopt Ruth Frankenberg's injunction that cultural practices considered to be white need to be seen as contingent, historically produced, and transformable. White culture is not monolithic and its borders must be understood as malleable and porous. It is the historically specific confluence of economic, geopolitical, and ethnocultural processes. According to Alastair Bonnett, whiteness is neither a discrete entity nor a fixed, asocial category. Rather, it is an 'immutable social construction' (1996, p. 98). White identity is an ensemble of discourses, contrapuntal and contradictory. Whiteness — and the meanings attributed to it — are always in a state of flux and fibrillation. Bonnett notes that 'even if one ignores the transgressive youth or ethnic borderlands of western identities, and focuses on the "centre" or "heartlands" of "whiteness", one will discover racialized subjectivities, that, far from being settled and confident, exhibit a constantly reformulated panic over the meaning of "whiteness" and the defining presence of "non-whiteness" within it' (1996, p. 106). According to Frankenberg, white culture is a material and discursive space that:

> is inflected by nationhood, such that whiteness and Americanness, though by no means coterminous, are profoundly shaped by one another. . . . Similarly, whiteness, masculinity, and femininity are co-producers of one another, in ways that are, in their turn, crosscut by class and by the histories of racism and colonialism. (1993, p. 233)

Whiteness needs to be seen as *cultural*, as *processual*, and not ontologically different from processes that are non-white. It works, as Frankenberg notes, as 'an unmarked marker of others' differentness — whiteness not so much void or formlessness as norm' (1993, p. 198). Whiteness functions through social practices of assimilation and cultural homogenization; whiteness is linked to the expansion of capitalism in the sense that 'whiteness signifies the production and consumption of commodities under capitalism' (1993, p. 203). Yet capitalism in the United States needs to be understood as contingently white, since white people participate in maintaining the hegemony of institutions and practices of racial dominance in different ways and to greater or lesser degrees. Ruth Frankenberg identifies the key discursive repertoires of whiteness as follows:

> [first] modes of naming culture and difference associated with west European colonial expansion; second, elements of 'essentialist' racism . . . linked to European colonialism but also critical as rationale for Anglo Settler colonialism and segregationism in what is now the USA; third, 'assimilationist' or later 'colour- and power-evasive' strategies for thinking through 'race' first articulated in the early decades of this century; and, fourth, . . . 'race-cognizant' repertoires that emerged in the latter half of the twentieth century and were linked both to US liberation movements and to broader global struggles for decolonization. (1993, p. 239)

While an entire range of discursive repertoires may come into play, jostling against, superseding, and working in conjunction with each other, white identity is constructed in relation to an individual's personal history, geopolitical situatedness, contextually specific practices, and his or her location in the materiality of the so called 'racial order'. In other words, many factors determine which discursive configurations are at work and the operational modalities present. Whiteness has no formal content. It works rhetorically by articulating itself out of the semiotic detritus of myths of European superiority. These are myths that are ontologically empty, epistemologically misleading, and morally pernicious in the way that they privilege descendants of Europeans as the truly civilized in contrast to the quaint, exotic or barbaric character of non-European cultures.

Whiteness is a sociohistorical form of consciousness, given birth at the nexus of capitalism, colonial rule, and the emergent relationships among dominant and subordinate groups. Whiteness operates by means of its condition as a *universalizing* authority by which the hegemonic white bourgeois subject appropriates the right to speak on behalf of everyone who is non-white, while denying voice and agency to these 'others' in the name of civilized humankind. Whiteness constitutes and demarcates ideas, feelings, knowledges, social practices, cultural formations, and systems of intelligibility that are identified with or attributed to white people and which are invested in by white people as 'white'. Whiteness is also a refusal to acknowledge how white people are implicated in certain social relations of privilege and relations of domination and subordination. Whiteness, then, can be considered as a form of social amnesia associated with certain modes of subjectivity within particular social sites considered to be normative. As a lived domain of meaning, whiteness represents particular social and historical formations that are reproduced through specific discursive and material processes and circuits of desire and power. Whiteness can be considered to be a conflictual sociocultural, sociopolitical, and geopolitical process that animates commonsensical practical action in relationship to dominant social practices and normative ideological productions. Whiteness constitutes the selective tradition of dominant discourses about 'race', class, gender and sexuality hegemonically reproduced. Whiteness has become the substance and limit of our commonsense articulated as cultural consensus. As an ideological formation transformed into a principle of life, into an ensemble of social relations and practices, whiteness needs to be understood as conjunctural, as a composite social hieroglyph that shifts in denotative and connotative emphasis, depending upon how its elements are combined and upon the contexts in which it operates.

Whiteness is not a pre-given unified ideological formation but is a multifaceted collective phenomenon resulting from the relationship between the self and the ideological discourses which are constructed out of the surrounding local and global cultural terrain. Whiteness is fundamentally Euro-or western-centric in its episteme, as it is articulated in complicity with the pervasively imperializing logic of empire. Whiteness in the United States can be understood largely through the social consequences it provides for those who are considered to be non-white. Such consequences can be seen in the criminal justice system, in prisons, in schools, and in the board rooms of multinational corporations. It can be defined in relation to immigration practices and social policies and practices of sexism, racism, and nationalism. It can be seen historically in widespread acts of imperialism and genocide and linked to an erotic economy of 'excess'. Eric Lott writes:

> In rationalized western societies, becoming 'white' and male seems to depend upon the remanding of enjoyment, the body, and aptitude for pleasure. It is the other who is always putatively 'excessive' in this respect, whether through exotic food, strange and noisy music, outlandish bodily exhibitions, or unremitting sexual appetite. Whites in fact organize their own enjoyment through the other, Slavoj Zizek has written, and access pleasure precisely by fantasizing about the other's 'special' pleasure. Hatred of the other arises from the necessary hatred of one's own excess; ascribing this excess to the 'degraded' other and indulging it — by imaging, incorporating, or impersonating the other — one conveniently and surreptitiously takes and disavows pleasure at one and the same time. This is the mixed erotic economy, what Homi Bhabha terms the 'ambivalence' of American whiteness. (1993, p. 482)

Whiteness is a type of articulatory practice that can be located in the convergence of colonialism, capitalism, and subject formation. It both fixes and sustains discursive regimes that represent self and 'other'; that is, whiteness represents a regime of differences that produces and racializes an abject other. In other words, whiteness is a discursive regime that enables real effects to take place. Whiteness displaces blackness and brownness — specific forms of non-whiteness — into signifiers of deviance and criminality within social, cultural, cognitive, and political contexts. White subjects discursively construct identity through producing, naming, 'bounding', and marginalizing a range of others (Frankenberg, 1993).

Whiteness constitutes unmarked (white American male) practices that have negative effects on and consequences for those who do not participate in them. Inflected by nationhood, whiteness can be considered an ensemble of discursive practices constantly in the process of being constructed, negotiated, and changed. Yet it functions to instantiate a structured exclusion of certain groups from social arenas of normativity. Coco Fusco remarks:

> To raise the spectre of racism in the here and now, to suggest that despite their political beliefs and sexual preferences, white people operate within, and benefit from, white supremacist social structures is still tantamount to a declaration of war. (1995, p. 76)

Whiteness is not only mythopoetical in the sense that it constructs a totality of illusions formed around the ontological superiority of the Euro-American subject, it is also metastructural in that it connects whiteness across specific differences; it solders fugitive, break-away discourses and rehegemonizes them. Consumer utopias and global capital flows rearticulate whiteness by means of relational differences.

Whiteness is dialectically reinitiated across epistemological fissures, contradictions, and oppositions through new regimes of desire that connect the consumption of goods to the everyday logic of western democracy. The cultural encoding of the typography of whiteness is achieved by remapping western European identity onto economic transactions, by recementing desire to capitalist flows, by concretizing personal history into collective memory linked to place, to a myth of origin. Whiteness offers a safe 'home' for those imperiled by the flux of change.

Whiteness can be considered as a conscription of the process of positive self-identification into the service of domination through inscribing identity into an onto-epistemological framework of 'us' against 'them'. For those who are non-white, the seduction of whiteness can produce a self-definition that disconnects the subject from his or her history of oppression and struggle, exiling identity into the unmoored, chaotic realm of abject otherness (and tacitly accepting the positioned superiority of the western subject). Whiteness provides the subject with a known boundary that places nothing 'off limits', yet which provides a fantasy of belongingness. It is not that whiteness signifies preferentially one pole of the white–non-white binarism. Rather, whiteness seduces the subject to accept the idea of polarity as the limit-text of identity, as the constitutive foundation of subjectivity.

Ross Chambers (1996) notes that whiteness is able here to retain a mythic status of aparadigmaticity. The presumed indivisibility of whiteness ensures that whiteness has a uniform quality. By contrast, non-whiteness is portrayed as a paradigm of heterogeneity, as a multiplicity of different ways of being (non-white). The invisibility of whiteness depends on a dichotomization of the white–non-white relation. In this instance, Whites are perceived as singular, individual historical agents whose differences among themselves are largely unclassifiable. Their whiteness is secondary to their individual self-identity. Non-Whites, however, are first pluralized and then homogenized and classified as members of a given group (for example, as black or Latino). Whereas non-Whites are pluralized through a classification into various group affiliations and then homogenized through stereotyping, white hegemony works by atomizing whiteness as constituted by individual historical agents, thereby masking the power of white hegemony. The perceived singularity of whiteness, Chambers observes, produces a sense of indivisibility among Whites that facilitates their invisibility. By contrast, the pluralization of the 'other' on the part of Whites creates a sense of divisibility between and homogenization of others that puts non-Whites into a position of examinability. Chambers further argues that differences between white and non-white depend upon the existence of multiple categories that constitute the paradigm of non-whiteness. The pluralization and divisibility of non-whiteness as black, brown, African, Latino, Asian, mestizo (mixed) or 'pure' are what enable whiteness to stake out its claim as non-paradigmatic or singular. Whiteness is opposed to blackness, it becomes in this instance an absolute form, it claims to exist outside of the pluralized 'mix' that defines its others. By examining or classifying non-white others, Whites exempt themselves from the category of the examined. They become beyond examination, naturalized beyond scrutiny. Their power is thus less likely to be made visible, named as such, and challenged.

Whiteness also offers coherency and stability in a world in which capital produces regimes of desire linked to commodity utopias where fantasies of omnipotence must find a stable home. Of course, the 'them' is always located within the 'us'. The marginalized are always foundational to the stability of the central actors. The excluded in this case establish the conditions of existence of the included. So we find that it is impossible to separate the identities of both oppressor and oppressed. They depend upon each other. To resist whiteness means developing a politics of difference. Since we lack the full semantic availability to understand whiteness and to resist it, we need to rethink difference and identity outside of sets of binary oppositions. We need to view identity as coalitional, as collective, as processual, as grounded in the struggle for social justice.

Alastair Bonnett notes that the reified concept of whiteness 'enables "white" people to occupy a privileged location in antiracist debate; they are allowed the luxury of being passive observers, of being altruistically motivated, of knowing that their "racial" identity might be reviled and lambasted but never actually made slippery, torn open, or, indeed, abolished' (1996, p. 98). Bonnett further notes:

> To dismantle 'blackness' but leave the force it was founded to oppose unchallenged is to display both a political and theoretical naivety. To subvert 'blackness' without subverting 'whiteness' reproduces and reinforces the 'racial' myths, and the 'racial' dominance, associated with the latter. (1996, p. 99)

In his important volume, *Psychoanalytic-Marxism* (1993), Eugene Wolfenstein describes the whiteness of domination as the 'one fixed point' of America's many racisms. He argues that whiteness is a social designation and a 'history disguised as biology' (1993, p. 331). Whiteness is also an attribute of language. Wolfenstein claims that:

> Languages have skin colours. There are white nouns and verbs, white grammar and white syntax. In the absence of challenges to linguistic hegemony, indeed, language is white. If you don't speak white you will not be heard, just as when you don't look white you will not be seen. (1993, p. 331)

Describing white racists as 'virtuosos of denigration', Wolfenstein maintains that the language of white racism illustrates 'a state of war' (1993, p. 333). Yet the battles are fought through lies and deceit; most notably, as we have already seen, through the idea of 'colourblindness'. Wolfenstein notes that colourblindness constitutes more than a matter of conscious deceit:

> White racism is rather a mental disorder, an ocular disease, an opacity of the soul that is articulated with unintended irony in the idea of 'colourblindness'. To be colourblind is the highest form of racial false consciousness, a denial of both difference and domination. But one doesn't have to be colourblind to be blinded by white racism. . . . Black people see themselves in white mirrors, white people see black people as their own photographic negatives. (1993, p. 334)

Wolfenstein links white racism here to what he terms 'epidermal fetishism'. Epidermal fetishism reduces people to their skin colour and renders them invisible. It is a form of social character that is formed within a process of exchange and circulation. As such, whiteness represent the super-ego (the standard of social value, self-worth, and morality). Since the ego is affirmatively reflected in the super-ego, it also must be white. What is therefore repressed is blackness which 'becomes identified with the unwanted or bad parts of the self' (1993, p. 336). In order to resist this epidermal fetishism, Wolfenstein argues, two epistemological tasks need to be undertaken. Black people need to look away from the white mirror; white people need to attempt to see black people as they see themselves and to see themselves as they are seen by other black people. In short, oppressed people need a language and a politics of their own.

In so doing, however, it is important to recognize that white racism is neither purely systemic or purely individual. Rather, it is a complex interplay of collective interests and desires. White racism in this instance 'becomes a rational means to collective ends' (Wolfenstein, 1993, p. 341) when viewed from the standpoint of ruling class interests. Yet for the white working-class it is irrational and a form of false consciousness. White racism also circumscribes rational action for black people in that they are encouraged to act in terms of their 'racial' rather than their class interests.

Ian Haney López's (1996) book, *White by Law*, offers a view of white transparency and invisibility that is at odds with Gallagher's (1994) thesis that Whites are growing more conscious of their whiteness. López cites an incident at a legal feminist conference in which participants were asked to pick two or three words to describe themselves. All of the women of colour selected at least one 'racial' term, but not one white woman did so. This prompted Angela Harris to remark that only white people in this society have the luxury of having no colour. An informal study conducted at Harvard Law School underscores Harris' remark. A student interviewer asked 10 African-Americans and 10 white Americans how they identified themselves. Unlike the African-Americans, most of the white Americans did not consciously factor in their 'whiteness' as a crucial or even tangential part of their identity.

López argues that one is not born white but becomes white 'by virtue of the social context in which one finds oneself, to be sure, but also by virtue of the choices one makes' (1996, p. 190). But how can one born into the culture of whiteness, one who is defined as white, undo that whiteness? López addresses this question in his formulation of whiteness. He locates whiteness in the overlapping of chance (e.g., features and ancestry that we have no control over, morphology); context (context-specific meanings that are attached to 'race', the social setting in which 'races' are recognized, constructed, and contested); and choice (conscious choices with regard to the morphology and ancestries of social actors) in order to 'alter the readability of their identity' (1996, p. 191).

In other words, López maintains that chance and context are not racially determinative. He notes:

> Racial choices must always be made from within specific contexts, where the context materially and ideologically circumscribes the range of available choices and also delimits the significance of the act. Nevertheless, these are racial choices, if sometimes only in their overtone or subtext, because they resonate in the complex of meanings associated with 'race'. Given the thorough suffusion of 'race' throughout society, in the daily dance of life we constantly make racially meaningful decisions. (1996, p. 193)

López's perspective offers new promise, it would seem, for abolishing racism since it refuses to locate whiteness only as antiracism's 'other'. We agree with Bonnett when he remarks that 'to continue to cast "whites" as antiracism's "other", as the eternally guilty and/or altruistic observers of "race" equality work, is to maintain "white" privilege and undermine the movement's intellectual and practical reach and utility' (1996, p. 107). In other words, Whites need to ask themselves to what extent their identity is a function of their whiteness in the process of their ongoing daily lives and what choices they might make to escape whiteness. López outlines — productively in our view — three steps in dismantling whiteness:

> First, Whites must overcome the omnipresent effects of transparency and of the naturalization of 'race' in order to recognize the many racial aspects of their identity, paying particular attention to the daily acts that draw upon and in turn confirm their whiteness. Second, they must recognize and accept the personal and social consequences of breaking out of a white identity. Third, they must embark on a daily process of choosing against whiteness. (López, 1996, p. 193)

Of course, the difficulty of taking such steps is partly due to the fact that, as López notes, the unconscious acceptance of a racialized identity is predicated upon a circular definition of the self. It is hard to step outside of whiteness if you are white because of all the social, cultural and economic privileges that accompany whiteness. Yet, whiteness must be dismantled if the United States is to overcome racism. Lipsitz remarks: 'Those of us who are "white" can only become part of the solution if we recognize the degree to which we are already part of the problem — not because of our "race", but because of our possessive investment in it' (1995, p. 384).

The Editorial in the book, *Race Traitor*, puts it thus:

> The key to solving the social problems of our age is to abolish the 'white race'. Until that task is accomplished, even partial reform will prove elusive, because white influence permeates every issue in US society, whether domestic or foreign. . . . 'Race' itself is a product of social discrimination; so long as the white race exists, all movements against racism are doomed to fail. (Ignatiev and Garvey, 1996, p. 10)

Whilst we lack the semantic availability to capture fully the meaning and function of whiteness we can at least describe it as a discursive strategy, articulation, or modality; or we can refer to it perhaps as a form of discursive brokerage, a pattern of negotiation that takes place in conditions generated by specific discursive formations and social relations. Historically, whiteness can be seen as a tattered and bruised progeny of western colonialism and imperialism.

Whiteness is crisscrossed by numerous social dynamics. It is produced through capitalist social relations or modes of domination. The marker 'whiteness' serves as a discursive indicator or social hieroglyph (Cruz, 1996) — an 'effect' of systematic social relations of which those who are marked as 'white' have little conscious understanding. Whiteness, therefore, is socially and historically embedded; it is a form of racialization of identity formation that carries with it a history of social, cultural, and economic relations. Whiteness is unfinalizable but compared to other ethnic formations, its space for manoeuvring in the racialized and gendered permutations of US citizenship is infinitely more vast. The task here for critical educators is to *denaturalize* whiteness by breaking its codes and the social relations and privileging hierarchies which give such codes normative power. The codification of whiteness as a social hieroglyph associated with civility, rationality, and political advancement is part of inherited social and cultural formations (cf. May, this volume), formations that were given birth after the marriage of industrialism and militarism. Whiteness is linked in a fundamental — if not dramatic — way to the racialization of aggression. Inherited categories and classifications that made whiteness the privileged signifier over blackness is a theme that has been addressed before (see McLaren, 1995), and we will not rehearse that argument here.

We believe that the relation between whiteness and privilege can be better understood by locating whiteness in the context of what Howard Winant calls 'racial formation' (1994) and what David Theo Goldberg (1993) describes as 'racial modality'. A racial modality refers to 'a fragile structure of racist exclusions at a space-time conjuncture' that is sustained by the power of socio-economic interests and the intersection of discursive fields and strategies of representation (Goldberg, 1993, p. 210). Winant defines 'race' as 'a concept that signifies and symbolizes sociopolitical conflicts and interests to different types of human bodies' (1994, p. 115). This signals an understanding of 'race' as an everyday phenomenon — an ontological category, as we described it earlier, that is historically and socially con-structed, and is implicated in social structures, identities, and signification systems. The concept of 'racial formation' also addresses the 'expansion and intensification of racial phenomena' on a global basis. Further, it suggests 'a new conception of racial history and racial time' (1994, p. 116). Concerning the latter, then, whiteness can be seen as implicated in the progressive expansion of capitalism throughout the world and the genealogical racial time of European conquest, what Winant calls:

> . . . archetypal *longue durée*: a slow agony of inscription upon the human body, a murder mystery, if you will, but on a genocidal scale. The phenotypical signification of the world's body took place in and through conquest and enslavement, to be sure, but also as an enormous act of expression, of narration. (1994, p. 117)

Whiteness, of course, is also a product of historical time in terms of what Winant calls 'contingency', or the contextual specificity of its hegemonic articula-tions. Whiteness is implicated on a global basis in the internationalization of capital which is being accompanied by the internationalization of 'race'. We are witnessing growing diasporic movements as former colonial subjects immigrate to the western metropoles, challenging the majoritarian status of European groups. Winant remarks that we are also witnessing 'the rise of "diasporic" models of blackness, the creation of "pan-ethnic" communities of Latinos and Asians (in such countries as the United Kingdom and the United States), and the breakdown of borders in both Europe and North America all [of which] seem to be hybridizing and racializing previously national policies, cultures and identities' (1994, p. 118).

We follow Winant in maintaining that the focus of our struggle at this present juncture should be on the racialized dimensions of capitalism and the mobilization of white 'racial' antagonisms. Prior to the Second World War in the United States there existed a well-developed racial ideology, 'a caste-based social structure developed to guarantee white workers their racial identity as a signifier of their "freedom"' (1994, p. 125). White people represented the *Herrenvolk* — a democracy of white males. Winant observes that the *Herrenvolk's* supremacy was seriously eroded during the civil rights era. Of course, the post-civil rights era is another matter altogether. As racial domination gave way to racial hegemony, the task was no longer to subdue the masses of disenfranchised minorities but to accommodate them. The caste-based logic of 'race' was discarded by Whites in favour of an egalitarian politics underwritten by a culture of poverty thesis: people of colour should pull themselves up out of the 'underclass' through their own initiatives. Consider the recent case in point of the University of California's dismantling of affirmative action (positive discrimination), championed by Ward Connerly, a conservative African-American and University of California (UC) Regent. When reports commissioned by the UC provost projected that the numbers of white and Asian UC undergraduates would grow markedly and numbers of under-represented minority students would diminish, Connerly responded: 'This is the most tacit admission of the extent that we are using race for under-represented students that one could ever find' (quoted in Wallace, 1996, p. 1, 18). Connerly's comment is underwritten by a belief that African-American and Latino/a students, for instance, are being given an unfair advantage by affirmative action programmes. However, this presumes that the playing field is now level, and that we have arrived at a point in our society where meritocracy exists in reality. It ignores issues of culture, economics, and ideology and how these and other factors work in relation to public institutions and the (re)production of structural racism. Consequently, Connerly is unable to fathom how his position on affirmative action acts in the service of white privilege.

We don't believe in reverse racism since we don't believe white people have transcended 'race', nor do we believe that Latinos/as or African-Americans have acquired a systematic power to dominate Whites. Yet along with the editors of *Race Traitor*, we argue for reversing racism by systematically dismantling whiteness. Even so, we are acutely aware that people of colour might find troubling the idea that white populations can simply reinvent themselves by making the simple choice of not being white. Of course, this is not what López and others appear to be saying. The choices one makes and the reinvention one aspires to as a 'race traitor' are not 'simple' nor are they easy choices for Whites to make. Yet from the perspective of some people of colour, offering the choice to white people of opting out of their whiteness could seem to set up an easy path for those who don't want to assume responsibility for their privilege as white people. Indeed, there is certainly cause for concern. David Roediger captures some of this when he remarks: 'Whites cannot fully renounce whiteness even if they want to' (1994, p. 16). Whites are, after all, still accorded the privileges of being white even as they ideologically renounce their whiteness, often with the best of intentions. Yet the reality that Whites might seriously consider non-whiteness and anti-white struggle is too important to ignore, dismiss as wishful thinking, or to associate with a fashionable form of code-switching. Choosing not to be white is not an easy option for white people, as simple as deciding to make a change in one's wardrobe. To understand the processes involved in the racialization of identity and to consistently choose non-whiteness is a difficult act of apostasy, for it implies a heightened sense of social criticism and an unwavering commitment to social justice (Roediger, 1994). Of course, the question needs to be asked: If we can choose to be non-white, then can we choose to be black or brown? Insofar as blackness is a social construction (often 'parasitic' on whiteness) we would answer yes.

Theologian James Cone, author of *A Black Theology of Liberation*, urges white folks to free themselves from the shackles of their whiteness:

> . . . if Whites expect to be able to say anything relevant to the self-determination of the black community, it will be necessary for them to destroy their whiteness by becoming members of an oppressed community. Whites will be free only when they become new persons — when their white being has passed away and they are created anew in black being. When this happens, they are no longer white but free. (1986, p. 97)

Again we would stress that becoming non-white is not a 'mere' choice but a self-consciously political choice, a spiritual choice, and a critical choice. To choose blackness or brownness merely as a way to escape the stigma of whiteness and to avoid responsibility for owning whiteness, is still very much an act of whiteness. To choose blackness or brownness as a way of politically disidentifying with white privilege and instead identifying with and participating in the social struggles of non-white peoples is, on the other hand, an act of transgression, a traitorous act that reveals a fidelity to the struggle for justice. Lipsitz sums up the problems and the promise of the abolition of whiteness as follows:

> Neither conservative 'free market' policies nor liberal social democratic reforms can solve the 'white problem' in America because both of them reinforce the possessive investment in whiteness. But an explicitly antiracist pan-ethnic movement that acknowledges the existence and power of whiteness might make some important changes. Pan-ethnic, antiracist coalitions have a long history in the United States — in the political activism of John Brown, Sojourner Truth, and the Magon brothers, among others — but we also have a rich cultural tradition of pan-ethnic antiracism connected to civil rights activism . . . efforts by whites to fight racism, not out of sympathy for someone else but out of a sense of self-respect and simple justice, have never completely disappeared; they remain available as models for the present. (1995, p. 384)

George Yúdice gives additional substance to Lipsitz's concerns related to coalition-building when he points out some of the limitations of current identity politics:

The very difficulty of imagining a new social order that speaks convincingly to over 70 per cent of the population requires critics to go beyond pointing out the injustices and abuses and move on to an agenda that will be more effective in transforming structures. What good is it to fight against white supremacy unless Whites themselves join the struggle? (1995, p. 268)

Stowe echoes a similar sentiment when he writes:

race treason has its limits as a workable strategy. Consider the economistic language in which it is described. Whites are exhorted to renounce the wages of whiteness, to divest from their possessive investment in whiteness, to sabotage the exchange value of racial privilege. . . . How many social movements have gotten ahead through the renunciation of privilege, though? (1996, p. 77)

Yúdice makes a lucid point when he criticizes *Race Traitor* for lacking a notion of political articulation. We agree with him that it is not enough to simply have faith in Whites of goodwill to disidentify with their whiteness. He argues that change will not come suddenly as Whites rise up against their whiteness. This position ignores that:

(1) We are living in a time of diminishing expectations and (2) what binds together a society is an overdetermined configuration or constellation of ideologemes: democracy, individuality, free enterprise, work ethic, upward mobility, and national security are articulated in complex ways that do not simply split apart when anyone of them is challenged. Social formations tend to undergo processes of rearticulation, according to Ernesto Laclau, rather than the kind of upheaval that *Race Traitor* seeks. (Yúdice, 1995, pp. 271–2)

What is needed, argues Yúdice, is a multicultural politics that is capable of projecting 'a new democratic vision that makes sense to the white middle- and working-classes' (1995, p. 273). Whites must be interpolated in rearticulating the whiteness of the dominant class. Whites need to 'feel solidarity with those who have suffered deprivation as members of subordinated groups' (1995, p. 276). They must be offered more than a rationalized rights discourse. They need to struggle over the interpretation of needs through the proliferation of public spheres in which the struggle for democracy can take place. The key, Yúdice maintains, is to centre the struggle for social justice around resource distribution rather than identity:

Shifting the focus of struggle from identity to resource distribution will also make it possible to engage such seemingly nonracial issues as the environment, the military, the military-industrial complex, foreign aid, and free-trade agreements as matters impacting local identities and thus requiring a global politics that works outside of the national frame. (1995, p. 280)

Because ethnic identity is constructed diacritically, whiteness requires the denigration of blackness and brownness (López, 1996). Therefore we do not argue for the construction of a positive white identity, no matter how well intentioned. Rather, we argue against celebrating whiteness in any form. As López notes, whiteness retains its positive meaning only by denying itself. We call for the denial, disassembly, and destruction of whiteness as we know it and advocate its rearticulation as a form of critical agency dedicated to social struggle in the interests of the oppressed.

That whiteness was reproduced in the petri dish of European colonialism cannot be disputed but in our estimation it is wrong to think of whiteness as an incurable disease. Multiculturalists whose identities depend on whiteness being the static 'other' to antiracist efforts will perhaps resist the abolition of whiteness even though its destruction is their stated aim. We need to transgress the external determinations of white identity which have brought about the unique conjuncture we have labelled the social hieroglyphics of whiteness — an ensemble of discourses informed, in part, by a perceived lack of ethnicity, and also by issues of 'race', sexual identification, religion, and nation. Since the meanings that suture whiteness to special options denied to other groups within the United States are socially and historically constituted through circuits of ideological investment and exchange, such meanings are mutable and can be transformed, but certainly not by self-willed efforts at refashioning whiteness into a new liturgy of self-critique accompanied by a new white cultural etiquette. Not until the social relations of (re)production and consumption are recognized as class relations linked to whiteness and thus challenged and transformed can new ethnicities emerge capable of challenging white privilege.

Euro-Americans still constitute the gatekeepers of the white 'racial order' known as the United States. Its *Herrenvolk* democracy of white supremacy remains largely camouflaged under the logic of egalitarianism and meritocracy and the denial of the significance of 'race' expressed by calls to abolish the 'colourline' through anti-affirmative action measures. This 'colourline' is no longer bipolar — black versus white — but rather multipolar; Asians and Latinos increase their pressure on white majoritarian constituencies in the larger struggle for racial democracy. Winant argues for the elimination of racial discrimination and inequality but emphasizes as well the liberation of 'racial' identity itself. We agree with Winant that this will involve 'a re-envisioning of racial politics and a transformation of racial difference' (1994, p. 169).

Critical Pedagogy, Multicultural Education and Classless Antagonisms

Critical pedagogy is a way of thinking about, negotiating, and transforming the relationship among classroom teaching, the production of knowledge, the institutional structures of the school, and the social and material relations of the wider community, society, and nation-state. Developed by progressive teachers attempting to eliminate social class inequalities, it has sparked a wide array of antisexist, antiracist, and antihomophobic classroom-based curricula and policy initiatives. Critical pedagogy has grown out of a number of theoretical developments such as Latin American philosophies of liberation, the pedagogy of Brazilian educator Paulo Freire, the sociology of knowledge, the Frankfurt school of critical theory, feminist theory, and neo-Marxist cultural criticism. In more recent years it has been taken up by educators influenced by Derridean deconstruction and post-structuralism. Yet at the level of classroom life, critical pedagogy is often seen as synonymous with whole-language instruction, adult literacy programmes, and new 'constructivist' approaches to teaching and learning based on Vygotsky's work. While critics of critical pedagogy often decry this educational approach for its idealist multiculturalism, its supporters, including Freire, have complained that critical pedagogy has often been domesticated and reduced to student-directed learning approaches devoid of social critique (see also Kalantzis and Cope, this volume).

It is painfully evident that critical pedagogy and its political partner, multicultural education, no longer serve as an adequate social or pedagogical platform from which to mount a vigorous challenge to the current social division of labour and its effects on the socially reproductive function of schooling in late capitalist society. In fact, critical pedagogy no longer enjoys its status as a herald for democracy, as a clarion call for revolutionary praxis, as a language of critique and possibility in the service of a radical democratic imaginary, which was its promise in the late 1970s and early 1980s.

A nagging question has resurfaced: can a renewed and revivified critical pedagogy serve as a point of departure for a politics of resistance and counter-hegemonic struggle in the twenty-first century? On the surface, there are certain reasons to be optimistic. Critical pedagogy has, after all, joined antiracist and feminist struggles to articulate a democratic social order built around the imperatives of diversity, tolerance, and equal access to material resources. But surely such a role, while commendable as far as it goes, has seen critical pedagogy severely compromise an earlier, more radical commitment to class struggle.

Once considered by the faint-hearted guardians of the American dream as a term of opprobrium, critical pedagogy has become so completely psychologized, so liberally humanized, so technologized, and so conceptually postmodernized, that its current relationship to broader liberation struggles seems severely attenuated if not fatally terminated. The conceptual net known as critical pedagogy has been cast so wide, and at times so cavalierly, that it has come to be associated with anything dragged up out of the troubled and infested waters of educational practice, from classroom furniture organized in a 'dialogue friendly' circle to 'feel-good' curricula designed to increase students' self-image. Its multicultural education equivalent is linked to a politics of diversity that includes 'respecting difference' through the celebration of 'ethnic' holidays and themes such as 'black history month' and 'Cinco de Mayo'. If the term 'critical pedagogy' is refracted onto the stage of current educational debates, we have to judge it as having been largely domesticated in a manner that many of its early exponents, such as Brazil's Paulo Freire, so strongly feared.

Many educationalists who are committed to critical pedagogy and multicultural education propagate versions of it that identify with their own bourgeois class interests. One doesn't have to question the integrity or competence of these educators or dismiss their work as disingenuous — for the most part it is not — to conclude that their articulations of critical pedagogy and multicultural education have been accommodated to mainstream versions of liberal humanism and progressivism (see also Kalantzis and Cope, this volume). While early exponents of critical pedagogy were denounced for their polemical excesses and radical political trajectories, a new generation of critical educators have since that time emerged who have largely adopted a pluralist approach to social antagonisms. Their work celebrates the 'end of ideology'; the critique of global capitalism is rarely brought into the debate.

The reasons for the domestication of critical pedagogy are various but space permits us to elaborate only a few. There has been a strong movement among many critical educators infatuated by postmodern and poststructuralist perspectives to neglect or ignore profound changes in the structural nature and dynamics of US late capitalism. Why should political economy be a concern to educators in this era of post-Marxist sympathies and multiple social antagonisms? Precisely because we are living at a particular historical juncture of doctrinaire unregulated capitalism with overwhelming income reconcentration at the top. Millions are unemployed in 'First World' economic communities and millions more in 'Third World' communities; three quarters of the new jobs in the capitalist world are temporary, low-paid, low-skill and carry few, if any, benefits. In the US in 1989 the top 1 per cent earned more collectively than the bottom 40 per cent. Overconsumption — the political subsidization of a sub-bourgeois, mass sector of managers, entrepreneurs, and professionals — has occurred during a time in which we are witnessing a vast redistribution of wealth from the poor to the rich as corporations are benefiting from massive tax cuts and reorientation of consumption towards the new middle-class. This is also accompanied by a general retreat of the labour movement (Callinicos, 1990).

There has been a shifting of positions among many North American critical educators from earlier Marxist perspectives to liberal, social-democratic, neo-liberal and even right-wing perspectives. We have even seen on the theoretical front the conscription of some Marxist writers, such as Antonio Gramsci, into the service of a neo-liberal political agenda. In all, we have witnessed the evisceration of Marxist politics in current education debates and the accommodation of some of its positions into the capitalist state apparatus. Discussions of political and ideological relations and formations are being engaged by many North American leftist educators as if these arenas of social power exist in antiseptic isolation from class struggle. It is clear that a renewed agenda for critical pedagogy must include more than the postmodernist goal of troubling fixed notions of identity and difference, or an unsettling of the notion of a bounded, pre-given or essential 'self'.

What Must Be Done

Both critical pedagogy and multicultural education need to address themselves to the adaptive persistence of capitalism and to issues of capitalist imperialism and its specific manifestations of accumulative capacities through conquest (which we know as colonialism). In other words, critical pedagogy needs to establish a project of emancipation centred around the transformation of property relations and the creation of a just system of appropriation and distribution of social wealth. Neo-Marxist accounts have clearly identified imperialistic practices in recent movements towards global capital accumulation based on corporate monopoly capital and the international division of labour. The West has seen a progressive shift in its development that some liberals would champion as the rise of individuality, the rule of law, and the autonomy of civil society (see also May, this volume). Yet from a Marxist perspective these putative developments towards democracy can be seen, in effect, as 'new forms of exploitation and domination, (the constitutive "power from below" is, after all, the power of lordship), new relations of personal dependence and bondage, the privatization of surplus extraction and the transfer of ancient oppressions from the State to "society" — that is, a transfer of power relations and domination from the State to private property' (Wood, 1995, p. 252). Since the triumph of European capitalism in the seventeenth century, the bourgeoisie have acquired the legal, political, and military power to destroy virtually most of society in its quest for accumulation (Petras and Morley, 1992)

Capitalism in advanced western countries must be dismantled if extra-economic inequalities — such as racism and sexism — are to be challenged successfully. While it is true that people have identities other than class identities that shape their experiences in crucial and important ways, anticapitalist struggle is the best means to inform educators as to how identities can be conceived and rearticulated within the construction of a radical socialist project. As Ellen Wood notes:

> Capitalism is constituted by class exploitation, but capitalism is more than just a system of class oppression. It is a ruthless totalizing process which shapes our lives in every conceivable aspect, and everywhere, not just in the relative opulence of the capitalist North. Among other things, and even leaving aside the direct power wielded by capitalist wealth both in the economy and in the political sphere, it subjects all social life to the abstract requirements of the market, through the commodification of life in all its aspects, determining the allocation of labour, leisure, resources, patterns of production, consumption and the disposition of time. This makes a mockery of all our aspirations to autonomy, freedom of choice, and democratic self-government. (1995, pp. 262–3)

Critical educators need to consider how racisms in their present incarnations developed out of the dominant mode of global production during the seventeenth and eighteenth centuries of colonial plantations in the New World with slave labour imported from Africa to produce consumer goods such as, among others, tobacco, sugar, and cotton. How the immigrant working-class has been divided historically along racialized lines is a process that needs to be better understood and more forcefully addressed by multicultural educators. How, for instance, does racism give white workers a particular identity which unites them with white capitalists (Callinicos, 1992)?

Critical pedagogy as a partner with multicultural education needs to deepen its reach of cultural theory and political economy, and expand its participation in social-empirical analysis in order to address more critically the formation of intellectuals and institutions within the current forms of motion of history. Critical pedagogy and multicultural education need more than good intentions to achieve their goal. They require a revolutionary movement of educators informed by a principled ethics of compassion and social justice, a socialist ethos based on solidarity and social interdependence, and a language of critique that is capable of grasping the objective laws of history (San Juan, 1996). Given current US educational policy with its goal of serving the interests of the corporate world economy — one that effectively serves a de facto world government made up of the IMF, World Bank, G-7, GATT and other structures — it is imperative that critical and multicultural educators renew their commitment to the struggle against exploitation on all fronts (Gabbard, 1995). In emphasizing one such front — that of class struggle — we want to emphasize that a renewed Marxist approach to critical pedagogy that we envision does not conceptualize 'race' and gender antagonisms as a static, structural outcome of capitalist social relations of advantage and disadvantage but rather locates such antagonisms within a theory of agency that acknowledges the importance of cultural politics and social difference. Far from deactivating the sphere of culture by seeing it only or mainly in the service of capital accumulation, critical pedagogy and multicultural education need to acknowledge the specificity of local struggles around the micropolitics of racialized relations, ethnicity, class, gender and sexual formation. A critical pedagogy based on class struggle that does not confront racism, sexism and homophobia will not be able to eliminate the destructive proliferation of capital.

In its attempt to rehabilitate the meaning of democratic community prior to its displacement and dismemberment within late capitalist social formations, critical pedagogy and critical multiculturalism seek a future that avoids both *telos* and radical contingency, a future that is unstable yet can be concretely locatable in multiple racial formations. A world in which multiple racisms can be identified is one in which multiple challenges can be brought against them.

The central task for critical pedagogy and multicultural education is the construction of what Mohan calls 'creative resolutions and contingent alliances'. As he elaborates:

> multiculturalist pedagogy takes as its starting point a notion of culture as a terrain of conflict and struggle over representation — conflict for which resolution may not be immediate and struggle that may not cease until there is a change in the social conditions that provoke it. Rather than present culture as the site where different members . . . coexist peacefully, it has to develop strategies to explore and understand this conflict and to encourage creative resolutions and contingent alliances that move students from interpreting cultures to intervening in political processes. Implicit in this agenda is a shift in pedagogical emphasis from transmitting to transforming knowledge, though the full analysis of this shift had a slow start because of its alarmist construction as an irresponsible abdication of intellectual standards. (1995, p. 385)

Because interests are not immediately self-present to agents, critical pedagogy encourages self-reflection as a practice of everyday life in which a normative democratic theory of knowledge production and conception is a prominent feature. In other words, critical pedagogy needs to re-embrace macro-concepts such as 'totality', 'exploitation', and 'patriarchy' and it must do so without denigrating a critical understanding of micro-structures of experiential engagement and micro-intimacies of everyday communal and family life. Yet in affirming a rational project of emancipation, critical multiculturalists need to resist the irrational myth that rationality conceals. Such a project must resist the peripheralizing of the 'other' as the irrational; the consignment of the 'other' to the category of sub-reason. Edward Said remarks:

> the so-called objective truth of the white man's superiority built and maintained by the classical European colonial empires also rested on a violent subjugation of African and Asian peoples, who, it is equally true, fought that particular imposed 'truth' in order to provide an independent order of their own. (1996, p. 90)

Critical pedagogy must assume a position which Enrique Dussel calls 'trans-modernity':

> Trans-modernity (as a project of political, economic, ecological, erotic, pedagogical, and religious liberation) is the co-realization of that which it is impossible for modernity to accomplish by itself: that is, of an *incorporative* solidarity, which I have called analectic, between centre/periphery, man/woman . . . different ethnic groups, different classes, civilization/nature, Western culture/Third World cultures, et cetera. For this to happen, however, the negated and victimized 'other-face' of modernity — the colonial periphery, the Indian, the slave, the woman, the child, the subalternized popular cultures — must in the first place, discover itself as innocent, as the 'innocent victim' of a ritual sacrifice, who, in the process of discovering itself as innocent may now judge modernity as guilty of an originary, constitutive, and irrational violence. (1993, p. 76)

The critical pedagogy to which we are referring needs to be made less *informative* and more *performative*, less a pedagogy directed towards the interrogation of written texts than a corporeal pedagogy grounded in the lived experiences of the students. Critical pedagogy, as we are revisioning it, is a pedagogy that brushes against the grain of textual foundationalism, ocular fetishism, and the monumentalist abstraction of theory that characterizes most critical practice within multicultural classrooms. We are calling for a pedagogy in which multicultural ethics are performed rather than simply reduced to the practice of reading texts. Teachers need to displace the textual politics that dominate most multicultural classrooms and engage in a politics of bodily and affective investment. A critical pedagogy for multicultural education should serve to quicken the affective sensibilities of students as well as provide them with a language of social analysis and cultural critique. Opportunities must be made for students to work in communities where they can spend time with ethnically diverse populations in the context of community activism and participation in progressive social movements (see Sleeter and Montecinos, this volume).

Students need to move beyond simply knowing *about* critical multiculturalist practice. Rather, they need to take the required steps towards an embodied and corporeal understanding of such practice and an affective investment in such practice at the level of everyday life such that it deflects the invasive power of capital.

Critical educators would do well to develop those qualities of the intellectual of which Edward Said has written so eloquently. According to Said, the intellectual must possess an 'unbudgeable conviction in a concept of justice and fairness that allows for differences between nations and individuals, without at the same time assigning them to hidden hierarchies, preferences, evaluations' (1996, p. 94). Further, Said notes that intellectuals possess 'an alternative and more principled stand that enables them in effect to speak the truth to power' (1996, p. 97). 'Yes, the intellectual's voice is lonely', Said goes on to say, 'but it has resonance only because it associates itself freely with the reality of a movement, the aspirations of a people, the common pursuit of a shared ideal' (1996, p. 102). In other words, this is more than an issue of intellectual probity but rather an issue of critical self-reflexivity. It is in this sense that critical educators need to adopt the distinction made by Said between the professional and amateur intellectual:

> the professional claims detachment on the basis of a profession and pretends to objectivity, whereas the amateur is moved neither by rewards nor by the fulfillment of an immediate career plan but by a committed engagement with ideas and values in the public sphere. The intellectual over time naturally turns towards the political world partly because, unlike the academy or the laboratory, that world is animated by considerations of power and interest writ large that drive a whole society or nation, that, as Marx so fatefully said, take the intellectual from relatively discrete questions of interpretation to much more significant ones of social change and transformation . . . the intellectual who claims to write only for him or herself, or for the sake of pure learning, or abstract science is not to be, and must not be, believed. (1996, p. 110)

Racisms: Breaking Out of the Black–White Dichotomy

The unproblematized 'commonsense' acceptance of 'race' as a legitimate means of framing social relations has found its way into the classroom. Since to a large extent schools mirror the ideological and material structure of the society-at-large, they serve as powerful vehicles for socialization — for shaping students' 'racial' perceptions of subordinate groups through the hidden and racialized dimensions of the official curriculum, textbooks, and pedagogy. These racialized practices are embodied by students of both subordinate and dominant populations and, in turn, are used to frame or make conclusions about existing social relationships. These racialized practices also influence how these students define racism and how they perceive and respond to different forms of racialized discourses and events that involve African-Americans as well as other subordinate populations.

To address seriously the issues raised in our chapter requires a willingness to shift from talking about 'race' to talking about *racisms*. It requires understanding the concept of racialization as a historically specific ideological process. Critical educators should not be trying to seek a critical theory of 'race' for this will lead only to the further domestication of multicultural education. Critical educationalists and scholars who have an interest in multiculturalism should seek to develop an understanding of historically defined racialized relations from the perspective of a global economy. Further, they need to acknowledge the plurality of racisms at work, including those which we have termed the practices of 'whiteness'. We are not playing with semantics here but rather proposing an alternative analytical framework from which to identify the structures and practices of racialization. To construct a new language for examining the nature of these racisms requires an understanding of how complex relationships of exploitation and resistance, grounded in differences of class, gender, and ethnicity, give rise to a multiplicity of ideological constructions of the racialized other. This knowledge challenges the traditional notion of racism as solely a black–white phenomenon and directs us toward a more accurately constructed, and hence more politically useful, concept of racisms and those relations of power that shape the social conditions faced by racialized groups on a daily basis in schools and society.

In discussing our analytical framework of racisms and the politics of whiteness in the preceding sections, we have attempted to draw attention to competing and complementary theoretical narratives in the area of multicultural education and 'race relations'. One issue is clear to us. Despite recent criticisms of Marxist analyses of class as a politics of economic determinism, we welcome a renewed interest in class analysis as this could eventually lead to a more profound understanding and transformation of racialized identities among various populations within the United States. We recognize that there is an apparent political tension between our insistence on the need for a renewed class analysis at a time when it has become fashionable to question its usefulness, and post-Marxist constructivist and textual accounts of 'race' and racialized identities. We argue, nonetheless, that much of the new analysis of racialized social relations will be influenced by new approaches to class relations, class structure, and class formations inspired by contemporary Marxist formulations.

In a recent interview, Stuart Hall expresses a serious concern with both the Left's current silence on issues dealing with social class and its failure to articulate sufficiently the relationship between the economic and the political in discussions of globalization:

> I do think that's work that urgently needs to be done. The moment you talk about globalization, you are obliged to talk about the internationalization of capital in its late modern form, the shifts that are going on in modern capitalism, post-Fordism, etc. So those terms which were excluded from cultural studies . . . now need to be reintegrated. . . . In fact, I am sure we will return to the fundamental category of 'capital'. The difficulties lie in reconceptualizing *class*. Marx it seems to me now, was much more accurate about 'capitalism' than he was about class. It's the articulation between the economic and the political in Marxist class theory that has collapsed. (see Chen, 1996, pp. 400–1)

Our criticism of current approaches to 'race' and multiculturalism has attempted to foreground and redress some of these concerns. Multicultural education as it presently stands, denuded of effective strategies of resistance to the wrecking train of globalization, bears the stigmata of its liberal humanist underpinnings. To reinvigorate antiracist struggle, multicultural educators need to learn from but decidedly move beyond the cultural politics initiated by the categories of syncretism, hybridity, pastiche and the literary conceits of undecidability and indeterminacy so prominent in postmodernist formulations. In short, they need to move beyond the demystifying interrogations of Eurocentric discourse and western cultural imperialism that have been exercised by postcolonial critics. A revolutionary multiculturalism must be developed that is able to put into operation strategies and tactics that exceed and break out of the socio-historical determinations of bourgeois humanism and an addiction to *haute politique*. What must be forcefully challenged is the uneven and combined development of the 'Third World', as well as the unbridled accumulation of power and the exploitative practices of the oligarchic industrialized powers. San Juan (1996) has convincingly argued (after Wallerstein) that since capitalism, as a world system, denominates as racism and universalism, the major axis of liberation must be anticapitalist struggle. Since postcolonial criticism is unable to account for the construction of subjectivity outside of the 'epistemological necrophilia' that accompanies such deconstructive efforts, the struggle against transnational capitalism is, according to San Juan, the only viable option for critical multiculturalists. Failure both to intervene in the compradorization and refeudalization of the 'Third World' at the level of anticapitalist mobilization, and to work towards the development of counter-hegemonic struggles by the poor and the dispossessed of the planet is to suspend multiculturalism indefinitely over 'the specular abyss of *differánce*' that will doom it to oblivion.[1]

Note

1 This chapter draws from a number of other chapters and articles. See, in particular: Peter McLaren's *Revolutionary Multiculturalism: Pedagogies of Dissent for the New Millennium* (Boulder Col: Westview Press, 1997); Peter McLaren's, 'Unthinking whiteness, rethinking democracy', *Educational Foundations*, **11**, 2, Spring 1997, pp. 5–40.

    Rodolfo Torres wishes to acknowledge the significance of his collaborative work with Antonia Darder in informing his contribution to this chapter. Both authors wish to thank Stephen May for his excellent editorial suggestions and assistance in completing the chapter.

References

ALCOFF, L. (1996) 'Philosophy and racial identity', *Radical Philosophy*, **75**, pp. 5–14.

BONNETT, A. (1996) 'Antiracism and the critique of white identities', *New Community*, **22**, pp. 97–110.

CALLINICOS, A. (1990) *Against Postmodernism: A Marxist Critique*, New York: St Martin's Press.

CALLINICOS, A. (1992) 'Race and class', *International Socialism*, **55**, pp. 3–39.

CALLINICOS, A. (1993) *Race and Class*, London: Bookmarks.

CASHMORE, E. (1996) *Dictionary of Race and Ethnic Relations* (fourth edition), New York: Routledge.

CHAMBERS, R. (1996) 'The unexamined', *The Minnesota Review*, **47**, pp. 141–56.

CHEN, K-H. (1996) 'Cultural studies and the politics of internationalization: An interview with Stuart Hall', in MORLEY, D. and CHEN, K-H. (eds) *Stuart Hall: Critical Dialogues in Cultural Studies*, London: Routledge, pp. 484–503.

CONE, J. (1986) *A Black Theology of Liberation*, New York: Orbis Books.

CRUZ, J. (1996) 'From farce to tragedy: Reflections on the reification of race at century's end', in GORDON, A. and NEWFIELD, C. (eds) *Mapping Multiculturalism*, Minneapolis: University of Minnesota Press, pp. 19–39.

DUSSEL, E. (1993) 'Eurocentrism and modernity' (Introduction to the Frankfurt Lectures), *Boundary*, **2**, 20, 3, pp. 65–76.

FRANKENBERG, R. (1993) *The Social Construction of Whiteness: White Women, Race Matters*, Minneapolis: The University of Minnesota Press.

FUSCO, C. (1995) *English is Broken Here: Notes on Cultural Fusion in the Americas*, New York: The New Press.

GABBARD, D. (1995) 'NAFTA, GATT, and Goals 2000: Reading the political culture of post-industrial America', *Taboo*, **II**, pp. 184–99.

GALLAGHER, C. (1994) 'White construction in the university', *Socialist Review*, **1**, 2, pp. 165–87.

GILROY, P. (1987) *There Ain't No Black in the Union Jack*, Chicago: University of Chicago Press.

GOLDBERG, D. (1993) *Racist Culture: Philosophy and the Politics of Meaning*, Cambridge, MA: Blackwell Publishers.

GUILLAUMIN, C. (1995) *Racism, Sexism, Power, and Ideology*, London: Routledge.

HARRIS, C. (1993) 'Whiteness as property', *Harvard Law Review*, **106**, pp. 1709–91.

HERRNSTEIN, R. and MURRAY, C. (1994) *The Bell Curve: Intelligence and Class Structure in American Life*, New York: Free Press.

IGNATIEV, N. and GARVEY, J. (eds) (1996) *Race Traitor*, New York: Routledge.

LIPSITZ, G. (1995) 'The possessive investment in whiteness: Racialized social democracy and the "white" problem in American studies', *American Quarterly*, **47**, pp. 369–87.

LÓPEZ, I. (1996) *White by Law*, New York: New York University Press.

LOTT, E. (1993) 'White like me: Racial cross-dressing and the construction of American whiteness', in KAPLAN, A. and PEASE, D. (eds) *Cultures of United States Imperialism*, Durham: Duke University Press, pp. 474–98.

McLAREN, P. (1995) *Critical Pedagogy and Predatory Culture: Oppositional Politics in a Postmodern Era*, New York: Routledge.

MILES, R. (1993) *Racism after 'Race Relations'*, London: Routledge.

MILES, R. and TORRES, R. (1996) 'Does "race" matter? Transatlantic perspectives on racism after "race relations"', in AMIT-TALAI, V. and KNOWLES, C. (eds) *Resituating Identities: The Politics of Race, Ethnicity and Culture*, Peterborough, Ontario, Canada: Broadview Press, pp. 26–46.

MOHAN, R. (1995) 'Multiculturalism in the nineties: Pitfalls and possibilities', in NEWFIELD, C. and STRICKLAND, R. (eds) *After Political Correctness: The Humanities and Society in the 1990s*, Boulder, CO: Westview Press, pp. 372–88.

PARENTI, M. (1996) *Dirty Truths*, San Francisco: City Lights Books.

PETRAS, J. and MORLEY, M. (1992) *Latin America in the Time of Cholera: Electoral Politics, Market Economies, and Permanent Crisis*, New York: Routledge.

ROEDIGER, D. (1994) *Towards the Abolition of Whiteness: Essays on Race, Politics, and Working Class History*, New York: Verso.

SAID, E. (1996) *Representations of the Intellectual*, New York: Vintage Books.

SAN JUAN, E. (1996) *Mediations: From a Filipino Perspective*, Pasig City, Philippines: Anvil Publishing.

STOWE, D. (1996) 'Uncolored people: The rise of whiteness studies', *Lingua Franca*, **6**, 6, pp. 68–77.

WALLACE, A. (1996) 'Less diversity seen as UC preferences end', *Los Angeles Times*, October 2, A1, 18.

WEST, C. (1993) *Keeping Faith: Philosophy and Race in America*, New York: Routledge.

WINANT, H. (1994) *Racial Conditions: Politics, Theory, Comparisons*, Minneapolis: University of Minnesota Press.

WOLFENSTEIN, E. (1993) *Psychoanalytic-Marxism: Groundwork*, New York: The Guilford Press.

WOOD, E. (1995) *Democracy Against Capitalism: Renewing Historical Materialism*, Cambridge: Cambridge University Press.

WRAY, M. and NEWITZ, A. (eds) (1997) *White Trash: Race and Class in America*, New York: Routledge.

YÚDICE, G. (1995) 'Neither impugning nor disavowing whiteness does a viable politics make: The limits of identity politics', in NEWFIELD, C. and STRICKLAND, R. (eds) *After Political Correctness: The Humanities and Society in the 1990s*, Boulder, CO: Westview Press, pp. 255–85.

3   Racism, 'Postmodernism' and Reflexive Multiculturalism

Ali Rattansi

What I propose to do in this chapter is to posit a 'postmodern'[1] frame, in order to provide a particular 'take' on issues around racism, ethnicity and identity. My elaboration of the issues will, wherever possible, highlight educational processes, although not exclusively so. My general discussion of racism, ethnicity and identity will be followed by a sketching out of the implications of my 'postmodern' framing for the so-called politics of identity and what I call 'reflexive multiculturalism', especially in relation to education.

The 'Postmodern' Frame

The following features of a 'postmodern' frame as an analytic device are highlighted, and their implications explored, in the understanding of questions of racism and ethnicity, multiculturalism and antiracism.[2]

1   The 'postmodern' condition as primarily an intellectual condition characterized by reflection on the nature and limits of western modernity. This intellectual reflection itself has, of course, certain historical conditions of existence. Thus, although some considerations on the pretensions of western modernity can be found in the writings of Nietzsche, for example, the current form of 'postmodern' analysis draws crucially upon the manner of western modernity's forms of development in the twentieth century. In other words, the postmodern sensibility that informs the discussion here is itself the outcome of, and contributes to, key recent transformations in the discursive-institutional complexes of western modernity and their global ramifications.

2   'Modernity' as a theoretical category. The form of conceptualization adopted here focuses especially on the dualities of modernity: for example, between the formation of democratic institutions on the one hand and disciplinary complexes of bureaucracy and power/knowledge on the other hand, a point particularly relevant to educational institutions; between the excitement of rapid change and the simultaneous anxiety of societies seemingly out of control; and the constant destabilization of identities and continuous reinvention of 'traditions'.

3   The role of western modernity's 'others', both internal and external, real and imagined, especially in the context of various imperialisms and colonialisms. Also, as potent forces in the formation and continuous reconstruction of western identities, in particular by processes of the marginalization of others as binary opposites of supposedly western characteristics. Derridean 'deconstructive' strategies

are brought into play to display the artifice involved in the construction of binarities in western discourses and cultural identities. This also helps to destabilize the way in which oppositions such as male–female, active–passive, culture–nature, rational–emotional, civilized–savage, white–black, and so forth, have become superimposed on each other to hold together, precariously — a phallocentric 'Occidentalism' against feminized 'Orients' and barbaric 'Africans' to take just two examples (Rattansi, 1994, 1997). At the same time, it is important to understand the images of the 'West' that have become embedded in non-western cultures (Carrier, 1995).

4   An exploration of the profound impact of new phases of globalization, theorized as uneven processes, but as corrosive of old national boundaries and playing a creative role in the formation of new, hybrid, syncretic transnational identities (see Appadurai, 1996; Hall, 1992a, 1992b).

5   The project of 'decentring' and de-essentializing both 'subjects' and the 'social': the individual is no longer conceptualized as a fully coherent, 'rational', self-knowledgeable agent capable of direct access to reality and truth, and is theorized as living within the tension of a variety of potential and actual subject positions; social formations are no longer regarded as tightly knit complexes of institutions with necessary, predetermined forms of connection or logics of development — there are no final determining instances or levels such as the economy, and no laws of motion as posited in most versions of Marxism.

6   Analyses of temporality and spatiality as constitutive features of the social, of subjectivities, and of processes of identification. Neither time nor space are privileged over the other (Adam, 1990; Lash and Urry, 1994; Soja, 1989; Urry, 1991), both are seen as being in a constant state of flux, in contrast to a widespread tendency to view time as dynamic and space as static — a form of conceptualization which, among other things, has allowed time to be associated with 'progress', activity, and the masculine, while space has been construed as passive and 'feminine' (Massey, 1993). Moreover, in conditions of 'late modernity' and its associated intensified globalization, there is an emphasis on what Harvey (1989) has called 'time-space compression', that is, the diminution of space by technologies of mass communication and travel and the increasing simultanity of experience across the globe (see also Brunn and Leinbach, 1991). There are specific 'postmodernist' aesthetic strategies and cultural movements associated with these transformations which are crucial to a sense of the 'postmodern' as a cultural and political formation (Boyne and Rattansi, 1990).

7   A reconsideration of the relation between the 'psychic' and the 'social' which takes seriously a specifically psychoanalytic decentring of the subject, positing it as constitutively split between a conscious self and the disruptions of unconscious desire, emotional attachments and hostilities, the operations of ambivalence, splitting, fantasy, paranoia, projection, and introjection (Craib, 1989; Elliott, 1994; Rattansi, 1994; Rustin, 1991).

8   An engagement with questions of sexuality and sexual difference, both as theorized within poststructuralist and 'postmodern' feminisms, which destabilize and de-essentialize the categories of 'woman' and 'women' and question the simple binaries of sex/gender and public/private (Butler, 1990; Elam, 1994; Flax, 1990, 1993; Hekman, 1990), and as analysed in attempts to understand the sexualization of

'race' (Fanon, 1986; Frosh, 1989; Gilman, 1992; Kabbani, 1986; Nandy, 1983, 1990; Rattansi, 1994; Stepan, 1990) and the multifarious intersections between 'race' and 'sex' (Zack, 1997).

Having set in place, albeit in outline form, the elements of a particular 'postmodern' framework I turn now to exhibiting some of its uses in tackling questions of racism and ethnicity.

Defining Ethnicities and Racisms

A 'postmodern' frame's intrinsic suspicion of doctrines of 'pure' origins makes it inherently corrosive of discourses that invoke notions of historically formed cultural essences. Its de-essentializing and decentring tendencies inevitably provoke conflict with political projects which rely on strong classificatory systems, whether based on conceptions of 'ethnicity', 'nation', or 'race'. Moreover, conventional ideas of ethnicity and racism as elaborated in the truth-regimes of the human sciences find themselves equally vulnerable to the deconstructive power of 'postmodern' analysis.

The social sciences have had predictably little success in furnishing uncontentious definitions of ethnicity and racism. There is little agreement except around the points that the term 'ethnicity' derives from the Greek *ethnos*, meaning a people, a collectivity sharing certain common attributes; and that ethnicity ought essentially to be regarded as a cultural marker or, indeed, container in which some conception of shared origin and characteristics is crucial (Rex, 1986, pp. 26–9, 79–98). But what precisely is meant here by 'culture'? Is any particular shared 'cultural' attribute more important than any other — for instance, language, territoriality, or religion? Do not notions of 'shared origin' smuggle in ideas of shared biology (Nash, 1989, p. 5)? How is 'ethnicity' to be consistently and usefully distinguished from 'race', and 'ethnocentrism' from 'racism', and both of these from 'xenophobia' and 'nationalism'? How distinctive is the current notion and practice of 'ethnic cleansing' from the Nazi project of 'racial cleansing', especially in view of the manner in which 'racial scientists' before the Second World War discussed differences between Croats and Muslims in biological terms (Kohn, 1995, p. 12)?

The inherent conceptual difficulties of strong classificatory programmes in the human sciences have, around these questions, been hopelessly exacerbated by becoming intertwined. Not only that, they have had to come to terms with the astonishingly complex manner in which populations appear to draw and redraw, and maintain and breach, and narrow and widen the boundaries around themselves and others.

Decentring and De-essentializing Ethnicity, 'Race', and Racism

In this context, the first 'postmodern' move must be to decentre and de-essentialize, by postulating what is often glimpsed but rarely acknowledged and accepted with any degree of comfort: *there are no unambiguous, water-tight definitions to be had of ethnicity, racism, and the myriad terms in between* (Omi and Winant, 1986, pp. 68–9). Indeed, all these terms are permanently *in-between*, caught in the impossibility of fixity and essentialization. There is a 'family resemblance' between them, a merging and overlapping of one form of boundary formation with another, coupled with strong contextual determinations. One programmatic conclusion would be for 'postmodern' frame analyses to eschew tight definitions, and instead engage in Foucauldian genealogical and archeological projects, exploring the accretion of meanings, political affiliations, subject positions, forms of address, regimes of truth, and disciplinary practices involved in the construction of particular myths of origin, narratives of evolution, and forms of boundary marking and policing engaged in by different 'communities' in particular historical contexts. 'Ethnicity', 'race', 'the nation', and so on, carry infinitely rich connotations and continue to be harnessed to a wide variety of political and cultural projects. Such genealogies and archeologies can and have explored the continuities and discontinuities in the discursive practices involved.[3]

The debate about whether there is now a 'new racism' (cf. Short and Carrington, this volume) serves to provide a telling illustration of the necessity for decentring and de-essentializing concepts of 'race', 'ethnicity', and 'nation'.

Racisms 'Old' and 'New': Undoing a Binary Opposition

The political projects and the disciplinary matrices involved in the formation of 'race' as a marker in western modernity have, of course, been extensively studied, especially in the forms of nineteenth century and early twentieth century 'scientific racism' which were intertwined with conceptions of non-European others, sexual difference, anti-Semitism, and the culturally assimilationary thrust of the nation-state. 'Scientific racisms' have had two enduring characteristics: a biological definition of 'race', therefore 'racializing' the body and conceiving of a population as having a commonality of 'stock' and phenotypical features;[4] and, secondly, attempts to create a hierarchy of 'races' which, despite representing some 'white races' as racially inferior to others, have consistently consigned 'non-white' populations to the lowest rungs of the racial ladder (Banton and Harwood, 1975).

But the difficulty of extrapolating from 'scientific racism' to contemporary forms of inferiorization, discrimination, and exclusion in order to define racism is evident in the controversy over the 'new racism' as well as in attempts to provide legislative and judicial protection to populations subjected to discriminatory practices. The term 'new racism' is already burdened by having two different referents. Martin Barker (1981), who appears to have first used the label, mainly targeted the relatively recent appropriation of the doctrines of sociobiology by the British New Right, who have deployed sociobiological conceptions in postulating a supposedly 'natural' equivalence between cultural, especially national difference, and cultural and political antagonisms against those deemed to be 'obviously different', that is, foreign and alien. They have attempted thereby to legitimize policies for the repatriation of British Asian and British African-Caribbean populations, and to underwrite de facto segregation in schooling, especially in areas with a large concentration of British Asian, particularly Muslim, populations. Balibar (1991), also keen to highlight the relatively novel phenomenon in which overt doctrines of biological inferiority have been abandoned in Europe (although legitimation for domination, discrimination, repatriation, and forms of segregation or separation continue to be found there), speaks of the new racism as primarily a form of 'cultural racism'; a 'differentialist racism', in which cultural difference replaces the earlier and now scientifically discredited biological theorizations. Support for culturalist interpretations of new forms of racism has also come from a number of other influential commentators (see, for example, Gilroy, 1987, pp. 43–51).

But at least two problems arise immediately in any serious consideration of this issue. Firstly, how 'new' is the 'new racism'? Its credentials for novelty have been questioned by Miles (1987), whose argument that the 'scientific racism' of the nineteenth and twentieth centuries, although rooted in biological features, always revolved around a conception of cultural/national character and uniqueness and that there has always been a powerful connection between racist and nationalist discourses, challenges the claims of Barker, Balibar, and the rest. Secondly, as Kohn (1995) has demonstrated, even today, strong biological notions of 'race' are surviving and regrouping in a variety of institutions and scientific disciplines, and also in versions of Afrocentrism (see also May; Nieto, this volume).

My purpose in referring to this discussion is not to adjudicate between these particular disputants — I return to some of these questions later. Rather, it is to suggest that inside a 'postmodern' frame it seems clear, on the one hand, that without a very detailed archeological and genealogical exercise it would be impossible to grasp the continuities and discontinuities between the two, but also that a simple old/new binary homogenizes each discourse and delimits its field of application, effectiveness, and articulation in a singularly unhelpful manner. Both 'scientific racism' and 'differentialist racism' are complex enough formations to merit being referred to in the plural, and any effective comparative exercise requires an understanding of their articulation with discourses and disciplinary practices not merely around the 'nation' as has hitherto been the case, but also around sexual difference, and the cultural codes of social class difference. My argument acquires particular relevance at a period in European history that has seen the resurgence of racisms which combine older fascist, anti-Semitic ideologies with a 'new' scientific racism as discussed by Kohn (1995) and with a differentialist rhetoric mobilized against migrant communities with 'Third World' origins. Some of these movements are not afraid to speak openly of a commitment to racism, while still maintaining a rhetoric of differentialism, for example the British National Party (see Rattansi, 1994).

The Discourses of 'Race', Nation and Ethnicity: No Necessary Political Belonging

Note, too, the ways in which racializing, exclusionary discourses can take antiracist campaigning principles based on multiculturalism and equal respect for all cultures, and egalitarian appeals based on rights of citizenship, and turn them around so that multiculturalism becomes transmuted into a defence of the rights of white cultures to retain their 'purity', and the rhetoric of citizenship is mobilized to underwrite demands for forms of segregation in schooling, for example (cf. Carrim and Soudien, this volume). This can then be conjoined with claims that the real problem is that Whites have become 'second-class citizens' in their own countries, all ploys which are evident in the discourse of the Ku Klux Klan, or in the appeals of the British extreme right as well as in British popular culture (on the latter, see Cohen, 1993; Rattansi, 1994). Moreover, while the British extreme right has generally espoused a traditional stance on the role of women and 'family values', there has in fact been an internal struggle over attempts by some members to articulate their racism with feminism, and attract more women members, by arguing for more egalitarian approaches (Durham, 1991, p. 274). The only way to make sense of these complex and ever-changing reconfigurations of what one might call colour, culture, and political discourse is to decentre and de-essentialize concepts of 'race', ethnicity, and nation as recommended here and to acknowledge that *they have no necessary political belonging*. Although it is arguable that historically concepts of 'race' have contained a strong biological element, the degree of centrality accorded to biology is obviously subject to enormous variation, as is its articulation with conceptions of nationality, sexual difference, class, and democratic rights. There are, moreover, shifts of discourse and policy depending upon targeted populations — 'black', 'Asian', 'Oriental', 'Celtic', and so on. In other words, *there are racisms, not a singular racism*.

Nor can it be assumed that the concepts of 'race' and nation will only function in a manner that underwrites projects of domination and inferiorization. Their capacity for mobilization as resources for resistance is evident in conceptions of Afrocentrism and in other projects which rely on a notion of an African 'race' and nation, particularly in the populations of the African diaspora in the United States and Britain. And it certainly cannot be ruled out that some of the discourses and practices of those committed to doctrines of 'racial' and cultural purity amongst ethnic minorities might be regarded in some respects and contexts as 'racist'. Hence, in part, the futility of merely proclaiming the scientific falsity of the concept of 'race'. From 'postmodern' perspectives, as from others, such attributions of fixed origin appear reprehensible in their attempts at closure around mythic collectivities, but there is no denying their potential for cultural and political mobilization (cf. McLaren and Torres, this volume).

Thus, as with 'race', the various elements that go to make up the notion of ethnicity — language, religion, notions of common origin, codes of kinship, marriage, and dress, forms of cuisine, and so forth — can be mobilized for apparently incongruous alliances.[5] Examples of such alliances include those between the 'cultural racists' of the British New Right and British Muslim communities demanding the right to separate schooling, between the black nationalism of the African-American Louis Farrakhan and elements of the white American extreme right — anti-Semitism being one of the uniting political strands — (and in South Africa, not so long ago, between sections of the Zulu population and white right-wing groups, each demanding separate 'homelands'), thus demonstrating the complex articulations that become possible around projects of nationalism, racism, and ethnicity, white and black. To reiterate, the language of cultural difference, as part of ethnicity, 'race', and nation has no necessary political belonging.

Ethnicity, Representation, and Racialization

A 'postmodern' framing conceptualizes ethnicity as a lived experience as well as part of a cultural politics of representation. It involves processes of 'self-identification' as well as formation by disciplinary agencies such as the State, and includes the involvement of the social sciences, given their incorporation in the categorization and redistributive activities of the State and campaigning organizations. 'Representation' in this conceptualization is being used in a double sense. On the one hand, it refers to issues of authority and accountability in the articulation of communal views and 'interests'. It poses questions about who is authorized to speak for whom, and immediately opens up the issue of conflicts within designated ethnic communities. It also encourages analyses of projects of hegemony within and between ethnic communities (Cohen, 1988; Winant, 1994). Moreover, by foregrounding institutional politics, it reveals what is so often at stake in the conflicts within and between collectivities: a voice in the allocation and redistribution of resources, often from local and national state agencies. But the emphasis on 'representation' is also important for its focus on the significance of the construction and constant recreation of ethnic identities through the production of images and narratives in visual and written texts of 'popular' and 'high' culture: newspapers, novels, television documentaries and drama, cinema, the theatre, music, painting, and photography. Ethnic identity is a 'social imaginary', to adapt a term from Castoriadis (1987), or to borrow Anderson's term, an 'imagined community' (1991), that is, amongst other things, a collectivity bonded together by forms of literary and visual narration which locate in time and space, in history, memory, and territory.

The formation of ethnic identities may be regarded as part of a process of racialization when categories of 'race' are explicitly invoked or when popular or specialized biological and quasi-biological discourses are drawn upon to legitimate projects of subject-formation, inclusion and exclusion, discrimination, inferiorization, exploitation, verbal abuse, and physical harassment and violence. However, individual acts and collective projects of boundary formation, discrimination, exploitation, and violence may or may not involve explicit inferiorization and may or may not contain references to biological notions of 'stock', 'blood', genetic differences, and bodily attributes such as colour and capacities such as 'intelligence'. Note, too, that appeals to ethnicity and cultural difference, by invoking ideas of shared origin, 'kith and kin', and 'nation' may in fact smuggle in quasi-biological conceptions (Nash, 1989). Moreover, as Cohen (1988) in particular has emphasized, rhetorics of social class have often contained appeals to biology, enshrined in ideas of 'codes of breeding'.

The decentring and de-essentialization of 'race' and ethnicity that is being recommended here makes for a much more fruitful analytical engagement with these processes of flux, contextual transformation and dislocation, and the complex overlapping and crosscutting of boundaries that characterize the formation of ethnic and racialized identities. This is not to argue that definitions of racism are not necessary — both for purposes of legal protection and redress, and the specification of objects of social, political, and economic analysis — but that strict definitions are always liable to find themselves confounded by the complex intertwining of the very wide range of cultural repertoires being drawn upon by individuals and collectivities.

The difficulties of drawing neat boundaries around concepts such as ethnicity, ethnocentrism, 'race', racism, and so forth, are now becoming more widely acknowledged, as are the difficulties of finding unambiguous and acceptable ethnic labels in practices of regulation and policy, as for example, in census questions. Some have even doubted the value of the notion of ethnicity (Omi and Winant, 1986, although see May, this volume). Others (Anthias, 1992) appear to regard ethnicity as the primary concept, with 'race' as a subset, although this then leads to another set of classificatory conundrums around definitions of racism (see Mason's, 1992 critique of Anthias).

The significance of a 'postmodern' framing of these difficulties lies in elaborating a framework that makes these problems intelligible in a specific manner, and in proposing avenues for research. The 'postmodern' point is not merely one of highlighting a perennial excess of 'things' over 'words', that is, that definitions and analyses are always partial, but one of exhibiting particular forms of interpenetration between 'words' and 'things' in which discourses of 'race' and ethnicity are *productive* of objects of analysis in forms that prevent simple 'empirical' adjudication between competing discourses. This involves an undermining of the cultural/material distinction, and is overlaid by the potential destabilizing effects of *différance* as a property of language and discourse, both in everyday life and specialized disciplines, and deconstruction as an analytical strategy that allows the unraveling and displacement of binaries, for example, that of 'old/new' racism. These general aspects of a 'postmodern' framing raise a number of questions and open up several avenues for elaboration. Given the constraints of space, four issues only are now briefly highlighted to exhibit further the particular emphases of 'postmodern' framing. The discussion that follows will thus be confined to (a) the effects of a 'postmodern' decentring, de-essentialization, and 'detotalization' or 'undoing' of the social; (b) a decentring of the racist subject; (c) issues of sexual difference, ambivalence, and pleasure in racializing processes, in the context of time/space relations and new forms of global/local configurations; and (d) the phenomenon of the so-called 'new ethnicities'.

Racism and the Decentring of the Social

Decentring and detotalizing the social has the consequence, amongst the other things referred to, of treating the 'social' within a 'postmodern' frame as always relatively open, in the process of becoming 'closed', but always subject to the play of contingency, dislocation, opposition, and disintegration, which prevents closure around discursive practices within and between contextual, institutional sites. Framed in this mode, the variety and contradictions of ethnic and racialized discourses, as constitutive of the social, are particularly highlighted, painting up the complexity and relative contingency and openness of the processes by which identities are constructed in 'routine' everyday practices, as well as in more explicit political projects of ethnic and racialized hegemony. Take the case of 'stereotypes' of British Asians and British African-Caribbeans, as part of the cultural repertoire of inferiorization, exclusion, abuse, and discrimination in contemporary Britain. A 'postmodern' framing is alert to significant dislocations in a process often portrayed as all-encompassing and monolithic, smoothly reproducing racialized stereotypes and practices of discrimination in institutional sites, for example, schools. To put it differently, a 'postmodern' framing requires that we break with 'reproductive' models in which, say, the academic performance, suspension rates, and so forth, of British Asian and British African-Caribbean pupils are portrayed as an outcome of 'stereotypes' of these pupils held by teachers which lead to acts of discrimination against them, for example, placing them in less academic streams and sets. This picture oversimplifies. I have discussed much of the earlier educational research documenting the complexity of the processes involved elsewhere (Rattansi, 1992). Further research has continued to support this interpretation of the disjointed character of processes of racialization (see for example, Wright, 1995; Verma, 1995). Racialization processes in schools are coming to be seen as uneven and contradictory in their operation. Not all teachers hold stereotypes; the stereotypes are often contradictory in their attributions of characteristics such as 'lazy', 'unacademic', 'stupid', 'bright', as between different British Asian and British African-Caribbean pupils; and other forms of discrimination may or may not follow from the expression of stereotyping abuse in the classroom. Wright (1995, pp. 48–9), in her study of British primary (elementary) classrooms, remarks on the complexity and ambivalences of teacher responses to ethnic minority pupils, and especially on the intersections of gender and ethnicity in the classroom context, with Asian boys and white girls being most favourably perceived — a point which I discuss in greater depth later. Verma's overall judgment on his findings from a study of nine British multiethnic secondary schools was that 'The picture that emerged is complex and at times contradictory' (1995, p. 66). This is revealed in his study to be as true of patterns of teacher racism as of other features, a point also registered by Bhatti (1995) in her research on Asian students.

While British research monographs in the social sciences more generally (Genders and Player, 1989; Jenkins, 1986, 1992) have noticed the occurrence of contradictory stereotypes, neither their general significance, nor the import of their gendered mode, have been sufficiently noticed. As we shall see, the role of 'modernity' as a constitutive category, and the significance of time and space in the operation of these dislocations and contradictions, have also been similarly neglected. In understanding these problems, a shift of conceptual vocabulary from conventional social science to a more poststructuralist one is useful. One translation to make here is again a Foucauldian one: studies of recruitment of ethnic minorities to employment (Jenkins, 1986, 1992), of discriminatory treatment in schools (Rattansi, 1992; Verma, 1995; Wright, 1995) and allocation procedures for public housing (Henderson and Karn, 1984, 1987), for example, may be said to point up the extent to which stereotyping discourses — working as legitimation for exclusion from jobs, higher streams and sets in schools, and better public housing — are based on normalizing, disciplinary judgments. This forms part of what Foucault has called 'bio-politics' — enshrined in managerial and allocatory practices which regard good time-keeping, lack of 'trouble-making', and possible attributes of cleanliness, hygiene, bodily deport-ment and technique, and so forth, as the relevant criteria which determine access and the allocation of resources. These considerations override conceptions of skill, academic ability, and need, and neglect the possibility of greater acceptance of cultural relativism in matters of 'taste' and lifestyle. Moreover, these judgments are gendered and class-specific as well as racialized. To elaborate upon just one of the instances mentioned above, it is clear that judgments which have worked against certain families being allocated public housing on the basis of size of family, type of 'taste' in decoration, lifestyle, and so forth, are the product of a form of professional and managerial disciplinary, bio-political gaze and practice, routinized in the proced-ures of modern public bureaucracies, which have disadvantaged both ethnic minorities and particular sections of the white working-class. This is how Henderson and Karn's (1987) research, for example, may be read within a 'postmodern' frame.

Institutional Racism

The concept of 'institutionalized racism', of course, has been deployed to point up processes of this kind, but a 'postmodern' frame sees this not as a smooth, repro-ductive machine but as an internally contradictory set of processes, bound up with the specificity of modern disciplinary institutions, which amongst other things embody particular 'standards' of deportment and hygiene, involving not merely racialized, but gendered and class-specific discursive practices of judgment and discrimination involving bodily attributes, everyday aesthetics, capacities for self-control (drinking, time-keeping, lack of disruptive behaviour), and ordering the immediate environ-ment (tidiness, cleanliness, etc.). Moreover, the assumption of 'uniform' judgments, consistently 'applied', cannot necessarily be made — Bhatti (1995), for example, emphasizes the existence of a diversity of discourses in the school she researched — although the consistently discriminatory outcomes of allocatory processes may provide particular clues to the forms of 'normalizing' discrimination involved.

Undoing the social in this manner has, of course, general implications for the way in which the operation of racialized power relations is theorized. That is, it cannot be conceptualized as working and reproducing through a small number of tightly knit sites such as those of state and capital, aided and abetted by a capitalist media supposedly only interested in dividing black and white workers, as set out in some influential British Marxist works (for cruder versions of this thesis see, for example, Sivanandan, 1974; for a more sophisticated but nevertheless class-reductionist rendering of this type of argument, see Sarup, 1986, pp. 40, 95–8). Instead, racialized power relations may be seen more usefully in neo-Foucauldian terms which do not deny the importance of the State and capital but see these as far more fragmented and internally divided, together with a multiplication of sites for the operation of racisms — playgrounds, streets, classrooms, doctors' surgeries, mental hospitals, offices, etc. — with an important constitutive role assigned to specialized configurations of power/knowledge such as psychiatry or educational psychology, and professional ideologies. For example, among British teachers, the popular liberal notion of treating individual students in supposedly 'colour-blind' terms has the effect of ignoring the consequences of racism and racialized economic disadvantage on students — a form of 'professionalism' criticized in the British state-commissioned Rampton Report (Department of Education and Science, 1981). The continuing prevalence of this ideology amongst British teachers is documented by Bhatti (1995, pp. 70–1; see also Moodley, this volume).

Moreover, attempts to understand struggles to improve the treatment of ethnic minorities, for instance, in the workplace, have to give much greater importance to the question of discursive contestations. Jewson and Mason's (1992) analysis of the rhetorical ploys and counter-moves in struggles over the meaning of 'equal opportunities' in particular workplaces furnishes an especially well-researched illustration of a widespread strategy of resistance by those opposed to such policies.

Sexuality, Time/Space, the Body, Pleasure, Ambivalence, and the Spectacular in Racialization

The question of the gendering of racialized discursive practices has already featured in my discussion above. Several other dimensions can be highlighted. For instance, the ways in which the black and Asian presence in British inner-cities — in other words 'the inner-city' as a racialized 'place' — is also sexualized by reference to the 'threat' posed to white women by black men in a variety of discourses, including those of the popular press, politicians, and the police (Ware, 1992). The British extreme right has certainly been adept at exploiting this particular form of appeal to its male and female members in texts likely to generate fear in the women and masculine protectiveness in the men (see Rattansi, 1994). Amongst other things, these examples also manage to convey the significance of the articulations between 'family' and 'home' as symbols of 'race' and space (Cohen, 1993). They also repeat, at a temporal and spatial distance, the colonial discourse whereby the idea of the empire as a dangerous place where women needed protection and were to stay at 'home' allowed the construction of aggressive and protective masculinities, with a privileged placing in the 'public' arena, confining women to the 'domestic' sphere.

Of course, the racializing of space, especially in the city, takes a variety of forms, from the relative segregation of communities by housing policies and the phenomenon of 'white flight' (Cohen, 1993), as well as black expulsion — ethnic minority families forced out by vicious harassment — to the connotative 'fixing' of drug and crime issues to the black presence. And the sexualization of the inner-city also has an autonomous logic involving prostitution and the activities of pornographers, and 'panics' around the gay and lesbian presence, although here again the racialization and the sexualization can be articulated to each other via the supposed power of black pimps[6] and panics about black homophobia (Burston, 1993). The gendering and sexualization of the nation is another important element in the dynamics of the sexualization of 'race'. Women, as Yuval-Davis and Anthias (1989, pp. 8–10) have pointed out, and as is evident from the discussion of the discourse of the extreme right above, play a pivotal role in the construction of ethnicity and nationality: as biological reproducers; as boundary markers — hence the attempts to police their sexual relations with 'others'; as transmitters of the culture; as crucial symbols, for example, in notions of the motherland; and, of course, as actual participants in national struggles. Hence, surely, the significance of the metaphor of 'rape' in discussions of the impact of immigration on British culture (see, for example, the speech by John Stokes, MP, reproduced, although not with this point in mind, by Barker, 1981, p. 18), and the actuality of rape in so many projects of what have come now to be called 'ethnic cleansing'. If 'woman' is a key signifier of both culture and territory, then the sexual violation of her body is an assertion of masculinist ethnicity, or nationality, or 'race', which emasculates the other (although thereby enmeshing the rapist in the contradictions of defilement by such biological intercourse and the probable birth of a 'miscegenated' population). But masculinization may function in an oppositional mode — for example, in struggles for nationhood — while simultaneously being part of the discursive practices which subordinate women in that community. An instance may be found in Yuval-Davis and Anthias' recounting of a popular, presumably male, Palestinian saying of the 1980s which referred to the higher birthrates among the Palestinian population: 'The Israelis beat us at the borders but we beat them in the bedrooms' (1989, p. 8).

Space, then, is not only feminized but masculinized. This sexualization too feeds into the racialization of locales. In British cities this often happens through the staking out of territorial claims, and their continued policing by young working-class males to keep an area 'clean' of 'wogs', 'Pakis', and 'niggers'. Amongst other things, the discursive practices involved attempt to humiliate these others by physical assaults and verbal abuse which 'prove' the masculinity of the attackers and 'reduce' the victims to 'sissies': a form of emasculation and effeminization (Willis, 1977). And the significance of masculinist cultures was emphasized by the Macdonald Enquiry into the murder of an Asian pupil at Burnage High School in Manchester, England, by a white schoolmate: a strong masculinist culture of violence in the all-boys school was, the report argued, an important constitutive feature of the racism in the school (Macdonald, et al., 1989). But it is important to remember that there may be complex variations in the racializing dynamics involved, with alliances between white and African-Caribbean males against Asians or, as in some areas, the skirmishes being confined to Whites and Asians, coexisting with the presence of African-Caribbeans in local colleges of further and higher education (Cohen, 1993). The Macdonald Enquiry also had some interesting remarks on the complexity of racialized networks of alliance and cooperation, borne out by the recent research of Back (1996) which documents the marginalization of Asian, particularly Vietnamese youth, in Britain.

There is beginning to be some important research on the complex interrelations between gender, sexuality, 'race' and schooling which bears out the general argument of this chapter on the significance of this set of issues; research which was only in its very early stages or non-existent when I attempted to highlight its importance in an earlier, much discussed contribution to debates on racism and education (Rattansi, 1992). As I argued there, it had already become clear by the late 1980s that codes of black femininity and masculinity were involved in the differential school experiences and educational achievements of black boys and girls. Black girls' resistance to formal schooling fell short of the confrontational styles of black boys which affirmed particular forms of black masculinity but which also had the effect of creating a spiral of conflict and alienation between teachers and black boys that had serious consequences for the educational performance of the boys.

The research of Mac An Ghaill (1994) and Sewell (1995, 1997) has since shed considerable light on the processes and psychic investments involved in these spirals of confrontation. Sewell confirms the role of the school as a masculinized space where many black boys see resistance and non-conformity as the only 'manly' way to respond to many of the humiliations of racialized processes in schools and in other sites, disparagingly effeminizing conformist black boys as 'pusses'. The black diaspora and its manifold cultural expressions are drawn upon as resources, with misogynist African-American rap music and Jamaican conceptions of the macho 'Yardie' figuring in the identities created in the confrontational space of the school. Moreover, sexuality and the body are crucial elements in these processes. For one thing, there is considerable valorization of the sexual exploits of the non-conformist black boys. But also, the supposed 'size' and deportment of black boys' bodies become invested with powers and threats which have important effects on teacher–student interactions. The black body appears to serve as a metonym for the myriad ways in which black boys are seen as challenging the 'normalizing' institutional procedures of schooling with their injunctions regarding bodily discipline and deferential postures in encounters with teachers.

Relatedly, the question of the specificity of the spatial and masculinity in racialization is well analysed by Connolly (1995) whose research demonstrates that the 'public' arena of the playground can become a site of racialization where displays of masculinity become associated with the ability to use racially abusive language and where the exclusion of Asian boys from football games also serves to signify masculine and racialized dominance.

However, there still remains a dearth of research on the connections between *classed* masculinities, the territorialization of social relations, and white racism in Britain (Cohen's work being a notable exception). I would suggest that amongst the elements that such research would need to consider are the pleasures of male bonding and (racist) violence in various urban contexts where there is a perennial search for excitement thwarted by a chronic lack of material and cultural resources and opportunities. The possibilities for gaining fame and notoriety through media coverage gives added pleasure and affirmation, and provides motivation for a continuation of the racist violence despite the threat and actuality of prison and other sanctions (see Ascherson, 1993; Weale, 1993). Moreover, what applies to racist activities can surely also be true of the pleasures of antiracist involvements and of the bondings of black boys in their resistance to schooling.[7]

The body and its insertion into an economy of the cultural politics of pleasure and spectacle thus emerges as an important site for exploration that future research into racializing processes must address. Think, for example, of the ways in which so many younger members of the extreme right fashion distinctive bodily adornments from tattoos to skinhead and 'Mohican' haircuts. These are 'badges' of membership, identification, and affirmation directly imprinted on the body, but are also allied to particular conceptions of bodily hygiene and a lifestyle which allow them to construct their identities in often imaginary differentiation from both Blacks and 'Pakis' and groups like 'new-age travellers'. Musical preferences for raucous rock and modes of dance — often accompanied by violence — set their bodies in motion, to borrow a phrase from Mort (1983).

These features give added weight to Silverman's suggestion that an understanding of contemporary forms of racism, and racist violence in particular, requires an acknowledgment of Bauman's emphasis on the symbolic nature of the 'struggle for survival' today and its desire to imprint itself on 'the public imagination' (Silverman, 1993). A shift to a relatively novel racism in which the symbolic has a more privileged role, whether in the form of the desecration of Jewish graves or attacks on Muslim and other places of worship, takes place as part of a change of emphasis in racialized discourses to the language of 'difference', which I have discussed earlier. Silverman usefully yokes his argument to recent discussions of economic and political transformations in western Europe — whether theorized in terms of 'postmodernization' or, as Wieviorka has done in his *L'Espace du Racisme* (1991; see also, 1994), under the rubric of 'postindustrialism' — an analysis which points to the marginalization of older labour movements and the numerical decline and fragmentation of the communities built around the male manual working-class due to a fundamental restructuring of the industrial and urban infrastructure, combined with crises of national identity and state institutions (see McLaren and Torres, this volume). This is the 'space' in which there is a relatively new politics of cultural difference organized around 'new' social movements, including racist and antiracist movements.

One consequence of the new industrial, urban, and cultural transformations is a disembedding of traditions and a collapse of employment and other infrastructures, and feelings of rootlessness, generating anxieties which become exploited and mobilized around endless searches for 'roots' and projects of racialized nationalisms. There is a sense in which this gives rise to particular racisms which are novel, and enable the thesis of a 'new racism' to be reformulated in a more convincing fashion.

But as I have argued above, such analyses will have to accomplish far more than a documentation of some of these sorts of processes of 'postmodernization' or the crisis of 'modernity'. We need to theorize them rigorously by a more direct rethinking of the formation of identities, subjectiveness, and the social — one in which issues of sexuality, pleasure, temporality, and spatiality have a role, in contrast to their neglect in the work of both Wieviorka and Silverman. And although Silverman refers to the significant role of the media, the analysis here needs to add several other dimensions. After all, the media does not merely provide a spectacle and a stage for the acting out of various forms of racist activity, it has itself become an active constituent of identities of both the social and the self. I take this discussion a little further in the next section.

It is important to note, too, that the form of analysis I am recommending is different in quite fundamental ways from discussions of urban racism based either on albeit sophisticated versions of the 'false consciousness' thesis as posited by Phizacklea and Miles (1980; for an appreciative but critical discussion see Rattansi, 1992, pp. 31–3) or a resource-conflict model of the type proposed by Wellman (1977) in which white racism is seen primarily as a legitimating ideology for white privilege.

The differences involved are further underscored once the question of *ambivalence* and its great significance is appreciated. Racialized discourses, and those involving degrees of sexualization in particular, are not merely differentiating, inferiorizing, and legitimating, but involve forms of ambivalence which interrupt their subordinating charge. I have remarked elsewhere on the ambivalence around the figure of the British Asian woman, at once the guardian and pillar of the 'tightly knit' Asian family — much admired, especially by the Right for its 'family values' and discipline — but also a symbol of the 'backwardness' of Asians. For she is both seen as subject to extraordinary subordination — and, by her adherence to Asian conventions, regarded as an obstacle to the assimilation of Asians into British culture or 'the English way of life' — and as sexually alluring, the dusky heiress to the Karma Sutra and the Oriental harem (Rattansi, 1992).

But in this instance, and others around the discussion of 'the Asian woman' and 'the Asian family', we can also see how the category of 'modernity', conceptions of time and space, and the sexualization of discourses around cultural 'others' can combine in distinctive ways. That is, discourses around British Asians, their families, 'their women', their supposed business success, and so forth can be understood by analogy with Bauman's analysis (1989, 1991) of the Jew as eternal 'stranger', falling foul of modernity's drive for classificatory order and its abhorrence of the disruptive, inassimilable figure. It is arguable, that is, that British Asians generate a series of contradictory responses in discourses in modern British culture, partly because of their transgression of a series of culturally produced boundaries which attempt to hold British modernity in place: *British Asians are, in effect, too premodern, too modern, and too postmodern.* The 'premodernity', the lack of coevality in time of British Asians, is symbolized by the supposedly all-effective subjugation of 'their women', as well as by patterns of dress, religious 'fundamentalism', 'uncivilized' and 'backward' practices of ritualized animal slaughter, and so forth (cf. Short and Carrington, this volume). Their modernity-in-excess is symbolized, as with the Jews, by their supposedly disproportionate involvement in commerce, their eagerness to accumulate, and by their shops replacing the 'traditional' English corner shop, symbol of the cosy British working-class community-neighbourhood — the 'kith and kin' element is important here. But they are also too 'postmodern', too mobile, a diasporic, 'deterritorialized' community with links in India, Pakistan, Canada, the United States, Singapore, Hong Kong, and elsewhere, disturbing the settledness of Britain's 'island race' culture, bringing in brides and husbands from India, while setting up transnational businesses and refusing to support the British cricket team in its (often disastrous) encounters with India, Pakistan, and the West Indies. And yet, this is a form of cultural disruption always overlaid with the ambivalence of unconscious desire and the more explicit pulls of admiration and envy. So there is not just the often-noted *double bind* of racist discourses which traps the racialized subject into inferiorization and transgression — as Fanon put it, 'When people like me, they tell me it is in spite of my colour. When they dislike me, they point out it is not because of my colour.

Either way, I am locked into the infernal circle' (1986, p. 116) — but also a *triple bind* which is revealed when temporality and spatiality are more explicitly built into the analysis of racializing processes.

Other important forms of ambivalence are evident in the contradictory pulls of racism, on the one hand, and the attractions of many forms of black popular culture for young white people of both sexes, on the other. This, however is a subject best discussed in the sections to come.

Decentring the Racist Subject

If the proliferation of contradictory and ambivalent discourses is indicative of dislocations internal to, and constitutive of, the social and its relative openness, it is also to be seen as part of the structuration which makes available a series of different 'subject positions'. In effect, this is part of the process by which, in this instance, racist identities are decentred by being invited to occupy a variety of enunciative modes and engage in a range of practices. A 'postmodern' frame posits racist identities — like other identities, including that of the 'antiracist' — as decentred, fragmented by contradictory discourses and by the pull of other identities. As such, racist identities are not necessarily consistent in their operation across different contexts and sites, or available in the form of transparent self-knowledge to the subjects.

British researchers like Michael Billig (1978, 1984), more aware of the complexities of racialized identity formation, have furnished a range of examples of relevant subjects and contexts. For instance, the trade union official, a member of the explicitly racist British National Front, who appeared to have been elected to his union position by both Blacks and Whites because of his record of fighting equally for both sets of members, and his personal relations of friendliness to black colleagues; the white girl interviewed at school, who expressed strong racist views, but was then seen leaving school arm in arm with an Asian girl. Amongst the other documentations of the complexity of racist expression by young people, in schools and youth clubs, and in the context of a shifting network of friendships, the recent ethnographic studies by Hatcher (1995) and Back (1996) stand out. Both emphasize the ways in which some forms of racist name-calling and abuse occur in brief episodes of conflict among friends or acquaintances or as part of masculinist 'windups', which can start as friendly banter and then turn into more serious hostility when the situation escalates beyond the control of the participants. Relatedly, Connolly (1995) points to the playground as a space in which football games create situations in which brief episodes of racist name-calling and exclusion can co-exist with otherwise friendlier relations between white, black and Asian boys.

Even the MacDonald Enquiry into the murder of a British Pakistani pupil at Burnage High School in Manchester was forced to conclude that the racism of his killer, a white fellow pupil, was not of a 'simple' kind: he had earlier established alliances and friendships with other black and Asian pupils (see Rattansi, 1992 for a more detailed discussion). Moreover, as I pointed out earlier, the Enquiry also, in effect, argued that what has to be understood is not only the complexity of his racism, but the effect of his masculinity as embedded in the aggressive and violent culture of his all-boys school.

The form of decentredness of racist and racializing subjectivities and identities cannot, however, be understood simply in Foucauldian terms as the structured effect of different discourses and the subject positions thus made available, for example around both 'race' and masculinity. Thus, disavowal statements of the kind 'I'm not a racist, but . . . (there are too many of them)', or 'Some of my best friends are black, but . . . (it's the rest)', need to be seen as part of complex rhetorical strategies by subjects as *reflexive agents*, attempting to articulate different subject positions within a framework of perceived interests and drawing upon a variety of what Wetherell and Potter (1992) have called 'interpretive repertoires'. Wright cites a particularly striking instance of this reflexivity on the part of a very young white boy who contests any suggestion that his dislike of Asian children makes him racially prejudiced by retorting: 'If I'm prejudiced I wouldn't like Blacks at all, but I do like Blacks. Some of me friends are black . . .' (1995, p. 56)

An important source of decentring of white young people in Britain is the attractiveness of black popular culture, especially musical forms such as reggae and rap, and black styles in dress and language. For many white male youths this is compounded by the attractions of 'hard' versions of black masculinity and envy with regard to black achievements in sport and on the dance floor (Back, 1996; Hewitt, 1986; Jones, 1988; Sewell, 1995, 1997). Involvement in black cultural forms splits strong investments in 'white' identifications in a variety of ways and it has even been suggested that the new 'hybrid' identities and syncretic cultures may be seen as the possible seedbeds of new, popular multiculturalisms and antiracisms (Back, 1996).

On the other hand, discourses of liberalism and even egalitarianism may be rhetorically mobilized not merely against racialized forms of discrimination and exclusion but to legitimate them. Wetherell and Potter's (1992) discourse analysis frame for the exploration of the highly complex rhetoric involved in the 'working out' of white New Zealanders' construction of the indigenous Maori as 'racial' problems, and their legitimation of exclusionary and exploitative practices against Maori, may be regarded as a particularly fruitful illustration of a type of 'postmodern' analysis of racism. Eschewing reductive accounts of racism as simply 'false consciousness', and the 'racist' as a unified subject, they explore how social categories and arguments are deployed by white New Zealanders around specific instances and fields such as education, crime, land claims, and so forth. But, for Wetherell and Potter, this is always with a view to understanding these rhetorical moves in a historical context of relations of power, domination, and advantage, while drawing out the tension of contradictory pulls of 'racist' and 'antiracist' positions.

Amongst other things, Wetherell and Potter's (1992) *Mapping the Language of Racism* accomplishes a critique of the common conception of racism as 'prejudice', with its psychologically reductive, individualistic, and pathologizing tendency. It reveals at the same time the Enlightenment residue of the 'rational/prejudiced' binary which underlies much of this type of analysis (see also Rattansi, 1992 for a critique of 'prejudice' as used in the discourse of 'multicultural education'). And it establishes the productiveness of the strategy recommended in this chapter, of avoiding supposedly water-tight definitions of racism in favour of actually examining how 'racial' logics and categories work in relation to specific events and social fields.

However, amongst a number of my reservations with regard to Wetherell and Potter's project, three interrelated ones are particularly relevant here. First, while justifiably sceptical of attempts within social psychology to construct typologies of subjects along a spectrum of adherence to racist views (Wetherell and Potter, 1992, p. 194), by default they end up not merely decentring but almost completely denuding subjects of identities altogether: 'Conflict, ambivalence, inconsistency and contradiction seem to be endemic. They do not, that is, seem to be associated with just one group of individuals or one type of person. Everybody is a dilemmatician — anti-racists to the same extent as racists' (1992, p. 198). But this evades the issue of the different 'investments' that individuals may have in particular identities and identifications in a wide range of contexts. To take rather extreme cases to illustrate the point, while both the long-standing British National Front activist and the 'liberal' or other kind of antiracist activist may both draw on conflicting logics and face discursive dilemmas in justifying their (subject) positions, to homogenize them as 'dilemmaticians' — Wetherell and Potter's term — is to ignore vital differences in how each may engage in social practices towards racialized groups at work and in other fields, and the degree to which each is likely to initiate and respond to various projects of racialized or racializing mobilization. Unwittingly no doubt, Wetherell and Potter appear to be aligned to the crasser forms of 'postmodernist' conceptions of 'multiple identities', mainly as a consequence of wanting to avoid equally problematic theorizations of 'identity' in social psychology (1992, pp. 43–9).

At this point a second difficulty becomes apparent: the neglect of psychoanalytic accounts. Wetherell and Potter distance themselves, not without good reason, from the Frankfurt School's 'Authoritarian Personality' studies (1992, pp. 49–57), but apart from a passing nod of approval to the possibilities of mobilizing Horney's 'neo-Freudian' work for reading racist discourse (1992, p. 54), they fail to engage with the psychoanalytic possibilities that might prove fruitful. Not surprisingly, while borrowing from aspects of Bhabha's work (Wetherell and Potter, 1992, pp. 142–3), his use of psychoanalytic theory, and the related emphasis on 'ambivalence' go unnoticed. It is also tempting here to attribute Wetherell and Potter's complete neglect of the gendering and sexualization of racial discourse, and this is my third reservation, in part to the absence of psychoanalytic theory in their construction of discourse analysis.

Psychoanalysis and the Decentred Racist Subject

Psychoanalytic theorizations, as an earlier part of this chapter has suggested, must be regarded as important to a 'postmodern' decentring of the subject and in principle could yield interesting accounts of decentred, racialized subjects — here to include those with investments in racist and antiracist positions, and also those who are the objects of racism. Franz Fanon's *Black Skins, White Masks* (1986) is a key reference point for understanding some of the psychic costs of racism to its victims — I use the latter term without imputing passivity to them. However, it is not at all clear that, to date, the psychoanalytic literature has produced work of serious power and scope in understanding the psychic economy of racism, although Fanon himself offers some interesting observations, and the work of Kovel (1988), Kristeva (1991), Rustin (1991, pp. 57–84) and others (see Gordon, 1992 and Young, 1993 for brief surveys), may be regarded as having made a start (see also McLaren and Torres, this volume). Amongst those I have already discussed, Bhabha, Gilman, and Cohen, from different theoretical stances, have deployed psychoanalytic concepts productively. A more Jungian inflection is evident in Adams' *The Multicultural Imagination* (1996).

The *ambivalence* of racism, although deriving from a variety of sources that I have remarked upon, is particularly open to psychoanalytic interpretation, for it is in psychoanalysis that the notion has its strongest root. Curiously, the Klein-influenced commentators, Gordon, Young, and Rustin, appear not to grasp its significance; indeed, they neglect it altogether, one consequence being their noticeable pessimism (this being slightly less true of Rustin), the effect of reducing racism to an uncontradictory pathology.

'Postmodern' framing obviously requires a form of psychoanalytic theorization which, in addition to being aware of the racist involvements of psychoanalytic theory and politics, does not reduce all racisms merely to supposedly eternal and universal psychic mechanisms, but also reflects on the specificity of modernity and its constitutive role in the formation of racism. Psychoanalytic attempts to grapple with colonialism and the Holocaust have been forced to confront racism in a more historically specific register, with the Frankfurt School's 'Authoritarian Personality' studies perhaps being the most explicit in their efforts to delineate some of the interconnections between modernity and racism. One of the more interesting recent attempts is that by Stephen Frosh (1989; see also 1987, 1991), who sketches out the links between racism and modernity, sexuality, and masculinity, while mindful of the significance of ambivalence. Frosh analyses racism as one response of the threatened ego, an ego that is generically fragile, split, and fragmented in both Kleinian and Lacanian senses, but under further pressure from the multiplicitous, disintegrating, constantly changing, fast-moving forces of social life under conditions of modernity. Sexuality is crucially important in his account: in the Fanonian sense, with the white man seeing the black man as biological other — a vehicle for the projection of unwanted feelings about the body — as well as a sexual threat (Fanon, 1986, pp. 163–78). Repressed homosexual desire creates an ambivalence that connects up with other forms of ambivalence that permeate feeling toward others, whether Jews, Blacks, or Asians. Modernity is one of the other sources of ambivalence. It is experienced as threatening, but in part exciting. Other forms of ambivalence see the objects as not only disgusting and hateful, but powerful, fascinating, and erotic and possessors of qualities admired by racist subjects. Hence the plausibility of conspiracy theories in which the enemy is seen as having conquered what terrifies the racist — chaos, change, disorder, fragmentation, disintegration.

This is not an appropriate place to enter into a lengthy consideration of the merits of psychoanalytic approaches to issues of racism. Here I only wish to register the general point that in my view neither the general decentredness of the (racist) subject nor the sexualization and ambivalences of racism can be fully grasped without some hypothesization of the self as constitutively divided between the conscious and the unconscious, without understanding the centrality of sexuality, and without some consideration of splitting, fantasy, pleasure, introjection, projection, and so on, as possible mechanisms by which identifications and subjectivities operate and change. Clearly, complex issues arise for practices of antiracism, too, if psychoanalytic insights are granted credibility.

Ethnicities, 'New' and 'Old'

The 'decentring' and 'de-essentializing' moves of the 'postmodern' frame have played a key role in this chapter: in mobilizing a general conception of identities, in pointing to its effects on the dissolution of 'woman' as a figure in feminism, in suggesting its possible ramifications for understanding the nature of 'race', in the formation of racist identities, subjectivities, and discourses, and in emphasizing that ethnicities, nationalisms, and other forms of collective identity are products of a process to be conceptualized as a cultural politics of representation, one in which narratives, images, musical forms, and popular culture more generally, have a significant role.

Contemporary forms of globalization, the formation of diasporas and diasporic identities, and the creation of new hybrid and synthetic cultural forms, I have earlier argued, are also of key interest within a 'postmodern' frame, as is Hall's conception of the 'new ethnicities' (1992a), for similar reasons, in what he now refers to as a 'notorious' piece (1992d). Written in the context of a debate on the place of 'black film' in British cinema, Hall's 'New Ethnicities' (1992a) reflects on the particularities of an apparently curious conjunction between poststructuralism, a series of iconoclastic 'black' cinematic projects — Kureishi's *My Beautiful Launderette* and Sankofa's *Passion of Remembrance* being two outstanding examples — and the formation of a new configuration in ethnic minority politics in Britain where the saliency of 'black' as a unifying signifier has been gradually losing its potency. This is in effect a double interwoven transition. A shift, first, from an earlier period characterized by a struggle over *relations of representation* — taking the form of demands for access to the apparatuses and technologies of representation, and the contestation of gross stereotypes and their replacement with 'positive' images — to a *politics of representation* where the demands of the 'positive' image are now regarded as suffocating the possibilities for exploring the huge variety of ethnic, subcultural, and sexual identities pulsating in the minority communities. Moreover, there is an experimentation with modernist and 'postmodernist' forms which breaks from an equally stifling aesthetic of 'realism' imposed by the demands of the 'positive image' (usually privileging middle-class heterosexuality). And relatedly, we see the beginnings of a new phase which Hall describes as the demise of 'the essential black subject' in which the oppositional political unity forged by ethnic minorities of African-Caribbean and South Asian descent under the sign of blackness — influenced by the Black Power movement in the United States — is giving way to new types of political 'subjects' involving new forms of identity-formation and a new phase in the politics of cultural difference.

Poststructuralism doubles here as both a form of analysis, which reads this as a de-essentializing moment, and a constitutive element in the formation of the new ethnicities insofar as some of the cultural workers and activists involved have themselves been influenced by poststructuralist currents (not least by the writings of Hall himself). By the same token, the 'postmodern' frame as defined here is also doubly valorized (although I hasten to add that the essential black subject is being undermined by rather more than the adoption of versions of poststructuralism by artists and film-makers).

Questions of sexuality have been crucial to the projects comprising the new ethnicities, for many of the de-essentializing cultural and political projects have been produced by black feminists and gay and lesbian activists intent upon challenging the codes of black masculinity that had hitherto marginalized other sexual identities in the minority communities. Issues of globalization and diaspora are also central, given the impetus provided by decolonization processes in general, the influence of 'Third World' cinema, and the creation of new 'hybrid' cultural forms, which I have referred to earlier, by borrowing from western, Asian, African, African-American, and other cultural practices.

Commenting on these new cultural politics, and indeed deploying the term 'new ethnicities' is, for Hall, also a way of rescuing the concept of ethnicity from its connotative links with nation and 'race' (see also May, this volume). Here we encounter another doubling, for at the same time that Hall himself contributes to a de-essentialization of the black subject by pointing to the cultural and political possibilities opened up by the new cultural politics, he also wants to emphasize that there can be no form of representation, no sort of political enunciation, no kind of positioning which does not have to operate with historically given languages and cultural codes; in other words, with ethnicities. The 'new ethnicities', then, is Hall's way of conceptually inserting the minority communities into the more generally commented upon politics of cultural difference of late modernity or 'postmodernity', a politics that has also seen the demise and fracturing of other previously essentialized subjects: social classes and women.

The precise meaning of 'ethnicity' still remains elusive, but in my view Hall's general project is nevertheless indispensable, for it attempts to chart and indeed to recommend new, more open, non-absolutist forms of cultural politics within and between the minority communities and their articulation with the politics of the 'centre' — a project to which Paul Gilroy (1992, 1993b) has also made powerful contributions — while not falling into the trap of assuming a utopian emancipation from all forms of cultural essentialization, an escape from the positionings of time and space, narrative, memory, and territorialization which make cultural production and politics possible. It is here that the 'strategic essentialism' recommended by Spivak (1990) and others finds its place in an oppositional politics of coalition and cooperation rather than an endless multiplication of identities and fragments incapable of effective collective mobilization. In all these senses Hall's account of the 'new ethnicities' can be mined for its suggestiveness for what in very general terms may be regarded as the political implications of the 'postmodern' frame, especially as they relate to questions of 'race' and ethnicity.

But this is a politics that has to contend with a variety of different political projects of cultural difference in the minority diasporic communities of Britain and the United States, and the 'blacklash' they have had to endure. For one thing, versions of the 'old' ethnicities are very much alive, a point hardly to be laboured in the wake of the Salman Rushdie affair in Britain in which revamped Islamic 'fundamentalisms' were met in turn with a retreat into virulent assimilationism by some white liberals. Fay Weldon's *Sacred Cows* (1989) provides an instructive illustration of the arguments of Mendus (1989) and Parekh (1995) about the strong limits to 'liberal' toleration. At the same time, many new black cultural forms and projects, from rap to the films of Spike Lee, have attempted to reconstruct traditional masculinities, have colluded with or actively promoted misogynistic and homophobic currents, and have supported black nationalisms which run quite counter to the optimistic openness tracked in Hall's 'new ethnicities' (on Spike Lee, see, for instance, the critiques by Michelle Wallace, 1992 and Paul Gilroy, 1993b).

Rap is clearly a contradictory cultural form here. There is, on the one hand, a strong strand of misogyny evident in rap, with some black cultural critics making a particularly strong stand against it (Baker, 1992, 1993). Stephens (1991), on the other hand, regards rap as a 'clearly postmodern artform', characterized by 'indeterminacy, decanonization, hybridization, performance and participation, and immanence', although his oxymoronic construction of rap as a form of Afrocentric 'postmodernism' fails to convince. A more likely candidate for the label 'postmodernist' rap in the sense used in this chapter is the music and performance of the British South Asian rapper Apache Indian, who not only mocks the misnaming of Native Americans — although this may be an unwitting consequence of borrowing the name from an Indo-Caribbean musical hero (see Back, 1993a) — and borrows a musical form produced by members of the African diaspora, but in songs like 'Arranged Marriage', 'Sharabi' (alcoholic), and 'Caste System' he also challenges cultural practices amongst the British South Asian communities which subordinate women, valorize hard-drinking displays of masculinity, and reinforce boundaries of caste, class, and ethnicity (Back, 1993a, 1993b).

This is not to argue that only 'progressive' forms of rap can qualify as 'postmodernist' but that the essentialism of a strongly committed form of Afrocentrism surely disqualifies (cf. May; Nieto, this volume). Stephens (1992), however, does usefully place rap as a 'postmodern' musical form and reflects on the mixed audiences for it, and now the 'interracial' performers of the music. Recently, the cultural politics of Asian expressive cultures are beginning to receive welcome, serious treatment by researchers aware of the complexities of the new youth identities rapidly emerging in Britain, while being mindful of similar efflorescences in the United States (Sharma *et al.*, 1996).

However, a glaring omission in most of these discussions of the new ethnicities and their implications for cultural politics is the issue of social class (see also McLaren and Torres, this volume). While researchers are aware that they are engaging primarily with working-class youth, for instance, there appears to be precious little attention to the ways in which expressive cultures and their cultural politics are affected by socio-economic structuring. What, for example, are the specific new identifications of middle-class black, Asian and white youth? How different are they from ways in which black and Asian youth are forging specific syncretic black-Asian-working class cultures and identities? Raising these questions immediately plunges us into the wider set of issues of 'identity politics' that has become such a feature of current political discussion.

Racialization and the Politics of Identities

A distinctive thrust of this chapter has been the recommendation of a strategy of 'postmodern', especially poststructuralist, 'deconstruction' which decentres racist and antiracist subjects and de-essentializes and detotalizes racialized social structures. Attention has been focused on the mobility and variability of 'race' as a signifier in political processes, and an attempt has been made to treat the 'racist' and the ethnic subject as the site of contradictory identities which result from the contextual juggling of the variety of subject positions that 'western' capitalist liberal demo-cracies make potentially available: citizen, democrat, worker, employer (note the significance of class here), man, woman, or masculine and feminine. These articulate with many others, but especially with various ethnic and racialized positions — white, black, African, Asian, and all the myriad others, forged in long struggles for recognition, entitlements, and freedoms. Very often the tensions between positions have been explicitly acknowledged, especially by subordinated minorities — one only has to think of 'African-American' or 'black British' — in an attempt to work within syncretic spaces and desynchronized temporalities. That is, to work with frag-ments, from the margins, attempting to get some place in the structures, narratives, and imaginations of the centres.

But these emphases are often taken to imply that the institutionalization, the sheer 'materiality' of power, and the necessity and possibility of broadly based struggles for transformation are dissolved and denied in this type of 'postmodern' politics. Fragmented, 'local' struggles are all we are supposedly left with in the debris that remains after the demolition of centred subjects and brute, enduring socio-economic oppressions. If individual subjects are fragmented, what hope can there be for the formation of collective subjects and movements? If the 'social' is de-essentialized such that no necessary links between power structures are posited, how can strategic programmes of broad reform be formulated which might allow alliances between 'antiracists', 'feminists', workplace struggles, and so forth?

Although such political and strategic implications *may* be inferred from a 'deconstructive' approach, they are by no means the only points of destination. Other routes are equally plausible, for there has been another set of thematics consistently present in my analysis. The interpretive strategy advocated here has emphasized, for one thing, the institutional forms of bio-power and the *material* effects of discursive regimes of power which inscribe the bodies and subjectivities of individual subjects. Forms of racialized discrimination in education, employment, public housing allocation, and so forth, have been shown to operate within patterned structures of power and domination — that is, public and private bureaucracies. Although these are no longer posited as monolithic, reproductive machines, there is no denial of the embeddedness of power relations in these institutions, sedimented over long periods. The operations of power within these fields can be analysed in their historical and contemporary actualities, and the strategies, rules, and procedures activated by dominant and subordinate reflective agents through the use of institutional resources, can be excavated by various forms of struggle and research. The detailed workings of discriminatory practices can be scrutinized, central nodal points of subject-formation and power networks identified, and weak points hypothetically specified where strategic pressure may make parts of institutions susceptible to reform in the direction of nondiscriminatory and redistributive practices. In this chapter a number of studies of racist discrimination in schools, private enterprises, and public bureaucracies have been cited which can form the basis of strategies to challenge, dismantle, and restructure the regimes of power and 'truth'.

An emphasis on historical and cultural specificities in the workings of power relations does not necessarily condemn struggles to the desert of infinite difference and permanent fragmentation. Analyses of discriminatory practices in Britain discussed in this chapter have shown the ways in which the procedures and practices which disadvantage one group, for example, black and Asian pupils, black and Asian workers seeking employment, or black, Asian and Irish families applying for public housing, may also work against white English working-class individuals and families. The white professional and managerial, often male bio-political gaze which attempts to identify and exclude the 'abnormals' — the subversive or recalcitrant student, the 'undisciplined' worker, or the unhygienic family — creates both *classed and racialized* collectivities of the disadvantaged (cf. McLaren and Torres, this volume). In specific historical and political circumstances this may create the possibility of broader 'race'-class alliances, for example, in the inner city. The gendered and sexualized forms of 'racial' and ethnic conflicts and discriminations create the potential for local and national alliances which target hyper-masculinities (themselves classed and territorialized in form). The 'locales' or sites of struggle may even extend beyond the whole national polity, given the regulatory reach of corporations and state agencies, on the one hand, and the existence of diasporas on the other — the 'Black Atlantic' (Gilroy, 1993a) and the Indian, Irish, and Jewish diasporas (as well as movements of indigenous peoples) immediately spring to mind as collectivities that have been able to mobilize transnationally.

Moreover, the operation of decentred subjectivities and identities can work both ways. Potentially they can fragment as well as unite. If racist subject positions in liberal democratic polities are also open to the pull of others such as 'liberal', 'good citizen', 'unprejudiced', and thus other political discourses too — 'fairness', 'equal opportunities', 'justice' — then the potential always exists for the mobilization of otherwise disparately located subjects by movements struggling for antidiscriminatory and redistributive reform. Note too the possibly progressive effects of various forms of ambivalence highlighted in this chapter.

However, my conceptualization does not regard identities as completely 'free-floating', nor does it assume that each subject position has equal salience for any particular individual. There is no collapse into what I have earlier called a 'vulgar postmodernism' of multiple selves. Individual subjects have different degrees of 'investment' in particular identities which have effectiveness over a number of contexts. Thus reformist alliances cannot be guaranteed. Perhaps one of the most important lessons of the present era is that there are no guarantees, period. But the point is that these are all grounds for optimism as well as pessimism. The 'postmodern', especially Foucauldian, emphasis on the ubiquity of relations of power, domination, and resistance opens up the whole terrain of the 'social', however its boundaries are drawn in specific circumstances, to political practice. And the emphasis on the significance of new hybrid and syncretic identities shows the potential for crossover identities which destabilize old ethnic absolutisms; this was part of the point of my discussion of rap and new youth identities in Britain. The contemporary politics of 'race' and ethnicity in all the liberal democracies of Europe and in the United States are witnessing a struggle between forms of 'ethnic absolutism' on the one hand — white supremacist movements, neo-fascisms of various types, forms of black nationalism — and, on the other hand, attempts to build broader, 'rainbow' coalitions to contest racialized disadvantage, subordination, and violence. While there are transnational patterns, they take local, historically specific forms (Lloyd, 1994; Miles, 1994; Wieviorka, 1994). No universal programmes of reform can be prescribed. And no particular types of struggle and strategy can be universally proscribed, although it is worth pointing out that one implication of the type of analysis recommended in this chapter is the need to recognize the limitations of overly 'rationalist' (Enlightenment) strategies which neglect the strength of emotions, fantasy, and pleasure in sustaining racisms (see Rattansi, 1992 for a discussion of the significance of this in projects of antiracist education). But what forms of reform are likely to be effective and what discourses will be capable of progressive mobilization — 'citizenship', 'equal rights', 'democracy', 'justice', 'fairness' — can only be contextually decided. Strategies can only be forged in active politics and have to be endlessly revisable in the light of struggles and results.

Coda: Reflexive and Critical Multiculturalisms

The term 'multiculturalism' has acquired considerable currency in the struggles to transform the racist cultures and structures of western societies. The valency of the idea has, of course, been subject to the vagaries of particular national histories. In Britain the main focus until recently has been a series of debates between (supposedly 'liberal') multiculturalists and (left-radical) antiracists, particularly in the arena of education. In the United States a variety of multiculturalisms — of which more later — has been battling it out with WASPish monoculturalists who have warned of the supposedly imminent collapse of (western-American) 'civilization' in the face of 'cultures of complaint', 'political correctness', and those who want to 'close' American-western minds and disintegrate and disinter everything that has made American-western culture the best that humankind has thought and done (see also May, this volume). Moreover, while a key arena for American debates has been the university, in Britain it is the curriculum and practices of the primary and secondary school that have been the sites of the main debates.

Although the British multicultural/antiracist divide has not finally been laid to rest, the foundations of the opposition between the two have been thoroughly shaken (see Rattansi, 1992 for one version of the critique) and there appears to be a growing chorus of voices recommending a constructive *rapprochement* (see, for example, May, 1994). In the American context, although the monoculturalists continue to moan, a great deal of the interest appears to have shifted to the *varieties* of multiculturalisms and *their* political 'correctness' (see Goldberg, 1994a for a useful collection). Goldberg's (1994b) introduction to his volume, for example, leaves the reader in no doubt that the 'politically correct' version of multiculturalism is one or other variety of 'critical' multiculturalism, as opposed to varieties of 'liberal' and 'left-liberal' multiculturalisms. Goldberg's critique is echoed in a number of other contributions to his volume, most notably a powerful chapter by McLaren (1994). In some respects, the debate between 'critical' and 'liberal' multiculturalisms is the American version of the British divide between antiracists and multiculturalists, although this comparison should not be carried too far.

One important reason why the positions in Britain and the USA do not coincide is that the American version of 'critical' multiculturalism has already moved beyond some of the reductionisms and oversimplifications of both the British multiculturalist and British antiracist movements by incorporating important elements of poststructuralist and 'postmodern' analyses which were being recommended by the British critics of the multiculturalist/antiracist divide (see Rattansi, 1992). Thus McLaren's (1994) critique of 'liberal' and 'left-liberal' multiculturalisms is explicitly 'postmodern' in its basic stance. Not surprisingly, then, the general framework for a reflexive multiculturalism that I shall outline here bears many similarities to the 'critical' multiculturalism of McLaren and his colleagues such as Giroux (Aronowitz and Giroux, 1991; Giroux, 1994; Giroux et al., 1996) and also to the arguments set out for 'critical' multiculturalism by Goldberg in his introduction (1994b).

Why then should a distinction be made between 'reflexive' and 'critical' multiculturalism? To begin with, let me register my misgivings about the ubiquitous term 'critical' that self-professed left-radicals usually adopt to distinguish themselves from what they regard as the less than 'radical' positions of the 'liberals'. One problem is that this polarizes, and divides when this is not especially necessary or constructive. For example, a 'critical' distance is established from the 'reformism' of the liberals (McLaren, 1994, p. 51), or a line is drawn against the deradicalizing tendencies that become evident when 'nonacademic corporate and administrative agencies' become involved in multiculturalist initiatives (Chicago Cultural Studies Group, 1994, p. 115). It is not merely that somewhere underneath this distancing lurks a now highly problematic binary division between 'reform' and 'revolution', but two other unhelpful tendencies appear. One attempts to completely delegitimize a homogeneous 'liberalism' just at the point when a constructive *rapprochement* between 'liberal', 'socialist' and 'communitarian' conceptions of the political community is under way (Held, 1984, 1996; Mouffe, 1992, 1996). A second tendency which is encouraged is one which has in the past prevented 'radicals' from cooperating with professionals — for example in social services, education and private corporations — where some gains are possible but where certain institutional constraints also have to be creatively negotiated. A policy of critique and non-involvement or critique and unrealistic demands may keep one's hands and spirit unsullied, but does little to improve the life chances of ethnic minority employees, clients or pupils who would benefit from 'reformist' equal opportunity programmes and even limited changes in the racialized cultures of private and public bureaucracies. 'Mere reform' is better than none, and may indeed provide the basis for further institutional change.

Two caveats must immediately be entered to avoid possible misunderstanding of the arguments I am advancing. First, there is little doubt that a critique of the limitations of liberalism when confronted with issues of racism and cultural difference is fundamentally necessary, and has been effectively made by a number of authors (see, for example, Goldberg, 1993; Mendus, 1989; Parekh, 1995; see also May, this volume). Secondly, it is arguable that my reservations about 'critical' multiculturalism as presently formulated are still made from *within* this paradigm of 'critical' multiculturalism and that the term 'reflexive multiculturalism' only indexes a further development or, better still, a different inflection of the tenets of the 'critical' tradition. In other words, I do not wish to create further unnecessary divisions in a set of movements with rather more important adversaries to challenge. On the other hand, there has to be some way of marking differences of emphasis in what is itself a broad set of constantly developing positions rather than a static doctrine.

One final set of considerations is necessary. It may appear contradictory that in this chapter I am about to set out a series of general thematics about 'reflexive multiculturalism' while at the same time apparently affirming a 'postmodern' aversion to meta-narratives. However, as should be amply clear from the whole architecture of my chapter, I do not believe that it is possible to do without relatively general frameworks of interpretation. These have to be well aware of their historical specificity and their cultural boundedness and the need to accommodate constant revision. Thus what are being offered here are provisional theses that are constructed in dialogue and have to be endlessly revisable in the face of historical and cultural specificities and criticism from a variety of other interpretive frameworks.

These caveats having been entered, it is now possible to proceed to a brief sketch of the framework of reflexive multiculturalism. In the first place, the very idea of reflexivity itself needs some clarification. As deployed here, it is an eclectic mix of Derridean deconstruction and Giddens' work on the condition he variously labels 'radicalized' or 'late' modernity. The Derridean element is important in foregrounding the constant, 'reflexive' deconstruction of binary oppositions before they ossify into irreversible polarities. Hence, for one thing, my deconstructive remarks on the dangers of a polarization between 'liberalism' and 'critical' standpoints. And the same goes for my own attempt to prevent any unnecessary divide between entrenched 'reflexive' and 'critical' multiculturalisms. It is my argument that one reason for the possibility of the 'liberal'/'critical' difference ossifying into an unhelpful binary opposition in the work of McLaren and others is partly owing to the absence of this form of deconstructive reflexivity.

The significance of this type of reflexivity also becomes evident, in my view, when the arguments of Goldberg (1994b) on the 'foundations' of 'critical' multiculturalism are examined. Goldberg argues that the necessity for multiculturalism to become a key aspect of modern institutions derives from the ubiquity of *heterogeneity* as part of the human condition, with the constancy of migrations and movements in human history as one of the prime reasons for the omnipresence of heterogeneity (1994b, pp. 20–33). Goldberg posits the principle of heterogeneity to counter the emphasis on *homogeneity* which in his view underlies the standpoints of the monoculturalists. But it is surely clear that to create a binary opposition between homogeneity and heterogeneity as defining features of the human condition is to reify and essentialize in an unhelpful manner (see also May's comparable discussion in this volume of the unhelpful juxtaposition of ethnicity and hybridity). *Both* homogeneity *and* heterogeneity appear to be constants in human histories when discussed at this sort of level of generality, and while the elevation of heterogeneity as a principle allows for a temporary victory over the positions of the monoculturalists, it is the simplest of intellectual manoeuvres to display the partiality of Goldberg's own 'foundations' as it has been for him to undercut the one-sidedness of the monoculturalists. Instead of *either/or*, a central plank of deconstructive reflexivity is *both/and* (Bernstein, 1991), thus building in a constant cautionary device against the erection of unnecessary and unviable binary divisions.

The notion of reflexivity as adapted from Giddens (1990, 1991, 1994) highlights two aspects of 'late/postmodern' social configurations. One is the reflexivity of agents and subjects. It not only builds in the idea of agency as part of the essential architecture of my proposed framework, but hopefully can act as a counterweight against the tendency to view racism as part of a pathology of irrationality. As I have argued earlier in this chapter, the articulation of racist discourses and the performance of racist acts must be seen as part of the 'rational', that is, 'reasoned' activities of 'normal' subjects who bring to bear a variety of what Wetherell and Potter (1992) have called 'interpretive repertoires'. It is important to emphasize that this does not undermine the concept of *decentred* subjects. Reflexive agency as posited here does not imply singular subject positions nor does it deny the decentredness and lack of self-transparency that derive from the possible operations of the unconscious (although this is perhaps under-emphasized by Giddens himself).

The second element of reflexivity adapts Giddens' insistence on the significance of 'expert systems' and the social as a series of hermeneutic loops (this is my phrase, not his). What I would like to draw out here is the routine circulation of expert knowledges, via education systems and the media, which create individual and collective subjects who are constantly monitoring and changing their rhetorics and strategic interventions in the light of specialized academic and political discourses. A striking illustration of this process is the way in which, as I have remarked earlier, the arguments of multiculturalists are adapted by racists to argue for the protection of 'white' cultures and even separate 'homelands' for different cultural groups.

Another is the way in which the arguments of sociobiologists have gained common currency amongst monoculturalists and various types of racists, and the ways in which the work of psychologists such as Jensen, Eysenck, Murray and so forth, are repackaged by a variety of agencies, including far-right political groups in an attempt to undermine egalitarian multicultural initiatives.

One key element of reflexive multiculturalism, then, becomes the constant attempt to engage the monoculturalists and racists in *dialogue*. From this perspective, the recent refusal by publishers of a probably racist book by the British academic psychologist Christopher Brand (*Times Higher Education Supplement*, 15 August, 1997, p. 19) is regrettable. Far better a constant, reasoned public challenge to views such as his as part of a more general project of radical and dialogic democracy than an attempted censorship. This is not to argue that 'anything goes' and that there are never any grounds for delimiting the dissemination of particular views even in radicalized democratic polities. Rather, it is to suggest that from the standpoint of a reflexive multiculturalism, dialogue and debate can only be overriden in very exceptional circumstances, including in schools. The circulation of various knowledges and discourses is set to grow dramatically with the new information technologies, and one of the fundamental strategies of reflexive multiculturalism is going to have to be the contestation of monoculturalist and racist discourses at *all* the nodal points of the new information networks.

Deconstructive and other forms of reflexivity carry further implications for the notion of reflexive multiculturalism. The latter must incorporate in all its forms, whether in classroom materials or political interventions, an acute, constant and deconstructive attention to processes of boundary formation in social groups at all levels, from ethnic communities to academic disciplines. Reflexive multicultural education should strive to query disciplinary boundaries as well as enable students to engage with the artifice of boundedness when it comes to the discussion of historically constructed cultures. However, given what I have said in relation to the false dichotomization of heterogeneity and homogeneity, reflexive multiculturalisms cannot ignore socially constructed traditions and their institutionalization, nor should they attempt to minimize the ways in which 'tradition' is not simply a constraint but an enabler. Here again it is useful to be mindful of Giddens' argument about the enabling as well as constraining powers of structures and Hall's point that utterances have to be spoken from somewhere, a 'foundation' of language and culture that even in his argument translates into 'ethnicity' (cf. May, this volume). However, a reflexive multiculturalism in education and the wider fields of politics must be constantly attentive to the arena of culture as one of power, domination, hegemony and struggle. In my discussion of cultural politics as one of representation, I emphasized that in one of its forms the issue of representation is about who speaks for whom, who has the power and authority to define what a community is and what its 'interests' are. This is one of the points at which reflexive/critical multiculturalisms must part company with the non-antagonistic conceptions of cultural pluralism stubbornly embedded in most forms of liberalism (see Mouffe's, 1996 critique of Rawls' recent work for a good illustration of the issues involved).

No doubt, a major focus for reflexive multiculturalisms must be the new ethnicities and 'hybrid' identities, the liminal spaces and the 'border' cultures and spaces that Giroux, in particular, has emphasized and which have been much discussed in Britain too (e.g. Aronowitz and Giroux, 1991; Back, 1996; Hall, 1992a; McLaren, 1994). But two notes of caution here (see also May; McLaren and Torres, this volume). First, the tendency to over-glamorize these spaces and cultures must be resisted given what we know about the elements of homophobia, misogyny and what Cornel West has called the cultures of nihilism that have often disfigured these cultures/identities and colonized these spaces (a point I have discussed earlier). Secondly, liminality by its very nature is transitional and transitory. The cultures and identities under discussion are usually those of young people, often in marginal situations in more ways than one. The strength and durability of their transformative potential can only be guessed at and is likely to fluctuate widely in different time-spaces, in different locales, in different historical and political conjunctures. These are not the same as the 'new social movements' and reflexive multiculturalists would do well to formulate their strategies and alliances forewarned that the new ethnicities and border cultures and identities have no necessary political belonging. On the other hand, perhaps what amongst other things can be learnt from the new spaces and cultures of liminality is how to live with cultural difference, rapid social change and the complexities of the local/global interface.

In framing racism from a particular 'postmodern' standpoint, I have been at pains to emphasize the centrality of gender and sexuality as constitutive of racialization. In keeping with this interpretation of the dynamics of 'race', reflexive multiculturalisms must regard considerations of sexual difference as being of the utmost importance in any educational and political interventions. In education, at whatever level, issues of racism and sexuality will constantly have to be conjoined in pedagogic projects and the formulation of policies. The double investments in masculinity and racism that I have highlighted will have to generate particularly innovative curricula and practices for the transformation of student subjects, both white and black. Mac An Ghaill's *The Making of Men* (1994) and Hopkins' *Educating Black Males* (1997) are indicative of the very different directions that such projects will inevitably take.

It is worth ending this coda with a mention of two areas in which there is almost complete coincidence between 'reflexive multiculturalism' as conceived of here and the project of 'critical multiculturalism' as envisaged by McLaren, Giroux and others. First, there is the emphasis on cultural and media studies as an intrinsic part of multiculturalism. The powerful influences of the mass media and popular culture, and their narratives in the construction of identities, call for a critical engagement that is indubitable and urgent (Giroux, 1996; Giroux et al., 1996). And the 'postmodern' questioning of the legitimating narratives of western modernity should be central to any such project, as McLaren and his colleagues have rightly highlighted in their contributions to current debates.

This, however also opens up a whole arena of engagement around issues of the 'Enlightenment Project', western definitions of rationality, the role of science and questions around environmentalism, linked inevitably to concerns over global inequalities and the complex ways in which 'race' figures in these questions (see Hodson, this volume). Reflexive multiculturalism as envisaged here would draw attention to these issues in a form that appears to differ somewhat from critical multiculturalism's apparent failure to break with a 'productivism' in which the feasibility and desirability of never-ending economic growth seem not to be questioned. This may be because 'critical multiculturalism' as presently constituted has failed to distance itself sufficiently from the ways in which even its neo-Marxism is suffused with assumptions from the European Enlightenment which require critical engagement.

However, finally, I fully concur with McLaren's point (1994, p. 63; McLaren and Torres, this volume) that calls for 'reflexivity' can result in a culturalism that avoids engagement with the issues of class inequalities and the need to grasp the real scale and impact of the changing political economy of globalized capitalism, and an academicism that fails to enter the public sphere via political movements. In other words, I do not envisage a form of multiculturalism that falls into these traps. But nor does the conception of reflexivity advanced here underestimate the signficance of *intellectual* engagements, for the complex intertwining between 'expert' narratives and those of the public sphere, and the institutional centrality of education will continue to ensure that intellectual and academic interventions will never remain 'merely academic'.[8]

Notes

1 By placing the term 'postmodern' consistently in quotation marks, I am registering reservations about its distinctiveness and indicating a provisionality about its usage and usefulness which are discussed at length elsewhere (Rattansi, 1994).

2 My construction of the 'postmodern' frame draws eclectically upon a wide range of authors — Appadurai (1996), Bauman (1989, 1991), Bhabha (1983, 1984, 1994), Butler (1990), Derrida (1977, 1978, 1981), Elam (1994), Foucault (1977, 1979, 1980), Giddens (1990), Hall (1992a, 1992b, 1992c, 1992d), Hekman (1990), Laclau (1990), and Said (1978, 1993), among others (see Rattansi, 1994 for an earlier elaboration).

3 Elsewhere, I have discussed the intersections between these notions in British immigration policy towards black and Asian communities (Rattansi, 1995).

4 These phenotypical features have included coloration, hair type, shape of nose and skull, and, as Gilman (1991, pp. 38–59) has pointed out, even type of foot in the case of representations of Jewishness.

5 See Laclau (1977, pp. 160–72) and (1990, pp. 28–9) for a discussion of the relative motility of various discursive figures in the 'trench war' of political struggles.

6 A representation circulated by various forms of media including film: take the case of the British film *Mona Lisa*, whose racializing and sexual dynamics, involving a world of black pimps and black and white prostitutes, are acutely explored by Pajaczkowska and Young, 1992.

7 For discussions of 'pleasure' in cultural politics, see the pioneering attempt in Bennett, et al. (1983).

8 This chapter has been adapted and developed from two earlier chapters: 'Western racisms, ethnicities and identities in a "postmodern" frame', in Rattansi, A. and Westwood, S. (eds) *Racism, Modernity and Identity*, Cambridge: Polity Press, 1994 and 'Just framing: Ethnicities and racisms in a "postmodern" framework', in Nicholson, L. and Seidman, S. (eds) *Social Postmodernism: Beyond Identity Politics*, New York: Cambridge University Press, 1995.

References

ADAM, B. (1990) *Time and Social Theory*, Cambridge: Polity Press.

ADAMS, M. (1996) *The Multicultural Imagination: 'Race', Colour and the Unconscious*, London: Routledge.

ANDERSON, B. (1991) *Imagined Communities: Reflections on the Origins and Spread of Nationalism* (revised edn.), London: Verso.

ANTHIAS, F. (1992) 'Connecting "race" and ethnic phenomena', *Sociology*, **26**, pp. 421–38.

APPADURAI, A. (1996) *Modernity at Large: Cultural Dimensions of Globalisation*, Minneapolis: University of Minnesota Press.

ARONOWITZ, S. and GIROUX, H. (1991) *Postmodern Education*, Minneapolis: University of Minnesota Press.

ASCHERSON, N. (1993) 'Scenes from domestic life', *Independent on Sunday*, 17 October.

BACK, L. (1993a) 'X amount of sat siri akall: Apache Indian, reggae music, and intermezzo culture', Mimeo.

BACK, L. (1993b) 'The unity beat', *The Guardian*, 13 October.

BACK, L. (1996) *New Ethnicities and Urban Culture*, London: University College Press.

BAKER, H. JR (1992) '"You caint' trus" it: Experts witnessing the case of rap', in WALLACE, M. and DENT, G. (eds) *Black Popular Culture*, Seattle: Bay Press, pp. 132–49.

BAKER, H. JR (1993) *Black Studies, Rap, and the Academy*, Chicago: University of Chicago Press.

BALIBAR, E. (1991) 'Is there a neo-racism?', in BALIBAR, E. and WALLERSTEIN, L. (eds) *Race, Nation, and Class*, London: Verso, pp. 17–28.

BANTON, M. and HARWOOD, J. (1975) *The Race Concept*, Newton Abbot: David and Charles.

BARKER, M. (1981) *The New Racism*, London: Junction Books.

BAUMAN, Z. (1989) *Modernity and the Holocaust*, Cambridge: Polity Press.

BAUMAN, Z. (1991) *Modernity and Ambivalence*, Cambridge: Polity Press.

BENNETT, T., BURGIN, V. and DONALD, J. (eds) (1983) *Formations of Pleasure*, London: Routledge.

BERNSTEIN, R. (1991) *The New Constellation*, Cambridge: Polity Press.

BHABHA, H. (1983) 'The other question . . .', *Screen*, **24**, 6, pp. 18–36.

BHABHA, H. (1984) 'Of mimicry and man: The ambivalence of colonial discourse', *October*, pp. 125–33.

BHABHA, H. (1994) *The Location of Culture*, London: Routledge.

BHATTI, G. (1995) 'A journey into the unknown: An ethnographic study of Asian children', in GRIFFITHS, M. and TROYNA, B. (eds) *Antiracism, Culture and Social Justice in Education*, Stoke on Trent: Trentham Books, pp. 61–76.

BILLIG, M. (1978) *Fascists: A Social Psychological View of the National Front*, London: Harcourt, Brace, Jovanovich.

BILLIG, M. (1984) 'I'm not National Front, but . . .', *New Society*, **68**, 21, pp. 255–8.

BOYNE, R. and RATTANSI, A. (eds) (1990) *Postmodernism and Society*, London: Macmillan.

BRUNN, S. and LEINBACH, T. (1991) *Collapsing Time and Space*, London: Harper Collins.

BURSTON, P. (1993) 'Batties bite back: Gays, homophobia, and racism', *The Guardian Weekend*, 20 November.

BUTLER, J. (1990) *Gender Trouble: Feminism and the Subversion of Identity*, London: Routledge.

CARRIER, J. (1995) *Occidentalism: Images of the West*, Oxford: Oxford University Press.

CASTORIADIS, C. (1987) 'The imaginary', in APPIGNANESI, L. (ed.) *The Real Me: Postmodernism and the Question of Identity*, London: Institute of Contemporary Arts.

CHICAGO CULTURAL STUDIES GROUP (1994) 'Critical multiculturalism', in GOLDBERG, D. (ed.) *Multiculturalism: A Critical Reader*, Oxford: Basil Blackwell, pp. 114–39.

COHEN, P. (1988) 'The perversions of inheritance: Studies in the making of multiracist Britain', in COHEN, P. and BAINES, H. (eds) *Multiracist Britain*, London: Macmillan, pp. 9–118.

COHEN, P. (1993) *Home Rules: Some Reflections on Racism and Nationalism in Everyday Life*, London: New Ethnicities Unit, University of East London.

CONNOLLY, P. (1995) 'Racism, masculine peer-group relations and the schooling of African Caribbean infant boys', *British Journal of Sociology of Education*, **16**, pp. 75–92.

CRAIB, I. (1989) *Psychoanalysis and Social Theory*, Brighton: Harvester Wheatsheaf.

DERRIDA, J. (1977) *Of Grammatology*, Baltimore, MD: Johns Hopkins University Press.

DERRIDA, J. (1978) *Writing and Difference*, London: Routledge.

DERRIDA, J. (1981) *Positions*, Chicago: University of Chicago Press.

DEPARTMENT OF EDUCATION AND SCIENCE (1981) *West Indian Children in Our Schools* (The Rampton Report), London: Department of Education and Science.

DURHAM, M. (1991) 'Women and the National Front', in CHELES, L., FERGUSON, R. and VAUGHAN, M. (eds) *Neo-Fascism in Europe*, London: Longman, pp. 264–83.

ELAM, D. (1994) *Feminism and Deconstruction*, London: Routledge.

ELLIOTT, A. (1994) *Psychoanalytic Theory*, Oxford: Basil Blackwell.

FANON, F. (1986) *Black Skins, White Masks*, London: Pluto Press.

FLAX, J. (1990) *Thinking Fragments: Psychoanalysis, Feminism, and Postmodernism in the Contemporary West*, Berkeley: University of California Press.

FLAX, J. (1993) *Disputed Subjects: Essays on Psychoanalysis, Politics, and Philosophy*, New York: Routledge.

FOUCAULT, M. (1977) *Discipline and Punish*, London: Allen Lane.

FOUCAULT, M. (1979) *The History of Sexuality: Vol 1, an Introduction*, London: Allen Lane.

FOUCAULT, M. (1980) *Power/Knowledge: Selected Interviews, 1972–7*, GORDON, C. (ed.), Brighton: Harvester Press.

FROSH, S. (1987) *The Politics of Psychoanalysis*, London: Macmillan.

FROSH, S. (1989) 'Psychoanalysis and racism', in RICHARDS, B. (ed.) *Crises of the Self*, London: Free Association Books, pp. 229–44.

FROSH, S. (1991) *Identity Crisis: Modernity, Psychoanalysis, and the Self*, London: Macmillan.

GENDERS, E. and PLAYER, E. (1989) *Race Relations in Prisons*, Oxford: Clarendon Press.

GIDDENS, A. (1990) *The Consequences of Modernity*, Cambridge: Polity Press.

GIDDENS, A. (1991) *Modernity and Self-identity*, Cambridge: Polity Press.

GIDDENS, A. (1994) 'Living in a post-traditional society', in BECK, U., GIDDENS, A. and LASH, S. (eds) *Reflexive Modernization*, Cambridge: Polity Press, pp. 56–109.

GILMAN, S. (1991) *The Jew's Body*, London: Routledge.

GILMAN, S. (1992) 'Black bodies, white bodies: Toward an iconography of female sexuality in late nineteenth-century art, medicine, and literature', in DONALD, J. and RATTANSI, A. (eds) *'Race', Culture, and Difference*, London: Sage, pp. 171–97.

GILROY, P. (1987) *There Ain't no Black in the Union Jack*, London: Hutchinson.

GILROY, P. (1992) 'Cultural studies and ethnic absolutism', in GROSSBERG, L., NELSON, C. and TREICHER, P. (eds) *Cultural Studies*, London: Routledge, pp. 187–98.

GILROY, P. (1993a) *The Black Atlantic: Modernity and Double Consciousness*, London: Verso.

GILROY, P. (1993b) *Small Acts: Thoughts on the Politics of Black Cultures*, London: Serpent's Trail.

GIROUX, H. (1994) 'Insurgent multiculturalism and the promise of pedagogy', in GOLDBERG, D. (ed.) *Multiculturalism: A Critical Reader*, Oxford: Basil Blackwell, pp. 325–43.

GIROUX, H. (1996) *Fugitive Cultures: Race, Violence and Youth*, London: Routledge.

GIROUX, H., LANKSHEAR, C., McLAREN, P. and PETERS, M. (1996) *Counternarratives: Cultural Studies and Critical Pedagogies in Postmodern Spaces*, London: Routledge.

GOLDBERG, D. (1993) *Racist Culture*, Oxford: Basil Blackwell.

GOLDBERG, D. (ed.) (1994a) *Multiculturalism: A Critical Reader*, Oxford: Basil Blackwell.

GOLDBERG, D. (1994b) 'Introduction: Multicultural conditions', in GOLDBERG, D. (ed.) *Multiculturalism: A Critical Reader*, Oxford: Basil Blackwell, pp. 1–41.

GORDON, P. (1992) 'Souls in armour: Towards a psychoanalytic understanding of racism', Mimeo.

HALL, S. (1992a) 'New ethnicities', in DONALD, J. and RATTANSI, A. (eds) *'Race', Culture, and Difference*, London: Sage, pp. 252–9.

HALL, S. (1992b) 'The question of cultural identity', in HALL, S. and McGREW, A. (eds) *Modernity and Its Futures*, Cambridge: Polity Press, pp. 274–316.

HALL, S. (1992c) 'The west and the rest: Discourse and power', in HALL, S. and GIEBEN, B. (eds) *Formations of Modernity*, Cambridge: Polity Press, pp. 275–320.

HALL, S. (1992d) 'What is this "black" in black popular culture?', in WALLACE, M. and DENT, G. (eds) *Black Popular Culture*, Seattle: Bay Press, pp. 21–33.

HARVEY, D. (1989) *The Condition of Postmodernity*, Oxford: Blackwell.

HATCHER, R. (1995) 'Racism and children's culture', in GRIFFITHS, M. and TROYNA, B. (eds) *Antiracism, Culture and Social Justice in Education*, Stoke on Trent: Trentham Books, pp. 97–114.

HEKMAN, S. (1990) *Gender and Knowledge: Elements of a Postmodern Feminism*, Cambridge: Polity Press.

HELD, D. (1984) 'The contemporary polarization of democratic theory: The case for a third way', in HELD, D. *Political Theory and the Modern State*, Cambridge: Polity Press, pp. 174–88.

HELD, D. (1996) *Models of Democracy* (2nd edn.), Cambridge: Polity Press.

HENDERSON, J. and KARN, V. (1984) 'Race, class, and the allocation of public housing in Britain', *Urban Studies*, **21**, pp. 115–28.

HENDERSON, J. and KARN, V. (1987) *Race, Class, and State Housing*, Aldershot: Gower.

HEWITT, R. (1986) *White Talk, Black Talk: Inter-racial Friendship and Communication amongst Adolescents*, Cambridge: Cambridge University Press.

HOPKINS, R. (1997) *Educating Black Males: Critical Lessons in Schooling, Community and Power*, Albany, NY: SUNY Press.

JENKINS, R. (1986) *Racism and Recruitment*, Cambridge: Cambridge University Press.

JENKINS, R. (1992) 'Black workers in the labour market: The price of recession', in BRAHAM, P., RATTANSI, A. and SKELLINGTON, R. (eds) *Racism and Antiracism: Inequalities, Opportunities, and Policies*, London: Sage, pp. 148–63.

JEWSON, N. and MASON, D. (1992) 'The theory and practice of equal opportunities policies: Liberal and radical approaches', in BRAHAM, P., RATTANSI, A. and SKELLINGTON, R. (eds) *Racism and Antiracism: Inequalities, Opportunities, and Policies*, London: Sage, pp. 218–34.

JONES, S. (1988) *Black Culture, White Youth*, London: Macmillan.

KABBANI, R. (1986) *Europe's Myths of Orient*, London: Macmillan.

KOHN, M. (1995) *The Race Gallery: The Return of Racial Science*, London: Jonathan Cape.

KOVEL, J. (1988) *White Racism: A Psychohistory*, London: Free Association Books.

KRISTEVA, J. (1991) *Strangers to Ourselves*, New York: Columbia University Press.

LACLAU, E. (1977) *Politics and Ideology in Marxist Theory: Capitalism, Fascism, Populism*, London: New Left Books.

LACLAU, E. (1990) *New Reflections on the Revolution of Our Time*, London: Verso.

LASH, S. and URRY, J. (1994) *Economies of Sign and Space*, London: Sage.

LLOYD, C. (1994) 'Universalism and difference: The crisis of antiracism in France and the UK', in RATTANSI, A. and WESTWOOD, S. (eds) *Racism, Modernity, and Identity*, Cambridge: Polity Press, pp. 222–44.

MAC AN GHAILL, M. (1994) *The Making of Men: Masculinities, Sexualities and Schooling*, Milton Keynes: Open University Press.

MACDONALD, I., BHAVNANI, R., KHAN, L. and JOHN, G. (1989) *Murder in the Playground*, London: Longsight Press.

MASON, D. (1992) 'Some problems with the concept of racism', Leicester: Leicester University Discussion Papers in Sociology.

MASSEY, D. (1993) 'Politics and space/time', in KEITH, M. and PILE, S. (eds) *Place and the Politics of Identity*, London: Routledge, pp. 141–61.

MAY, S. (1994) 'The case for antiracist education', *British Journal of Sociology of Education*, **15**, pp. 421–8.

MCLAREN, P. (1994) 'White terror and oppositional agency: Towards a critical multiculturalism', in GOLDBERG, D. (ed.) *Multiculturalism: A Critical Reader*, Oxford: Basil Blackwell, pp. 45–74.

MENDUS, S. (1989) *Liberalism and the Limits of Tolerance*, Cambridge: Cambridge University Press.

MILES, R. (1987) 'Recent Marxist theories of nationalism and racism', *British Journal of Sociology*, **38**, pp. 24–43.

MILES, R. (1994) 'Explaining racism in Europe', in RATTANSI, A. and WESTWOOD, S. (eds) *Racism, Modernity, and Identity*, Cambridge: Polity Press, pp. 189–221.

MORT, F. (1983) 'Sex, signification, and pleasure', in BENNETT, T., BURGIN, V. and DONALD, J. (eds) *Formations of Pleasure*, London: Routledge, pp. 36–43.

MOUFFE, C. (1992) 'Democratic citizenship and the political community', in MOUFFE, C. (ed.) *Dimensions of Radical Democracy*, London: Verso, pp. 225–39.

MOUFFE, C. (1996) 'Democracy, power and the political', in BENHABIB, S. (ed.) *Democracy and Difference: Contesting the Boundaries of the Political*, Princeton: Princeton University Press, pp. 245–56.

NANDY, A. (1983) *The Intimate Enemy: Loss and Recovery of Self under Colonialism*, Delhi: Oxford University Press.

NANDY, A. (1990) *The Tao of Cricket: On Games of Destiny and the Destiny of Games*, New York: Viking.

NASH, M. (1989) *The Cauldron of Ethnicity in the Modern World*, Chicago: University of Chicago Press.

OMI, M. and WINANT, H. (1986) *Racial Formation in the United States: From the 1960s to the 1980s*, New York: Routledge.

PAJACZKOWSKA, C. and YOUNG, L. (1992) 'Racism, representation and psychoanalysis', in DONALD, J. and RATTANSI, A. (eds) *'Race', Culture, and Difference*, London: Sage, pp. 198–219.

PAREKH, B. (1995) 'Liberalism and colonialism', in PIETERSE, J. and PAREKH, B. (eds) *The Decolonization of Imagination: Culture, Knowledge and Power*, London: Zed Books, pp. 81–98.

PHIZACKLEA, A. and MILES, R. (1980) *Labour and Racism*, London: Routledge.

RATTANSI, A. (1992) 'Changing the subject? Racism, culture, and education', in DONALD, J. and RATTANSI, A. (eds) *'Race', Culture, and Difference*, London: Sage, pp. 11–48.

RATTANSI, A. (1994) ' "Western" racisms, ethnicities, and identities in a "postmodern" France', in RATTANSI, A. and WESTWOOD, S. (eds) *Racism, Modernity, and Identity*, Cambridge: Polity Press, pp. 222–44.

RATTANSI, A. (1995) 'Forget postmodernism?', *De Bunker. Sociology*, **29**, pp. 339–49.

RATTANSI, A. (1997) 'Postcolonialism and its discontents', in *Economy and Society*, **26**, pp. 480–500.

REX, J. (1986) *Race and Ethnicity*, Milton Keynes: Open University Press.

RUSTIN, M. (1991) *The Good Society and the Inner World*, London: Verso.

SAID, E. (1978) *Orientalism*, London: Routledge.

SAID, E. (1993) *Culture and Imperialism*, London: Chatto and Windus.

SARUP, M. (1986) *The Politics of Multiracial Education*, London: Routledge.

SEWELL, T. (1995) 'A phallic response to schooling: Black masculinity and race in an inner-city comprehensive', in GRIFFITHS, M. and TROYNA, B. (eds) *Antiracism, Culture and Social Justice in Education*, Stoke on Trent: Trentham Books, pp. 21–41.

SEWELL, T. (1997) *Black Masculinities and Schooling*, Stoke on Trent: Trentham Books.

SHARMA, S., HUTNYK, J. and SHARMA, A. (1996) *Dis-Orienting Rhythms: The Politics of the New Asian Dance Music*, London: Zed Press.

SILVERMAN, M. (1993) 'Symbolic violence and the new communities', Paper presented to Antiracist Strategies and Movements in Europe Workshop, University of Greenwich, London.

SIVANANDAN, A. (1974) *Race, Class, and the State*, London: Institute of Race Relations.

SOJA, E. (1989) 'Spatializations: A critique of the Giddensian version', in SOJA, E. (ed.) *Postmodern Geographies*, London: Verso, pp. 138–56.

SPIVAK, G. (1990) *The Post-Colonial Critic: Interviews, Strategies, Dialogues*, London: Routledge.

STEPAN, N. (1990) 'Race and gender: The role of analogy in science', in GOLDBERG, D. (ed.) *Anatomy of Racism*, Minneapolis: University of Minnesota Press, pp. 38–57.

STEPHENS, G. (1991) 'Rap music's double-voiced discourse: A crossroads for interracial communication', *Journal of Communication Inquiry*, **15**, 2, pp. 70–91.

STEPHENS, G. (1992) 'Interracial dialogue in rap music', *New Formations*, **16**, pp. 62–79.

URRY, J. (1991) 'Time and space in Giddens' social theory', in BRYANT, C. and JARY, D. (eds) *Giddens' Theory of Structuration*, London: Routledge, pp. 160–75.

VERMA, G. (1995) 'Ethnic relations in secondary schools', in TOMLINSON, S. and CRAFT, M. (eds) *Ethnic Relations and Schooling*, London: Athlone Press, pp. 60–78.

WALLACE, M. (1992) 'Boyz n the hood' and 'Jungle fever', in WALLACE, M. and DENT, G. (eds) *Black Popular Culture*, Seattle: Bay Press, pp. 123–31.

WARE, V. (1992) *Beyond the Pale: White Women, Racism, and History*, London: Verso.

WEALE, S. (1993) 'Foreign fields of violent dreams', *The Guardian*, 16 October.

WELDON, F. (1989) *Sacred Cows: A Portrait of Britain, Post-Rushdie, Pre-utopia*, London: Chatto and Windus.

WELLMAN, D. (1977) *Portraits of White Racism*, Cambridge: Cambridge University Press.

WETHERELL, M. and POTTER, J. (1992) *Mapping the Language of Racism*, Hemel Hempstead: Harvester Wheatsheaf.

WIEVIORKA, M. (1991) *L'Espace du Racisme*, Paris: Seuil.

WIEVIORKA, M. (1994) 'Racism in Europe: Unity and diversity', in RATTANSI, A. and WESTWOOD, S. (eds) *Racism, Modernity, and Identity*, Cambridge: Polity Press, pp. 173–88.

WILLIS, P. (1977) *Learning to Labour*, Farnborough: Saxon House.

WINANT, H. (1994) 'Racial formation and hegemony: Global and local developments', in RATTANSI, A. and WESTWOOD, S. (eds) *Racism, Modernity, and Identity*, Cambridge: Polity Press, pp. 266–89.

WRIGHT, C. (1995) 'Ethnic relations in the primary classroom', in TOMLINSON, S. and CRAFT, M. (eds) *Ethnic Relations and Schooling*, London: Athlone Press, pp. 30–59.

YOUNG, R. (1993) 'Psychoanalysis and racism: A loud silence', Mimeo.

YUVAL-DAVIS, N. and ANTHIAS, F. (1989) *Woman–Nation–State*, London: Macmillan.

ZACK, N. (ed.) (1997) *Race/Sex*, London: Routledge.

4   Forging Partnerships for Multicultural Teacher Education

Christine Sleeter and Carmen Montecinos

What is multicultural education fundamentally about? What should it be about? To a great many people in the United States, particularly those who are members of the dominant society, multicultural education seems primarily to entail adding recognition of cultural differences to the education enterprise, despite the efforts of many educators over the past 25 years to argue for a much broader conception (Bartolomé, 1995; Nieto, 1995). As this conception of multicultural education is enacted in the schools, it also becomes endorsed and perpetuated by members of subordinated groups (Montecinos, 1994). In this conception of multicultural education, schooling is taken for granted as basically sound and well-structured, but as sometimes too culturally homogeneous in its curriculum and special events. Multicultural education, therefore, is understood to mean changing teachers' and administrators' choices regarding which groups are represented in the curriculum and changing the curriculum's ability to adapt to individual differences in students (i.e., teaching to diverse learning styles). These views are embedded in commonsense understandings of predominantly white, western capitalist societies such as the United States and Canada, and correspondingly their institutions, as fair, open, democratic, and meritocratic.

This prevailing conception can be contrasted with the commonsense understanding that one of us (Montecinos), an immigrant to the United States, made of the term 'multicultural education' when she first heard it. During her high school years her country underwent drastic political changes when in 1970 a democratically elected Marxist government took office following a centrist administration. During the third year of what was supposed to be a six-year term, this government was overthrown in a military coup with a consequent shift to the extreme right of the political spectrum. Prominent among the various justifications given by supporters of the coup was the educational reform programme that the Marxist government had embarked upon. This reform aimed at providing one national school system, thus eliminating significant disparities in the educational quality afforded by the State to those who were wealthy and those who were poor. Needless to say, the fiercest opposition to the idea of one national school system came mainly from the wealthy, not from those who had their children attending underfunded, overcrowded schools. This controversy, as well as the changes in education that immediately followed the coup, made it plainly obvious to her that schooling was a site of struggle between opposing views on how wealth and power should be distributed in a given society.

Consequently, as an educational reform movement that was led by people of colour, it was 'commonsense' to her that multiculturalism had to be about reworking existing power arrangements and not just about the representation and celebration of cultural diversity.

Whereas the prevailing conception of multiculturalism focuses on a struggle for the recognition of diversity within existing social structures, the latter conception stresses the importance of linking the struggle for recognition to a broader struggle for social justice. Teachers who understand that education must be both multicultural and social reconstructionist must, by necessity, be politically literate. The politically educated teacher is one who:

> can make judgments about the distribution of power and resources . . . to effect changes in these power and resource holdings if these do not fit a rational image of the good life or of human virtue. . . . They would be able to protect themselves and others from inequalities in the distribution of income and wealth and other valued possessions. (Allen, 1992, p. 138)

Freire (1985) and others have noted that learning how to ask critical questions about existing social arrangements must start from an examination of one's immediate reality. In the case of teachers, one place to start is through an examination of how decision-making power in schooling is distributed and the limitations of schooling models that concentrate power in the hands of school professionals. But as teacher educators we need to move beyond critique and help teachers envision alternative power arrangements in the process of schooling. In this chapter we suggest that asking preservice teachers to engage in community-based learning projects that are structured around the principles of egalitarian partnerships can show them ways in which power can be shared among school professionals and with other school constituencies.

Currently in the United States the necessity of forming partnerships among schools, universities, businesses, and other community agencies is a notion widely accepted by conservatives, liberals, and progressives alike. But, as we illustrate through examples of alternative models for structuring service learning projects, partnership is a concept that lends itself to multiple interpretations and applications. In this chapter we draw from Eisler and Loye's (1990) distinction between dominator and partnership models of social interactions, and Koegel's (1995, 1996) distinction between partnership and dominator intelligence, to characterize alternative approaches for structuring school–community partnerships. We suggest that partnering for social change entails challenging the professional mystique, to use the words of Biklen (1995), that concentrates power in the hands of experts. As we discuss next, understanding multicultural education as a social movement instead of simply an educational reform has implications for preparing teachers and for challenging the notion that professional experts' viewpoints about education are the only legitimate viewpoints.

Multicultural Education as a Social Movement

Multicultural education in the US grew out of the Civil Rights movement, and, as such, is grounded in a vision of democracy, social justice, pluralism, and equality. These are words that fall lightly off the tongues of most people in western nations, but they are very difficult to act upon in highly unequal societies. Most educators and other citizens have learned to take for granted huge discrepancies in wealth and living conditions, control over national decision-making by a small elite, and 'professionalism' as a means of restricting who can make decisions over what. These conditions are continually contested from society's margins, and have been explosively contested during times such as the Civil Rights movement. That vibrant affirmation of the ideals of democracy, equality, pluralism, and justice is the legacy of multicultural education.

As such, multicultural education has served as a mobilizing site for struggle within education (Gay, 1983). James Banks (1992), for example, has traced the intellectual roots of multicultural education to the scholarship of African–Americans such as W.E.B. DuBois, whose work challenged dominant paradigms about African–American people, 'race', and society, and laid the intellectual groundwork for the liberation struggle. As the field has drawn in more and more groups, and focused on an increasingly complex array of oppressions, it has drawn theory and intellectual inspiration from additional sources, such as feminism, Marxism, and bilingualism. Multicultural education in the US also connects with social reconstructionism, which is usually traced at least back to the early 1930s, as a critique of Great Depression conditions following the stock market crash of 1929 (Stanley, 1992). More recently, it has built on the thought and practices of Paulo Freire (1973, 1985).

The social movement metaphor is useful for engaging with education that is multicultural and social reconstructionist — more so, we would argue, than the educational reform metaphor (Sleeter, 1996). When multicultural education is viewed as an educational reform, professional educators tend to view themselves as the most appropriate people equipped to decide what in schools should be reformed and how. Professional educators taking the lead in multicultural education is problematic, however, because the great majority are white and middle-class, which leaves the main locus of decision-making about schools in the hands of members of the dominant ethnic and social class group. As Catherine Walsh argues:

> A close examination of the substance and focus of most current, system-based and organized reforms, indicates that few prescribe radical change; the structures, policies, and practices that advantage some and disadvantage others remain stable. An examination of who directs, controls, and envisions most of these reforms is similarly demonstrative. Education reform is overwhelmingly top-down, institutional rather than grassroots and community-based, and homogeneous in terms of race, class, politics, and gender. (1996, p. xii)

Educational reforms do not generally challenge fundamental power relations; social movements do.

A social movement can be defined as a 'sustained challenge to powerholders in the name of a population living under the jurisdiction of those powerholders by means of repeated public displays of that population's numbers, commitment, unity, and worthiness' (Tilly, 1993, p. 7). Such movements aim to redistribute power and resources by confronting power relations in which a dominant collective has attained the power to define the society for the masses, to construct an ideology in which that definition makes sense, and to achieve hegemony — to get most people to accept that ideology and act in accordance with it, viewing it as natural (Gramsci, 1971; Touraine, 1988). Social movement theorists distinguish among four kinds of actors in a movement: the constituent base, the powerholders, the activists, and the general public who are not directly involved.

While professional reforms are largely initiated and controlled by powerholders, social movements are initiated and controlled mainly by a grassroots constituent base, led by activists. Professional educators can act as allies and collaborators, and that relationship is what many multicultural education advocates have sought since the field's inception. One can identify many examples of community-based reform efforts initiated by marginalized communities (see, for example, Densmore, 1995; Moses, et al., 1989; Phillips, 1995). In some cases professional educators become active allies, but in many cases they resist community-based grassroots efforts to change schooling.

When multicultural education is situated within historic social movements led by oppressed communities, the changes and agents of change it entails are quite different than when it is framed as merely an educational reform. The social movement metaphor brings into focus concerns with group rights and agency and the commitment to teaching students how to exercise power and responsibility as they materialize democratic ideals. The above discussion is rooted primarily in a US frame of reference, but the same issues have been framed in other national contexts as differentiating a benevolent form of multicultural education from an actively critical form (see, for example, Gillborn, 1992; May, 1994; Ng, et al., 1995; Troyna, 1987).

Challenging the Ideology of Professionalism

We do not believe that resistance to power-sharing results in most instances from educators not caring about students or their desiring to dominate others. Rather, resistance largely comes from the technical-rational understanding that has permeated prevailing conceptions of the professions in general and the teaching profession in particular. From this perspective, teaching entails a series of technical decisions made by experts who have a claim to authority. This claim rests on two premises: ownership of a domain of a morally neutral set of facts and the belief that those facts represent law-like generalizations that can be applied to particular cases (MacIntyre, 1984). Within a technical perspective school professionals, therefore, are encouraged to apply techniques that have been shown to improve their ability to predict and control students' learning. These professionals are not encouraged to critically interrogate the social arrangements that shape their lives and the lives of their students, nor are they encouraged to see students and their parents as people who have something meaningful to say about how school experiences are selected, organized, and regulated.

Dominant ideologies function as 'regimes of truth' (Foucault, 1972). The professional mystique is one regime of truth that leads experts, who are disconnected from the everyday struggles and systems of meaning through which inner-city dwellers shape their lives, to believe that they can provide solutions to the problems of inner-city schools. The power of such regimes of truth lies in their taken-for-grantedness by most members of the society and their ability to define, describe, delimit, and circumscribe how and what can be said about a given phenomenon (Kress, 1985).

For oppressed groups, framing teaching as a series of technical decisions made by experts constitutes cultural invasion — the dominant society renders as illegitimate systems of meaning and reality originating in oppressed communities (Freire, 1970). Such systems, or 'counter-memories', give voice to oppressed groups, including political critiques of their position in society (Gay, 1995). As San Juan has explained:

> Popular memory, a sense of history inscribed in the collective resistance against, racist, patriarchal, and exploitative forces, is one of the necessary means for oppressed peoples to acquire a knowledge of the larger context of their collective struggles, equipping them to assume transformative roles in shaping history. . . . The struggle to define and articulate a politics of popular memory in the face of the populist amnesia which consumerism induces occupies centre stage in formulating an agenda for an ethnopoetics sensitive to the racial politics of the twenty-first century. (1992, p. 77)

Counter-memories situate subordinant groups historically in a manner that articulates a group consciousness, redefines their relationship with the dominant society, and suggests changing that relationship (Aronowitz, 1992). The more powerful a counter-memory, the more forcefully it will be suppressed. Professional 'experts' who represent the dominant ideology generally regard powerful counter-memories as too divisive, too political, or simply irrelevant.

Educators who successfully teach children from oppressed communities actively affirm the cultures, ideologies, memories, languages, and communities of the children, an assertion documented by research on effective teaching of cultural minority students in the US and elsewhere, and experiences of cultural minority educators (see, for example, Ladson-Billings, 1994; Lucas *et al.*, 1990; May, 1994). To do this well, however, educators must view culture and community as dynamic, complex, living, contemporary, and historically situated. As Antonia Darder argues, the concept of culture is usually framed in dominant discourse as politically neutral: 'What is readily apparent from the standpoint of any critical analysis of much of this work is the obvious absence of specific reference to the issue of power and its relationship to the nature in which cultural relations are structured and perpetuated within and between groups' (1991, p. 26). When power relations are considered, culture becomes not just something passed down from one generation to the next, but also everyday ways in which dominant groups impose or maintain their power, and subordinated groups cope with, survive, and resist subordination.

Most educators find it quite hard to acknowledge that we rarely understand a culture or community to which we do not belong as well as we might believe that we do. As teachers we are used to knowing more than our students and are often very threatened by possibilities that students or their parents might know more than we do. As a result, in cross-cultural classrooms well-intentioned multicultural teachers too often attempt multicultural teaching by presenting superficial versions of other people's cultures and communities; failing to affirm learning processes that allow complexity to emerge in the classroom as well as in the larger community.

Geneva Gay (1995) describes the process of cultural affirmation as 'giving voice' to students and allowing them to help shape the content, processes, style, and language of the classroom. Giving voice to students does not invalidate what the teacher knows, but rather restructures teacher–student relationships from mono-logical relationships in which the teacher has all the power to define curriculum and instruction, to dialogical relationships in which teacher and students co-construct curriculum and instruction. Catherine Walsh, for example, describes how she en-gaged students in a collaborative research project to restructure their own school. Her main argument is that 'a meaningful and expert source for understanding the significance and substance of [a different approach to schooling] are the students' (1996, p. 229). As her work exemplifies, when students are taken seriously they can design meaningful and substantive ways that schools could serve them more effect-ively. Walsh argues that educators should not rely mainly on the literature to figure out how to create better schools, but that they should also work collaboratively with students and their communities (see also Nieto, this volume; Shor, 1996).

Alternative Models for School–Community Partnerships

The kinds of educational structuring advocated by Gay (1995), Walsh (1996), and others require that educators and those with whom they work develop the counter-ideology of partnership as it has been described by Eisler and Loye (1990) and Koegel (1995, 1996). But before we discuss an ideology that supports the forging of egalitarian partnerships, it is important to understand how these authors characterize the 'regime of truth' that structures contemporary relationships among various social groups in the United States, the ideology of domination. These authors have char-acterized partnership and dominator models for social interactions as reflecting a continuum rather than a dichotomy. In what follows we conceptually articulate them as opposites — as ideal-types, in effect. Keep in mind that when enacted within institutions and by individuals, what often happens is that characteristics of each model are present in different degrees, with one or the other pole of the continuum usually prevailing.

Dominator Intelligence

The static divisions of constituencies into groups with varying amounts of power and resources that characterize traditional schools follow what Eisler and Loye

(1990) called the dominator model of social relations. Koegel (1996) has further elaborated this model to examine the structural roots, social patterns, and personal dimensions of distinct patterns of thinking, being, and relating that make up what he calls 'dominator intelligence'. Dominator intelligence continuously seeks to frame relationships among groups and individuals in terms of the enforced hierarchization of social differences, making it difficult to relate to others as equals. Ranking can be based on a multiplicity of criteria, depending on the context, but it always serves as a basis for the unequal distribution of power and resources in ways that systematically perpetuate the hierarchy. For example, in schools we tend to rank students based on scores obtained on aptitude and achievement tests, defining those who are superior as well as those who are inferior. As Oakes' (1985) studies on tracking (streaming) have shown, those who are identified as superior get a higher quantity and quality of resources. In other words, schools act to perpetuate and to legitimate their superior status. As Darder (1991) and others have shown, students of colour who are tracked in the lower rungs find ways, passively and actively, of resisting this hierarchization.

Having 'power-over' others becomes addictive and the organizational structures that are established, therefore, seek to perpetuate the dominance of those who wield power. A system based on dominance is set up to give incentives to those who are willing to play by rules that have been established unilaterally by the dominant group and to instil chronic fear among those who think of challenging that dominance. In the wider society, dominance is always backed by force and usually maintained through the various socialization agents that form our consciousness (what we come to regard as 'human nature' or commonsense), such as schooling and the media. For example, early in our schooling experiences we quickly realize that our classmates who do not follow the rules established by those in power are punished. This fear of punishment — the fear of having someone take away the little power or resources we have been able to garner for ourselves — frames our interactions with people in authority and peers. And it shapes our beliefs and the institutions we create.

Social relationships that follow dominator intelligence engender fear not only in those who are subordinated, but also in those who dominate. Dominators are constantly afraid that someone else might want to dominate them (Koegel, 1996). In the context of school, an excellent example of fear-based relationships established by those who have an institutional position of power is found in the work of O'Hair and Blase (1992) who studied teachers' political orientations toward students. They described two types of orientations. The first type characterizes teachers who try to influence their students. These teachers stress the importance of tactfulness, friendliness, communication, and role modeling. The second type of orientation characterizes teachers who are concerned with protecting themselves from the criticism of students, parents, and colleagues. This protectionist orientation is found among teachers who feel vulnerable to others who exercise coercive forms of power, such as threats and criticism. To protect themselves they make compromises in areas such as grading, homework, and discipline. Fear promotes insecurity and a sense of urgency which inhibits dominators and subordinates from paying enough attention to the long term consequences of the means used to maintain dominance.

Dominator intelligence either crushes resistance or accommodates it through alliance building. When dominators seek to cooperate with others, they are largely motivated by the fear of losing power if that alliance is not established at a given juncture. This alliance, however, will be easily erased and replaced if it threatens the dominator's ability to define for others the rules by which exchanges at the social, political, and economic level are governed.

Eisler (1987) contends that when we structure social relationships as force-backed rankings, then we generate a system that leads to chronic violence, social injustices, and ecological imbalance that jeopardizes the sustainment of life. The dominator model, as Eisler illustrates, is not the only reflection of human nature. She provides numerous historical examples where human beings have constructed societies that are not based on relationships of domination and oppression. These societies are based on cultural patterns and institutional structures that foster what Koegel (1996) calls 'partnership intelligence'.

Partnership Intelligence

The ideological and structural elements described above are present to a much lesser degree in partnership societies. In these societies the basic principle for social organization is the egalitarian and caring linking of groups (as opposed to adversarial ranking). When people within a country and among countries are largely linked through relations of reciprocity, and conscious efforts are made to minimize relations of domination and subordination, then there is no need for a political and ideological apparatus of social control that entails coercion, hatred, fear, and the threat of violence. From this perspective, social relations are created through ideologies and institutions that support cooperation (not competition) based on trust, caring for others, and the egalitarian distribution of wealth, power, and resources. Conflict is recognized as natural among people who have different skills, resources, beliefs, interests, and desires but it is believed that these can be resolved peacefully through life-enhancing and life-maintaining activities.

When we believe that the joint struggle for the common good results in winners and winners (not winners and losers), then social differences are no longer a basis for ranking and domination. Once we eliminate the notion of the inevitability of the winner/loser dichotomy, we become less interested in determining *who* is superior and more interested in understanding *what* social arrangements can benefit all at the expense of none. When no one group has a claim to the authority to make decisions for others, then we can maximize participatory decision-making and democracy.

Within partnership ideological and institutional structures power is understood as the ability to create, nourish, and avail the resources for oneself and others to enjoy their actualization to the highest potential. This entails 'power-with' others (not 'power-over' others) to enhance both individual and communal well-being (Koegel, 1996). Partnership intelligence motivates us to cooperate with one another, not out of a chronic fear of losing the little 'power-over' the resources we have been able to attain but out of caring for ourselves in relationship to our community. Caring is possible because everyone's basic needs tend to be fulfilled at a much higher rate than they are frustrated.

Power is not seen as the property of some but as a shared process for all. In the classroom, partnership intelligence will lead teachers and students jointly to construct rules to govern their interactions, passing the 'power ball' to those who at a given point in time have more expertise in a subject. Schools are organized to meet the needs of children, teachers, and the community at large. These needs are jointly identified as such, not arbitrarily named by those with more institutional power. The different requirements that people have to achieve their actualization are met by distributing resources according to need, not by power wielding.

Building social relationships on the partnership model enables us to pursue three interrelated goals: a) meeting our needs as we further our development, b) responding to others' needs as we foster their development, and c) developing mutually empowering relationships (Koegel, 1996). Working in one's relational self-interest is inextricably linked to working in the interests of others as we see the 'I in the We and the We in the I'. Under dominator intelligence, these would be understood as incompatible goals.

The distinction between dominator and partnership intelligence can be illustrated by looking at social service programmes for inner-city communities. Keith (1996) identified three distinct assumptive frameworks social service programmes use regarding the main barriers to the development of inner-city communities. First, programmes can be structured under the assumption that the main barrier to community development is the community itself: deficiencies in students and families who inhabit the schools account for poor performance on standardized achievement tests, truancy, dropping-out, and so on. Programmes based on this assumption emphasize the provision of services to remedy recipients' deficits, ultimately constructing service recipients as the problem. A second framework assumes that barriers stem largely from inadequacies or irrationalities in how the bureaucratic institutions and organizations that are designed to assist in community development, such as schools, use existing resources. In this case, school professionals are blamed for failing to be skilful enough in their use of the technologies science offers us for improving student learning. Both of these approaches reflect dominator intelligence because they organize services and activities that secure the dominance of mainstream views as they are structured hierarchically around the understandings of benevolent or philanthropic experts. They also fail to incorporate recipients' visions of what needs to change and how this can be accomplished.

A third assumptive framework asserts that barriers to development can be traced largely to the solutions that have been proposed by organizations that structure services without substantive input from those whose needs, concerns, perspectives, and interests these organizations purportedly want to assist. This last assumptive framework is coherent with partnership ideology because it believes that experts as well as inner-city dwellers can draw on each other's perspectives on the nature of the problems as well as the identification and implementation of solutions. When school professionals start from this assumptive framework, the disproportionate numbers of school drop-outs and 'underachievers' found among students who come from low-income and ethnic minority backgrounds are viewed as reflecting discontinuities between communities' cultures and the structure and content of the schools that serve them (Cummins, 1986). School personnel who are disconnected from certain segments of the community they serve, end up developing policies that do little to challenge hegemonic views on the causes of disenfranchisement.

For instance, the high school in the largely middle-class community in which one of us (Montecinos) lives instituted a policy that would allow truant students who had a drug habit to be spared an expulsion for violating attendance rules if they agreed to attend drug rehabilitation. In practice, this sensible idea clearly resulted in privileging those students whose parents could afford the cost of a rehabilitation programme. Low-income students who did not qualify for aid from the government to pay for such a programme could not take advantage of this waiver and ended up getting expelled from school, as was the case of a youth who was temporarily living in the home of one of the authors (Montecinos). If those who sat on the board that developed this policy included the poor and uninsured, would such a policy have been instituted in the first place without making accommodations for those who, for financial reasons, could not obtain rehabilitation services?

Dominator models generate distinct patterns of beliefs among individuals who come from the dominant group and these tend to differ from patterns of beliefs found among those who come from the oppressed group. Table 4.1 characterizes how powerholders and social activists view the various aspects of schooling we have been discussing when operating from a dominator model, and when they move to a partnership model. Social activists' beliefs are more congruent with partnership than are powerholders' beliefs, but because they are enacted within a culture and social institutions structured by the logic of domination, they do not necessarily disrupt adversarial relationships and foster reciprocal caring. It is important to point out too, that activists committed to one emancipatory cause too often continue to reproduce dominator dynamics in their relationships with other subordinated groups (a prime example is the historically conflictual relationships between white feminists and feminists of colour in the USA).

Whether one deploys more of a dominator than a subordinated viewpoint tends to be situational. Acting as a partner, or as a dominator, is not a characteristic inherent to the person but rather a patterning in the social relations that we may establish at any given time. Adair and Howell have elaborated on the patterns of surviving that operate at the subjective level to complement oppressors' views with the oppressed's views in ways that perpetuate relations of domination. People tend to adapt to relations of dominance or subordination by developing or being social-ized into reciprocal behaviour patterns. For instance, an individual from a dominant group will 'tend to be presumptuous, does not listen, interrupts, raises voice, bullies, threatens violence, becomes violent'. An individual from an oppressed group often 'finds it difficult to speak up, [is] timid, tries to please. Holds back anger, resent-ment, rage' (1989, p. 11). An individual from a dominant group often 'fears losing control, public embarrassment', whereas one from an oppressed group often 'laughs at self, others, sees humour as a method of dealing with hypocrisy' (1989, p. 13).

Table 4.1: *Dominator and partnership beliefs*

	Dominator Model		Partnership Model
	Powerholders' Beliefs	*Social Activists' Beliefs*	*Partners' Beliefs*
Nature of the social system	Taken for granted to be highly stratified	Dominant groups have constructed as highly stratified	Work toward an egalitarian structure
Ideology about schooling	Meritocratic, fair, open	High degree of institutionalized oppression	Emphasis on relationships of interdependence that are democratic and egalitarian
Nature of school professionals	Fairminded, enlightened, benevolent, protectors, superior	Mostly well intended, but too many blindly carry out racist/classist/sexist practices	Used to dominating but capable of partnering
Nature of children and families who are members of subordinated groups	Culturally deficient, cannot be trusted to provide leadership	Strong, capable, resourceful	Strong, capable, resourceful, capable of partnering
Sources of school failure	Individuals' personal and groups' cultural deficiencies, lack of information or misunderstandings	Dominant groups and the institutions they have created	Patterns of interactions among groups that are marked by fear, distrust, dominance, resistance, coercion
Professional roles in resolution of these problems	Leaders, social control; don't trust others' ability to provide leadership	Need to be willing to be re-educated or get out of the way	Learn to collaborate, share resources and power
Parents'/community's role in resolution of these problems	Follow and support professionals' lead or at least not interfere	Their perspectives need to be included; they can exert leadership in designing solutions as actions for social change	Shared leadership, collaborate to achieve mutually agreed upon goals, interdependence
Direction of communication	One-way	Two-way	Two-way/multiple ways

As a female professor one might thus find it difficult to confront male domination among senior colleagues while at the same time behaving presumptuously in relationships with students and junior colleagues. As Table 4.1 illustrates, the dominator model generates conflict, distrust, and finger-pointing. While social activists may be more congruent with partnership than are powerholders' beliefs, their relationship within a dominator model is still conflictual. When both move toward a partnership model, both begin to exhibit different behaviours.

The pervasiveness of dominator ways of structuring social life are not just reduced to subjective ways in which we come to accept and protect any of our privileges, and accept and protect ourselves from oppressive relations. We live in a society whose major institutions and prevailing cultural patterns are far more oriented to the dominator model than to the partnership model (Eisler, 1987). This often makes us vulnerable to reproducing the dominator model even when we might be explicitly committed to promoting partnerships. Educational and political interventions are necessary for people to recognize how in their social interactions they contribute to maintaining a system that hurts them and others — when they are in a position of domination as well as when they are in a position of subordination. Resisting hegemony becomes a crucial task for those who are committed to partnership. This entails a conscious and sustained effort to identify social forces that pressure us to accept dominator dynamics and to challenge and transform those dynamics both at the personal and institutional levels (Koegel, personal communication 25 May, 1997).

In what follows we exemplify how the dominator model and the partnership model play themselves out when used to structure practices in multicultural teacher education that intentionally seek to form partnerships between school and community groups. We use the case of service learning projects to illustrate these models because, although community-based learning experiences are usually couched in the language of partnership, we believe they very often embody dominator intelligence. The process for breaking out of the dominator intelligence that permeates much of how we have come to understand what it means to be a school professional necessitates that we unveil the taken-for-granted modes of thought about the relationship between schools and the wider community. When they are structured on the basis of partnership intelligence, school–community partnership projects offer great potential for undermining the certainties that preservice teachers have regarding life in marginalized communities.

The following are fictionalized composite portraits based on specific service learning projects with which we are familiar. These examples demonstrate the types of projects that perpetuate dominator intelligence and those that afford students opportunities to develop the counter-ideology of partnerships. It is important to keep in mind that social practices, institutions, and people rarely enact pristine versions of these models. In practice, organizations based on the dominator model distinguish themselves from those based on the partnership model more in terms of the degree or emphasis given to things such as cooperation versus competition, fear versus trust, ranking versus linking, and so on (Eisler and Loye, 1990).

Application of Dominator/Partnership Distinction to Community-based Learning Projects

Teacher preparation programmes in the United States are increasingly discussing the use of community-based learning experiences as a part of preparation for cultural diversity (see, for example, Kahne and Westheimer, 1996; Tellez, et al., 1995; Wade, 1995). Service learning, which is becoming ever more popular on US university campuses, can be viewed as a form of community-based learning. Service learning is commonly defined as: 'a credit-bearing educational experience in which students participate in an organized service activity that meets identified community needs, and reflect on the service activity in such a way as to gain further understanding of course content, a broader appreciation of the discipline, and an enhanced sense of civic responsibility' (Bringle and Hatcher, 1996, p. 222). Service learning and other community-based learning experiences are usually structured as partnerships between the university and various community agencies. These partnerships, however, can be structured quite differently depending upon how programme developers define barriers to community development (Keith, 1996).

A Service Learning Project Based on Dominator Intelligence

At Everready University, teacher education students complete one of their field experiences working in a literacy programme that serves a low-income section of the city in which most of the residents are African–American or Latino. Most of the students in this teacher education programme are young white women from suburban areas. The main stated purpose of the service learning programme is to sensitize them to inner-city communities by having direct contact with members of that community. The faculty members teaching the service learning course chose this literacy programme as a placement primarily because its focus — teaching reading — relates directly to the work of the classroom teacher. The programme relies on volunteers and welcomes the university students, and the programme director — a white woman who used to be a classroom teacher — relates well with the university faculty.

At the beginning of every semester, the literacy programme director makes a short presentation to the teacher education students, prior to their work in the programme, in which she orients them to the programme and their role in it. Her presentation usually stresses the following ideas: a) the programme serves a very low-income area in which most people are poorly educated and many adults are illiterate; b) illiteracy is a result of the culture of poverty and perpetuates poverty; c) programme volunteers can help attack poverty by promoting literacy; d) people who are served by the programme appreciate it a great deal and will appreciate the volunteers' efforts, and; e) the volunteers will gain great satisfaction knowing they have helped someone else, and many volunteers return to serve year after year because they know they are helping.

The programme incorporates the preservice students fairly easily. It uses a particular literacy programme that includes a set of materials and teaching strategies that requires minimal training time. Most of the programme staff are white women, and they relate easily to most of the preservice teachers. The work of the programme is highly structured, asking both volunteers and service recipients to stick to a schedule of sessions.

This is a fairly popular field placement among the teacher education students. Most of them describe it as an 'eye-opener', as it is their first sustained inner-city experience. By the end of the semester, they describe the programme as having given them a better sense of the problems inner-city families face, and they also feel they are able to give something positive: education. Most of them feel they struggled while teaching literacy to adults, but also achieved some success. The volunteers' biggest complaint about the programme is that most clients do not follow the schedule very well, for a variety of reasons related to their own personal and familial lives. While most of them still do not wish to teach in inner-city schools, several of the teacher education students now feel excited about the possibility of 'helping' needy students.

As teacher education programmes in the US increasingly incorporate community field experiences as part of multicultural education initiatives, programmes like the one described above are frequently implemented. For reasons we will enumerate, we regard the above composite picture as illustrative of community–university collaborations that represent to a greater degree characteristics of the dominator model than those of the partnership model. Partnership is represented in the caring that drives most of these preservice teachers to volunteer in a community that they perceive as in need of assistance. It is also present in the idea of reciprocity — these students have something to learn from their interactions with people who differ from themselves. The programme itself is set-up in ways that foster a friendly and cooperative relationship among the various participants. Learning occurs in the absence of the coercive elements too often found in school-based learning activities.

The ideology of domination, however, looms more loudly. First, the leadership and most of the staffing for the programme are not from the community being served, but rather comes from white, wealthier neighbourhoods. When one considers the social location of the director, the staff, and the volunteers, collectively they are socially positioned quite differently from the clients they serve. Rather than interrogating the implications of this differential positioning, however, this service learning activity allows university students to enter into the social world of inner-city dwellers as it is organized and structured around the culture, lifestyle, assumptions, and power advantages of the white suburban people who run the programme.

Second, the structure and content of the programme are disconnected from African–American and Latino efforts to connect literacy with cultural empowerment (see, for example, Macedo, 1993; Peterson, 1991; Shannon, 1989). As a result, students are not given opportunities to question the programme's core assumptions. For instance, the programme is predicated on the assumption that the culture of inner-city people is the main source of their poverty, and that poverty can be alleviated by changing that culture. It follows then, that the materials and teaching strategies used have been imported from programmes developed in suburban cultural contexts, only minimally adapted to the local community. As such, the materials and teaching strategies operate as top–down mechanisms for defining and controlling literacy and the perpetuation of marginalization of people of colour these practices serve. By taking for granted where materials and implementation strategies should come from (experts), teacher education students' attention is diverted from analyses of culture and poverty, and from critique of the systemic social injustices that create pockets of illiteracy in one of the wealthiest countries in the world. If most of them do not think to find out how African–American and Latino educators, either locally or nationally, are framing and working with literacy, this programme is not raising questions about the alternative meanings of literacy or about the political implications of each of these meanings.

Third, the programme itself operates procedurally in ways that work better for the staff than for the clients. The schedule is a good example. Most of the volunteers like the highly structured schedule despite the fact that many of the clients miss sessions because of it. By not giving volunteers an opportunity to connect absentee-ism to established procedures, the programme can easily lead volunteers to view the clients as 'problem-ridden' and sometimes as 'irresponsible', reinforcing their belief that the community is 'culturally deprived' and the creator of its own underpriv-ileged position (see Weis, 1985).

Fourth, the source of communication and decision-making about the pro-gramme is largely one-way: *from* the programme director and staff *to* individual members of the community. As a former teacher, the director feels that she has expertise to offer the community whereas her clients, none of whom graduated from high school, lack that expertise. She is offering a service; the main choice of the clients is whether or not to accept it. This is a mode of communication most of the teacher education students view as natural and normal to their future role as teachers, particularly if they find themselves teaching in low-income areas. The director herself is unaware of this mode of communication partly because she does have some communication with directors of other agencies who are local to the com-munity. That communication, however, does not invite critique of her programme, but rather it revolves around occasionally coordinating her programme's events with other programmes and coordinating clients' needs with services offered by other programmes. The community has no substantive input into the programme; there is no 'feedback loop' in which assumptions undergirding the programme can be examined and renegotiated from the points of view of community members.

Fifth, the stated purpose of the programme, helping the predominantly white, middle-class preservice teachers to become sensitized to the inner-city, contributes to securing the dominance of whiteness in teacher preparation. Preservice teachers who come from the inner-city themselves might find little value in educational activities designed to bring awareness among their white, middle-class classmates. By this, we are not advocating the transparency of identity politics but we are suggest-ing that to disrupt the dominance of whiteness, strategies for consciousness raising must take into account the social location of all students, not just of those who are white (cf. McLaren and Torres, this volume). Elsewhere we have argued that because of their life experiences, most preservice teachers of colour and others who come from socially subordinated groups, do not need to be made aware by teacher education curricula of what it is like to be poor or to be an ethnic minority. To materialize the promises of greater educational equity that have been associated with increasing the numbers of teachers of colour in US primary and secondary schools, teacher education needs to make available experiences that help them to *politicize* their understanding of racism, help them to understand how formal schooling can be connected to the home and community life of their students, and help them understand how to translate their cultural knowledge into pedagogical practices (Montecinos, 1994; Sleeter, 1993).

A Service Learning Project Based on Partnership Intelligence

Central College's teacher education programme has a network of field experiences throughout the programme that attempt to link the college, community organizations, schools, and progressive community grassroots movements. Like Everready University and most other teacher education programmes in the US currently, the majority of the students are white and a sizable proportion are from either suburban or small town communities. Unlike Everready University, Central College has been working hard to recruit future teachers from urban and rural communities of colour in the local area through this college–community–school network.

As is true in most low-income communities, a wide variety of community agencies exist, run by a wide variety of people. The network began informally, and although it now has some formal structure, it still rests on an informal basis of mutuality. The college faculty members who developed the service learning component of the curriculum have over time developed collaborative relationships with people in a few community organizations and schools. For example, one faculty member is on the board of the local affiliate of the National Urban League (a predominantly African–American social service and civil rights organization), and another is on the board of the local chapter of LULAC (League of United Latin American Citizens, also a civil rights organization). About half of the faculty live in or adjacent to the inner-city. Some are members of local black or Latino churches. As a result of interacting with the black, Latino, and low-income communities in a variety of settings, they can orient their thinking regarding the needs of the community largely around the perspectives of the community members.

The faculty in Teacher Education at Central College have identified three goals for their students: to learn about the community from the perspectives of people who live there, to become acquainted with issues faced by the community, and to become acquainted with the political and educational work community people engage in to address these issues. To accomplish these goals, they sought partnerships with community agencies and community centres that were run primarily by community members. The University faculty got to know some of the directors and staff members of these agencies, and explored ways in which college student volunteers might be of help to the agencies and centres. For example, the local Urban League and a partner community centre had several programmes that could use volunteer help; they also needed help developing a newsletter and upgrading computer systems. The faculty were also especially interested in political action and advocacy efforts in the community, wanting teachers to critique and begin to challenge mainstream views that represented inner-city dwellers as the source of their problems in the areas of housing, health, education, safety, and so on (cf. Rattansi, this volume). In the case of the Urban League, although its mission was to serve the community rather than to work politically, many of its members were also members of the local chapter of the NAACP (National Association for the Advancement of Coloured People) — which was very active politically, and met regularly at the Urban League facility — and were willing to discuss with the university students their perspectives on the political tasks involved in community development.

At the same time, faculty members were also developing collaborative relationships with local schools. For example, several teachers were interested in improving literacy instruction, and were especially interested in using multicultural children's literature, helping Spanish-speaking students develop biliteracy skills, incorporating traditional family stories into literacy instruction, involving parents, and teaching students to create books about their own communities. The faculty and teachers worked together to develop strategies that fit the students in the schools, involving teacher education students in this process.

As they went through the teacher education programme, students experienced field placements in both community centres and schools. From their perspectives, there was remarkable continuity among the schools, the college, and the community, since the various people they worked with knew each other and worked together in a variety of contexts. No one seemed to be 'the' expert on issues, since the various professionals they worked with — knowledgeable as they were — also encouraged them to seek perspectives of other people. The students also experienced a fair amount of dissonance and disagreement, however. Their own perspectives and assumptions were challenged regularly, but they also discovered that the various people they had contact with did not necessarily agree with each other. There was no monolithic 'inner-city' perspective, but rather great variety in how people identified and viewed issues and situations. For example, parents, teachers, and community centre staff regularly had heated debates about how to approach Black English. These offered students and their instructors opportunities to understand how 'race', class, and gender intersect to find both allies and adversaries. By the time they finished student teaching, the teacher education students appreciated the complexity of issues teachers face, and the impossibility of representing cultural groups in monolithic terms, and they respected the diverse perspectives and areas of expertise of adults in the local community.

Central College's community-based learning programme clearly differs in important ways from Everready's, and exemplifies several dimensions of a partnership model. There was no dichotomy between service provider and recipient; rather, there was a fairly horizontal network of service exchange. The community organizations with which Central College worked were largely from the local community itself. Even the Urban League, an affiliate of a national organization, was directed by an African–American professional who lived in the community and was staffed by people who also lived in the community. While many of the people involved were not necessarily politically active, they shared the social locations, perspectives, cultures, and languages of the local community. The community organizations themselves worked as partners with local residents. In addition, the college faculty had developed partnership relations with the organizations, and with some local residents and teachers. Most of the teacher education faculty had not grown up in the local area and about two-thirds were white. As such, they made conscious choices to avoid taking on the role of experts. The partnership relationship was manifest in a variety of ways.

First, students' volunteer work in the community was structured around community needs, not around college convenience. Community centre directors selected volunteers based on information students supplied about their skills and available time; some students had to change their own schedules and often their time commitments extended beyond the traditional semester time structure. Students often had to rely on others in the community organization to teach them what to do. For many of the white teacher education students, this was the first time they were expected to learn from an adult of colour outside of the college. College faculty communicated regularly with the organizations to make sure the time they spent working with the students was worthwhile to the organization.

Second, the college, community organizations, and schools had developed organic collaborative working relationships that were visible on a regular basis as decisions were made. It was not unusual for teacher education students to see a college professor conferring with a community centre director in the director's office, or college faculty and teachers meeting with parents and community centre staff to solve a problem or initiate a programme. The structure and basic content of the teacher education programme was, in fact, a product of such collaboration.

Third, through this collaborative working relationship, teacher education students learned to teach in ways that connected with the children's cultural resources. For example, rather than learning to view literacy as a resource the 'haves' give to the 'have nots', they were learning to see language as richly woven into the daily fabric of cultural life, and literacy as a tool oppressed groups can master and appropriate for their own self-determination. In addition, they were learning to construct their notions of 'culture' around the complex, syncretized, lived cultures of real people. So often culture is presented to teachers as a static body of beliefs and practices presumed to belong to monolithic, bounded groups (cf. May, this volume). This view is more likely to go unquestioned when curriculum is enacted as something one imposes on children rather than as a product of co-construction with them.

Fourth, by connecting students with local political activity, the teacher education programme helped them to critique power relations between the community and sectors of the dominant society, recognize various forms of action that groups in the community are taking to attempt to shift the balance of power, critique the ideology of cultural deprivation many of them began the programme with, and learn how they can support ongoing community empowerment efforts. For example, through his work with computers in a community agency, a white student critiqued his initial assumption that the black community did not value computer literacy and realized that people cannot buy computers they cannot afford; he also gained some appreciation of the black community's use of the computer as a tool for national networking. The 'breakthrough' in his thinking occurred when he redirected his attention from what he had presumed was a cultural characteristic, to what he now understood as an economic issue. Consequently, he then began to ask how computer technology can be made more affordable to low-income communities.

Fifth, from its inception the programme had inclusive goals, designed to meet the needs of preservice teachers of colour as well as their white counterparts. It purported to go well beyond sensitizing its largely white, female, middle-class student body to the 'realities' of the inner-city. Flexibility, opportunities for linking with others in shifting roles, emphasis on dialogue, co-construction, understanding of multiple perspectives, and so on, provided ample opportunities for students to recognize how schooling could be constructed around the strengths of the community. Central College's approach to service learning provided students opportunities to frame four fundamental questions (Giroux, 1992) regarding the organization of schools, and to seek answers from school personnel as well as students, parents, and grassroots organizations in the communities they serve: a) what knowledge do we teach? b) how does this knowledge relate to students' lives? c) how can students engage with that knowledge? and d) how does curriculum and pedagogy facilitate individual and group empowerment?

Sixth, the structure and activities of the programme enabled students to see the problematics of assuming that pedagogical techniques that are advocated within the context of formal schooling can be unproblematically transported to other contexts, such as community youth centres, women's shelters, runaway shelters, and so on. Education in the community differs from school-based education in two important ways. First, education in the community is not structured around lesson plans. Risk, unpredictability, dialogue, and bonding are the words that define education outside of school bureaucracies (Smith, 1994). In fact, one of the hallmarks of this programme was that it allowed these future teachers to see how curriculum could emerge from social interactions. Second, schools are run by professionals who 'invite' students to join a space that has been territorialized and highly regulated by these professionals (Oliveira and Montecinos, in press). In contrast, school professionals do not have a legitimate claim to inhabiting the community centres and other places where education in the community occurs. In these places, the educator's presence is rendered authentic by securing, from the youth, an invitation to be there. The educator has to learn how to gain a space among the many social actors that compete to influence those who are to be educated.

In addition to fostering the political education of these prospective teachers, the type of immersion in community life afforded by Central College opens up the possibility for learning about pedagogical practices that are used by educators who work outside the formal schooling system. Community-based learning, in this way, provides alternative pedagogical frameworks that can be used to help prospective teachers to critique and improve what they are being taught in their teacher education courses. Additionally, by working with educators from the informal sector they can expand their instructional repertoire as they acquire pedagogical knowledge generated by various community educators students encounter. This pedagogical knowledge can, in turn, help teachers build bridges between students' school life and their community life. For example, Faltis (1993) recommends that teachers learn about community-based organizations that serve immigrant groups to be able to make parent referrals and seek assistance when communicating with parents (i.e., free translation services). Additionally, prospective teachers' involvement with the community should give them opportunities to figure out how to tap into the 'funds of knowledge' that families rely upon in their daily lives (Faltis, 1993; Moll, 1992).

Uncovering the Model of a Proposed Partnership

We end this chapter by offering the following set of interrelated questions that can help partners in education critically interrogate the structure and content of the partnership they are seeking to forge. Community-based learning as a part of the multicultural teacher education curriculum offers a way of helping teachers learn to engage in partnership models of institution-building. Community-based learning, however, must be carefully constructed, since the dominator context in which we structure these learning activities makes us vulnerable to impose dominator dynamics.

1 What is the assumptive framework regarding the barriers to community development that undergird the programme?

Any conception of multicultural education that views pluralism as a problem for professionals to solve embodies dominator intelligence. This can range from teacher-controlled multicultural curricula to community-based learning projects that frame the recipients of services as the problem. Projects that seek to expedite and make more efficient the bureaucratic organization for delivering services that have been structured with little or no input from those who are being served also represent dominator intelligence. Partnerships that prepare teachers for the exigencies of sharing power with children, and the wider communities they serve, need to be structured around programmatic needs and delivery systems that have been developed with substantive input from those who are being served.

2 Is the programme mainly framed as charity work or as addressing the root causes of issues?

Community-based learning experiences embody dominator intelligence when they are framed as charity rather than as social change — as providing *service to* communities rather than engaging in *service with* communities. In a thoughtful discussion of service learning, Kahne and Westheimer (1996) asked: 'In service of what?' They went on to contrast projects that teach young people to engage in charity with those that teach them to analyse community issues politically in order to learn to create political solutions. Charity — which frames oppressed communities as merely unfortunate and dominant groups as benevolent — is usually the view volunteers bring to service learning (Barber and Battistoni, 1993; Kahne and Westheimer, 1996; Serow,

1991). For example, primary-level students in one school collected 140 pairs of sneakers for Haitian children as their way of affecting world poverty (Kinsley, 1994). Why are Haitian children impoverished? What role do historic as well as contemporary relationships between rich and poor (and between predominantly white and predominantly black) nations play in their poverty? Those questions, which would lead to a vibrant multicultural curriculum and dialogue with Haitian people, and to social change initiatives, went unanalysed. In a partnership model, such questions come to the fore because they are central issues the service recipients face.

3   How are the various stakeholders' needs prioritized?

Dominator intelligence is used when, by virtue of their being initiated and controlled by professionals, multicultural efforts place professional educators' purposes first. For example, university-controlled community-based learning for multicultural teacher education usually places the needs of the university before the needs of the community. Research studies that evaluate the impact of these programmes are more likely to focus on what students gain from them than on what communities gain, even if the project has been framed in terms of social change rather than charity (see, for example, Serow, 1991; Wade, 1995). While many educators recognize the importance of partnership relationships, their interest is still often mainly in field experiences as an instructional model for students, more so than in strengthening strategies for meeting community needs (cf. Bringle and Hatcher, 1996).

4   How are roles assigned?

Dominator intelligence is present in activities that assign the parties to rigid roles that involve unequal hierarchical relationships (recipient/provider) versus flexible roles where each party is both a recipient of help as well as a help giver (Maybach, 1996). Teacher–parent relationships are very often based on a distinct hierarchy. Flexibility in roles requires that each partner makes explicit the contributions that one hopes one's partners can make to one's learning, to learn about the contributions that one's partners want to make, and the conditions under which these contributions and expectations can be materialized. This, in turn, gives each one opportunities to understand the strengths and weaknesses that each one brings to the relationship, critically examine the extent to which the structure and context of the activities are designed to capitalize on each other's strengths, and the possibilities that this partnership offers for everyone to grow together in ways that none could have accomplished had they remained isolated from each other.

5   Whose knowledge is considered most worthy of consideration when framing problems and solutions?

Dominator intelligence is present in curricula and programmes that privilege 'expert' knowledge over other community-based ways of knowing. This usually happens when curricula are chosen and taught by people from outside the community. It also tends to happen when teacher education students are expected to engage in skilful application of the techniques and theory they have learned in their university-based courses, when they enter classrooms or communities. Activities that are largely structured around course content tend to foster a separation between the teaching or service activity, and community life — for both the university student and the recipient. Partnerships on the other hand, seek connections and continuities as needs are jointly defined for both parties and shared decision-making is encouraged. A partnership model emphasizes co-creation, imagination, emancipation and ability to change.

6   How is feedback obtained and used?

Feedback in the dominator model is either ignored or used to figure out how to improve social control to attain the goals defined by those who are in charge. In partnership models, feedback is used to examine assumptions, renegotiate mutually agreed upon goals, and evaluate the extent to which the service provided is meeting the needs of both university students and the community.

7   How is conflict understood?

In the dominator model conflict is either ignored, suppressed, or attributed to inadequacies in the recipients. Partnerships address conflict in ways that allow both parties to grow and to learn. For example, absenteeism is not treated as a problem of the recipients of the service; rather, it is understood as a symptom of a disjuncture between service partners. To resolve conflict both parties must critically interrogate the context under which they are working together, their taken-for-granted assumptions, and the areas of misinformation they have about each other. On this basis, they can then develop solutions that take into consideration each other's needs, strengths, and limitations.

8   How are service activities structured throughout the curriculum?

In the dominator model, activities are structured in ways that commit students to form, at best, a short-term alliance with those who are seen as in need of help. Partnerships go beyond helping to solve an immediate need. They seek to structure activities that promote a commitment to participate in grassroots movements designed to remove barriers that created the need in the first place. Multicultural education efforts that are designed to help students understand the roots of social problems, and work to remove barriers as they work collectively with others, necessitate the coordination of activities across the curriculum, instead of such activities being attached to a single course or fragmented throughout. This continuity is critical because prolonged engagement with the community, access to a variety of contexts and resources, and ample time and experiences are required to revisit taken-for-granted assumptions and to learn how to develop cooperative relations with people preservice teachers see as different from themselves.

Conclusion

In the United States there is a widespread concern regarding the fragmentation of the civil society. To address this concern social policies that propel citizens towards community work and volunteerism are being widely advocated. In schools of education this has mainly taken the form of requiring prospective teachers to engage in service-learning projects. In the United States — contrary to the prevailing ideology that represents the country as open and fair — the visions of democracy, pluralism, and equality are largely unrealized for the poor, for people of colour, for women, for those who have disabilities, and for members of other socially subordinated groups. Under these conditions, building the civil society cannot be limited to asking university students to engage in charitable work. When multicultural education is understood as a social movement, teacher preparation that is multicultural must seek pedagogical practices that help prospective teachers move from charity towards justice, and from dominance to partnership.[1]

Note

1   We are grateful to Rob Koegel and Stephen May for their helpful comments and questions on earlier drafts of this chapter.

References

ADAIR, M. and HOWELL, S. (1989) *The Subjective Side of Politics*, San Francisco: Tools for Change.

ALLEN, G. (1992) 'Active citizenship: A rationale for the education of citizens?', in ALLEN, G. and MARTIN, I. (eds) *Education and Community: The Politics of Practice*, London: Cassell, pp. 130–44.

ARONOWITZ, S. (1992) *The Politics of Identity*, New York: Routledge.

BANKS, J. (1992) 'African American scholarship and the evolution of multicultural education', *Journal of Negro Education*, **61**, pp. 273–86.

BARBER, B. and BATTISTONI, R. (1993) 'A season of service: Introducing service learning into the Liberal Arts curriculum', *PS: Political Science and Politics*, **26**, pp. 235–41.

BARTOLOMÉ, L. (1995) 'The methods fetish', *Harvard Educational Review*, **64**, pp. 173–94.

BIKLEN, S. (1995) *School Work: Gender and the Cultural Construction of Teaching*, New York: Teachers College Press.

BRINGLE, R. and HATCHER, J. (1996) 'Implementing service learning in higher education', *Journal of Higher Education*, **67**, pp. 221–39.

CUMMINS, J. (1986) 'Empowering minority students: A framework for intervention', *Harvard Educational Review*, **56**, pp. 18–36.

DARDER, A. (1991) *Culture and Power in the Classroom*, New York: Bergin and Garvey.

DENSMORE, K. (1995) 'Education for literacy', *The Urban Review*, **27**, pp. 299–320.

EISLER, R. (1987) *The Chalice and the Blade*, San Francisco: Harper and Row.

EISLER, R. and LOYE, D. (1990) *The Partnership Way: New Tools for Living and Learning, Healing Our Families, Our Communities, and Our World*, New York: Harper San Francisco.

FALTIS, C. (1993) *Joinfostering: Adapting Teaching Strategies for the Multilingual Classroom*, Englewood Cliffs, NJ: Merrill/Prentice Hall.

FOUCAULT, M. (1972) *The Archaeology of Knowledge*, New York: Harper Colophon Books.

FREIRE, P. (1970) *Pedagogy of the Oppressed*, New York: Seabury Press.

FREIRE, P. (1973) *Education for Critical Consciousness*, New York: Seabury Press.

FREIRE, P. (1985) *The Politics of Education: Culture, Power, and Liberation*, MACEDO, D. (Trans.) South Hadley, MA: Bergin and Garvey.

GAY, G. (1983) 'Multiethnic education: Historical developments and future prospects', *Phi Delta Kappan*, **64**, pp. 560–3.

GAY, G. (1995) 'Mirror images on common issues: Parallels between multicultural education and critical pedagogy', in SLEETER, C. and McLAREN, P. (eds) *Multicultural Education, Critical Pedagogy, and the Politics of Difference*, Albany, NY: SUNY Press, pp. 155–90.

GILLBORN, D. (1992) 'Citizenship, "race" and the hidden curriculum', *International Studies in Sociology of Education*, **2**, pp. 57–73.

GIROUX, H. (1992) 'Post-colonial ruptures and democratic possibilities: Multicultural as antiracist pedagogy', *Cultural Critique*, **21**, pp. 5–39.

GRAMSCI, A. (1971) *Selections from Prison Notebooks*, New York: International Publications.

KAHNE, J. and WESTHEIMER, J. (1996) 'In service of what? The politics of service learning', *Phi Delta Kappan*, **77**, pp. 592–8.

KEITH, N. (1996) 'Can urban school reform and community development be joined? The potential of community schools', *Education and Urban Society*, **28**, pp. 237–68.

KINSLEY, C. (1994) 'What is community service learning? Children who can make a life as well as a living', *Vital Speeches*, **61**, pp. 40–4.

KOEGEL, R. (1995) 'Responding to the challenge of diversity: Domination, resistance and education', *Holistic Education Review*, **8**, pp. 5–17.

KOEGEL, R. (1996) 'Partnership intelligence and dominator intelligence: Their social roots, patterns, and consequences', Unpublished manuscript.

KRESS, G. (1985) 'Ideological structures in discourse', in VAN DIJK, T. (ed.) *Handbook of Discourse Analysis*, vol 4, London: Academic Press, pp. 27–42.

LADSON-BILLINGS, G. (1994) *The Dreamkeepers*, New York: Jossey-Bass.

LUCAS, T., HENZE, R. and DONATO, R. (1990) 'Promoting the success of Latino language-minority students: An exploratory study of six high schools', *Harvard Educational Review*, **60**, pp. 315–40.

MACEDO, D. (1993) 'Literacy for stupidification: The pedagogy of big lies', *Harvard Educational Review*, pp. 183–206.

MACINTYRE, A. (1984) *After Virtue* (2nd ed.), Notre Dame, IN: University of Notre Dame Press.

MAY, S. (1994) *Making Multicultural Education Work*, Clevedon, England: Multilingual Matters.

MAYBACH, C. (1996) 'Investigating urban community needs: Service learning from a social justice perspective', *Education and Urban Society*, **28**, pp. 224–36.

MOLL, L. (1992) 'Bilingual classroom studies and community analysis', *Educational Researcher*, **21**, 2, pp. 20–4.

MONTECINOS, C. (1994) 'Teachers of color and multiculturalism', *Equity and Excellence in Education*, **27**, 3, pp. 34–42.

MOSES, R., KAMII, M., SWAP, S. and HOWARD, J. (1989) 'The algebra project: Organizing in the spirit of Ella', *Harvard Educational Review*, **59**, pp. 423–43.

NG, R., STATON, P. and SCANE, J. (eds) (1995) *Antiracism, Feminism and Critical Approaches to Education*, Westport, CT: Bergin and Garvey.

NIETO, S. (1995) 'From brown heroes and holidays to assimilationist agendas: Reconsidering the critiques of multicultural education', in SLEETER, C. and McLAREN, P. (eds) *Multicultural Education, Critical Pedagogy, and the Politics of Difference*, Albany NY: SUNY Press, pp. 191–220.

OAKES, J. (1985) *Keeping Track: How Schools Structure Inequality*, New Haven, CT: Yale University Press.

OLIVEIRA, W. and MONTECINOS, C. (in press) 'Social pedagogy: A matter of presence, commitment, identification, and availability', *Teaching Education*.

O'HAIR, M. and BLASE, J. (1992) 'Power and politics in the classroom: Implications for teacher education', *Action in Teacher Education*, **14**, pp. 10–17.

PETERSON, R. (1991) 'Teaching how to read the world and change it: Critical pedagogy in the intermediate grades', in WALSH, C. (ed.) *Literacy as Praxis: Culture, Language and Pedagogy*, Norwood, NJ: Ablex, pp. 156–80.

SAN JUAN, E., JR. (1992) *Racial Formations/Critical Transformations*, Atlantic Heights, NJ: Humanities Press, International.

SEROW, R. (1991) 'Students and voluntarism: looking into the motives of community service participants', *American Educational Research Journal*, **28**, pp. 543–56.

SHANNON, P. (1989) *Broken Promises: Reading Instruction in Twentieth-century America*, Granby, MA: Bergin and Garvey.

SHOR, I. (1996) *When Students Have Power*, Chicago: University of Chicago Press.

SLEETER, C. (1993) 'How white teachers construct race', in McCARTHY, C. and CRICHLOW, W. (eds) *Race, Identity, and Representation in Education*, New York: Routledge, pp. 167–71.

SLEETER, C. (1996) *Multicultural Education as Social Activism*, Albany, NY: SUNY Press.

SLEETER, C. and GRANT, C. (1993) *Making Choices for Multicultural Education: Five Approaches to Race, Class, and Gender* (2nd edn.), New York: Merrill.

SLEETER, C. and McLAREN, P. (eds) (1995) *Multicultural Education, Critical Pedagogy, and the Politics of Difference*, Albany, NY: SUNY Press.

SMITH, M. (1994) *Local Education: Community, Conversation, Praxis*, Buckingham, England: Open University Press.

STANLEY, W. (1992) *Curriculum for Utopia*, Albany, NY: SUNY Press.

TELLEZ, K., HLEBOWITSH, P., COHEN, M. and NORWOOD, P. (1995) 'Social service field experiences and teacher education', in LARKIN, J. and SLEETER, C. (eds) *Developing Multicultural Teacher Education Curricula*, Albany, NY: SUNY Press, pp. 65–78.

TILLY, C. (1993) 'Social movements as historically specific clusters of political performances', *Berkeley Journal of Sociology*, **38**, pp. 1–30.

TOURAINE, A. (1988) *Return of the Actor*, Minneapolis, MN: University of Minnesota Press.

TROYNA, B. (1987) 'Beyond multiculturalism: Towards the enactment of antiracist education in policy, provision and pedagogy', *Oxford Review of Education*, **13**, pp. 307–20.

WADE, R. (1995) 'Developing active citizens: Community service learning in social studies teacher education', *Social Studies*, **86**, pp. 122–9.

WALSH, C. (ed.) (1996) *Education Reform and Social Change*, Mahwah, NJ: Lawrence Erlbaum Associates.

WEIS, L. (1985) *Between Two Worlds*, New York: Routledge and Kegan Paul.

5   Antiracist Education through Political Literacy: The Case of Canada

Kogila Moodley

Comparative Context

One can usefully distinguish between three types of ethnically divided societies. These three types derive from specific historical beginnings, different kinds of problems for state policies, and distinct forms of resistance and conflict resolution. They are: a) indigenous peoples, b) immigration societies, and c) nationalities in competition. All three types can be found within the same state boundary, as in Canada.

Indigenous Peoples

Indigenous minorities such as the San speakers (Bushmen) in Namibia and Botswana, the aboriginal peoples in North America and Australia, and the Maori in New Zealand, perceive themselves as the conquered owners of the original land. Although they claim title to large parts of state land and resources, they lack the voting strength or economic clout to achieve their aims, and usually appeal through the legal system to the self definition of liberal democracies. This symbolic power as 'First Nations' — in some cases, reinforced by treaties with the colonial power — can embarrass liberal states or even lead to mini-revolts by severely aggrieved people.

Even when indigenous peoples represent sizeable minorities, as in Mexico and other Latin American states, and in some regions in India, modern states often suppress their protests, if necessary by renewed genocide. In more liberal democracies, state policies towards the legitimate grievances of subjugated minorities have wavered between forced assimilation in residential areas and schools, legal suppression of cultural traditions, conversion by missionaries, benign neglect, or a welfare colonialism in Canada and Australia. More recently, limited autonomy and self-rule in education and policing on reservations has been granted (for educational developments see May, 1998). This corresponds with a cultural revivalism and ethno-exclusivism stressed by once nearly extinct but now growing and politically conscious aboriginal minorities, who do not consider themselves bound by the laws of the State of which they are 'forced citizens'.

Above all, indigenous peoples all over the world demand recognition of their special aboriginal status, with claims to the land as original owners dispossessed by conquest. In liberal democracies, such as Canada, courts decide about the entitlement of indigenous peoples. In some cases, court decisions and lengthy negotiations with state representatives have led to the recognition of substantial land claims, with compensation flowing from such newly confirmed ownership. Native title remains a controversial issue wherever democratic regimes followed conquest.

Immigration Societies

Immigration societies (or polyethnic states, see Introduction) can be divided into those that soon grant recognition to newcomers as equal citizens (the US, Canada, Australia) and those which treat foreign migrants as sojourners or 'guest workers' (Germany, Switzerland). The Central European countries do not perceive of themselves as immigration societies. Normally they do not allow double citizenship even to those second or third generation migrants born in the country. Only after stringent criteria of cultural assimilation are met do a small number receive passports of their country of residence. Xenophobia and anxiety about cultural alienation characterize some European countries which house up to 25 per cent official foreigners. By contrast, Canada and Australia grant citizenship quickly and easily. They have adopted (at least in recent times) an official policy of multiculturalism, celebrating diversity as a source of enrichment and national unity. A common patriotism based on loyalty to the constitution and the ideology of upward mobility serves as a binding glue for the newcomers in traditional immigration societies. In the United States, the immigrants are supposed to melt into an American society that is perceived as a mixture of people with different origins. This 'melting pot' ideology has not prevented the continued survival of ethnic identities. In contrast, ethno nationalism derived from ancestry excludes those not of the same mythical descent in Europe.

It is important to note that immigrants everywhere primarily hope for individual integration and mobility and not autonomy or special treatment as in the case of indigenous peoples. Immigrants do not aim at establishing a new state but strive to adapt as individuals into the new homeland and take advantage of its better opportunities.

Nationalities in Competition

The most problematic of the three categories is that of divided societies with competing nationalities bound to a geo-historical territory in which they strive collectively for dominance, or equal treatment, or even secession. Nationalist mobilization of a distinct group of people trying to maintain their own institutions based on different cultural, linguistic, religious or ethno-racial mythologies can lead to severe strife, unless federalism or power sharing satisfies the elites on all sides to adhere to agreed-upon political rules. Self-reliant competing nationalities in multiethnic states have the capacity to change the balance of political power or even destroy the state, which is not possible in the first two cases discussed.

In the case of Canada, all three types of minorities may be found within the national context. Hence educational programmes based on an integrative multiculturalism face some challenges. Such programmes attempt to improve inter-group relations through recognition of each other's cultural backgrounds, and awareness of shared similarities and differences. They also aim to teach a moral abhorrence of racist practices which are disrespectful of 'difference'. While this approach may appeal to immigrant groups, it is received very differently by Canadian aboriginal groups and by Québec nationalists. Their particular and unique identities and prior claims to resources and territory, they argue, are threatened by an equalizing multiculturalism. It nullifies their claims.

Forms of Racism

Teachers and administrators throughout Canada experience various forms of racism among the multiethnic populations they teach. Sometimes this is blatant, explicit, overt, while at other times tensions are covert and less visible. Individual pupils engage in name-calling or violence, sometimes entire groups battle each other. These animosities may emanate from a range of sources: more powerful groups take advantage of less empowered ones, majority group students line up against newer minorities, recent immigrants attempt to assert a threatened identity. Throughout, First Nations students continue as victims in one form or another. The question is how to deal with these issues in a school system that is already 'stretched' with numerous demands such as for different kinds of instruction and recognition of difference. Nor are these problems only present in inner-city, lower income schools. They now invade the peaceful surroundings of suburbia as well. All this takes place within a culture of 'politeness' and 'tolerance' which chooses to overlook such unpleasantries in the hope that 'things will work themselves out'. To locate this we need to understand what racism is all about, how it fits within the context of a multicultural society, and how schools and educators respond (Moodley, 1995).

What is racism? It can be defined as the ideology of ascribing inferior characteristics to physically different people. In the nineteenth century version of racism people of colour or different origin (Jews) were said to behave in distinct ways because of their inherent 'nature'. European colonialism and slavery justified its conquest with the superior 'racial' qualities of the colonizers. The alleged superior products of genetic evolutionary selection were destined to rule over intellectually backward humans. Nowadays a 'new racism' (cf. May; Rattansi; Short and Carrington, this volume) is said to use cultural difference instead of biology for discrimination. The attribution of ability or lack of ability to individuals' immutable cultural traits is grounded in similar essentialist explanations as biologically-based racism. At the overt political level, minority ethnic groups are presented as the eternal cultural 'outsider', threatening national identity and unity.

Lately, any attitudes that rely on universally valid norms originating in the European tradition are considered racist or ethnocentric because of the European history of exclusion and subjugation with its in-built arrogance for people of colour. Yet racism or ethnocentrism are not confined to Europeans alone. Indians or Japanese are known to be as racist toward outsiders as are Tutsis toward Hutus or Arabs toward Africans. What is common to all these intergroup relations is that some groups have greater power and cultural currency to affect the lives of others; their greater power translates into higher status and denigration of inferior, low status outgroups.

Oppression and racism are heavy accusations. They should not be bandied around lightly and without evidence, notwithstanding the fact that victims know when they are being discriminated against and that it is not always easy to demonstrate the barriers and hostilities experienced. As Morton Weinfeld reminds us 'if everything is harassment, racism and genocide, then nothing is harassment, racism or genocide' (1996, p. 122). Analytical insights cannot be free of passion but must avoid distortion by inflationary language and dubious categories. A rhetoric of indignation should not substitute for an analysis of why people denigrate others. Preaching hardly even penetrates an authoritarianism predisposed to hate. Those individuals harbour deep seated resentments. They are often persons with low self-esteem who try to make themselves superior by debasing others. Racists almost need more empathy than contempt. Nor can reprehensible attitudes be legislated. Only their behavioural expressions need to be criminalized.

'Zero tolerance', as advocated in Britain, allows antiracist advocates to claim victory in public, 'whilst the informal cultures of racism which actually sustain these practices are relegated to an untouchable realm of "private attitudes"' (Cohen, 1992, p. 96). When racism awareness training attempted to intervene at this level with the same procedures as were applied in the public realm, this enforced privatization 'in many cases resulted in more secretly coded forms of expression, which actually strengthened popular resistance to antiracism' (Cohen, 1992, p. 97). 'Political correctness' pressure drives unpopular expressions underground. Contested issues such as immigrant quotas become a taboo instead of being subject to an informed public debate and input (cf. Rattansi, this volume).

Particularly for the learning experience in the classroom it would seem important that students are allowed to work through their own stereotypes without being embarrassed or silenced from the outset. All too often antiracist advocates display a self-righteous superior morality that by definition exempts the speaker from the sins of racism. Antiracist pedagogues patronizingly lecture others in proper behaviour, spread enlightenment about neglected voices and hope that their own indignation or alleged victimhood will either persuade or cow racists into submission. This assumption is not only naive but may well be counterproductive.

Similar critiques of antiracism have been expressed by the political Left in Britain. Gilroy, for instance, proposes:

> that we reject the central image of ourselves as victims and install instead an alternative conception which sees us as an active force working in many different ways for our freedom from racial subordination. The plural is important here for there can be no single homogeneous strategy against racism because racism itself is never homogeneous. It varies, it changes and it is always uneven. (1990, p. 83)

Gillborn (1995) on the other hand, cautions against the abandonment of the antiracist cause based on this critique. Instead he calls for a more reflexive, self-critical approach which continues to see the need to address 'race' and racism as indispensable concepts. He argues:

> A critical and reflexive antiracism cannot be constrained by the narrow politics of 'racial dualism' which denies the importance of culture and cultural racisms; but neither must it lapse into ethnic absolutism that mirrors the New Right's ethnicist discourse. Cultures are never fixed; the dynamic relations between changing ethnic categories are reflected in everyday interactions, including the school-lives of young people. An awareness of the new cultural politics of difference offers a lens on the racism at work between and within various minority communities — a reality often denied by previous antiracist analyses. An awareness of hybrid identities and 'cultural syncretism', however, should not blind us to the continuing power of traditional 'racial' dichotomies — categories that have genuine currency in countless contexts and can still prove fatal. (1995, p. 90)

Canadian Bigotry Compared

How prevalent is racism in Canadian society? Are Canadians more or less prone to xenophobia and stereotyping of others than the US, Britain, France or Germany? Is Canadian ethnocentrism different from the distrust of 'uncivilized foreigners' in China or the disdain and social distance of a Brahmin towards lower caste members in the Hindu caste system?

The evidence from representative opinion surveys among Canadians is contradictory. All opinion surveys reveal substantial approval of multiculturalism and at the same time some anxiety about the pace of ethnic transformation. In a 1996 Angus Reid Poll, 80 per cent agreed with the statement: 'Canada's multicultural make-up is one of the best things about this country'. However 41 per cent also approved that 'Canada is changing too quickly because of all the minorities we have now'. A 1993 poll shows that a significant minority of the general public feels that new Canadians should be restricted in terms of how much influence they are permitted to exercise over the future of the country. Over one third say that they are angered when they see new immigrants on television demanding the same rights as other Canadians. Contrary to the goals of official multiculturalism, 57 per cent of Canadians urge minorities to become more like most other Canadians rather than preserve their cultural or linguistic traditions. Canadians are particularly angered when they perceive immigrants importing their political troubles from 'back home'. However, only 15–20 per cent can be described as hard core anti-immigrant in the sense that they wish to preserve a white Canada, deny the material benefits from immigration, and advocate a (hypothetical) return of immigrants. This figure is not higher than comparable right wing support for Le Pen in France, the National Front in Britain, or neo-Fascist parties in Germany. All western democracies have to cope with anti-democratic populist fringe groups, who are generally not a threat by themselves but by their subtle pressure in pushing establishment parties to the right.

The best indicator for the levels of racism in Canada is provided in a survey among potential victims. While a majority of Canadians as a whole label racism as a significant problem in the country and 60 per cent 'sense racism has been growing' (Reid Report, 1991, p. 6) only 39 per cent of urban Chinese-Canadians in Toronto and Vancouver report that they have experienced discrimination (Reid Report, 1994, p. 9). This relatively low figure of a representative sample of 800 Chinese is truly surprising and could lead to the suspicion that many victims engage in denial, or blame themselves, in order to live with an unpleasant reality. The low 39 per cent of reported personal discrimination remains constant with length of stay in the city and is slightly lower in Toronto (where Blacks seem a more obvious target) than in Vancouver, without a significant black population, but with Indo-Canadians and First Nations people as equally ready targets. However, the explanation of self-denial of outsider status cannot be upheld in light of the fact that in the same sample 81 per cent of Chinese-Canadians report that they 'do not feel accepted' in Canada. Obviously, Canadian racism nowadays expresses itself less in direct personal discrimination and much more in a cultivated social distance to the constructed 'other'. Our very everyday language reflects this distance between 'us' and 'them', the ingroup and the outgroup: the term 'ethnic' is used only for so called 'Third World' immigrants, as if Scottish or French people had no ethnicity (cf. Kalantzis and Cope; May, this volume).

Euphemisms about the unfamiliar arrivals abound. Since racist discourse became a taboo, a government Green Paper on immigration in the 1980s focused all its attention on 'people with novel and distinct features', as if those phenotypical characteristics were the cause of all problems. Colour is seen as the potential barrier for integration. The difference however lies always in the eye of the beholder who socially constructs otherness. It is not the colour difference that matters but the stereotypes we attribute to and associate with different appearance.

There is no doubt that the majority of Canada's bigots view their political home in the Reform Party, which regularly receives 20 per cent of the popular vote nationally, and much higher percentages in British Columbia and Alberta in provincial elections, swelled by protest voters and disillusionment with provincial governments. However, an important difference between right wing parties in Europe and the Reform party in Canada, lies in the ideology of the leadership. Le Pen in France, or Frey in Germany are ethnocentric and racist to the core. Like the National Front in Britain, they explicitly mobilize and stimulate latent racist sentiment. The populist Reform Party leader Preston Manning, on the other hand, does not encourage overt racism in his party but attempts to contain it, whether for reasons of expediency or conviction. Privately, the autocratic Manning is a Christian fundamentalist, but (he would argue) not a racist. The name-calling and labelling of the Reform Party leadership by its political foes in a recent fierce election campaign should not be taken at face value. To label all Reform voters racist is as false as calling voters of the New Democratic Party, communists. To be sure, the Reform Party has benefitted from widespread anti-immigrant sentiment. But by disavowing and expelling some of its more outspoken racists, the party leadership keeps a lid on the public expression of bigotry. In Germany or France, in contrast, anti-foreigner attitudes can be openly expressed. During the long debate about asylum restrictions, German ethnocentrism in different guises has almost acquired a certain political respectability. As far as the right-wing political parties stand in a symbiotic relationship with the long-time ruling Christian Democrats in Germany, they exercise influence far beyond their support in moving the government to the right.

In the Canadian political system on the other hand, all political parties have to look to the centre for votes if they wish to grow. This reinforces the fundamental Canadian consensus and moderates ethnic extremism. Without proportional representation, ethnic or racist parties have no chance in a Westminster parliamentary system of winner-takes-all. All parties have to compete for the sizeable non-Anglo Saxon/non-French vote, if they wish to be players on the national scene. With the exception of regional parties, such as the Bloc Québécois, the national parties (including the aspiring Reform Party) cannot afford to alienate important segments of the electorate. They would all rather treat sensitive issues such as immigration or 'race relations' as a taboo in an election campaign than debate different viewpoints openly. This explains the strangely depoliticized elections in Canada. Important issues, such as environmental protection, women's concerns, foreign policy or education are not discussed at all and voters are merely exposed to variations of apple pie and motherhood themes, like job creation and deficit reduction. In contrast, the political debate in Germany and Europe as a whole remains far more grounded in intractable ideological positions and principles in which the 'foreigner' figures as an important symbolic threat to collective purity and solidarity.

Visible minority members are confronted with the majority attitude that they 'own' the country. The 'visibly different' are expected to be forever grateful for having been let in. They are seen to never truly belong, because the sense of belonging includes the imagined prior ownership in which the visibly different immigrants do not partake in the very history of initial European settlement. This makes the 'visibles' eternal trespassers, both in the view of the dominant group but also sometimes in the eyes of the 'intruders' who internalize majority attitudes towards them.

A dialectic of multiculturalism results in similar unintended consequences. Multiculturalism is intended to ensure equity through representation by highlighting origins elsewhere. At the same time, origins of dominant white groups wane into irrelevance as they exercise dominance and a 'natural' claim to ownership (cf. May; McLaren and Torres, this volume). However, the more the culture of the 'others' is celebrated, the less their claim to the local is emphasized.

Everyday Racism

How is everyday racism produced and reproduced within the educational system? The school simultaneously holds out the promise of mobility and opportunity, yet at the same time teaches and reinforces hierarchy and stratification in its day to day operations.

What are the social processes in everyday practices through which ideologies of superiority and inferiority are reproduced? Three areas stand out: firstly the content of education, secondly, hierarchies of language, and thirdly, the hidden curriculum.

Most curricula privileges whiteness as the norm, and in that sense is a racialized text (cf. McLaren and Torres, this volume). Like women, ethnic minorities are seldom portrayed as active agents in history, geography or literature for instance. They seldom transcend stereotyped roles. As Toni Morrison puts it: 'certain absences are so stressed, are so ornate, so planned, they call attention to themselves: arrest us with intentionality and purpose like neighbourhoods that are defined by the population held away from them' (1989, p. 28). In literature, writing by ethnic minorities is referred to as 'postcolonial' or 'Commonwealth' writing, seldom entering the hallowed confines of 'literature'. For the most part colonialism is not presented as economic exploitation, conquest and slavery but almost a form of paternalistic benevolence through which primitive savages became civilized, westernized Christians. Yet the very term 'privileging' is inaccurate, if one considers, as Pinar (1993) points out, that it is not only the marginalized who suffer, but the privileged as well in so far as they live in ignorance that their knowledge is racialized knowledge.

The culture of de facto monolingualism, albeit in a bilingual, multicultural country like Canada,[1] implicitly teaches a ranking of other languages. Other languages are benignly labelled 'heritage' languages, as though English or French are not 'heritage' languages as well. However, beyond this is the informal culture of a carefully learned 'embarrassment' which non-English or non-French speaking students experience when their languages are used in the public domain of school. What is it that is communicated in the hidden curriculum that transmits this lack of value of difference? How does this laundering of difference take place? What happens to those who can launder their accents but not their skin colour?

Internalized domination and self racism are indelibly etched in students' conceptions of themselves and 'received as truth because they are transmitted in the context of authority, that is the classroom' (Brittan and Maynard, 1985, p. 158). Furthermore, these views are also shaped by the family and wider society. In schools in British Columbia, Canada, students in group discussions speak openly about their experiences with racism.[2] They speak of routine racist slurs in school corridors, classrooms and on the sports grounds. This is frequently reported to be accompanied by acts of violence. Graffiti in gyms, on playground walls and toilet doors sometimes include swastikas. What some students find abhorrent is that no provisions are made to remove them immediately. Others complain that school 'supervisors' within whose hearing racist slurs are made, do nothing about this. As one Indo-Canadian student put it, 'You see these supervisors wearing antiracism badges, but what's the worth in that if you're going to stand around and not do anything'. All too often schools see racial incidents as a conflict of personalities, and as nothing more than that. Teachers should be given workshops to know what racism is all about, so that they can detect their own biases. A student of Filipino descent who claims to have been roughed up and demeaned by name-calling, speaks of how it shattered his confidence and left him with 'no courage to go to school'. The hardest thing for him was that like many other minority children he kept the hurt to himself, since he did not wish to burden his immigrant parents with the problem. 'They don't have the language to face the school system, so its better if they're left out of it . . . they believe in schools as fair places . . . why should I shatter that belief!' (cf. Nieto, this volume).

Other outcomes of a racially charged climate are when minority students engage in outbursts of self hate, putting down their own group members and joining more powerful peer groups in denigrating people like themselves. Recent arrivals acquiring English as a second language are often the victims of scapegoating by other group members who have become acculturated and learnt the new currency of intra-group dominance. Students also spoke of their own efforts to educate their parents, and agreed that everyone has to take responsibility for combatting racism.

On the subject of racialization and children and its implications for schools, Hatcher and Troyna (1993) make five useful points. Firstly, they recognize the significance of racism for minority children. Secondly, they argue that 'race' is a significant element in the lives of the majority group child, both in their social relationships as well as in their understanding of society. Thirdly, 'race' does not work in isolation but is 'interfused with other ideologies and social processes in children's lives' (1993, p. 123). Fourthly, 'among white children there is a spectrum both of beliefs about "race" and of ways in which "race" operates in social inter-action' (1993, p. 123). The relationship between the two is not one of simple correspondence: interactional processes have their own dynamics. Finally, processes of racialization of children's attitudes and social behaviour are often fluid, fragmented and inconsistent.

Hatcher and Troyna therefore argue 'that schools need to establish effective procedures to implement a clear and firm policy to deal with racist incidents, as part of a wider policy addressing issues of conflict between children' (1993, p. 124). Yet while this may reduce the occurrence of racist incidents, it may not get at the roots of racism.

> Schools therefore need to find ways in the curriculum to help children to engage with how 'race' works in their lives. To reflect cultural diversity positively and to teach about racism in society are both vital, but it is equally important to connect these interventions with children's own lives by bringing children's relationships and the conflicts within them including racialized forms, into the curriculum itself. (1993, p. 124)

In a similar vein, George Dei, a Canadian antiracist theorist attributes black student underachievement to the institutionalized policies and practices of exclusion and marginalization that organize public schooling and make them feel unconnected to the system. Their experiences are considered irrelevant, and they are suspicious of teachers' pedagogies. He proposes as a response, that 'skin colour should be an important criterion around which to rally in the fight for a just redistribution of material means' (1996, p. 19). To implement this, he promotes the concept of an 'African-centred' secondary school model, to meet the needs of black students facing frustration and alienation (cf. Nieto, this volume). Antiracist education in this view serves as a unifying force for oppressed groups who abhor social oppression and are prepared 'to fight the prevailing culture of dominance' (1996, p. 24).

In contrast to other forms of antiracist education, models such as this differ in that they aim at strengthening the excluded minority in order to deal with the effects of racism. Other studies in implementation aim at institutional transformation for multiethnic schools. Two exemplary works stand out as theoretically sophisticated and nuanced in conceptualization. These are Stephen May's (1994) careful documentation of structural reorganization at Richmond Road School in New Zealand, which led to the successful implementation of a *critical* multicultural education within the school, and David Gillborn's (1995) study of antiracism across the curriculum in selected British schools.

Canadian Teachers' Views

That said, considerable difficulties remain in implementing successful multicultural and antiracist education programmes in schools, not least because of the often ambivalent responses of teachers to such programmes. In a recent study by Solomon and Levine-Rasky (1994) the views of over 1000 teachers, school administrators, multicultural and antiracist advisors in 57 elementary (primary) and secondary schools from five school boards across Canada were sought on the subject of multi-cultural and antiracist education. Educators varied widely in their philosophies, concepts and practices of antiracist and multicultural education. In many instances these ideas were seen as unwelcome challenges to their teaching practices. For the most part, antiracist education was viewed as merely reactive to potentially explosive racial conflicts. Multicultural education was perceived as additive in nature, not a core issue for all sensitive teachers.

Solomon and Levine-Rasky reiterate the findings of several previous studies, such as the Fisher and Echols (1992) study of the Vancouver School Board, that while there was a good deal of support *in principle* for antiracist and multicultural education, when considered from the view of practice, responses ranged from accommodation to resistance (cf. Carrim and Soudien, this volume). Accommodation they point out takes the shape of passive acceptance of multicultural education and antiracist education, to active advocacy and risk taking. Accommodating educators were engaged in revising their pedagogic orientations, classroom and school-wide practices, and challenging conservative political views represented by various school staff members. Educator resistance, which predominated in the study, involves anything from a seemingly harmless denial of the need for multicultural education or antiracist education, claims of curricular overload or inaccessibility of resource materials, to a more provocative unwillingness to question beliefs and philosophy.

Those who resisted often expressed a desire to adhere to a traditional interpretation of provincial curriculum guidelines. They viewed suggestions about curriculum innovation or intervention as a violation of their professional autonomy, and saw monitoring of antiracist programmes as superfluous and disruptive of their collegial relations. They feared 'affirmative action' as a way of addressing inequity, and were critical of paid 'race relations' consultants to advise school boards about reform. Lack of rewards for effective implementation of equity policies, as well as vague imprecise policies, caused discontent. Compared to their preference for ethnocultural equity, the language of antiracist education was experienced as negative. The articulation of 'race', racialization and racism in the schools was considered 'discomforting material for an educational arena'. The use of terms like racial anger and accusations of racism were considered offensive. Antiracist education, in their view, would be necessary if we had problems, but we don't, so 'if is isn't broke, don't fix it!'. Multicultural and antiracist education were seen as antithetical to teaching literacy and numeracy within an assimilative context. Contrary to its espoused goal of critical thinking, antiracist education was considered to be reverse indoctrination which was potentially inflammatory in creating social conflict and thus likely to be counterproductive. Another source of dissension was the inadequate provision of empirical evidence to convince teachers of the need for innovation. This was an affront to their professionalism. What they were expected to do in these antiracist programmes, it was argued, was simply good teaching practice, so why have a separate programme? Indifference, lack of time, and the need to focus on exam preparation were cited as reasons for non-compliance. Finally, the prevailing assimilative tone underlying practice is best summed up in the statement of one educator: Peoplehood can only be based on 'an absolute and ironic erasure of difference' (cited in Solomon and Levine-Rasky, 1994, p. 36).

It is not surprising therefore, that attempts to bring about change in education through professional development programmes meet with considerable resistance. Such transformative initiatives in pluralistic societies touch at the personal locus of teachers in terms of class, political ideologies, value orientations, and membership within the dominant-subordinate group spectrum. Similar resistance is reported for British schools (Brandt, 1986; Gillborn, 1990).

Multicultural and Antiracist Education as Official Ideology

Does official multiculturalism in Canada facilitate or obfuscate the school's struggle against racism? As a state policy designed by Trudeau's Liberals in 1971, it was meant to cope with the residual hostility towards immigrants, to garner the immigrant vote for the ruling party and to address the interests of the third force of non-English, non-French Canadians by elevating their claims to equal status with the English and French charter groups. It is therefore no wonder that Québec separatists as well as First Nations' nationalists reject multiculturalism because it equalizes their charter entitlement as well as undermines aboriginal rights. However, Canadian multiculturalism has undergone many changes from the song and dance days of its beginnings. An essentialist 'museums culture' has given way to official equity and antiracist efforts that are supposed not only to celebrate lifestyles but to guarantee equal life chances as well (Moodley, 1983).

Multiculturalism's right wing critics deplore an imagined divisiveness resulting from the official state policy that is said to undermine national unity. Left wing critics point to the symbolic manipulation that pretends power and class differentials in a common consumer society can be overcome by the celebration of diversity and mutual tolerance.

Both perspectives ignore valuable benefits of official multiculturalism. Psychologically, multiculturalism levels the traditional hierarchy. Official multiculturalism includes the newcomers in the cultural construction of 'Canadianness'. Multiculturalism makes immigrants officially welcome at little cost to the State. The symbolic acceptance prevents the official status of permanent strangers, both in the definition of 'the other' by the dominant majority, but even more importantly in the eyes of the newly arrived themselves.

At the same time the official tolerance patronizes. The tolerant majority and its State wallows in a self-congratulatory confirmation of its open-mindedness. The graciously accepted 'others' are expected to be thankful for the multicultural generosity. As Vijay Agnew has pointed out: 'Multiculturalism offers compensation to the powerless by 'accepting' them but not by giving them power or privilege. Rather than challenging Canadian political and social structures, it reinforces them' (1996, p. 35). Such a challenge can hardly be expected from official state policy, unless its targets exploit its inherent contradictions.

What recommendations can we then offer about the most successful strategy for combatting racism? Apart from the obvious sensitivity and leadership expected from opinion makers like educators in racist incidents, there is only one recommendation which can be wholeheartedly endorsed: the best way to eliminate prejudice is the *sociological understanding* of racism, its functions and ever changing forms. Racism is neither eradicated by preaching tolerance nor reduced by providing information that contradicts the stereotypes of the 'other'. Unless the predisposing conditions for denigration are addressed, the racist mind finds rationalizations for inferiorizing ever changing targets. The behaviour or appearance of the minority hardly influences the authoritarian character who is conditioned to hate, since the victim is interchangeable. Just as psychoanalytic therapy aims at making conscious the unconscious — transforming the id into ego, in Freud's terms — so the most lasting cure is to make the prejudiced individual understand why she or he cherishes such deep resentments. As we are all prejudiced to varying degrees, this political education in the most genuine sense should be geared to everyone, not just individuals singled out for special consciousness raising. Political literacy immunizes against racist temptations.

Policies, procedures, consequences and accountability for racist incidents obviously need to be in place in all schools. So too should compulsory education in the skills to deal with a multiethnic clientele for teachers, police personnel, social workers or hospital staff. Sadly, with few exceptions, this is not the case, despite all the lip service given to cross-cultural communication. Deterrence and communication skills, as necessary as they are, however, do not substitute for political literacy.

It is this wider context of understanding racist behaviour that is missing in all the noble attempts to fight an obvious evil. Instead of self-righteously demonizing racism, the widespread need for such a mentality has to be understood (cf. Rattansi, this volume). The need grows out of unfulfilled individuals who have no other options to establish a secure identity, but to debase others. Social conditions increasingly deprive people of the security and self-confidence that would militate against the need to stigmatize others. With the decline of such self-realization in a political economy where more and more people are declared superfluous, scapegoating and other artificial forms of self-realization increase.

Such insights link individual psychology with the social structure at large in which character development is always embedded. Successful antiracism in this deeper sense is predicated upon societal transformation. However, an apolitical consumerism that glorifies the private realm at the exclusion of the 'tainted' public sphere does not grasp the political significance of racism, let alone envisage the alternative that would eliminate the need for racial stigmatization. In short, the best job we as educators can do to combat racism is to ensure a cosmopolitan political literacy.

Cosmpolitan Political Literacy

What would such a cosmopolitan political literacy entail? It would be based on a sound education aimed at providing an *historical* understanding about the nature of prejudice, discrimination and racism. This historical knowledge would draw upon a *comparative* and *international* perspective, cosmopolitan in nature. The underlying questions would focus on how local specifics differ from discrimination elsewhere and why particular manifestations of inequality develop in the way they do. What role do the State, public compliance and specific group interests play in allowing unique characteristics to unfold? Critical analytical skills constitute the motivating force to decode mythologies and demystify popular ideologies. Students would be encouraged to question conventional wisdom. Students would develop analytical skills in distinguishing, for instance, apartheid from fascism, old and new forms of racism, as well as ethnic, cultural and gender based essentialism. Racism as an explanatory concept could itself become the focus of critical inquiry.

Peter McLaren and Rodolfo Torres (this volume) reiterate just this point when they refer to a lack of political imagination in discussions of multicultural and antiracist education that are anchored in a black–white binarism. The consequences of this, they maintain, camouflage 'the particular historical and contextual dimensions that give rise to differing forms of racism throughout the globe'. They argue: 'as long as a black–white dichotomy continues to be employed unproblematically, multicultural [and antiracist] education will remain deeply invested in its own generalized incapacity to elucidate and to challenge new racialized formations' (p. 46). Instead, the case is made for a plurality of historically specific *racisms*, not all of which employ explicitly the idea of 'race'.

What this means can be summarized best by clarifying seven different manifestations of racism:

- *Legal* racism, epitomized in apartheid South Africa and the 'Jim Crow Laws' of the southern US, both of which have now been abolished. As in the case of slavery previously, public opinion and effective forms of resistance such as the Civil Rights movement, strikes and economic boycotts turned against such obvious systems of inequality.
- *Scientific* racism, which was biologically rationalized, and that once justified colonial rule with its assertions of the superior intellectual and genetic qualities of European conquerors. It has also gone out of fashion and has become largely discredited.
- Subtle *social* racism is experienced subliminally through a cultural hierarchy of arrogance and may be even more debilitating in its effects than legalized collective discrimination. It has frequently replaced the previous cruder forms of discrimination and exclusion.
- *Cultural* racism, through a Eurocentric focus in the selection of what constitutes valuable and worthwhile knowledge, neglects non-European sources. Students learn to question the assumption of universal applicability of western values and are introduced to an understanding of cultural relativism without falling uncritically into the post modernist trap (cf. May, this volume).
- *Economic* racism which survives as the most significant indicator of an unaddressed past. Iniquitous educational and opportunity structures, and barriers in hiring practices, serve to reinforce unequal life chances. Ethnic groups are locked into positions without chances of mobility.
- The *religious* racism of the Hindu caste system likewise stigmatizes groups and places them firmly in an unequal division of labour. Students learn that racism is not only a black–white phenomenon but occurs wherever segments are discriminated on the basis of ancestry or group membership into which they are born.
- *Psychological* implications of denigration and exclusion based on racism, focuses on how denigrated groups often internalize the dominant view of themselves. Being disempowered and stigmatized from above predisposes them to ostracize others below them or identify with their own oppressors.

The insights gained from these broader understandings of iniquity, the similarities and differences from one context to the next, the relationships between class, ethnic and gender based inequality, the human costs involved — all serve to educate rather than indoctrinate. It should provide the intellectual scaffolding to deal with the tension between the ideal of colourblindness and the need to recognize just how 'race' works in order to abolish 'colour consciousness'. Students exposed to this kind of broad historical and comparative reasoning will inevitably acquire the skills to evaluate critically solutions and locally appropriate policies to deal with racism — from affirmative action, to personal involvement as active citizens in a democratic culture.

Notes

1 For a more detailed discussion of these issues, see Moodley (1995).
2 Videotape of student group discussion in Surrey, British Columbia, Canada, as part of school district wide multicultural forum. It was also reported in *Surrey Now*, 19 October, 1996.

References

AGNEW, V. (1996) *Resisting Women from Asia, Africa and the Caribbean, and the Women's Movement in Canada*, Toronto.

BRANDT, G. (1986) *The Realization of Anti-racist Teaching*, Lewes, England: Falmer Press.

BRITTAN, A. and MAYNARD, M. (1985) *Sexism, Racism and Oppression*, Oxford: Basil Blackwell.

COHEN, P. (1992) 'Hidden narratives in theories of racism', in DONALD, J. and RATTANSI, A. (eds) *'Race', Culture and Difference*, London: Sage, pp. 62–103.

DEI, G. (1996) *Anti-Racism Education: Theory and Practice*, Halifax, Canada: Fernwood.

FISHER, D. and ECHOLS, F. (1992) *Evaluation Report on the Vancouver School Board's Race Relations Policy*, Vancouver: Vancouver School Board.

GILLBORN, D. (1990) *'Race', Ethnicity and Education: Teaching and Learning in Multiethnic Schools*, London: Unwin-Hyman/Routledge.

GILLBORN, D. (1995) *Racism and Antiracism in Real Schools*, Buckingham: Open University Press.

GILROY, P. (1990) 'The end of anti-racism', *New Community*, **17**, pp. 71–83.

HATCHER, R. and TROYNA, B. (1993) 'Racialization and children', in McCARTHY, C. and CRICHLOW, W. (eds) *Race, Identity and Representation in Education*, New York: Routledge, pp. 109–25.

MAY, S. (1994) *Making Multicultural Education Work*, Clevedon, England: Multilingual Matters.

MAY, S. (ed.) (1998) 'Indigenous community-based education', Special issue, *Language, Culture and Curriculum*, **11**, 3.

MOODLEY, K. (1983) 'Multiculturalism as ideology', *Ethnic and Racial Studies*, **6**, pp. 320–31.

MOODLEY, K. (1995) 'Multicultural education in Canada: Historical development and current status', in BANKS, J. and BANKS, C. (eds) *Handbook of Research on Multicultural Education*, New York: Macmillan, pp. 801–20.

MORRISON, T. (1989) 'Unspeakable things unspoken: The African-American presence in American Literature', *Michigan Quarterly*, **28**, pp. 1–34.

PINAR, W. (1993) 'Notes on understanding curriculum as a racial text', in McCARTHY, C. and CRICHLOW, W. (eds) *Race, Identity and Representation in Education*, New York: Routledge, pp. 60–70.

REID REPORT (1991) 'Canadians' views on racism in their country', **6**, 9, pp. 11–15, Winnipeg: Angus Reid Group.

REID REPORT (1994) 'Chinese Canadians' views on life in Canada', **9**, 4, pp. 3–6, Winnipeg: Angus Reid Group.

SOLOMON, R. and LEVINE-RASKY, C. (1994) 'Accommodation and resistance: Educators' response to multicultural and anti-racist education', Unpublished Report.

WEINFELD, M. (1996) 'Social identity in the 1990s', in LITTLETON, J. (ed.) *Clash of Identities*, Englewood Cliffs, NJ: Prentice Hall, pp. 119–25.

6   Critical Antiracism in South Africa

Nazir Carrim and Crain Soudien

The transitional process presently underway in South Africa provides a useful opportunity to investigate the ways in which racism is constructed, deconstructed and reconstructed. This opportunity arises primarily as a result of the explicit ways in which the question of 'race' is being addressed in the process of reconfiguring the New South Africa. Of most interest in this process, but by no means the only site in which 'race' is a focus, is the new Constitution of the Republic of South Africa (Constitution, 1996). Given the blatantly racist nature of the system of apartheid, and its discursive heritage, the process of reform — and for our purposes, the reforms in education — provide the historical and material basis for such an overt addressing of questions of 'race' in South Africa. This chapter draws on research conducted between 1990–6 within the Gauteng (within which Johannesburg is located) and Western Cape (where Cape Town is located) provinces of South Africa. It explores the ways in which schools in these provinces are being desegregated and the patterns that may be discerned from these developments.

Our findings indicate that there are three emergent trends that may be noted in the experiences of schools in Gauteng and Western Cape: first, the predominance of an assimilationist approach; second, the shift from 'race' to ethnicity, and the consequent foregrounding of multiculturalism (cf. Carrim, 1995); and, third, the emergence of an approach which is sensitive to the need for dealing proactively and positively with 'differences', even within antiracist approaches. These findings — insofar as they point to the hegemony of assimilationist and, to a lesser extent, multiculturalist approaches — suggest that the distinctly racist logic of apartheid, and consequently the perpetuation of white domination, are being reconstructed in South Africa. They also point to the limitations of traditional forms and understandings of antiracism as a vehicle for deconstructing racism; and, it is here, we wish to argue, that the notion of 'difference' becomes crucial and suggests a need to develop what may be termed a 'critical antiracism'.

The notion of a 'critical antiracism' — which is used by David Gillborn (1995), and which draws on the influences of postmodernism on antiracism in the British context, in particular (cf. Donald and Rattansi, 1992) — bears significant resonances in, and for the South African situation. At best, a 'critical antiracism' may be described as a form of antiracism that is explicitly alert and sensitive to the multiple expressions of 'difference' in identity. Our findings in Gauteng and Western Cape schools emphasize the necessity of acknowledging and incorporating a notion of 'difference' in order to promote and maintain the importance, viability and sustainability of an antiracist project in South Africa.

A critical antiracist stance implies several things. Key, however, is its demand that antiracist approaches take seriously a 'de-essentialized' (Hall, 1992) notion of identity (cf. May; Rattansi, this volume). The significance of this for South Africa, where the identities of 'African', 'white', 'coloured' and 'Indian'[1] have been reified both in racial-biological and cultural permanentist terms, is profound and demands an understanding of identity which dispenses with what Hall (1992) has called 'innocent' subjects. A critical antiracism also points to the need to move away from 'doctrinaire' (MacDonald et al., 1989) and dogmatic forms of antiracism which homogenize and caricature Whites as proto-racists and Blacks as victims. It implies that the bipolarity inherent in the 'white' versus 'black' construction — common to both racist and antiracist arguments — is unhelpful in coming to terms with the complex ways in which racism expresses itself in various settings, particularly in regard to 'intra-black' dynamics. And, finally, a critical antiracism draws attention to the need for macro, antiracist interventions and policy formulations to take serious account of the ways in which people experience everyday life in all its micro manifestations. A critical antiracism, which incorporates a notion of 'difference' would, therefore, work with complex, non-stereotypical and dynamic senses of identity, and would 'talk to' the actual ways in which people experience their lives, worlds, and identities.

There is an emerging argument that what we are referring to as critical antiracism is similar to, if not the same as what is now becoming known as 'critical multi-culturalism' (see, for example, McLaren, 1995). A critical multiculturalism, it is argued, confronts cultural essentialism, acknowledges difference and incorporates the power dimensions of racism. In rejecting the notion of 'race' as an analytical category, critical multiculturalists choose instead to work with the notion of 'ethnicity', allowing them to uncover and critique new forms of cultural racism (see Carrington and Short; May, this volume). There are three major reasons why we choose to locate our discussion within critical antiracism and not critical multiculturalism. These reasons may be categorized as follows: the history of 'race' in South Africa; the nature of the emerging trends as reflected by our data, and; the nature of theoretical focus within our discussion here.

Since its inception in 1948, apartheid categorized and officially classified people in terms of 'race'. Four major 'races' were identified within the Population Registra-tion Act: 'Whites', 'Indians', 'Coloureds' and 'Africans'. Over the last 50 years the names appended to these categories were constantly changed. Indians, for example, were classified as 'Asians' at one stage. As another example, Africans were described successively as 'Natives', as 'Bantus', and as 'African'. Africans, moreover, were also further classified in cultural and ethnic terms such as Tswana, Venda, Xhosa and Zulu. This latter differentiation was aimed essentially at realizing the apartheid design of relegating the African population to 'bantustans' or 'homelands' — with each 'homeland' being for the designated use of a particular ethnic, African group — an example being Bophutatswana for Tswanas. The racial classification of South Africans influenced every aspect of their lives: where they lived, where they schooled, who they interacted with, which social amenities they had access to, their social relations, including who they slept with, and their political positions. Most, if not all people's social transactions were governed by legislation (e.g., the Group Areas

Act, the Immorality Act, the Separate Amenities Act) and officially policed. The discursive reach of racial ideology thus cut deep into the fabric of everyday society and did not exist only as a textual entry in the Population Registration Act. 'Race' influenced the *material* conditions of people's lives in explicit and direct ways, ensuring that South Africans lived segregated and unequal lives in almost every sense of the terms. Given these conditions and history, South Africans are not in a position to ignore 'race'. It is central to any understanding of South Africa, even in its current juncture.

The need to acknowledge 'race' in the South African context is an argument that has been made in various ways by the South African Communist Party (SACP), the African National Congress (ANC) and other stakeholders within the South African liberation movement for more than 50 years. The SACP argued, against the communists of the world, that 'race' was more than a mere superstructural manipulation within the South African context. It had direct effects in terms of people's material conditions and their relations to modes of production. It was not just false consciousness (see Wolpe, 1986, 1989 for a useful coverage of the race/class debates in South Africa). The argument of the ANC has been that while the concept of 'race' might be unsustainable, its social effects have been profound and that social interventions, actions and strategies engage with its complexity.

The second reason for locating our discussion within the language of critical antiracism, rather than critical multiculturalism, is because of the weight of our data. There is no evidence in our data, and certainly none in the history of South Africa, of the existence of a critical multiculturalist orientation. As we point out later in this chapter, the use of culturalist language in the schools we report on tends to be assimilationist and what we call 'bad' multiculturalist practices. These 'bad' multiculturalist practices essentialize cultures, homogenize and stereotype people's identities and do not address the power dimensions of racism. We also point out that such 'bad' multiculturalist tendencies bear stark resonances with the justifications of apartheid itself. Our purpose here is to interrogate these data in terms of notions of *difference* and *identity*; notions which emerge as consistent themes from the data. We do not review the literature on multiculturalism, culture, ethnicity, 'race relations' or even discourses about processes of racialization. To do that would require another paper with another focus.

Methodologically, we employed mainly qualitative methods of research. This entailed conducting interviews with school-based actors, teachers, students and, to a lesser extent, parents. Semi-structured observations of the daily routines of schools, both in classrooms and playing fields, were conducted. Quantitative methods were also used particularly in tracing statistically the rate of admission of black students into schools that were designated previously as being not for their use. However, it should be noted that the research work in Gauteng and Western Cape was conducted and designed separately. We do, nonetheless, share common methodological and theoretical assumptions, and our findings are convergent. It is upon these that we draw in this chapter.

The empirical research initially conducted in Gauteng (in 1992–3) surveyed all white, coloured and Indian schools in the region in regard to their admission rates of 'others' and the selection procedures they used. Thereafter two schools, one primary and one secondary school, in each racialized category were selected for further probing. All head teachers of these schools were interviewed, three teachers teaching at different grades and in different subjects were interviewed, and two groups of students, comprising eight students each, were also interviewed in groups. Thereafter, the same survey was administered to all Indian and coloured schools in the Gauteng region to discern changes in admission rates and patterns. The Gauteng Education Department's statistics were used to gauge the changes in white Gauteng schools. Two Indian schools and two coloured schools were then selected for interviews. The head teachers of these schools were interviewed, two teachers in each school were interviewed and one group of students, consisting of six students each, were interviewed in each school. Two white teachers, one in a primary school and the other in a secondary school, were also interviewed. This follow-up research was conducted in 1995 and 1996.

The research conducted in the Western Cape focused on desegregating coloured schools where, significantly more so than in white schools, the most important processes of 'opening up' were taking place. The information used in this chapter draws on research conducted with teachers and students in four formerly white schools, and two formerly coloured schools. In 1991 eight teachers and 20 students were interviewed in the four formerly white schools. Between 1991 and 1995, interviews and focus-group discussions were conducted with 40 students in the two formerly coloured schools, half of whom were classified coloured and half African. Three teachers in each school were also interviewed. The focus of the interviews was on the entry of African students into schools which had previously been predominantly coloured and how coloured and African students constructed and interpreted this experience.

The first section of this chapter deals with some of the historical details that are necessary to understand the ways in which the processes of school desegregation began to unfold in South Africa. The second section discusses the experiences within the Gauteng province. The third section outlines the ways in which Western Cape schools are addressing these processes. And the fourth and final section provides an analytical discussion of our findings.

'Open' Schools in South Africa

The choice of the focus on the period between 1990–6, is motivated by the official announcement in October 1990, by Piet Clase, the then Minister of Education in the apartheid, white, Nationalist government to allow white schools to enrol black students legally. The Clase Announcements, as they came to be known, coincided with the unbanning of liberation organizations in South Africa, like the African National Congress (ANC), Pan Africanist Congress (PAC) and the South African Communist Party (SACP). It was also accompanied by the release from prison of political leaders such as Nelson Mandela, and the return from exile of a number of South Africans who had been away from their places of birth for decades. The Clase announcements, therefore, were linked inextricably to the reformist initiatives of the Nationalist government.

Clase offered white schools three desegregation models from which to choose. Model A allowed white state schools to close down as state schools and to reopen as private schools. Model B allowed them to remain state schools, but to have an open admissions policy. Model C allowed them to convert themselves to semi-private and semi-state schools, where teachers' salaries would be paid for by the state, and all other operational expenses of the school would be borne by the school community itself. All three Models allowed such schools to enrol black students, the generic term used during the struggle years to refer to people who have been classified either as Indian, coloured or African. However, all of these Models were subjected to the same conditions:

1   All schools needed to ensure that 51 per cent of the school's student population remained white.
2   The cultural ethos of such schools remained intact.
3   The State and/or the school were not obliged to provide financial aid to black incoming students.
4   In the event of white parents or students refusing to remain in a school that had begun to enrol black students, and should they choose to move to another white-only school, the State would bear the costs of such a relocation.
5   The school and/or the State was under no obligation to provide any 'special' programme or support to facilitate the adaptation of black students into such schools.

These conditions accompanying the Clase announcements demonstrate clearly that the 'opening' of white South African schools was achieved in ways that were bent on ensuring continued white privilege and security. This is not surprising because the Clase announcements were framed by the apartheid constitution, which was still in place at the time. At the same time, the Clase announcements explicitly and officially put into place an assimilationist approach. Blatant here were the assumptions that Blacks needed to adopt the white schools' cultural ethos, to which they were also expected to adapt. Linked to this was also the assumption, so consistent in the arrogance of white supremacist logic, that the white cultural ethos was in fact better and superior, and one that needed to be maintained and into which 'others' needed to assimilate (Badat, 1992; Carrim and Sayed, 1991; 1992; Metcalfe, 1991; Muller, 1992).

By 1992, all previously white-designated schools were converted to Model C schools, despite 98 per cent of all white schools nationally opting to become Model B schools. The apartheid government argued that this was unavoidable because of its inability to continue providing financially for such schools. To avoid the closure of schools and/or the retrenchment of white teachers, previous white-only schools needed to be converted to Model C so that the financial costs could be shared by the State and the school community. Stark in this development is the fact that whilst black South African schools were (and in some cases still are) overcrowded and under-resourced, white schools in South Africa were being under-utilized and threatened with closure. This continued to be the case as late as 1993.

Nonetheless, in the wake of the Clase announcements, coloured and Indian schools in South Africa were officially permitted to admit into their schools students who were non-coloured or non-Indian. Thus, whilst the Clase announcements were targeted at white school communities, and were white-only affairs, they did signal nationally the desegregation of all South African schools.

Under apartheid, 19 racially and ethnically divided education departments existed. South African schools were segregated in terms of the categories of white, Indian, coloured and African, with the latter being further subdivided into ethnic cultural groups, such as Tswana, Zulu, Xhosa, etc. The Clase announcements allowed schools to register students from outside of their 'official' categories. A 'Tswana' school could now legally enrol non-Tswana students, a coloured school could accept non-coloured students, and so on. Whilst such enrolments did take place before the Clase announcements, they were unofficial and dependent upon the discretion of the school's principal. Principals, moreover, who chose to admit children who fell outside of the racial definitions which described their character, were legally transgressing the law and laid themselves open to disciplinary action. After the Clase announcements, however, such enrolments became public and official, and increased considerably (Carrim, 1992).

Model C schools continued to exist as such up until the end of 1996, when the South African Schools Act (Department of National Education, 1996) was passed. In this Act, the status of Model C schools was legally abolished and all schools in South Africa became either 'public' (meaning state/government) or 'private'. Most former Model C schools became 'public' schools, with special provisions allowing them to maintain the character of their schools. These provisions include a high level of autonomy for school governing bodies, so that on decentralized levels they may determine the policy and nature of their schools. However, such autonomy is circumscribed by national policies and the new Constitution of South Africa which categorically reject racist practices and uphold the rights of the child to a basic education. Thus, whilst schools do have autonomy, they cannot prevent a child of another 'race' access to a school. They do, however, have the latitude to stipulate other selection criteria that ought to be met for enrolment into their schools (Constitution, 1996; Department of National Education, 1996).

A few points need to be noted in this historical background. First, the 'opening' of schools in South Africa did not simply imply, and is not, a matter of Blacks going into white schools. It has entailed desegregation of schools within the broader black community as well. Second, an assimilationist approach to school desegregation has been set in place, prompted mainly by the conditions that accompanied the Clase announcements. Third, and as will be shown in more detail later, the experiences of reconstructed forms of racism mean different things in the different school contexts, and these include those within intra-black settings.

The Gauteng Experience

During 1990–4 — the period before the historic first non-racial democratic elections in the history of South Africa which installed Nelson Mandela as its first black

President — school desegregation processes within the Gauteng province were characterized by distinct patterns. These trends were: the use of admission tests; a low number of black student enrolments in white schools, non-Indian students in Indian schools, and non-coloureds in coloured schools, and; the predominance of an assimilationist approach.

All Model C schools — that is, previously white schools — used selection tests. 77 per cent of so-called Indian schools used selection tests, and 39 per cent of so-called coloured schools did likewise. In the instance of Model C schools, Indian, coloured and African students were put through selection tests. In the case of Indian schools, coloured and African students were tested, and in coloured schools African students were subjected to selection procedures. There is no record of white students going into either Indian or coloured schools, or Indian students to coloured schools. If they exist, they are exceptional cases, and not reflective of the norm.

In all cases, however, selection tests examined applicants in the areas of English or Afrikaans language proficiency and mathematical ability. In some instances, psychometric tests were also used. In addition, admission criteria included a parent's ability to pay the school fees, and whether students lived in areas close to the school. The latter two requirements had the effect of keeping black entrants to a minimum. School fees privileged middle-class black parents who could afford to pay (see Carrim and Sayed, 1992). Residential requirements have to be understood in relation to the racialized residential segregation of people under apartheid. Thus, it was unlikely that many black people would be found living in or close to the areas within which white schools, or for that matter Indian and coloured schools, were located.

The use of selection tests and other admission criteria thus had the effect of keeping the intake of black students at a low level. In general, the total enrolment of students to schools for whose use such schools were previously not designated, amounted to between 10–15 per cent of the overall student population of the school concerned. The low numbers of 'others' in white, Indian and coloured schools, were also informed and reinforced by the overtly assimilationist policies of such schools. Incoming students were expected to adopt and adapt to the existing cultural ethos of schools. In addition, the normal routines of the school, including its curriculum, remained unchanged. One white primary school girl said:

> I was excited about Blacks coming to our school. But I walked around the school for a week and only found one black girl in our school. Everything is still the same. (White primary school girl, Interview, 1992)

A group of coloured students said:

> So far things are alright. But once their (African students) numbers increase then things won't be the same. You see parents are already pulling out their children from our schools, and once their numbers increase this will happen more. (Coloured, male, high school student, Interview, 1992)

When an Indian teacher was asked how she was coping with the changes in her school, she replied by saying:

> Oh, it's not too bad. There aren't many of them, and they seem to fit in well. (Indian, female, high school teacher, Interview, 1992)

These comments by teachers and students, across Indian, coloured and white schools, make consistent reference to an 'us' and 'them' language which not only indicates the racially exclusivist ways in which they define their own identities, but also the predominance of assimilationism in their experiences of the desegregation of their schools. The assumption here being that 'they' are coming to 'us', and the more 'they' are like 'us' or the more 'they' become like 'us', the more acceptable 'they' become. The 'host' culture is not viewed as lacking in any way, since deficiencies, if any, are seen to be tied inextricably only to the incoming 'other'.

Nonetheless, occurring simultaneously with this experience were the daily pedagogical challenges that teachers faced at the chalk face. Teachers, whether white, coloured or Indian, were for the first time in their teaching confronted by multilingual, multiethnic, and multicultural classrooms. As such, teachers could no longer teach in their normal ways. They could not use the same examples to explain things, they could not uncritically reprimand students in the same ways, and they simply could not take the same things for granted. These daily pedagogical encounters pushed teachers away from assimilationist assumptions to adopting a more multicultural approach. In order to educationally reach the 'other', teachers were forced to recognize and acknowledge the 'other's' background, ways of making meaning, and difference. One Indian primary school teacher had this to say:

> For three months I could not get any of the black children in my class to say a word. Finally, I brought in the school caretaker to talk to them in Sotho, and these kids began to respond. I could not deny the fact that they spoke Sotho only, and I had to reach them in Sotho. After a while, these kids began to open up and now they are coping quite well. (Indian primary school teacher, Interview, 1992)

Another white primary school teacher pointed out:

> When I allow the black kids to talk of their own home experiences, the class as a whole is amazed at what these kids actually go through on a daily basis. The whole class benefits. I could not expect them to deny their own backgrounds. (White, female, primary school teacher, Interview, 1992)

Thus, pedagogically, teachers, in particular, were forced to shift from assimilationist approaches and assumptions to more multicultural ones that would acknowledge the different backgrounds and experiences incoming students were bringing with them into their schools. The policies and dominant approaches of these schools remained, nonetheless, assimilationist.

From 1994–6, however, the shift from assimilationism to multiculturalism became more prevalent. This shift was also influenced by major national developments in the country as a whole. First, in April 1994, the first non-racial democratic elections in South Africa took place. Mandela was President. South Africa was now being billed as the 'rainbow nation'. Second, the new South African Constitution — interim until 1996 when it was formally adopted — was in place. In this Constitution the multicultural nature of South African society was acknowledged officially, depicted most starkly in the statutory recognition of 11 official languages in South Africa. These macro developments were crucial in that they facilitated, on micro school levels, a shift from assimilationism to multiculturalism.

The macro developments signalled officially that all people's identities, along with the cultural, social and linguistic backgrounds these encompassed, were equally legitimate (at least in theory). They questioned the assimilationist assumption that some cultures were superior to others, and that some ways of looking at the world are necessarily and always better than others. However, it is important to note the ways in which these were experienced on the empirical levels of the schools themselves. Far from being a positive acknowledgement of 'difference', the multicultural trends in schools seem to be reconstructed forms of racism itself.

When asked how multicultural her school was, one Indian school teacher said:

> Oh, when we have our annual school concert, the Zulu kids put up a Zulu dance in traditional Zulu costumes. (Indian, female, primary school teacher, Interview, 1995)

When asked the same question, a white school teacher said:

> I always ask the black kids what these things mean in their culture. I must admit I am always shocked when they actually don't know. (White, female, primary school teacher, Interview, 1994)

Said another white teacher:

> Our parent days are like the United Nations. We have all the foods and costumes of all the cultures. We are very multicultural. (White, male, high school teacher, Interview, 1995)

In these teacher accounts, it is evident that the types of multiculturalism at work in these schools are at best stereotypical, and, at worst, caricatured. Comments like 'Zulu kids doing Zulu dances', or parent days being like the 'United Nations', or expectations that people of particular cultural groups would necessarily know everything there is to know about their particular culture, clearly reflect this. The possibility of Zulu kids actually doing a modern dance at the school concert, or Muslim kids dressing in western looking clothes at parent days, or black kids answering questions in ways that do not tie into their supposed, and assumed, cultural backgrounds do not seem to permeate these school experiences. Instead, students are positioned in stereotypical ways, are assumed to be fixed in their identities, are portrayed as necessarily representative of and loyal to their supposed cultures, and the prevalent understanding of culture seems to be narrowly defined as a reference to lifestyles, particularly in regard to dress, food and language. The effect is to project differences among people in negative ways and to reinforce rather than erode racist practices, as the following group of coloured students' comments indicate:

Oh, we do not mix really.
Why?
Well, you see they have their own culture and we have our own. They do things differently from us. So, they stick to themselves. And, we stick to ourselves. (Group of coloured male, high school students, Interview, 1995)

One white student remarked:

It's not a question of race, you know. It is more . . . eh . . . a cultural thing. Their's is very different from our's. (White, female, high school student, Interview, 1995)

Not only do these comments reflect that 'differences' are perceived negatively — 'difference' is rarely viewed as a strength, as a possibility for viewing the world with different eyes, or broadening one's understanding of things — they also camouflage the racial implications of such negative projections. White schools are by no means culturally homogeneous. They include Afrikaners, English, Greek, Portuguese and Jews, among others. Indians are made up of Muslims, Hindus, Tamils and Christians. Coloureds too are made up of Malays, Christians and Muslims. The cultural differences among these racialized groups tend to be under- or un-emphasized in these multicultural school experiences. They only get to be recognized in the cases of those who belong to other 'racial' groups, leaving one with the inescapable conclusion that such forms of multiculturalism are reconstructed forms of racism.

Nonetheless, the period between 1994–6 did witness a marked increase in the rate of enrolment of black students into white schools, non-Indian students into Indian schools, and non-coloured students in coloured schools. Existing figures indicate an increase of such student enrolments between 30–50 per cent of the entire school's student population. This is more than a 100 per cent increase in such enrolment rates when compared to the patterns before 1994. At the same time, admission tests, whilst still administered, are now predominantly used for placement purposes, rather than admission into schools. These changes in the ways in which admission procedures work have been propelled by provincial educational legislations that stipulate tests be used for placement purposes and not as mechanisms of exclusion. Thus, there is an increase in the number of 'other' students in desegregated schools within the Gauteng region, albeit characterized by racist, multicultural practices and assumptions.

The Western Cape Experience

The process of the 'opening up' of schools in the Western Cape Province was subject to the same macro conditions as those which shaped desegregation initiatives in the Gauteng Province. The context and history of the Western Cape, however, produced a somewhat different set of dynamics for the process of school desegregation. A central difference for the desegregation process was, and still is, that the Western Cape was demographically a predominantly so-called 'coloured' area. This, and the fact that a number of coloured schools attempted to resist, albeit with little success, the segregation of their institutions meant that racialization in the Western Cape proceeded along a slightly different path. There were teachers, for example, who had strong memories of what schools had been like before the introduction of apartheid. Moreover, during the period of apartheid itself, most coloured schools made little distinction between children classified 'Indian' and those classified 'coloured'. There were also significant numbers of teachers classified as 'white' working in these environments.

These differences served to present the Western Cape as a distinct locus of apartheid. It is, nonetheless, true that the region was ravaged by the deeply divisive policies of colonialism and apartheid which not only hierarchized Whites, Coloureds and Africans, but also nurtured specific forms of ethnocentrism and racism. Despite the more liberal history of the region, the central issue, of course, was that the apartheid regime had effectively blocked the movement of children deemed to be African from entering non-African schools. The numbers of African children in coloured schools prior to the era of desegregation were minimal (cf. Jacklin, 1991). African people were thus consistently vulnerable to a process of *othering*.

What this background sketch points to is the significance of coloured schools in the desegregation experience in the Western Cape. While the experience of desegregation in white schools has received most attention, it is important to signal the centrality of the larger constituency of coloured schools in this process.

During the mid-1980s, coloured schools began receiving increasingly large numbers of applications for admission from African students. As Jacklin (1991) comments, the factors behind this development were complex. Most important was what she called 'a loosening up of the spatial controls of apartheid'. The restrictive, and much resented, Influx Control Laws which prohibited African people from seeking domicile and employment in the Western Cape were being dismantled and were allowing rural people to seek their fortunes in the city of Cape Town. In addition, a perception was growing amongst African parents that their children were being wasted by the breakdown of schooling — the result of official neglect and the politicization of education in the African townships (see Soudien, 1996). The effect on enrolments in coloured schools was almost immediate. A small but significant number of African parents began seeking admission for their children.

The schools to which African students were most attracted were those which were found in areas contiguous to African townships and along significant transport routes. In a survey conducted in 1991, when the movement into coloured schools was reaching a high point, enrolment percentages of African students in coloured schools ranged between 5 and 33.3 per cent.

Enrolments of black children (Africans, Indians and Coloureds) into white schools, as suggested earlier, took place at a slightly later stage and in a somewhat different way. These differences were shaped by the fee levels of Model C schools and their cultural–linguistic environments. The more expensive Model C schools were in general inaccessible to most (except the black middle-class) because of their fee structures. Enrolments of black students into these institutions remained relatively low, seldom reaching above 5 per cent. In Model C schools in poorer white communities, however, the picture was significantly different. Three traditionally white lower-middle-class schools informally assessed during 1991 reported that coloured enrolments had broken the 50 per cent barrier (Soudien, 1994a).

With the opening up of schools a knock-on effect was produced. The entry of African students into coloured schools precipitated a flight of the coloured middle-class into white Model C schools. This change, in turn, stimulated the departure of middle-class Whites to the more expensive, and therefore more exclusive, public and private schools. Explicit and inexplicit selection procedures were in use in all the schools. Versfeld (1997), an educator working in the area of diversity in schools in the Western Cape, makes the claim that three major approaches were and still are used in schools to control admission: pegging fees beyond the reach of non-middle-class parents, demanding linguistic competence in either English or Afrikaans, and giving preference to children from school catchment areas.

As the work of Soudien (1994a, 1994b) seeks to show, the desegregation process in the Western Cape has been characterized by an entrenched and unproblematized philosophy of assimilation. To be sure, this philosophy is expressed most articulately in white or former Model C schools, but is pervasive too in coloured schools. For example, a study by Soudien (1994a) in 1992 and 1993 of how six white schools were responding to issues of 'race' showed that schools were going through a process of redefinition and were attempting to adjust to their new 'open' status. They had all attempted to set in place mechanisms for accommodating students who were not white. Examples of such mechanisms included cross-cultural music programmes, multi-faith assemblies, and so on. None of the schools, however, believed that they were departing fundamentally from what had existed prior to their conversion to Model C status (or simply Open in the case of the one private school in the group). Two of the schools explicitly emphasized that their broad ethos had not changed:

> I think Blacks in the school still respect the traditions and they really understand that it is a good school and that they must try to fit in and respect the school. So I think that they don't have to really adjust, they just come to the school. . . .

Flowing from this, there are two explicit features of 'open' schools to which we need to draw attention, as these could possibly obscure our understanding of what is happening within them:

1 In five of the six schools surveyed, stress was placed by teachers on qualities such as 'caring'. 'Our school is known as a caring school' said one, while another emphasized that 'we don't run away from academically weaker pupils'.

2 In each of the schools, much emphasis was laid on 'openness', in respect of both religious and political observance.

What is problematic about these features, however, are the implicit rules — or the hidden curriculum — governing them. In only one of the schools was there an acknowledgment of a changing school environment and a need for the school to reassess its ethos:

> (Our school is) in a state of transition at the moment . . . because it has changed radically from previous years . . . 60 per cent of our pupils don't live in the Cape Town area and have long travelling hours. So our sports programme has changed.

In all the other schools much was made of preserving what was perceived to be their primary function: i.e., maintaining as normal a learning environment as possible. Implicit in this approach, it could be said, is a reluctance to examine traditions assumed to be good in themselves. 'Our simple aim is to provide a basic, good grounding in education, not in terms of content, but in terms of values and morals'.

In three of the six schools in the study, teachers concluded emphatically that bringing children of colour into their classes had fundamentally changed their perceptions of issues relating to colour and even to class. In one instance a teacher admitted that 'he had operated off an all-white bias'. Similarly, another felt that 'we've been a bit presumptuous in the past . . . before, we believed that everyone we taught had 'our way of thinking'. All three teachers were conscious of the deep presumptions which had accompanied their previous practices. Issues were being raised in their classes which previously had not ever been considered.

While conceding that the presence of children of colour had brought new concerns into classroom discussion, such as the nature of the 'New South Africa' and 'getting the school to deal with real issues, rather than issues like uniforms, trouser styles, behaviour in the streets', three of the other teachers did not feel that their classrooms were different. 'One doesn't teach History to a race [sic], one just teaches History. So it shouldn't matter to whom you teach it' explained a teacher. This same teacher admitted, however, that some of the children of colour did not have the same resources as white children, and when it came to doing projects she had to adjust her expectations. Another teacher found no difference whatsoever in the 'open' context; that all the children, black and white, were coping well with each other and were 'secure, not alienated'. A specific 'black viewpoint' had not emerged in the classroom.

While the effects of the desegregation processes in coloured and white schools were similar, their articulation of what the problems were and how they should be approached was significantly different. A strong factor influencing the perceptions of coloured teachers was their exposure to the political discourse of the former liberation movements. Many of the teachers in the schools which were surveyed for the purpose of this and other exercises brought to their explanations the language of freedom and justice. Importantly, however, the problem of 'race' in most schools was consistently sublimated. Many teachers spoke of coloured and African children relating well. Where their counterparts in white schools claimed that white and black children were all the same, some coloured teachers sought to avoid the discourse of 'race' all together, arguing that 'race' as a descriptor had no validity whatsoever.

The effect of this was that while schools have instituted a variety of measures to deal with 'race' their approaches have failed to deal with difference. In white schools identity is invariably framed in the stable racial terms of the dominant order; in coloured schools a 'raceless' identity is invoked. The result, in both situations, is that the deeply 'othering' impulses of racism continue to run rampant because they are not explicitly addressed. A number of African students at a relatively mixed former coloured school exemplify these difficulties well as the quotations below suggest.

Jonas, a young man, commented, 'I don't think that I can say that I'm proud to be here. I don't feel it's good to be here. I'm black . . . I'm proud to be here? I wouldn't say that. I'm not proud to be here, because I'm not supposed to be here . . .'. He went on to explain that he had strong feelings about the historical circumstances which brought him to School X. 'It's because why,' he said, 'I should be in better places than this, you see. If the situation in South Africa wasn't here, or wasn't like this . . . like we are living in now. You see? That's what I mean' (Soudien, 1996, p. 175).

Another African student, Monde, made a similar point. He didn't feel great about school. He only came because he had to, '. . . I think when I said that I came here by force, I stated my reason. I actually said that I was doing it because it was a must in my life. I am told in order to prosper in future . . . that's why I'm forced to come to this school. It's not something I would wake up and say I want to go to school . . .' (Soudien, 1996, p. 175).

Lumko, a friend of Jonas, was also very deliberate in his explanation about the difficulties he had with School X. He made it very clear that it was not a 'privilege for him to be at the [coloured] school'. 'I can't say I like it', he said, 'because if this school is going to be like this, I won't come to school'. He went on to say that it was 'alright' mixing

> with some people who are not black like you. I can say it is nice you have now a different people from the township. But it is not nice because of this apartheid thing and what is happening. But if you're ignoring all these things it's okay. But you can't ignore all these things. You can say it's nice, but! Ja (yes), but you can see sometimes, that some of the Coloureds they don't accept Blacks, some of the teachers as well. . . . What I'm trying to say, is that . . . I'm not enjoying some of the things because of the things we are living under. (Soudien, 1996, p. 175)

Problems with Assimilationism and Multiculturalism in South Africa

As the data from both the Gauteng and Western Cape schools reveal, a range of approaches to difference exist. In the Gauteng area, and to a lesser extent in the Western Cape, a shift from assimilationism to multiculturalism is evident, but equally evident is the displacement of racial questions. However, rather than working with dynamic and complex senses of cultural identities, the multicultural practices that predominate in these schools' experiences tend instead to fix, stereotype and caricature people's identities. It is these that we now discuss as we argue for the importance of a critical antiracism in South Africa.

The problems with the assimilationist approach are widely known. Assimilationism denies the recognition of people's differences and the existence of cultural diversity. More so, assimilationist approaches have been found *not* to reduce racist practices or instances of racial abuse (cf. Brandt, 1986; Gillborn, 1990). In the South African case, assimilationism has been found to be insufficient in actually dealing with 'mixed' groups, since the denial of cultural diversity within assimilationism does not enable people to gain a better understanding of each other or facilitate improved relations among them. Hence, the motivation to shift from assimilationism to multiculturalism.

However, the multiculturalist practices in the Gauteng and Western Cape schools are not without problems either. As pointed out already these practices have tended to portray people of different 'racial' groups as being culturally different, implying a shift from 'race' to ethnicity. This is particularly evident in the fact that cultural diversity *within* racialized groups is ignored consistently. It is easier to talk of a Zulu as being culturally different, as opposed to an Italian in white school settings, for example. This denial of cultural differences within racialized groupings lends credence to the claim that this type of multiculturalism is a reconstructed form of racism itself. In South Africa this tendency has historical precedence.

During its inception, the system of apartheid itself was justified not only in racial but in cultural terms as well. Verwoerd's infamous Senate speech in 1953, which articulated the principles of apartheid education, is well worth quoting here:

> There is no place for him (the Bantu) in the European community above the level of certain forms of labour. Within his [sic] own community however, all doors are open. For that reason it is of no avail for him to receive a training which has as its aim absorption in the European community, where he cannot be absorbed. Until now he has been subjected to a school system which drew him away from his own community and misled him in showing him the green pastures of European society in which he was not allowed to graze. This attitude is not only uneconomic because money is spent for an education which has no specific aim but it is also dishonest to continue it. It is abundantly clear that unplanned education creates problems; disrupting the community life of the Bantu and endangering the community life of the European. (cited in Rose and Tunmer, 1975, p. 266)

Whereas Verwoerd used cultural differences between 'the Bantu' and 'European' as a justification for segregation and the establishment of apartheid education, the link in the argument between forms of racism and articulation of cultural differences is clear. As Cross and Mkwanazi (1992) have also argued, apartheid may be seen to be an extreme form of multiculturalism itself. The point of raising this here is to emphasize that an uncritical acceptance of multicultural practices in South Africa could quite easily perpetuate, rather than erode racism (cf. Rattansi, this volume). What enables such multicultural practices to take on racist connotations are due to the ways in which they highlight selectively when and among whom cultural differences are emphasized, the ways in which people's identities are construed, and the ignoring of power dimensions to questions of racism itself.

We have already shown that the multiculturalist approach recently adopted in South African schools does not acknowledge the cultural differences within racialized groups. Whites, whether they are Greek, English, Italian or Afrikaners, still get to be projected as if they are culturally homogeneous. Indians who are constituted by Muslims, Tamils, Hindus and Christians are still portrayed as if they are culturally all the same. Coloureds too are far from being culturally homogeneous, comprising Malays, Muslims and Christians. Yet, it is only when Coloureds, Indians and Africans come into contact with Whites that cultural differences are highlighted. Or when Africans and Coloureds come into Indian settings that cultural differences apparently become significant. Or, when Africans go into coloured spaces that it is important. This version of multiculturalism bears frightening resonances with the Verwoerdian manipulations of cultural diversity, and the racism within them is equally stark.

Yet, these versions of multiculturalism are also fraught with problematic assumptions about the nature of people's identities. In these particular multiculturalist accounts, people who are perceived to be culturally different are fixed and stereotyped within their assumed identities. A Zulu student in school is assumed to be representative of and loyal to Zulu culture. The fact that this student may have been living all of his or her life in an urban area, is immersed in westernized life-styles of rap-music, denim jeans, fast foods and shopping at urban malls, get conveniently edited out of the picture, since the Zulu is not supposed to be 'into' these sorts of activities. More disturbing is the fact that the Zulu is positioned as such, as a Zulu. The gender, class, ability, sexual orientation and other characteristics of the person are ignored almost entirely. The consequence of this is that these versions of multiculturalism deny the actual ways in which people live their lives and the various dimensions of their identities. As such, such multicultural practices land up constructing artificial and chimerical images of cultural difference that in fact are unhelpful.

These multicultural practices also ignore the power dimensions of racism. This, however, is an argument that antiracists have consistently levelled against such multicultural approaches by pointing out that the focus within multiculturalism is on lifestyles rather than life chances or opportunities (see, for example, Braham et al., 1992; Brandt, 1986; Gillborn, 1990; Troyna, 1993). The Gauteng and Western Cape schools that use multiculturalism to develop a 'United Nations' feel in their schools ignore the material differences that exist among differently 'raced' and racialized students in their schools. In these ways, the actual basis of the inequalities suffered by Blacks does not receive adequate attention, if at all, and the focus on the socially constructed nature of racism remains unexplored. The result is that racism gets displaced into considerations of different lifestyles, and racist practices, processes and assumptions continue almost unabated.

It could be argued that what we are pointing to here refers to 'bad' multicultural practices, and that it is possible and conceivable for multicultural practices to work with non-stereotypical and dynamic senses of identity. 'Good' multicultural practices or a critical multiculturalism would overtly confront questions about the power dimensions of racism and would insist that cultural differences among all people, including those within racialized groups, receive equal attention (cf. May, this volume). This possibility of 'good', critical multicultural practices is indeed conceivable, as this volume attests, but we do not have evidence of this existing in any of the South African experiences, either historically or in the contemporary situation. However, as we argue, this type of 'good', critical multiculturalism may be seen as being akin to a critical antiracism and it is to this that we now turn our attention.

A Critical Antiracism

The Gauteng and Western Cape school experiences indicate clearly that desegregation of South African schools is not just a black versus white issue. It is a matter of *intra*-black desegregation too. This is the case because Indian and coloured schools have also 'opened' their doors to non-Indian and non-coloured students. This broader process of inclusion has several implications.

First, the bipolarity between homogenized groups of Blacks and Whites, so consistent within both racist and antiracist logic, is untenable within the South African situation. Working with such a bipolarity will not equip us with the tools to investigate the intra-black dynamics that are currently unfolding. This also means that one cannot work with the assumptions that all Whites are necessarily and only proto-racists or that all Blacks are necessarily and always victims (cf. Moodley, this volume). This is clearly not the case.

The Gauteng and Western Cape schools show that Blacks manifest racist tendencies themselves. This comes through clearly in the ways in which Indians treat non-Indians, and Coloureds treat non-coloureds. As such, assuming an homogenized and essentialized sense of 'blackness' is not only counter-factual, it is also unproductive. To capture these intra-black dynamics one needs to work with a 'de-essentialized' (Hall, 1992) sense of what being black means. Not all Blacks are the same, and Blacks are actually much more than simply 'black'. A de-essentialized conception of blackness enables us to view the many ways in which people experience their 'race', the ways in which they position themselves within it, and the motley array of other identities that make up their persons. Being African in an Indian or coloured school is decidedly different from being African in a white school. Being African, middle-class and proficient in English is very different from being African, working-class, from a rural area and not having any English at all. Being Indian, female and lesbian too would have rather different implications in a white school environment as opposed to being Indian, male and heterosexual in the same school. A 'de-essentialized' conception of identity, therefore, more accurately captures the ways in which people live their lives, the nature of the experiences they have and the ways in which their identities are actually formed (cf. May; Rattansi, this volume).

The traditional antiracist logic, for us, therefore, needs to become more sophisticated by incorporating a more complex view of people's identities in order for the reality of their lives to be captured (cf. Gillborn, 1995). This is indispensable if we are to address the continuing and various ways in which racism is being reconstructed in current situations. This is crucial if the antiracist project itself is to remain a viable future strategy. This also means that macro policy formulations and interventions cannot continue to articulate antiracist strategies in general terms. They need to take into account the actual ways in which people experience their realities on micro levels. Such interventions need to 'talk to' the actual, 'on the ground' ways in which racism is perceived, understood, experienced and reconstructed. Failure to do so would render such interventions unimplementable, and thereby defeat the purposes for which they have been put into place in the first instance.

For us, a critical antiracism would ensure a 'de-essentialized' sense of people's identities, in that it would acknowledge and incorporate the notion of 'difference' within and among people. It would also pierce the bipolarity of Whites versus Blacks, and thereby get to grips with the various and varying ways in which racism is experienced within and across racialized groups of people. It would also inject the necessary specificities that ought to inform macro policy formulations and interventions. At the same time, critical antiracism would still carry with it the potency of the antiracist emphasis on the power dimensions of racism. A critical antiracism would maintain the focus on macro socio-economic and political forces and the ways in which they intersect with and influence people's micro, individual lives. These antiracist analytical strengths remain within the critical antiracist approach, which also means that a critical antiracism is but a sophistication and refinement of antiracism, not a betrayal or debunking of it.

Note

1   These designations are placed in quotation marks here so as to highlight their arbitrary and essentialized construction — the product of the racist apartheid system. We will continue to use these categories in what follows since they are part of the nomenclature and vocabulary of apartheid — and, to some extent still, post-apartheid — South Africa. However, we reject entirely the racism and racial essentialism embedded in their use.

References

BADAT, S. (1992) 'Open schools', in *New Era*, Cape Town: South African Research Services, p. 28.

BRAHAM, P., RATTANSI, A. and SKELLINGTON, R. (eds) (1992) *Racism and Antiracism: Inequalities, Opportunities and Policies*, London: Sage.

BRANDT, G. (1986) *The Realisation of Antiracist Teaching*, Lewes: Falmer Press.

CARRIM, N. (1992) *Desegregating Indian and Coloured Schools*, Education Policy Unit Research Report, Johannesburg: University of the Witwatersrand Press.

CARRIM, N. (1995) 'From "race" to ethnicity: Shifts in the educational discourses of South Africa and Britain in the 1990s', *Compare*, **25**, pp. 17–33.

CARRIM, N. and SAYED, Y. (1991) 'Open schools: Reform or transformation?', *Work in Progress*, **74**, Johannesburg: South African Research Services, pp. 28–9.

CARRIM, N. and SAYED, Y. (1992) 'Pay as you learn: Model C schools are not for working class kids', *Work in Progress/New Era*, **84**, Johannesburg: South African Research Services, pp. 28–9.

CONSTITUTION OF THE REPUBLIC OF SOUTH AFRICA (1996) Pretoria: Government Press.

CROSS, M. and MKWANAZI, Z. (1992) 'The concept of multicultural education and its relevance to South Africa', National Education Policy Investigations working paper, unpublished.

DEPARTMENT OF NATIONAL EDUCATION (1996) *South African Schools Act*, Pretoria: Government Press.

DONALD, J. and RATTANSI, A. (eds) (1992) *'Race', Culture, and Difference*, London: Sage.

GILLBORN, D. (1990) *'Race', Ethnicity and Education: Teaching and Learning in Multiethnic Schools*, London: Unwin Hyman/Routledge.

GILLBORN, D. (1995) *Racism and Antiracism in Real Schools*, Buckingham: Open University Press.

HALL, S. (1992) 'New ethnicities', in DONALD, J. and RATTANSI, A. (eds) *'Race', Culture, and Difference*, London: Sage, pp. 252–9.

JACKLIN, H. (1991) Unpublished transcripts and notes of interviews with teachers and principals in the Western Cape.

MACDONALD, I., BHAVNANI, R., KHAN, L. and JOHN, G. (1989) *Murder in the Playground: The Report of the MacDonald Inquiry into Racism and Racial Violence in Manchester Schools*, London: Longsight Press.

McLAREN, P. (1995) *Critical Pedagogy and Predatory Culture*, London and New York: Routledge.

METCALFE, M. (1991) *Desegregating Education in South Africa. White School Enrolments in Johannesburg 1985–1991: Update and Policy Analysis*, Education Policy Unit Research Report, Johannesburg: University of the Witwatersrand Press.

MULLER, J. (1992) 'Open schools', in *New Era*, Cape Town: South African Research Services, p. 28.

ROSE, B. and TUNMER, R. (1975) *Documents in South African Education*, Johannesburg: Donker.

SOUDIEN, C. (1994a) 'Dealing with race: Laying down patterns for multiculturalism in South Africa', *Interchange*, **25**, pp. 281–94.

SOUDIEN, C. (1994b) 'Equality and equity in South Africa: Multicultural education and change', *Equity and Excellence*, **27**, pp. 55–60.

SOUDIEN, C. (1996) 'Apartheid's children: Student narratives of the relationship between experiences in schools and perceptions of racial identity in South Africa', Unpublished PhD Dissertation, State University of New York at Buffalo.

TROYNA, B. (1993) *Racism and Education: Research Perspectives*, Buckingham: Open University Press.

VERSFELD, R. (1997) Personal communication.

WOLPE, H. (1986) 'Class concepts, class struggle and racism', in REX, J. and MASON, D. (eds) *Theories of Race and Ethnic Relations*, Cambridge: Cambridge University Press, pp. 110–30.

WOLPE, H. (1989) *Race, Class and the Apartheid State*, Paris: UNESCO.

7   Children's Constructions of Their National Identity: Implications for Critical Multiculturalism

Geoffrey Short and Bruce Carrington

Despite the need for pedagogic interventions to counter the influence of racism, ethnocentrism and xenophobia, such measures continue to be criticized by neo-conservatives on both sides of the Atlantic. In the United Kingdom, since the late 1980s, the influential cultural restorationist wing of the New Right has not only derided and lampooned such interventions, but has sought to impose its own narrow, exclusivist and cultural-racist construction of British national identity (as English and Christian) on the National Curriculum in England and Wales. British antiracist educators, with a few notable exceptions (see, for example, Cohen, 1988; Gillborn, 1995; Modood, 1992; Rattansi, 1992, this volume), have given little attention to what Barker (1981) has dubbed the 'new racism'. In so far as the latter is treated at all in the generality of antiracist literature, it is only ever mentioned in passing and its pedagogic implications appear never to have been addressed.

In this chapter, we briefly examine the reasons for this neglect before moving on to assess the impact of the new racism on the way children conceptualize their national identity. Drawing upon ethnographic data from a study undertaken in an elementary school in the US, three English primary schools and a Scottish primary school, we consider children's constructions of their national identity in relation to ethnicity, age and geographical location. Accepting the view that the dualism of antiracist and multicultural education is arbitrary and unhelpful (see, for example, May, 1994a, b), we conclude by exploring the relevance of our findings for critical multicultural pedagogy.

The New Racism

Just over 15 years ago, Martin Barker (1981) drew attention to an emergent form of racism in the United Kingdom that defined national identity in terms of cultural affiliation. This 'new racism' was directed against the country's African-Caribbean and South Asian communities and was alleged to be particularly prevalent among the right wing of the Conservative party. According to Barker, the new racism is distinguished from the old in three respects. It has no truck with notions of inferiority (either biological or cultural), no need for negative stereotyping, and no interest in blaming ethnic minorities for any of the country's problems, whether social or economic. The basis of the new racism is rather the instinctive need of the nation to protect itself against any perceived threat to its continued existence. With its philo-sophical roots in the writings of David Hume and its 'scientific' roots in sociobiology, the new racism contends that it is human nature to create bounded social groups (or nations) and for such groups to separate themselves from those they perceive to be different. The differences are defined culturally. Indeed, the importance attached to national culture within the new racism can be judged from the role it plays as both the source of individual identity and the guarantor of social and political cohesion. In the words of the Conservative journalist, T. E. Utley, 'No Tory can accept the view that the existence in one small and homogeneous island of a huge variety of divergent cultures and religions is in itself a source of strength' (cited in Rich, 1986, p. 64). Anything (such as a relatively large immigrant community with an alien culture) that endangers the national way of life, or disrupts what the British politi-cian Enoch Powell in 1977 referred to as the 'homogeneous we', will be disorienting and resented and will inevitably give rise to genuinely held fears. As Barker puts it: 'You do not need to think of yourself as superior — you do not even need to dislike or blame those who are different to you — in order to say that the presence of these aliens constitutes a threat to our way of life' (1981, p. 18).

Barker does not distinguish between racism and prejudice. It is evident, how-ever, that when alluding to the new racism, he actually has in mind a form of prejudice, for nowhere in his thesis does he consider the structural dimension of 'race relations' in the United Kingdom (for an elaboration of this critique, see Small, 1994). Rather less clear is whether he believes the new racism to have eclipsed the old or whether the two ideologies, to some extent, run in parallel. One thing though that is not in doubt is that new racist thinking has lost none of its appeal to sections of the Tory party, despite the fact that migration to Britain from the Caribbean and the Indian sub-continent, the chief pre-occupation of the new racism, has virtually ceased. Thus, in May, 1993, the Conservative MP, Winston Churchill (grandson of the wartime Prime Minister), said at a private meeting:

A halt must be called to immigration if the British way of life is to be preserved. The population of many of our northern cities is well over 50 per cent immigrant, and Muslims claim there are now more than two million of their co-religionists in Britain. Mr Major [then Prime Minister] seeks to reassure us with the old refrain 'There'll always be an England'. He promises us that 50 years on from now, spinsters will be cycling to Communion on Sunday mornings — more like the muezzin will be calling Allah's faithful to the high street mosque. (*The Times*, 29 May, 1993)

He reiterated these views a couple of months later.

We must not ignore or sweep under the carpet the impact on our society and the British way of life of the arrival in our midst. . . . of three to four million immig-rants from Africa, Asia and the Caribbean. (*The Times*, 20 July, 1993)

New Right, New Racism and Education

With the coming to power in the United Kingdom of the Conservative administration in 1979, the cultural restorationist wing of the party emerged as the dominant force in British politics. Central to its philosophy was the resurrection of a set of traditional values which effectively underwent an apotheosis during Mrs Thatcher's period in office (1979–90). They permeated every sphere of national life in a bid to arrest what was seen as an inexorable slide into moral decay and economic collapse. Schools became a prime site for intervention for it was here, according to party dogma, more than anywhere else, that the nation had lost its way following the alleged triumph of progressivism in the 1960s. Whilst successive Ministers of State focused obsessively on improving standards in 'the basics' (of English, maths, reading and science) they were no less zealous in purging the system of any vestige of cultural and moral relativism, a particularly unwelcome by-product of the supposedly permissive 1960s.

Although no longer in the ascendancy, especially after the massive electoral defeat of the Conservatives in May 1997, New Right thinking about various aspects of educational provision continues to exert a powerful influence on the new Labour government. For example, the recent White Paper *Excellence in Schools* (published in July 1997) outlines current strategies for state education, but does not differ substantially from those of the previous administration. Anti-progressivism is arguably its most clearly discernible *leitmotif* together with a continuing emphasis on centralized control and accountability. Social authoritarianism — a hallmark of New Right discourse — is largely unchallenged in the White Paper and measures such as those introduced by the previous administration to impose a curriculum on initial teacher education have been given a fresh lease of life. One of these measures, the requirement that new entrants to the profession are proficient in both spoken and written Standard English (DfEE, 1997, circular 1) reflects the view prevalent on the Right, both in Britain and the United States, that the dominance of such dialects is an essential precondition of national cohesion. (We elaborate on this point below.)

Over the past decade and a half, the media, aided by new racist ideologues, have portrayed multicultural education and its celebration of diversity as an alien and destabilizing intrusion, a threat, in other words, to the 'British way of life'. Antiracist education, with which multiculturalism is often associated, suffered similarly at the hands of the media and was frequently lampooned and derided by Conservative politicians, academics, and educationalists. It was thus no surprise to find the former Prime Minister John Major, telling the Tory party conference in 1992 that teachers in training 'should learn how to teach children to read' and 'not waste their time on the politics of gender, race and class'. Addressing a similar gathering five years earlier, his predecessor, Mrs Thatcher, accused 'hard-left education authorities and extremist teachers' of denying many young people the chance of a 'decent education'. She went on, 'children who need to be able to count and multiply are learning antiracist mathematics, whatever that may be' (see Troyna, 1993).

The culmination of these concerns was the Education Reform Act of 1988, the most far-reaching piece of legislation affecting educational provision in England and

Wales since the end of the Second World War. Not only was it to pave the way for a complex and prescriptive subject-based curriculum and system of national assessment at ages 7, 11, 14 and 16, but it also put in place various measures designed to enhance the power of 'consumers' (parents and employers) at the expense of the 'educational establishment'. As a result of the Act, the influence of various interest groups seen by the former government and right-wing polemicists as inimical to traditional values in education were marginalized (Ball, 1990; Troyna and Carrington, 1990).

The National Curriculum to which the Reform Act gave rise, represented a compromise between the assimilationist aspirations of the New Right and the forces of liberalism within the much maligned 'educational establishment' and in society-at-large. The battle over the place of religious education in the curriculum exemplified the compromise, for whilst the Act may have thrust Christianity 'into a position of embarrassing prominence' (Hull, 1989, p. 119), it nonetheless insisted that any new syllabus had to take into account the teaching and practices of other principal faiths. Compromise was also evident in the interim report of the History Working Group (established by the Secretary of State) which admitted to having British history at its core whilst managing to resist political demands for a more patriotic content. The working group noted that:

> Individual people in these islands have much in common but they also have many individual characteristics specific to country, ethnic grouping, religion, gender and social class. We do not believe that school history can be so finely tuned so as to accommodate all of these details all of the time, but at least it can make pupils aware of the richness and variety of British culture and its historical origins. (DES, 1989, p. 17)

With the passing of the Education Reform Act, there was to be no let up in the campaign waged by the New Right to set the educational agenda. For example, the Department for Education circular (1/94) on *Religious Education and Collective Worship* states that 'Religious education should seek to develop pupils' knowledge, understanding and awareness of Christianity as the predominant religion in Great Britain'. Likewise, the Schools Curriculum and Assessment Authority's (SCAA) proposals for the teaching of English (published in July 1994) stress the importance of standard English and also require children to be introduced to 'significant authors and works in the English literary heritage'.[1]

To be fair to the cultural restorationists, their spokespersons have never made any attempt to deny or disguise their purpose. They candidly admit their mission to stem the tide of cultural pluralism as can be seen in the following comment from Nick Tate, the Chief Executive designate of the government's Qualifications and Curriculum Authority:

> The proposals for British history, Standard English and the English literary heritage are designed to reinforce a common culture. A national curriculum, we imply, is more than simply a recipe for meeting economic needs, vital though these are; it is more than just the means to facilitate the infinitely varied life choices of collections of isolated individuals. It also plays a key part in helping society to maintain its identity. (Tate, 1994, p. 5)

We are not, of course, accusing Tate of being sympathetic to the new racism. None of his public statements lends credence to such an accusation and some clearly run counter to it. For example, when addressing a meeting of headteachers (principals) in July 1995, he said:

> The best guarantee of strong minority cultures is the existence of a majority culture which is sure of itself, which signals that customs and traditions are things to be valued and which respects other cultures. (*Daily Mail*, 18 July, 1995)

It would seem especially difficult to attack Tate when he pleads for a less disdainful attitude towards promoting a British identity in order to curb the nationalistic excesses of the British tabloid press. Recently, for example, with reference to the xenophobic coverage of the international football tournament Euro '96, he told the Association of Teachers and Lecturers: 'If you lack a worthwhile sense of group identity you become insecure and you begin to lash out at others' (*Times Educational Supplement*, 28 June, 1996). He claimed that a nation ill at ease with itself was taking solace in comic-book stereotypes.

We do not wish to impugn Tate's motives, for we have no doubt that he genuinely wishes to integrate Britain's ethnic minorities in ways that are acceptable to them and to the wider community. We have some reservations about his demand for a common curriculum — which we expand upon later — but our more immediate concern is with the effects of his frequent and highly publicized interventions on policy makers. Specifically, we fear the encouragement his words will give to those sympathetic to the new racism. The latter already appears to have influenced the National Curriculum and it is reasonable to assume that the changes have, in turn, influenced children to conceptualize their national identity in terms of cultural affiliation. We have no evidence that this is the case due to the lack of baseline data, but on *à priori* grounds the possibility cannot be dismissed and should not be treated lightly. Despite this, British antiracists have tended to show little or no interest in the new racism. Barring a few notable exceptions (e.g., Cohen, 1988; Gillborn, 1995; Modood, 1992; Rattansi, 1992), the subject has only ever surfaced *en passant* in antiracist literature and its educational implications appear never to have been addressed. One possible explanation for this neglect is the absence of any empirical evidence that children are, in fact, susceptible to new racist thinking. A second possibility is more serious for it is concerned not just with matters of evidence, but with the nature of antiracism itself. Antiracist education in the United Kingdom has, from the outset, eschewed any real interest in culture which it has viewed, at best, as an irrelevance and at worst, as a source of tension between ethnic groups (Troyna, 1987). However, the new racism, as we have seen, is a concept inextricably linked to culture.

Antiracist educators are faced with an irreconcilable dilemma. They wish to develop inclusivist notions of national identity (in order to safeguard the rights of ethnic minorities) but reject the means of bringing this about. Their seemingly implacable hostility towards multicultural education would appear to render them ideologically incapable of mounting any sort of challenge to the new racism. Critical multiculturalism (May, 1994a, b), offers the only way out of the dilemma for, in contrast to conventional antiracism, it sees no necessary incompatibility between the demands for cultural diversity on the one hand and for greater racial and ethnic equality on the other. Indeed, it maintains that such an integration is essential for the promotion of social justice. The problem for critical multiculturalism is practical rather than ideological, namely, how best to engage with the new racism.

More than a quarter of a century ago, Campbell and Lawton wrote that 'if we do not know the nature of children's thinking about society, it is difficult to plan appropriate learning contexts for them' (1970, p. 901). We believe this methodological imperative to be as relevant today as it was when originally enunciated. If we are to tackle effectively conceptions of national identity that run counter to democratic pluralism, we must first discover how children think about their national identity and how their thinking develops over time. In particular, we must uncover what Bill Damon has referred to as their 'central organizing principles', that is, 'the structural core that shapes [a child's] knowledge and gives it coherence and regularity' (1977, p. 25).

For this reason we have spent the past four years exploring the ways in which children of primary school age in the United Kingdom and the United States construe their national identity (Carrington and Short, 1995, 1996; Short and Carrington, 1996). Whilst undertaking this research we have been aware of both similarities and differences in how national identity is conceptualized in the two countries. One of the major similarities would seem to involve the treatment of linguistic diversity in populist discourse. Specifically, any attempt to undermine the hegemonic position of Standard English is invariably viewed, especially by the Right, as a potential threat to social cohesion. As Arthur Schlesinger (1992) has shown in *The Disuniting of America* the English-speaking political culture has been challenged not only by African-American secessionist ideologies but also by the increasing use of Spanish in the country (see May, this volume; Rex, 1996 for further discussion). It is not, of course, just academics who have underlined the importance of language to identity. The high-profile Republican, Newt Gingrich, during a debate in Congress on making English the country's official language (1 August, 1996), articulated widespread concern about the ramifications of linguistic diversity. He claimed that 'part of becoming American involves English. . . . It is vital to assert and establish that English is the common language at the heart of our civilization' (*Independent on Sunday*, 22 September, 1996).

The integral connection between a common language and national identity has been recognized for a long time. As Anthony Arblaster notes:

> In national and nationalist movements language has frequently been a focus for agitation and mobilisation. It is often one leading badge of a separate national identity, as in Catalonia or even Wales today. Conversely empires have often sought to prohibit and extinguish national languages and impose a single imperial language on their dominions. (1995, p. 202)

The crucial role of a common language in securing national cohesion has also been recognized for a long time and in many different contexts. In Australia, for example, as Bill Cope and Mary Kalantzis in this volume make clear, speaking 'English. . . . without a trace of the accent of another language' (p. 249) was a key component of the policy of assimilation which dominated government thinking in the 1950s and early 1960s.

Whilst Standard English might play a similar role in the construction of national identity in the United Kingdom and the United States, there are, as we have pointed out, some important differences between the two countries in respect of this form of identity. Tariq Modood, who has a particular interest in the sense of belonging of ethnic minorities, maintains that the British have no 'demonstrative expression of commonalty and national loyalty that can serve as a symbol of belonging'. Specifically, there is no British equivalent to the American Constitution and the acceptance of this constitution as a condition of citizenship. He posits that the absence of such a symbol of belonging poses particular problems for Britain's ethnic minorities who 'know they are not respected and yet are given little opportunity to express "Britishness"' (1992, p. 79).

A further difference between the two countries is that the Americans take seriously the notion of a hyphenated identity. To quote Modood again:

> They take pride not just in their Americanness, but in asserting that they are Irish-American, Black-American, African-American . . . and so on. . . . [It] is clear that a hyphenated identity does not imply that one is only half-American or any detraction from patriotism. Rather, it is seen as the claiming of an ethnic identity within the framework of a common nationality that is open to all forms of ethnic difference that do not challenge the overarching bonds of nation and citizenship. . . . 'British' by contrast is virtually a quasi-ethnic term, and being closely identified with whiteness, it excludes other ethnic terms, so it is not surprising that descriptions such as British-Black or British Pakistani are at present not much more than courtesy titles and carry limited conviction. (1992, p. 78)

David Miller explains the difference in the British and American responses to hyphenation as follows:

> Where the national identity includes as one of its cultural aspects the positive celebration of diversity, as in the case of the USA, it is relatively easy for people to adopt hyphenated identities to express their dual membership. . . . In most European states national identity is more heavily marked by the dominant ethnic group and hyphenation is less easy. (1995, p. 156)

Some prominent writers on national identity such as Bernard Crick (1995) regard Britain as a multinational state (see Introduction) and in this sense as fundamentally different from the United States. Britishness for them is a form of political and legal allegiance, a view summed up by Miller as follows:

> It is quite often argued that (the Scots, Welsh and Northern Irish) are separate nations so that rather than thinking in terms of British national identity at all, we should think of Britain as a multinational state in which common political institutions hold together communities with separate identities . . . (1995, p. 162)

Miller's own view is quite different. He argues that a 'shared historical experience, together with a very substantial level of cultural interchange . . . has sustained a sense of common nationality alongside an equally powerful sense of difference'. Claiming that there are many distinct and equally legitimate ways of 'being British', he cites the position of the Scots as illustrative: 'To be a Scot in Britain is to share in a common identity, but to have at the same time a powerful sense of the cultural distinctness of the group to which you belong . . .' (1995, p. 162). In support of this contention, Brand et al. (1993) found that when asked about their identity most Scots not only admit to being both British and Scottish, but attach greater importance to their Scottishness.

The empirical core of this paper examines whether different constructions of national identity within Britain and between Britain and the United States are reflected in children of primary school age. We report the findings before discussing their implications for critical multicultural pedagogy.

The Research

Background

Altogether we interviewed 265 children (136 boys and 129 girls). Those in the United Kingdom (numbering 204 in total) were drawn from three English primary (elementary) schools (two in the North East and one in the South East) and from one Scottish primary school. All four were situated in urban locations and were co-educational. The American sample of 61 children attended the same urban co-educational elementary school in Massachusetts. The schools were selected principally for reasons related to access.

All the participants (in England, Scotland and the United States) were aged between 8 and 12 and came from ethnically mixed backgrounds. However, the majority (80 per cent in Britain and 78 per cent in the United States) were white. Almost all the children (95 per cent) were born in the country where they were interviewed and while they represented a variety of social backgrounds, the parents' occupational profile was skewed towards white-collar and professional work.

Methodology

Semi-structured interviews were administered individually to the participants, all of whom were volunteers and had been given a guarantee of personal and institutional anonymity. They were informed that they could withdraw their co-operation at any time without explanation and without penalty (although in the event, none chose to exercise this option). The youngest of the British children (i.e. those aged 8 and 9) were initially asked, 'Have you heard the word British?'. Those responding affirmatively were then presented with the following core questions.[2]

- Are you British, or are you something else?
- What makes a person British?
- Is everyone who lives in this country British?
- Is it possible to stop being British and become something else?
- Is being British important to you?

Although the American children were presented with more or less the same questions — with appropriate substitutions — there were two main differences. They were asked an additional question, 'Are some people more American than others?', but they were not probed on whether their national identity was important to them.

The Findings

A number of interesting differences emerged between the American and British cohorts when they were asked to identify themselves in terms of nationality: 'Are you British/American, or are you something else?'. Whereas 94 per cent of the white children in English schools said that they were unequivocally British, only two-thirds of the white children in America referred to themselves simply as 'American'. The remainder either claimed a hyphenated identity (23 per cent) or a nationality other than American (13 per cent). This finding is clearly in line with the views of Modood and Miller referred to earlier. We cite below a couple of examples of American children explaining to the researcher the origins of their hyphenated identity. The detail may be significant, for it could well reflect the importance that children of primary school age attach to their sense of belonging to an 'imagined community' (Anderson, 1991).

> I'm Irish, Canadian; my dad's background is a little Russian (and) I think some France. (Shaun, 10 years)
> American, Irish, French and partly German. (Kevin, 10 years)

These comments may also be significant in so far as they reveal the embryonic grasp that some young children have of the problematic nature of 'whiteness'. The children appear to have rejected the monolithic view of white identity that has, for so long, been taken for granted in antiracist discourse on both sides of the Atlantic (see Bonnett 1993, 1996; McLaren and Torres, this volume). In contrast to the differences between the white children, the responses of the visible minorities in the two countries were almost identical, with about one-third viewing their national identity in hyphenated terms. A number of these children also gave detailed responses:

> My mum and dad are Chinese, but they were born in Taiwan and I was born here (so I'm) half Chinese and half American. (Benjamin, aged 10)

> Mum was born in England and she's British and my dad was born in Kenya. He's Indian. . . . I'm both, a bit British and a bit Kenyan. (Prashant, aged 9)

The tendency for ethnic minority rather than white children in the British sample to describe themselves in hyphenated terms lends support to Modood's view that African-Caribbeans and South Asians in Britain have far less opportunity to express 'Britishness'. However, 13 per cent of white children in Scotland (considerably more than the proportion in England) seemed to operate with a fluid conception of national identity rejecting the simple epithet 'British' in favour of a bifurcated description (e.g. 'Scottish and British'). As we have seen, the proportion of white Americans who defined themselves similarly was substantially higher.

The responses of the American cohort to the question, 'What makes a person American?' were broadly comparable to those of their British counterparts. They tended to define their national identity in concrete terms with most (64 per cent) claiming that being born in the United States was the key determinant. Other frequent responses fell into the following categories: 'living or working in the country' (31 per cent), 'having American citizenship' (16 per cent) or 'American ancestry' (11 per cent). There were, however, some significant differences between the British and American children. For example, whereas the latter made only the odd reference to linguistic factors when defining American identity, over a third of the English and more than a quarter of the Scottish children believed that the ability to speak English was a defining characteristic of Britishness.

Predictably, the question 'Is everyone who lives in this country American/ British?' prompted a varied response. The overwhelming majority were negative, with many simply answering 'No' without elaboration. The most frequently cited counter-examples were 'people from other countries', 'people born overseas' and 'immigrants'. There were no major differences between the British and American samples although subjective definitions of national identity, stressing the importance of self-regard, were more common among the Americans. In both groups of children it was rare to encounter instances of cultural racism (i.e., comments that express or imply a view of national identity defined partly in terms of assimilation to the dominant culture). One of the few came from an 8-year-old white boy who said: 'Some people who don't (go along with) the traditions, like don't celebrate Memorial day, might not be American'.

We were especially interested in the children's responses to the question, 'Is it possible to stop being British/American and become something else?', because of its potential for eliciting culturally racist remarks. In the event, only 14 per cent of the American children and a similar proportion of those in England and Scotland contextualized their comments in this way. The following transcripts from English schools are representative.

BC	Is it possible to stop being British and become something else?
Mark	(British white, aged 10) Yes, I think it is possible.
BC	Can you tell me how you'd do it?
Mark	Speak a different language. . . . just go to that country and try to be the same, wear the same clothes that they wear and do the same kind of things.

GS   If you are British, can you become something else? Can you become French or German or Chinese?

Dipesh   (British Asian, aged 10) Yes.

GS   How would I become French? What have I got to do?

Dipesh   Learn the language.

GS   So if I just stay at home here. . . . and I learn the language, does that make me French?

Dipesh   No.

GS   So what else have I got to do then to become French?

Dipesh   Learn the religion. You would have to go there. You would change your accent and change your lifestyle.

On both sides of the Atlantic, those answering the question in the affirmative were particularly inclined to think in terms of residence abroad as an entitlement to assume a different nationality. When seen in conjunction with the response to the question, 'What makes a person British/American?', we can be fairly confident that children of this age regard country of domicile as an important determinant of national identity and, perhaps, no less important than country of origin.

There were two principal differences between the American and British children. First, as we have noted, the Americans were far less likely to think in terms of learning the language as a means of adopting an alternative nationality. Only 3 per cent referred to it as a possibility, in contrast to both the English and Scottish samples where the proportion was significantly higher (34 per cent and 28 per cent respectively). Moreover, there were some English and Scottish children who claimed that difficulty in learning a foreign language was a reason for not being able to change one's nationality. No such responses were forthcoming from the American sample. The comparative dearth of references to language among the American children suggests that the fears voiced in certain academic and political circles in the country about threats to the hegemonic position of English may not enjoy widespread support. The data further suggest that there may be more tolerance of cultural diversity in the United States than in the United Kingdom. To quote Modood: 'pressures to conform in Britain are greater than they are in America' (1992, p. 80).

The second difference between the children concerns the importance attached to place of birth. Whereas around a third of the British children said it was not possible to change one's nationality because birthplace was crucial, just 1 per cent of the Americans thought likewise. (Whilst the historic role of the United States as a 'nation of immigrants' might account for this discrepancy, we recognize that the American figure might have been much higher had the research been undertaken in a part of the country with different demographic characteristics). The following comments are illustrative of those stressing the overriding importance of this aspect of national identity.

No — if you move to another country you can become part something else, but you are still American. (Lynne, 9 years, American white)

Not really because you were born in America. You can become a citizen of another place, but you are still American. (Alex, 9 years, American white)

> You can live in another country, but [you'd] still be American, if you were originally from America. . . . America is still part of your child[hood], or your adult[hood] — whenever you lived in America. (Mary, 10 years, American white)

The subjective or phenomenological dimension of national identity previously observed in the American sample was again evident in response to the question about altering one's national identity. Cindy (an 11-year-old Chinese-American) said that it would be necessary 'to go somewhere else and become something else *and stop thinking you're American*'. Fatima (an 11-year-old East Indian American) made a similar point. People could adopt another nationality, she declared, 'if they really hated it here, or were forced to live here and *didn't want to be American*'.

As pointed out, the American cohort was asked if some people are more American than others. The most common response — albeit largely confined to the 8- to 10-year-olds — was that those born in the United States were more American than those born elsewhere. Lynne, a 9-year-old white girl, summed up the dominant view when she said, 'If you're born in America, you are more American than someone who just moved here'. The younger children also tended to see those with relatives in the country and those who had lived in the country longer than others as having a stronger claim to American identity. In respect of the latter, the majority of older respondents (i.e., the 11-year-olds) seemed to regard the notion of being 'more American' as a category error. In their eyes, national identity is an absolute concept, not a relative one. As one 11-year-old put it: 'If you're American, you're American — there is no higher stage'. The only concession that some were prepared to make to 'Americanness' was in relation to the indigenous peoples. Thus, Lesley, a white American (aged 11), maintained: 'We're all basically the same — Native Americans can be called more American because their family originated from America'.

For a few of the older children, however, the idea of some people being more American than others not only made sense but was conceptualized as something that could be measured in cultural terms. In the words of José-Luis, a 10-year-old Puerto Rican American, 'People who celebrate Christmas may be more American than people who celebrate Chanukah'. Jim, a white American, who was a year older said: 'If they really like their original clothing and are in communication with their other country, they would be less American'.

We commented earlier that the English and Scottish children were asked whether their national identity was important to them. For the majority, it was, although in most cases it seems that it was the possession of *a* national identity rather than a specifically British one, that was important:

> Britain is the place I was born and also all my family are in Britain and all my friends as well. (Melanie, 9 years, British white)

> I understand this language. (Emily, 9 years, British white)

> I was born here and know lots of people here and I've never really lived in any other country. (Sarah, 9 years, British white)

As with a number of other questions, a small proportion of children contextualized their response in terms of cultural affiliation. For example:

BC	Is it important to you being British?
Stephen	(10 years, British white) Yes, quite.
BC	Why?
Stephen	I just feel I like the way we do things.
BC	What do you mean by the way we do things?
Stephen	Like the traditions and different kinds of things.

BC	Is it important to you, being British?
Claire	(11 years, British white) Not really, no. It's important being Scottish though.
BC	Why?
Claire	Because of the customs . . .

Policy Implications

So long as ethnic minorities in Britain are viewed by the white majority as British in a legalistic sense only, they will remain vulnerable to prejudice and discrimination and, ultimately, if Barker (1981) is correct, to repatriation. As was graphically illustrated in the case of the Jews in pre-war Germany, a sense of belonging that is not validated and reciprocated by the dominant majority is a delusion and potentially one with tragic consequences. However, as Modood (1992) points out, a genuine sense of belonging cannot be dependent on terms laid down by the majority; it must be acceptable to all ethnic groups. He therefore rejects any suggestion of equating national identity with assimilation to the dominant culture and has called for a concept of Britishness that would have no such implication. The latter, of course, is not something that can be imposed; it must evolve and teachers can play an important part in the process. They must ensure that new racist ideology, revolving around exclusivist notions of national identity, does not influence the way in which children conceptualize ethnic minorities.

Responses to the question of 'What makes a person British/American?' suggest grounds for optimism. For not only did most children claim that place of birth was of prime importance, none of the other frequently mentioned response categories (such as, 'living or working in the country') related to cultural affiliation.[3] Insofar as the children's responses in all three cohorts were broadly comparable, we may have identified an underlying reality, or 'central organizing principle'. Our confidence is bolstered by the relative dearth of culturally racist responses to other questions. Even the one considered most likely to evoke them ('Is it possible to change one's nationality?') largely failed to do so. However, we cannot rule out the possibility of an artefact accounting for the pattern of response as we do not know for sure how the children interpreted the questions. Some of them may have assumed that they called only for a technical or legal definition of national identity. If so, the findings would tend to underestimate the extent to which the children construed such identity as a cultural phenomenon.

Even if we exclude the possibility of an artefact and accept at face value the paucity of culturally racist remarks, we must be mindful of the threat posed by the new racism. For the undeniable reality, as our research has shown, is that children of primary school age are intellectually capable of absorbing new racist sentiments — even if the majority choose not to articulate them. Indeed, it is possible that some of the children, and the older ones in particular, were aware of the taboo status of assimilationist rhetoric and deliberately made no allusion to it in order to avoid being seen as 'politically incorrect'.

Having established the reality of the threat we turn now to consider the educational response. In accordance with the tenets of critical multiculturalism, we see that response involving elements of both conventional antiracism and a reconstructed form of multiculturalism. In respect of the former, it is essential that children of primary school age are able to recognize and challenge that dimension of racist folklore that links 'immigrants' with a range of social and economic problems.[4]

Our case study with a class of 10- and 11-year-olds in the north east of England (Short and Carrington, 1992) shows the feasibility of working with relatively young children to help them deconstruct racist myths and stereotypes. The class project — *In Living Memory* — initially focused on Britain in the immediate post-war period, dealing in particular with the difficulties posed by the acute labour shortage. Asking the children to consider how the difficulties might be overcome led naturally to the issues of 'race' and immigration. The scale and timing of the migration from the West Indies, the Indian sub-continent and elsewhere, and the problems the migrants encountered when they arrived in the United Kingdom, formed a substantial part of the project. Utilizing art, drama, creative writing and contemporary literature, the children were provided with a range of contexts in which they could reflect upon the harsh realities that have faced Britain's ethnic minorities since the war. Opportunities to replicate the project are certainly available within the current History National Curriculum in England and Wales at Key Stage 2 (for children aged 7 to 11). The Key Study Unit, 'Britain since 1930' is the ideal slot for such teaching.

Whilst tackling the 'old racism' may be a necessary precondition of coming to grips with the 'new', it should not be seen as a substitute. At some stage, teachers will have to confront directly the major ideological thrust of the new racism, namely, the contention that no society interested in its own survival can afford to make more than a token gesture towards cultural diversity.

As culture is the key concept in new racist ideology, we see no alternative to multicultural education as a means of combating it. However, if this form of education is to fulfil its role effectively, it has to do more than just supply the ethnic majority with information about the lifestyles and cultural achievements of ethnic minorities. It also has to do more than underline the similarities between ethnocultural groups, important though these are. However, one of the major problems associated with teaching about cultural diversity, as Troyna (1987) has pointed out, is the possibility of promoting the very opposite of social harmony. Put simply, there is a serious risk immanent in an unreconstructed multiculturalism of intensifying prejudice and, in the process, of shoring up the new racism (cf. Carrim and Soudien, this volume). Introducing minority faiths to the ethnic majority, for example, may do no more than demonstrate just how different and thus 'alien' they are. Regardless of the intention, the effect may be counterproductive, buttressing rather than undermining the claim that ethnic minorities have no place in Britain. To some extent, we are thinking of practices (such as the ritual slaughter of animals practised by Muslims and orthodox Jews) that some people might find difficult to accept (see, for example, Carrington and Short, 1993). But we also have in mind problems of a more subtle kind such as the inferences children are likely to draw from learning that certain religious groups pray in a foreign tongue. Grugeon and Woods (1990) illustrated this danger with a project on Judaism undertaken with a group of English 7- and 8-year-olds. Having noted that a number of children thought that Hebrew was 'the language of the Jews' and that many Jews spoke Hebrew at home, the authors concluded that there was a general feeling within the group that Jews were not British. This perception is hardly surprising in view of the data cited above showing the importance that primary-aged children in the UK attach to speaking English as a determinant of British identity.

A further drawback to conventional multiculturalism came to light in our own work on Judaism carried out in English schools with an older age group, i.e. 10–13-year-olds (Short and Carrington, 1995). These children had recently been taught about the Passover and it would seem that in the process some of them had acquired a number of misconceptions about the faith. Thus, one of the 13-year-olds said: 'We know about the Passover . . . that they have to put blood on their doors, otherwise the oldest child in the family — the Jewish family — will die'. A fellow student (the same age) made a similar remark: 'They have to put those things outside their doors — they put blood'. Such misconceptions can only play into the hands of the new racists, for they are clearly inimical to social harmony, tolerance and inclusivist notions of national identity.

In view of these problems we believe it necessary to offer a definition of multicultural education that departs from the conventional approach in three respects. First, it would teach children to distinguish unusual behaviour or cultural practices that are harmful to the interests of the wider community from those that are not. The feasibility of such teaching has been demonstrated with children of primary school age (Short and Carrington, 1991). Secondly, and on a related note, it would not just allow but actively encourage children to debate the merits of any cultural practice and argue for the proscription of those they find morally or socially unacceptable. Critically, though, children should be taught that to condemn some aspect of a culture, on whatever grounds, provides no warrant for discriminating against either other aspects of that culture or against those who practise it. The third respect in which a reconstructed multiculturalism would differ from a conventional approach is in the emphasis it places on identifying and correcting children's misconceptions of other cultures. Indeed, we would advocate attaching a higher priority to engaging with children's misconceptions than to teaching them anything new, for it is distorted or partial 'knowledge', rather than unadorned ignorance, that has the power to transform the unfamiliar into the threatening. The examples cited above of children believing that Jews put blood on their houses is hardly conducive to them viewing this minority group as British in anything other than a legal sense. There can be little doubt that similar misconceptions abound in relation to other minorities and have the same effect on the white majority's perception of their sense of belonging.

Thus far, we have discussed the different ways in which a reconstructed multiculturalism can challenge the new racism's central assertion that cultural pluralism is necessarily a threat to national cohesion. We believe that our recommendations are not only theoretically sound but, in the case of England and Wales, compatible with current curricular requirements. The need to identify misconceptions about different faith communities, for example, can be comfortably accommodated within SCAA's (1994) proposals for religious education. Likewise, teaching children to accept that 'unusual' cultural practices should not necessarily be viewed as anathema to the common good is entirely consistent with the claim in the National Curriculum Council's document *Education for Citizenship* that 'a variety of cultures and lifestyles can be maintained within the framework of (a democratic society)' (1990, p. 6). A critical multiculturalism is also able to exploit opportunities within the current British history curriculum to engage with the new racism. Specifically, teachers must show children that not only has Britain been a culturally diverse society for centuries, but that its social fabric has long been able to withstand tensions stemming from ethnic, religious, social class and regional differences.

Some writers, however, maintain that merely exploiting opportunities within the existing curriculum to undermine cultural racism is not enough. They want to go further and help ethnic minority children to develop a pride in both their ethnic and national identities. In this respect, Modood believes that the school's role is critical:

> Differences can only flourish where one can take a certain amount of commonality for granted: it must be the task of our schools to make both these things possible. To do so is to extend and enrich our understanding of our Britishness, a sense of belonging capable of embracing a number of hyphenated nationalities . . . (1992, p. 84)

Clearly, this is a view shared by Nick Tate who sees the current National Curriculum as a means of satisfying the need. He insists though that:

> Children need to learn about other countries, including Europe, and about other cultures and religions as well, and in some cases, to learn rather more than traditionally they have done. [Also, there should] be additional provision — for example community languages as part of the school curriculum — with the explicit aim of supporting the maintenance of minority cultural traditions where these are traditions that these communities wish to maintain. (1997, p. 3)

A major weakness in Tate's support for the National Curriculum in more or less its present form is 'that he fails to recognize the notoriously fine dividing line between healthy patriotism and negative nationalism' (Phillips, 1997, p. 31). The risk of tilting the balance towards nationalism is enhanced not just by the limited time available for teaching minority cultures but by the constant pressure from the Right (exerting a diminished but still significant influence) to restrict the time available still further.

In addition to sharing Phillips' concern, we are critical of Tate's advocacy of a form of multiculturalism that could well prove counter-productive to his own project. We have in mind Troyna's (1987) caution about the ease with which cultural differences can be construed as evidence that ethnic minorities have no place in British society. For this reason we have argued for a critical multicultural pedagogy, combining conventional antiracist education and a reconstructed multiculturalism, and have offered some practical guidance as to how such an amalgam might lead to a more inclusivist view of British identity. The success of our proposals will depend on the extent to which the ethnic majority disavows culturalist definitions of national identity and ethnic minorities genuinely feel a sense of belonging in Britain.

Notes

1 The fact that SCAA subsequently softened its opposition to non-standard dialects should not be seen, in the present political climate, as anything other than a temporary setback for the New Right.
2 Interviews conducted with older children began with the statement, 'You have obviously heard the word British'.
3 In other words, there was little evidence to suggest that the children construed their national identity in terms of a way of life.
4 As stated in our introduction, allegations of this kind play no part in the new racism. Nonetheless, it is self-evident that children (in the UK) who are ill-disposed towards African-Caribbeans and Asians for these reasons will be more susceptible to the spurious logic of the new racism.

References

ANDERSON, B. (1991) *Imagined Communities: Reflections on the Origins and Spread of Nationalism*, (rev. edn.) London: Verso.

ARBLASTER, A. (1995) 'Unity, identity, difference: Some thoughts on national identity and social unity', *New Community*, **21**, pp. 195–206.

BALL, S. (1990) 'Education, majorism and "the curriculum of the dead"', *Curriculum Studies*, **1**, pp. 195–213.

BARKER, M. (1981) *The New Racism*, London: Junction Books.

BONNETT, A. (1993) 'Forever "white"? Challenges and alternatives to a "racial" monolith', *New Community*, **20**, pp. 173–80.

BONNETT, A. (1996) 'Antiracism and the critique of "white" identities', *New Community*, **22**, pp. 97–110.

BRAND, J., MITCHELL, J. and SURRIDGE, P. (1993) 'Identity and the vote: Class and nationality in Scotland', in DENVER, D. et al. (eds) *British Elections and Parties Yearbook 1993*, Hemel Hempstead: Harvester Wheatsheaf.

CAMPBELL, R. and LAWTON, D. (1970) 'How children see society', *New Society*, 19 November.

CARRINGTON, B. and SHORT, G. (1993) 'Probing children's prejudice: A consideration of the ethical issues raised by research and curriculum development', *Educational Studies*, **19**, pp. 163–79.

CARRINGTON, B. and SHORT, G. (1995) 'What makes a person British? Children's conceptions of their national culture and identity', *Educational Studies*, **21**, pp. 217–38.

CARRINGTON, B. and SHORT, G. (1996) 'Who counts; who cares? Scottish children's notions of national identity', *Educational Studies*, **22**, pp. 203–24.

COHEN, P. (1988) 'The perversions of inheritance: Studies in the making of multi-racist Britain', in COHEN, P. and BAINS, H. (eds) *Multi-racist Britain*, London: Macmillan, pp. 9–118.

CRICK, B. (1995) 'The sense of identity of the indigenous British', *New Community*, **21**, pp. 167–82.

DAMON, W. (1977) *The Social World of the Child*, San Francisco: Jossey-Bass.

DES (DEPARTMENT OF EDUCATION AND SCIENCE) (1989) *National Curriculum: History Working Group Interim Report*, London: HMSO.

DfEE (DEPARTMENT FOR EDUCATION AND EMPLOYMENT) (1997) *Standards for the Award of Qualified Teacher Status*, London: HMSO.

GILLBORN, D. (1995) *Racism and Antiracism in Real Schools*, Buckingham: Open University Press.

GRUGEON, E. and WOODS, P. (1990) *Educating All: Multicultural Perspectives in the Primary School*, London: Routledge.

HULL, J. (1989) 'Editorial: School worship and the 1988 Education Reform Act', *British Journal of Religious Education*, **11**, pp. 119–25.

MAY, S. (1994a) *Making Multicultural Education Work*, Clevedon, England: Multilingual Matters.

MAY, S. (1994b) 'The case for antiracist education', *British Journal of Sociology of Education*, **15**, pp. 421–8.

MILLER, D. (1995) 'Reflections on British national identity', *New Community*, **21**, pp. 153–66.

MODOOD, T. (1992) 'On not being white in Britain: Discrimination, diversity and commonality', in LEICESTER, M. and TAYLOR, M. (eds) *Ethics, Ethnicity and Education*, London: Kogan Page, pp. 72–87.

NATIONAL CURRICULUM COUNCIL (1990) *Education for Citizenship*, York: National Curriculum Council.

PHILLIPS, R. (1997) 'Thesis and antithesis in Tate's views on history, culture and nationhood', *Teaching History*, **86**, pp. 30–3.

RATTANSI, A. (1992) 'Changing the subject? Racism, culture and education', in DONALD, J. and RATTANSI, A. (eds) *'Race', Culture and Difference*, London: Sage, pp. 11–48.

REX, J. (1996) 'National identity in the democratic multi-cultural state', *Sociological Research Online*, **1**, p. 2, (http://www.socresonline.org.uk/socresonline/1/2/1.html).

RICH, P. (1986) 'Conservative ideology of race in modern British politics', in LAYTON-HENRY, Z. and RICH, P. (eds) *Race, Government and Politics in Britain*, London: Macmillan, pp. 45–72.

SCAA (SCHOOL CURRICULUM AND ASSESSMENT AUTHORITY) (1994) *Model Syllabuses for Religious Education Consultation Document*, London: School Curriculum and Assessment Authority.

SCHLESINGER, A. (1992) *The Disuniting of America*, New York: W.W. Norton and Co.

SHORT, G. and CARRINGTON, B. (1991) 'Unfair Discrimination: Teaching the principles to children of primary school age', *Journal of Moral Education*, **20**, pp. 157–76.

SHORT, G. and CARRINGTON, B. (1992) 'Towards an antiracist initiative in the all-white primary school', in GILL, D., MAYOR, B. and BLAIR, M. (eds) *Racism and Education: Structures and Strategies*, London: Sage, pp. 253–68.

SHORT, G. and CARRINGTON, B. (1995) 'Anti-Semitism and the primary school: Children's perceptions of Jewish culture and identity', *Research in Education*, **54**, pp. 14–24.

SHORT, G. and CARRINGTON, B. (1996) 'Antiracist education, multiculturalism and the new racism', *Educational Review*, **48**, pp. 65–77.

SMALL, S. (1994) *Racialized Barriers: The Black Experience in the United States and England in the 1980s*, London: Routledge.

TATE, N. (1994) 'Off the fence on common culture', *Times Educational Supplement*, 29 July.

TATE, N. (1997) 'National identity and the school curriculum', Newsletter No. 11, Centre for Policy Studies in Education, University of Leeds.

TROYNA, B. (1987) 'Beyond multiculturalism: Towards the enactment of antiracist education in policy, provision and pedagogy', *Oxford Review of Education*, **13**, pp. 307–20.

TROYNA, B. (1993) *Racism and Education*, Milton Keynes: Open University Press.

TROYNA, B. and CARRINGTON, B. (1990) *Education, Racism and Reform*, London: Routledge.

8 Critical Multicultural Education and Students' Perspectives

Sonia Nieto

Even under the best of circumstances, the secondary school experiences of most students are characterized by uncertainty and tension. For culturally and linguistically dominated students, whose schooling can hardly be defined as occurring under the best conditions, such tensions are almost inevitable (Gillborn, 1995; Nieto, 1994; Olsen, 1988). Aside from the normal anxieties associated with adolescence, additional pressure for culturally subordinated students may be the result of several factors, including the physical and psychological climate of the schools they attend, the low status their native languages and cultures are accorded in the societies in which they live, the low expectations that society has of them, and their invisibility in traditional curricula.

Students are the people most affected by school policies and practices, but they tend to be the least consulted about them. Consequently, they are ordinarily the silent recipients of schooling. Indeed, it has been pointed out that their role as passive beneficiaries of educational reforms is in direct contrast to the widely accepted constructivist expectations for their learning (Corbett and Wilson, 1995). Even when students are not silent, as when they resist and challenge the education they receive (Kohl, 1994), their advice is ordinarily neither sought nor heeded.

The contribution of critical pedagogy to multicultural education has been especially important in this regard. That is, the insistence that students must be involved in the process of their own education, a central tenet of critical pedagogy, has inspired the inclusion of student voices that had heretofore been missing from most treatments of multicultural education. Further, because it recognizes the fundamentally political nature of education and the need to challenge both its content and form, critical pedagogy brings to multicultural education a sharp institutional analysis that might otherwise be missing (Sleeter and McLaren, 1995). This analysis has created a more self-consciously critical assessment of racism and of the negative impact of school policies and practices on students who have been the greatest victims of school failure.

How do students themselves understand and interpret their school experiences, and what can critical multicultural education offer in terms of its analysis? In this chapter, I will place current discussions concerning critical multicultural education within the framework of the experiences and perspectives of secondary school students who have been marginalized due to their ethnicity, culture, native language, social class, or other differences perceived as deficiencies by the mainstream society in which they live. Specifically, I will explore both the *sociopolitical context* of the lives and education of two students in the United States, and their *particular experiences* in school with racism, ethnocentrism, and unresponsive curriculum and pedagogy. The chapter will emphasize the importance of attending to student perspectives in order to inform and expand critical multicultural education.

The Sociopolitical Context of Education

Because the concept of *sociopolitical context* (Nieto, 1996) is central to my under-standing of critical multicultural education, I will define what I mean by this term before addressing the question of student perspectives. A sociopolitical context in education takes into account the larger social and political forces operating in a particular society and the impact they may have on student learning. Thus, the notion of *power* is at the very centre of the concept because it concerns issues such as structural inequality and stratification due to social class, gender, ethnicity, and other differences, as well as the relative respect or disrespect accorded to particular cultures, languages, and dialects. Hence, school reform strategies that do not ac-knowledge such macro-level disparities are sometimes little more than wishful thinking because they assume that all students begin their educational experiences on a level playing field.

In spite of the rhetoric of meritocracy espoused in most western capitalist countries, social stratification is based on *groups*, not on individuals (Ogbu, 1994). Given this perspective, educational decisions about such policies as ability grouping, testing, curriculum, pedagogy, and which language to use for instruction are also *political* decisions (Freire, 1985). Embedded within all educational decisions are also assumptions about the nature of learning in general, the worthiness and capability of students from various social groups, and the value or lack of value of languages other than the dominant one. Thus, even seemingly innocent decisions carry an enormous amount of ideological and philosophical weight, and these are in turn commun-icated to students either directly or indirectly (Cummins, 1996). David Corson, following Bourdieu (cf. May, this volume), describes the impact of decisions affect-ing school policies and practices on the most disadvantaged students in society: 'The members of some social groups, as a result, come to believe that their educational failure, rather than coming from their lowly esteemed social or cultural status, results from their natural inability: their lack of giftedness' (1993, p. 11). This is the ultimate educational legacy of an unequal society, and a sociopolitical context helps to uncover this truth.

Before proceeding with a discussion of student perspectives, a caveat is in order. Because I will be using case studies of two young people from the United States, the chapter is necessarily limited to the sociopolitical context of the United States, and specifically to these two young people who are respectively African–American and Chicano. I do not wish to claim any general wisdom from their cases to students in other societies, to students of other backgrounds in the United States, or even to other African–American or Latino students. That being said, however, it should also be clear that the particular educational problems faced by the two young men in the case studies are not unique; unfortunately, many students in many schools in the United States and even in other societies are faced with tremendous educational challenges that are at least partly based on their sociopolitical realities, and not just on their individual differences. Thus, it is my hope that readers will be able to glean some useful lessons for their particular context from these two case studies.

Research on Students' Perspectives

Students' perspectives about their schooling experiences are a relatively new and growing field of inquiry. This kind of research is especially significant in multicultural education because of the inherent student-centredness of the field. Thus, listening to what students have to say about their experiences and attending to their suggestions can result in a more critical conception of multicultural education. Likewise, students' views have important implications for transforming curriculum and pedagogy and for educational reform in general. I am not advocating that students' views should be adopted uncritically, a romantic notion at best. What I am suggesting instead is that if students' views are sought through a critical and problem-posing approach (Freire, 1970), their insights can be crucial for developing meaningful, liberating, and engaging educational experiences. In essence, educators lose a powerful opportunity to learn from students when they do not encourage their involvement. Suzanne Soo Hoo (1993) found this to be the case in a project where students were co-researchers. The question that was investigated in the project ('What are the obstacles to learning?') benefited tremendously from students' perspectives, and as Soo Hoo concluded: 'We listen to outside experts to inform us, and consequently, we overlook the treasure in our very own backyards: our students' (1993, p. 390).

Consequently, recent research has sought students' views in order to benefit from their ideas for improving schools. For example, how do students feel about the curriculum they must learn? What do they think about the pedagogical strategies of teachers? Do they believe that their involvement in school matters? Are their own cultural, ethnic, gender, and other identities important considerations for them? How do they view tracking (streaming), testing, disciplinary policies, and other school practices? Although these are key questions that affect the schooling of all students, few students have the opportunity to discuss them. When they are asked, they often seem surprised that anybody is interested; that is what I found repeatedly in the student interviews in my own research (Nieto, 1992, 1996). Moreover, students' views are often on target in terms of current thinking in education: Phelan et al. (1992), in a two-year research project in the US designed to identify students' thoughts about school, discovered that their views on teaching and learning were remarkably consistent with specialists of learning theory, cognitive science, and the sociology of work.

In terms of the *content* of their education, students are generally eager to express their opinions about both the tangible curriculum as manifested in books and other didactic materials and the 'hidden' curriculum, that is, the covert messages that can be discerned in the physical environment, extracurricular activities, interactions with adults, and school policies. For example, Christine Sleeter and Carl Grant (1991) found that a third of the students in a desegregated junior high school they studied said that *none* of the class content related to their lives outside class. Those who indicated some relevancy cited only current events, oral history, money and banking, and multicultural content (because it dealt with prejudice, a topic in which they were keenly interested, as are most students regardless of their backgrounds). Other examples of US research in which students were able to express their views have come to similar conclusions: students frequently report being bored in school and seeing little relevance for their lives or their futures in what is taught (Farrell et al., 1988; Hidalgo, 1991; Poplin and Weeres, 1992).

There is often a profound mismatch between students' cultures and the content of the curriculum. This is in stark contrast to Ira Shor's suggestion that 'What students bring to class is where learning begins. It starts there and goes places' (1992, p. 44). In fact, in many schools learning starts not with what students bring but with what is considered high-status knowledge, with its overemphasis on European and European American history, arts, and values. Without denying the importance of providing all students with the high-status knowledge that can open doors to otherwise unavailable life options for them, the case still needs to be made that it makes sense to begin with what students know. If not, rather than 'going elsewhere', students' learning often goes nowhere. Corroborating this lesson, Knapp et al. (1995), in the first large-scale study of the effect of using meaning-centred strategies in high-poverty classrooms in the United States, found that the *most* effective teachers were those who took active steps to connect learning to their students' backgrounds.

One way to use the experiences of students is to focus on the kinds of issues that they live with every day. In the case of disempowered students, these include such realities as poverty, racism, discrimination, and alienation. For instance, Karen Donaldson's (1996) study of an urban high school found that over 80 per cent of the students indicated that they had seen or experienced racism in their school. Yet these themes are conspicuously avoided in most classrooms, at least by teachers. Thus, Michelle Fine (1991) found that although over half of the students in the urban high school she interviewed described experiences of racism, teachers were reluctant to discuss it in class (cf. Moodley, this volume). Mary Poplin and Joseph Weeres (1992) also found that many of the students they interviewed brought up the issue of racism without being asked, while virtually none of the adults in the school even mentioned it. Perhaps this is because the majority of teachers in the United States are white Americans who are uncomfortable or unaccustomed to discussing these issues (Sleeter, 1994) because admitting that they exist challenges their most cherished ideals of democracy and equality (Tatum, 1992); perhaps it has to do with the tradition of presenting information in classrooms as if it were free of conflict and controversy (Kohl, 1993); or perhaps teachers are afraid of opening contentious discussions by involving students, as James Banks (1993) has suggested they might do, in debating such 'hot topics' as the literary canon or the extent to which Egypt might have influenced Greek civilization. Probably, the silence is a combination of all these factors.

Recent research focusing on students' views has found that they also have a great deal to say about the pedagogy they experience. Not surprisingly, students' views echo those of educational researchers who have found that teaching methods in most classrooms, and particularly those in secondary schools, vary little from traditional 'chalk and talk' methods; that textbooks are the dominant teaching materials used; that routine and rote learning are generally favoured over creativity and critical thinking; and that teacher-centred transmission models prevail (Cummins, 1994; Goodlad, 1984). In the case of my own research on students' perspectives, I found that although they often appreciated and applauded their teachers and the work they did, students were also critical of some practices and attitudes of their teachers (Nieto, 1994). Thus, I found striking agreement among students about the passive and text-based pedagogy that takes place in most classrooms: One young woman said: '. . . the teachers just, "Open the books to this page". They never made up problems out of their head. Everything came out of the book'. Another one said of her teacher 'She just does the things and sits down'. A young man said, 'They just teach the stuff. "Here", write a couple of things on the board, "see, that's how you do it. Go ahead, p. 25"'. Another young man stated that teachers can make classes more interesting if they teach from the point of view of the students: 'They don't just come out and say, "All right, do this, blah, blah, blah" . . . They're not so *one-tone voice*'. And another clearly connected what he saw as meaningless pedagogy with lack of caring when he said, 'Some teachers, they just go inside and go to the blackboard. They just don't care'.

Finally, students can teach educators enormously important lessons about unquestioned practices — what María de la Luz Reyes (1992) has called 'venerable assumptions'. For instance, one of the students in my research, Vinh, a Vietnamese immigrant, questioned teachers' practice of praising students for what he considered poor work. In his own case, he explained that his English was not very good, but that teachers uncritically praised his efforts anyway. He suggested instead, 'If my English is not good, she has to say, "Your English is not good, so you have to go home and study"'. He perceived teachers' praise as hollow and insincere.

It is clear from just this brief review of some of the recent research on students' perceptions of their education that they can provide a great deal of food for thought for critical multicultural educators. In what follows, I will focus on two specific students in order to draw out some of these lessons.

Case Studies of Educational Success and Failure

In an effort to determine how school, home, and community experiences affect young people of different backgrounds, and to explore how multicultural education when conceptualized as critical, comprehensive, and grounded in social justice might lead to positive adaptations in schools, a number of years ago several colleagues and

I interviewed 10 students from a wide variety of ethnic, social class, and family backgrounds (Nieto, 1992). The original intention of these interviews was to find out what it meant to be from a particular culture, how their culture might influence their school experiences, and what they would change about school if they could. The results of the first set of interviews were reported through a series of case studies, as well as in later analyses related to school policies and practices (Nieto, 1992, 1994).

As it happened, for it was unplanned, all 10 students in the original case studies were relatively academically successful. That is, although sometimes frustrated and alienated by school, they were for the most part fairly gratified with their school experiences. I was pleased it had turned out this way because research with linguistic, cultural, or ethnic minority students has consistently emphasized their failure in school rather than how they can learn despite difficult circumstances in their lives. According to Smith et al. (1993), in fact, the entire concept of academic failure has spawned a robust testing industry and a thriving niche in the academy, but it has done nothing to help those who are labelled as failures. In the end, they maintain, 'We must instead confront the very idea of school failure, seeing it for what it is, manifestations of classism and racism' (1993, p. 213). Significantly, a number of the students in my research were academically successful in spite of such challenges as abject poverty, lack of English-language skills when they began their schooling, single-parent families, a history of drug and alcohol dependence in their families, and the pressure of having to be cultural brokers for immigrant relatives at an early age.

Students in my research had a lot to say about the teachers they liked and disliked and why; about the overly important role that grades had acquired in school; about the tremendous faith their parents had in the promise of education and how schools could capitalize on it; and about the meaning their native languages and cultures had in their lives. The case studies implicated the need for schools to promote policies and practices that underscore diversity as a value to be affirmed rather than an obstacle to be confronted and obliterated. Notwithstanding the significant lessons that can be learned from successful students, their very academic success can be a serious limitation because these students tend to be the least marginalized in schools. They are, sadly, the exceptions to the rule of academic failure. Therefore, it is equally necessary to consider the experiences of students who have not been successful in school.

This chapter will centre on two students who had faced considerable failure in school but who were nonetheless having a more positive experience in alternative school settings at the time they were interviewed. Both are males and come from economically oppressed families. Paul is a Chicano from East Los Angeles, and Ron is an African–American who lives in Boston. Their case studies provide an in-depth examination of two young men who have been failed by schools and society.[1] Because at the time of their interviews both were attending public alternative schools where they were happier and more successful than in their previous schools, the case studies can serve as examples for what traditional schools can do to promote the academic achievement of many other young people in similar circumstances.

The fact that both of these case studies focus on young men of colour should come as no surprise. Although females in the United States are consistently victims of institutional bias in schools based on their gender, it is also true they earn higher grades as a group (Sadker and Sadker, 1994), probably due to their more docile and obedient behaviour in the classroom. Furthermore, young women of all groups, but especially Latinas and African–American females, are more likely to complete high school and attend college than their male counterparts (Bennett, 1995). Add to this the fact that young men of all backgrounds, but especially African–American and Latino males, are the most likely to have academic and disciplinary problems in school and to be assigned to special education (Ford, 1996), and it is understandable why these case studies concern young men of colour who live in poverty.

The lives of Paul Chavez and Ron Morris are in some ways remarkably similar: they have both faced sustained and consistent academic failure; they were both expelled from former schools; they each reported great frustration with their education before being admitted to the alternative schools they later attended; they have both been criminally involved, one with a gang; they come from female-headed households and live with large extended families struggling to make ends meet; they both admit there are serious problems at home. They also share a passionate desire to be successful in school and to go to college (university), in part to make their mothers, who they deeply love but who they have disappointed profoundly on numerous occasions, proud of them. In spite of these similarities, however, Ron and Paul are also quite different in many respects.

Before presenting the actual case studies, I will briefly describe the sociopolitical context of education for first, African–American, and then, Chicano, students in the United States. This will be followed by descriptions of Ron and Paul and then by their own words, in which they express their frustrations, hopes, and desires concerning education and their futures.

A Brief Review of the Education of African–American Students in the United States

A voluminous amount of research has been produced concerning the education of African–American students in US schools, and the major conclusions of all the reports, studies, and investigations have been accurately and succinctly stated by Kofi Lomotey:

> A threefold message is presented. First, the underachievement of African-American students is persistent, pervasive, and disproportionate; the severity of the problem has been well documented. Second, the reasons that this situation persists are varied; there is no simple explanation. Third, there are clear examples of environments that have, over long periods of time, been successful in educating large numbers of African-American students. These models can be replicated; the situation is not hopeless. (1990, p. 9)

Leaving aside the more racist and hopeless explanations cited in the literature concerning the educational failure of African–American students (deficit explanations focusing, for instance, on their supposed 'racial' and genetic inferiority, or on the pathologies or 'cultural deprivation' of their communities and families), which will not be considered here, one is still left with a plethora of theories. The more reasonable explanations cited in the US literature have ranged from the brutal and systematic exclusion of Blacks from education altogether, and later their de jure and de facto segregation from quality schooling (Weinberg, 1977); cultural and social class characteristics that place them at risk of failure (Pallas *et al.*, 1989); the negative attitudes and behaviours of their teachers (Irvine, 1990; New, 1996; Taylor, 1991) the effects of personal and institutional racism and the implications of 'stereotype stigma' on their learning (Steele, 1992); and the oppositional culture developed by African–American students as a result of a legacy of enslavement and domination, and the subsequent 'burden of acting white' in the face of educational success (Fordham and Ogbu, 1986; Ogbu, 1994). Some of the literature also rightly focuses on the characteristics of the schools that African–American students attend. For example, a study by Lee *et al.* (1991) found that African–American students with higher than average scores on reading achievement tests were actually similar to their lower-scoring counterparts in many respects; what differed were the schools attended by the higher-scoring students, which had a more positive environment.

Given the complexity of reasons cited in the literature for the widespread failure of African–American students in US schools (some of which are the subject of vigorous debate because of their focus on student or family characteristics rather than on structural inequalities in society or on the conditions of schooling that produce failure), it makes sense to instead focus on what has *helped* students achieve. Thus, for example, the evidence affirming that African–American students who perceive that their teachers care about them will be more academically successful (Patchen, 1982; Pollard, 1989) also makes commonsense. Similarly, African–American students for whom teachers hold high expectations, from elementary school through college, meet and even surpass those expectations (Bempechat, 1992; Irvine and Foster, 1996; Lomotey, 1990; Treisman, 1992). Moreover, a consistent finding in the more recent research has been that when the culture of African–American students is understood, appreciated, and used as the basis of their education, they can reach high levels of achievement (Boateng, 1990; Heath, 1983; Irvine, 1990; Ladson-Billings, 1994). This is not to imply that a simplistic or superficial 'feel-good' Afrocentric focus is what is called for. It is frequently overlooked that Afrocentrism can mean many different things and that positions on Afrocentric education in the United States have ranged widely from extremely conservative to progressive. Each of these conceptions has implications for educational practice. Consequently, both the wholesale rejection of Afrocentric education as 'essentialist' or its wholesale acceptance as 'culturally relevant' are problematic because they are incomplete and partial analyses of distinct ideological positions (cf. May, this volume). Thus, a critical stance toward Afrocentric education both coincides with basic tenets of critical pedagogy and challenges it to become less Eurocentric in its framework (Akinyela, 1995).

Kofi Lomotey's insistence that 'the situation is not hopeless' (1990, p. 9) for the education of African–American students in the United States is noteworthy. That is, there is ample evidence that African–American students can and do succeed academically in some situations. We will next review the case study of Ron Morris to consider how a critically conceived multicultural education that is grounded in an understanding of inequality and a respect for students' cultures can promote that success.

Ron Morris

Ronald Morris is 19 years old, highly expressive, and eloquent. He lives with his mother, three sisters, three nieces, and two nephews in a housing development in Boston just a few blocks from the alternative school he was attending at the time of his interviews. An older brother was in prison and an older sister was living in a shelter for the homeless. Several months before he was interviewed, Ron was mugged and, in the process of attempting to run away, he was shot six times. Miraculously, no vital organs were hit, but his recovery took many months.

Held back twice in elementary (primary) school and in and out of several high schools, Ron was attending a public alternative school the student body of which was primarily Latino and African–American. Ironically, the counsellor at this school was the same teacher who had most inspired Ron in his previous educational experience, the one who taught what he referred to in his interview as 'the first real class I ever had', a class in African and African–American history. The school offered a variety of educational, creative, vocational, and cultural opportunities for its 50 students. For example, in addition to his regular classes, Ron was participating in a small tutorial, an advanced history class on the Cuban Missile Crisis taught by a renowned retired professor of history who had previously worked at both Harvard University and Boston University. Ron loved this class because students had the opportunity to examine primary texts such as original documents and tapes in order to come to their own conclusions about decisions they would have made about this event.

The multicultural nature of the Pantoja School (named for a Puerto Rican educational and community activist) is one of the features that made it so appealing to Ron, as was its philosophy of empowerment and democratic participation by students and staff. The school also boasted an active sports programme. In addition, staff were helping Ron with decisions about college and a profession, two goals that until now had seemed unattainable to him. His future, however, was not as positive as it had been several months before: during one of his interviews, Ron confided that he was about to become a father with two different young women. Although he seemed willing to take some responsibility for the children who were coming and he had a serious relationship with one of the young women, he was determined to continue his education. He seemed largely unaware, however, of how profoundly this change was to affect his life.

Following are some of Ron's thoughts about the meaning of education:

> I didn't really like [school]. I used to always want to skip and go home or smoke or come to class and create ruckus or something. You know what you was going to

class for. You was going to class to be taught really nothing. They didn't really teach anything. I went to school. I come in, you sit down, you learn. Like in history, you learn the same thing over and over and over again.

They talked about Christopher Columbus like he was some great god or something. I never felt like I learned anything. I learned about this guy in the first grade. You went through three different segments of Christopher Columbus. You're saying now, okay, he's got to be a fake. He's a fictional character. They just keep pumping him up. Then you just get tired.

You learned about explorers and Malcolm, a little bit about Malcolm X, a little bit about Martin Luther King. You learned a little bit about slavery, a little bit about this. You learned a little bit about everything. You learned it just so many times. You just want to say, 'Well, isn't it time that we learned something different?' There's more than just what's in this book, 'cause what's in this book is not gonna let us know who we really are as people.

[Teachers should] probably just see what the students like and teach it how they would understand it and so that it's more helpful to them. More discussion instead of more reading, more discussion instead of just letting things be read and then left alone. People read things and then don't understand what they read.

Like if school was more — not all fun and games — but it was more realistic than just reading and doing the work and then you leave. You sit there for 45 minutes doing nothing, just reading a whole book and the teacher is doing nothing but letting you read and she's probably reading the newspaper or eating gum. And that's why the dropout rate is why [it is] because they just come to school and they ain't teaching us nothing, so why am I gonna sit here?

When a teacher becomes a teacher, she acts like a teacher instead of a person. She takes her title as now she's mechanical. Teachers shouldn't deal with students like we're machines. You're a person, I'm a person. We come to school and we all [should] act like people.

Proud to be Afro-American? Well, yeah and no. Yeah, I'm proud to be Afro-American because I'm a black male and all this and I have so many dreams and so many ways of being, that I come from a great 'race' of kings and queens who went through slavery and our 'race' still survives and all that. And no, because I have to accept the term Afro-American because I was born in America. I wasn't born where my ancestors come from. I'm not as pure as my ancestors were because your family's been raped and developed these different things.

Even though [Whites], they sit there and white history is the basic history, they don't really know anything about white. They look at it as white people have always been on top, which is not true for about — they don't know about before, five, six thousand years ago. Nobody even knew who white people were. To me, that's crazy. Everybody's running around not really knowing who they are. People think they know who they are. They think they know what their history is.

[I felt comfortable in school only] once, in eighth grade. Just this case, a history class I had. Just made me want to come to school and made me want to, made me say, 'Okay, now that I know there are so many false things in the world and that there's so much out there for me to learn, stop bullshitting'.

It was a black African history class. It was titled that. It was just so different from the textbook style. It was no books. It was just documents and papers and commonsense questions and commonsense knowledge. You'd just sit there, be like, 'This is real!' It was basically about black people. It showed us Latinos. It showed us

'Caucasians'. It showed us the Jews and everything how we all played a part what society in any country is like today. I just sat in that class and I used to go to that class once a week 'cause it was only a once-a-week class. I'd sit and just be like, I was just so relaxed. I just felt like the realest person on earth.

[This school] is more out to help you achieve instead of just sitting there doing nothing. Now I'm not in that 'they're not teaching me nothing, why should I come to school?' type thing. You learn more. You learn differently. It's realistic and my beliefs as an Afro-American are respected. [Teachers here] understand my identity and culture. They respect it.

I'm not perfect. I wouldn't call myself a good student. I call myself an all right student. I know what's right and what's wrong. I just have to apply [myself] to it. If you'd asked me about two, three years ago, I'd a told you I didn't have the slightest idea why I came to school; it's stupid, it's boring, they don't teach me nothing, I don't learn anything, I should just stay home. But you're asking me that now in the Pantoja School. Now I think about it differently because I'm not in the Boston Public Schools. I'm here, I'm learning, I'm learning more from people who know. It's not a book. Here, it's 'I can teach you through experience, through documents, through this, through that.'

I'm trying to get into Harvard. My mother told me I could do it. She'd say things like, 'If them women [the two women pregnant with his children] really understand what it is for you to be the correct father to your children, they don't burden you. They'll let you become these things and they'll let these things happen so their kinds won't have a typical black future' as if they're still living in the same house and I'm working making $6 an hour and killing myself and child support is taking all the money.

A Brief Review of the Education of Latinos in the United States

Although less so than in the case of African–American students, the educational failure of Latinos in the United States has also been the subject of sundry commissions, reports, and investigations. The picture that emerges from much of the research is that of unremitting and rampant educational failure (García, 1995; Nieto, 1995). This has been true of most Latinos, but is especially so of Mexican Americans (or Chicanos) and Puerto Ricans, the two Latino communities with a legacy of conquest or colonization by the United States. As aptly described by Richard Valencia, Chicano school failure is 'deeply rooted in history' (1991, p. 4). It has been characterized by a long history of negative conditions, including segregation, linguistic and cultural exclusion, racism, negative teacher–student interactions, consistent underfinancing of schools, and tracking (streaming). These same conditions have distinguished the educational history of Puerto Ricans in the United States (Rivera and Nieto, 1993; Walsh, 1991).

Latino students have frequently expressed feeling alienated and marginalized in their schools (Frau-Ramos and Nieto, 1993; National Commission, 1984; Upshur and Darder, 1993; Zanger, 1993). Furthermore, one study found that even when social class is held constant, Latinos still drop out at a higher rate than the general population (Steinberg et al., 1984). The researchers concluded that this condition may exist because the prejudice that exists against Latinos is widespread and impedes their educational progress. Yet, as is also true in the case of African–American students, much of the research has concluded that despite the bleak picture, Latino students can and indeed have been academically successful in numerous situations.

The explanations offered for the disproportionate failure of Latinos in US schools have paralleled those given for African–American students. The more mean-spirited among them have focused on Latinos' supposed lack of intelligence, cultural inferiority, lack of a value orientation to education, or uncaring parents (see Nieto, 1995 for a review). Even some well-meaning explanations have emphasized im-mutable or difficult-to-change characteristics. Thus, factors that have been identified as placing students 'at risk' of failure have included minority group status, poverty, single-parent household, non-English background, and having a poorly educated mother (Pallas et al., 1989), most of which apply to the vast majority of Latino students in the United States. Hence, their very identity — culturally, ethnically, and in other ways — places Latinos at risk. This reality has been borne out by a study of high-achieving and successful Chicano professionals by Patricia Gándara (1995). The study is more hopeful than previous research that focuses on students' identity as a risk factor because it addresses how Chicanos have been able to achieve academically in spite of what might be characterized as 'risk factors', specifically in this case, their low-income status. Here, too, however, the conditions that favoured the success of some over others would be at best difficult, or at worst impossible, to replicate for most Chicanos: light skin, attending middle- or upper-class and prim-arily white schools, and being tracked (streamed) in high-ability classes.

As I have argued elsewhere (Nieto, 1993), failure does not develop out of the blue, but is created partly through school policies and practices that in a very real way illustrate what a society believes its young people deserve. Thus, for instance, offering only low-level courses in schools serving Latino young people is a clear message that Latinos are not expected to achieve to high levels; labelling students 'at risk' because of their very ethnicity, native language, or social class is another sign that these students are expected to fail. Yet, research concerning what works with Latino students has consistently found that they respond positively to high expecta-tions, educational environments characterized by caring and respect, positive and close relationships with their teachers, and interventions such as bilingual education and other educational strategies that build on rather than demolish their native language and culture (Arias and Casanova, 1993; García, 1994; Gibson, 1995; Nieto, 1993, 1995; Zentella, 1992). As we will see in the case study that follows, few of these conditions existed in most of the schools that Paul Chavez attended.

Paul Chavez

The signs that Paul Chavez, 16 years old, has already lived a lifetime of gang activity, drugs, and adversity are apparent from his style of dress, the 'tag' (tattoo) on his arm, to his reminiscences of 'homeboys' who have been killed. Paul's is the third generation of his family to be born in Los Angeles. He does not speak Spanish, but said that both his mother and grandmother do in spite of the fact that they too were born and raised in the United States.

At the time of his interviews, Paul lived with his mother, three brothers, and sister in a small one-family home in east Los Angeles. Signs of gang activity were apparent in the tags on buildings and walls (a sign that the 'turf' belongs to a particular gang); according to Paul, an outsider suspected of belonging to another gang might be jumped for just walking down the street. Paul's mother, who had dropped out of high school many years before, was studying to obtain her high school equivalency diploma. She and Paul's father, an alcoholic living in a halfway house, had been separated for several years. Paul belonged to a neighbourhood ('hood) gang, along with 13 of his cousins and an older brother; an uncle and cousin had been killed as a result of their gang activity. Paul's parents also had been involved in a gang when they were younger.

Paul's academic and social problems in school began when he was in third or fourth grade. A few years later, he was suspended repeatedly from school for poor behaviour. The major problem had not been a lack of ability, but rather a lack of interest. He remembered Ms Nelson, his fifth grade teacher, as the only one with whom he had a meaningful relationship. In fact, he said she had been the only caring teacher he had during elementary (primary) school. Although he already wore gang-affiliated clothing and had a reputation as a troublemaker, Ms Nelson nevertheless held high expectations of him. It was in her classroom that he developed a fascination for history when he first read *The Diary of Anne Frank*.

When he began junior high school, the combination of negative peer pressure, family problems, and street violence had a decided influence on his school work. Consequently, he did very little in school, and he was expelled in eighth grade and stayed home for six months. By ninth grade, he was heavily involved in his gang. Several months later, he applied to a new alternative school, Nuestra Comunidad (Our Community) High School, designed for students who had dropped out or been expelled from other city schools. Heavily Chicano in population, the school was characterized by a multicultural curriculum that emphasized Chicano and Mexican history and it relied on students and staff for most decisions. After several months at the school, Paul was again expelled due to poor behaviour. After trying another programme and spending several months out of school, he applied again and had been in attendance for over a year at the time of his interviews. All of Paul's friends had by now quit school, and he confessed that he feared ending up like them. Since being accepted back into the programme, he had done quite well. Paul said that this school was different from any other he had attended because the entire staff cared about and encouraged the students, and because Chicano culture and history were central to the curriculum.

From his interviews, it was clear that Paul was at a crossroads. He had not quit his gang membership, and he seemed to both fear and be attracted to the lifestyle it represented. He was having success in school, and this was causing him to change some of his goals. Following are some of Paul's insights about these issues:

I'm from a gang and that's it, and just 'cause I'm from a gang doesn't mean I can't make myself better. But me, I do care. I have a life and I want to keep it. I don't want to lose it. I have two little sisters and I want to see them grow up too, and I want to have my own family.

I guess your peers . . . they try to pull you down and then you just got to be strong enough to pull away . . . I got to think about myself and get what I got to get going on. Got to have your priorities straight.

I came to [this school] and it was deep here. They got down into a lot of studies that I liked and there was a lot going on here. They get more into deeper Latino history here, and that's what I like. A lot of other, how you say, ethnic background. We had even Martin Luther King, we had Cesar Chavez. We had a lot of things.

I never used to think about [being Chicano] before. Now I do — being brown and just how our 'race' is just going out [being killed off]. You know, you don't want to see your 'race' go out like that. [In this school], they just leave the killings out and talk about how you can make it better, you know what I'm saying? Try to be more of the positive side of being a brown person, that's what I'm talking about.

[To make school better I would] talk about more interesting things, more things like that *I* would like, students would like. And I would get more involved, get more people involved. Get things going, not just let them vegetate or . . . on a desk and 'Here's a paper', teach 'em a lesson and expect them to do it. You know, get all involved. Try to find out what *we* think is important.

I'm getting out all I can get out [from this school]. There's so much to learn and that's all I want to do is just learn, try to educate my mind to see what I could get out of it. Now I take every chance I get to try to involve myself in something. Now it's like I figure if I'm more involved in school, I won't be so much involved in the gang, you know?

[I would want teachers to have] more patience and more understanding. [Teachers should] not think of a lesson as a lesson. Think of it as not a lesson just being taught to students, but a lesson being taught to one of your own family members, you know? 'Cause if it's like that, they get more deep into it, and that's all it takes. Teach a lesson with heart behind it and try to get your kids to understand more of what's going on. And don't lie to your kids, like to your students, saying, 'Everything is okay' and 'just say no to drugs, it's easy'. Let them know what's really going on. Don't beat around the bush. Let them know there's gangs, drugs.

I think they should get more of these aides, assistants, to be parents, okay? 'Cause the parents, I notice this: a parent in a school is more like they got *love*. That's it, they got love and they give it to you. They give it back to more students. I think they should get more like parents involved in the school like to teach this and that. Get more parents involved in the classroom too. Parents have a lot of things to say, I would think, about the schools.

After when I get my diploma, it's not the end of school, it's the beginning. I still want to learn a lot more after that. I basically want to go to college. Probably I would want to be either a teacher, a counsellor, something like working with youngsters to share my experience with them, you know? 'Cause I know there's a lot of people out there who talk down to youngsters, you know what I'm saying? Instead of talking *with* them, and just try to understand what they're going through.

You're gonna realize that you got to learn from day one . . . and education will never end. It's only when you stop it. I realize that now but I bet you there's a lot of kids that go to elementary school and [are] like I was. But see, me, I never really had somebody to push me. My mother pushed me and my mom, she just got tired. 'Paul, you're too much for me'. My father, he never really pushed me. He talked to me. That was like, 'Education, Paul, education', you know? And getting letters from my dad in jail, 'Stay in school', and that's all.

My mom, she's really proud of me. My friend was telling me that she was at church, at Bible study, a gathering at home of church people. And she was crying. She was proud. She said, 'Your mom was talking about you and she was crying. She's real proud'. And that's my mom, she's real sensitive. I love my mom so much it's even hard to explain.

I don't want to speak too soon, but I'm pretty much on a good road here. I'm pretty much making it. Trying to make something out of myself. I'm on that way, you know, I'm going that way. You can't talk about next month, at least at this time. I'm just today, get it done. That's it. The best I can. But I don't really like to build myself too high, because the higher you are, the harder you're gonna fall. I don't want to fall.

The Case Studies from a Critical Multicultural Education Perspective

Although the stories of Ron and Paul provide compelling examples of strength and resilience, they are also stories of defeat and despair within schools and in a society that hold out little hope for success for African–American and Latino students. Because their stories are vivid portraits of the complex interplay of relationships within families, communities, and schools, it may be helpful to view them from a critical multicultural education perspective.

How can the lens of critical multicultural education help us understand the case studies of Ron and Paul? Certainly, using multicultural education alone would uncover a number of important themes: the need to honour and respect students' cultures and identities; the urgency to diversify the curriculum; and the obligation to transform traditional pedagogy so that it better meets the needs of all students. Taken by themselves, however, these themes can remain within the categories of what Peter McLaren has called 'corporate' or 'liberal', in other words uncritical, multicultural education (McLaren, 1995). For instance, while it is true that using students' experiences as a basis of their schooling can help make their education more meaningful, it will not necessarily make students more critical thinkers. By the same token, adding a few characters of diverse ethnic background to the curriculum can be tremendously uplifting for students, but it may not help them critique how history is traditionally taught as unproblematic progress, regardless of the ethnic perspective. And changing pedagogical practices, while probably a good thing to do, will not likely in and of itself result in reversing the educational experiences of students such as Ron and Paul.

What I am suggesting is that multicultural education without a critical perspective can result in superficial changes that may not affect in any substantive way the life chances of students who have been as sorely miseducated as have Ron and Paul. On the other hand, applying a critical perspective to these case studies may prove helpful in understanding both the limits of multicultural education and its possibilities for transformative change. In what follows, I propose six ways in which a critical multicultural education can contribute to an understanding of the experiences of Ron and Paul and other young people who have been cast off by traditional schools.

1   Critical multicultural education affirms students' culture without trivializing the concept of culture itself

In the stories of Ron and Paul, it is clear that their community's culture and history, which had been glaringly missing from the curriculum in all their previous schools, has become a rich source of motivation and pride for both of them. In addition, they each expressed gratitude that the teachers in their new schools respected them and their backgrounds, a primary factor in academic success. However, a critical multicultural education perspective avoids what Anthony Appiah has called 'the tyranny of identity', that is, a tightly scripted identity based on 'the politics of compulsion' (1994, p. 163). We will remember, for example, that it was in Ms Nelson's fifth-grade classroom that Paul became fascinated with history, and it was not because he was learning about Mexican history but because he was reading the story of Anne Frank. Similarly, Ron's favourite classes at his alternative school were the history tutorial on the Cuban Missile Crisis and Spanish, not because they were about his life as an African–American, but because he found the pedagogy compelling and because he was passionately interested in the world outside his own experience.

Students of all backgrounds are captivated by the study of difference, as we have seen in some of the literature reviewed previously. But generally they can see through a superficial focus on diversity that emphasizes only cultural tidbits and ethnic celebrations. A critical multicultural education builds on students' interests without trivializing (or essentializing) the meaning of culture. This is important to remember because if we are serious about developing a truly liberating pedagogy, it means moving beyond an understanding of culture as a product or as the static symbol of a people (cf. Kalantzis and Cope; May, this volume). In the words of Frederick Erickson, 'I am concerned that our pedagogy and curriculum become genuinely transformative, not just cosmetically "relevant"' (1990, p. 23).

2   Critical multicultural education challenges hegemonic knowledge

Students learn to accept much of what is taught in schools as factual knowledge. If it is written in a textbook, it acquires an even more powerful authenticity (Apple, 1992). Yet as James Banks reminds us, 'Hegemonic knowledge that promotes the interests of powerful, elite groups often obscures its value premises by masquerading as totally objective' (1995, p. 15). Ron was acutely aware of this; he was clearly fed up with studying Christopher Columbus because with each passing year, Columbus became even more enshrined in mythology and mystique. However, it was not only Columbus who he saw treated this way: Ron also challenged the hegemonic way in which such African–American icons as Martin Luther King and Malcolm X were being taught. Thus, he challenged not the importance of studying historical figures, but the static and uncritical way in which it is done.

This same critical perspective needs to be applied to the entire curriculum. Ironically, the same Ron who was critical of the trivial and unproblematic portrayals of Christopher Columbus, Malcolm X, and Martin Luther King rather uncritically boasted of the 'great "race" of kings and queens' from which he descended. Yes, it is true that a society of great kings and queens may be a sign of an advanced civilization. However, it is also often the sign of a rigidly hierarchical society stratified by class, gender, and other differences in which those who are not favoured are destined to lives of servitude. Given the 'deculturalization' (Boateng, 1990) that has generally characterized the schooling of African–Americans, Ron's response is understandable. Not only have Africans and African–Americans been omitted from most school treatments of history, but even when included, they have as a rule been presented as savage and barbaric. Although slavery is bemoaned, the sting of oppression is softened with the impression that Africans were the beneficiaries of a benevolent civilizing on the part of Whites. In this way, a hideous part of US history is distorted and romanticized. Ron's statement that he felt 'like the realest person on earth' in his African history class is compelling testimony of the power of a curriculum that contests this hegemonic tradition.

A critical multicultural perspective demands that all knowledge, not only 'official knowledge', be taught critically. Thus, any history that is presented with a surplus of hyperbole by the use of such adjectives as 'majestic', 'magnificent', 'dazzling', or 'awe-inspiring' needs to be interrogated just as critically as official US history when it is taught in this way. All students deserve the right to be treated with respect; this means, among other things, affirming their backgrounds as well as trusting their intelligence. Having said this, however, it is equally important to be critical of those who bemoan the dangers of essentialism without truly understanding or taking into account the lives of young people who have been alienated from school and society. This point is eloquently made by bell hooks (1994) when she states that it is those from dominant groups who perpetuate essentialism, not just those from marginalized groups. She goes on to say, '. . . I am concerned that critiques of identity politics not serve as the new, chic way to silence students from marginal groups' (1994, p. 83; see also May, this volume).

3 Critical multicultural education complicates pedagogy

There is no one right way to teach, and a critical multicultural perspective helps us to understand this. For Ron, using primary texts such as documents and tapes was engaging; for Paul, reading biographies was often inspiring. The issue is not so much the particular pedagogical strategy used as is, in the words of Lilia Bartolomé, 'the teacher's politically clear educational philosophy' (1994, p. 179). A critical multicultural education perspective complicates the question of pedagogy; it challenges teachers who are interested in transformative education to re-think what and how they teach, and to constantly question their decisions. For instance, while it is probably true that Ron and Paul benefited from a more inspired pedagogy at their alternative schools than had been the case before, some of these same strategies were no doubt used in their previous schools. The major issue is not, then, the strategy or approach itself, but the environment in which it takes place. Cooperative learning, for example, can take place in the most uncooperative and oppressive of settings, while truly extraordinary and high-level discussions can happen in classrooms with nailed-down seats in rigid rows.

What is most striking in the words of Ron and Paul is the deep care and respect they felt from their teachers. This is an important lesson for multicultural education. It is not meant to discourage new and innovative pedagogical strategies; on the contrary, pedagogy, to be effective, needs to become more humanizing (Bartolomé, 1994). But there is no set 'bag of tricks' that will accomplish this awesome task (cf. Kalantzis and Cope, this volume). What matters are the intentions and goals behind the pedagogy.

4 Critical multicultural education problematizes a simplistic focus on self-esteem

Much has been written about the importance of multicultural education in building the self-esteem of students (Beane, 1991). The conventional wisdom, that students cannot learn unless they feel good about themselves, brings up the chicken-or-egg question: that is, do students need to feel better about themselves before they can be successful students, or does their academic success help them develop a higher self-esteem? As pointed out by Joseph Kahne, self-esteem is at best a 'slippery concept' (1996, p. 17). A critical multicultural education perspective problematizes the simplistic focus on self-esteem. An astute observation by Alfie Kohn is relevant here: 'Getting students to chant "I'm special!" — or to read a similar perfunctory message on cheerful posters or in prepackaged curricular materials — is pointless at best' (1994, p. 276).

Rather than think of it as a unitary concept, we need to understand that self-esteem operates *in relation to particular situations*. If self-esteem is used as an individual psychological construct, it overlooks the sociopolitical context of students' lives, downplaying or denying the racism and other oppressive behaviours that they experience. Therefore, how schools and society *create* low self-esteem in children needs to be considered. That is, students do not simply develop poor self-concepts out of the blue; rather, their self-esteem *in terms of schooling* is the result of policies and practices in schools that respect and affirm some groups while devaluing and rejecting others. Students from culturally dominated groups partially internalize some of the many negative messages to which they are subjected on a daily basis about their culture, ethnic group, class, gender, or language, but they are not simply passive recipients of such messages. They also actively resist negative messages through interactions with peers, family, and even school. This is one way of understanding Paul's connection with his gang, a relationship that raised his self-esteem but one that he began to question *once he became a more successful student*. The mediating role of families and communities, and in some cases schools, helps to contradict negative messages and to reinforce more positive and affirming ones.

5   Critical multicultural education encourages 'dangerous discourses'

According to Ellen Bigler and James Collins (1995), multicultural education is rightly perceived as a threat because it encourages 'dangerous discourses' and challenges existing arrangements in and out of school. Students such as Paul and Ron clearly understood this. Both, for instance, at last felt free to discuss issues that had been largely untouched in their former schools but that, as uncomfortable as they might be for teachers and other adults in their current schools, were important focal points of their learning. Why should this be the case in such schools? Unlike most traditional public schools, alternative schools are often the places where the most alienated students end up. In such schools, student alienation is generally understood not simply as pathological responses to individual circumstances but, at least partly, as the result of the sociopolitical context in which young people live.

Unfortunately, these 'dangerous discourses' have little place in most schools, as we have seen. Even in well-meaning schools where teachers have determined to develop a multicultural perspective, such discussions are usually missing because teachers are either unaware of the salience of such issues in the lives of students or they simply do not hear 'the hard questions' (Jervis, 1996) that children ask. Yet a critical multicultural perspective demands that schools become sites of freedom to learn even controversial issues. As such, critical multicultural education connects learning with democracy in a profound manner because it invites discussion and debate. It is not neat; it does not have all the answers. In this way, it is like life itself.

6   Multicultural education by itself cannot do it all

Multicultural education is a hopeful pedagogy. Because of this, it holds great promise for transforming the future of countless young people who would otherwise be rejected and devalued by the schools they attend and the societies in which they live. Nevertheless, a critical perspective makes it clear that multicultural education is not a panacea. For Paul and Ron, the road ahead is a difficult one. Crime, homelessness, and violence are just some of the manifestations of a society that is increasingly stratified and alienating, and massive structural changes in the economy are exacerbating the situation even further (cf. McLaren and Torres, this volume). Many young people in the United States, but especially those who are poor and black, Latino, or Native American, have little to look forward to but a life of unemployment or undemanding work in fast-food restaurants. To believe that changes in pedagogy and curriculum, or even the radical transformation of schooling itself could solve all these problems is illusory at best. The dilemmas faced by these young men obviously include far more than irrelevant curriculum and boring pedagogy, and that is why separating their reality from the sociopolitical context of society is like hiding one's head in the sand.

I do not mean to suggest that schools cannot make dramatic improvements in educating the large numbers of young people who are currently poorly served by both the educational system and by society itself. Indeed, that is what they have always promised to do: in the United States it is understood that schools have a social contract to educate *all* students, not just white, English-speaking, middle-class students who live with two parents. There have been numerous examples of teachers and schools who have provided environments of extraordinary academic success for students who might otherwise have been dismissed as possessing the 'intelligence' needed to achieve. Nevertheless, it is evident that schools alone cannot hope to achieve these results on a massive scale by themselves. In the case of Ron and Paul, their new schools were providing empowering models of education, but the limitations of such schools are evident. Poorly funded and small in number, although generally staffed by a corps of determined and dedicated teachers, alternative schools are a ray of hope where an entire constellation is needed. Social and structural barriers to learning as experienced by Ron and Paul are constant reminders that social justice cannot single-handedly be achieved even by caring, progressive teachers or by schools committed to multicultural education. What is needed, then, is committed and purposeful political activity, both within the classroom and outside of it, to ensure that the stated ideals of education in a democratic society are realized.

Conclusion

Paul and Ron are on the brink between triumph and disaster, and this is evident in the personal predicaments they talked about. Just over a year after they had been interviewed, I had the opportunity to speak with Beatriz McConnie Zapater and Mac Morante, my colleagues who had interviewed them. I was anxious to hear what had happened to Ron and Paul but I was determined not to repeat the sentimentalizing that goes on when specific educational strategies or programmes are simplistically proposed as the cure for the many difficult problems confronting schools and society. The outcomes of their specific situations again point out the need to face all such situations with a critical but hopeful perspective: Ron had dropped out of school and was living with one of the young women who had recently had his child; Harvard was a dream that would remain unfulfilled. Paul was still in school and would be graduating within a few months; he was looking forward to going to college.

In an essay on critical pedagogy, Maxine Greene (1986) asked what this kind of education might mean for teachers. She suggested that we need to begin by releasing our collective imaginations, and she continued:

> We might try to make audible again the recurrent calls for justice and equality. We might try to reactivate the resistance to materialism and conformity. We might even try to inform with meaning the desire to educate 'all the children' in a legitimately 'common school'. (1986, p. 440)

Like the words of Maxine Greene, the words of Ron and Paul were sometimes infused with a deep-seated belief in the power of education. How could this be? After all, both were prime examples of the failure of education to make good on its promise. But the ideal of social justice is powerful indeed, and the school as the site where social justice can best be achieved is a utopian vision that is irresistible. How else to explain Paul's desire to become a teacher? These young men were sometimes wise beyond their years, and they remind us of just how far we need to go in our schools and society to fulfill the promise of a life of equality and freedom for all our people.

Note

1 This chapter includes partial excerpts of the larger case studies of Ron and Paul. The names used in this chapter are pseudonyms, and other details (school names or the names of teachers or administrators) that might identify them, have also been changed. Paul Chavez was interviewed by Dr Mac Lee Morante, a mental health therapist and school psychologist in the Anaheim City School District, and Ron Morris was interviewed by Beatriz McConnie Zapater, the principal of the Greater Egleston Community High School in Boston. I am grateful for the many insights they provided as I developed the case studies. The interviews took place in 1994 and the case studies in their entirety are included in a second edition of the original research (Nieto, 1996).

References

AKINYELA, M. (1995) 'Rethinking Afrocentricity: The foundations of a theory of critical Afrocentricity', in DARDER, A. (ed.) *Culture and Difference: Critical Perspectives on the Bicultural Experience in the United States*, Westport, CT: Bergin and Garvey, pp. 21–39.

APPIAH, A. (1994) 'Identity, authenticity, survival: Multicultural societies and social reproduction', in GUTMANN, A. (ed.) *Multiculturalism*, Princeton, NJ: Princeton University Press, pp. 149–63.

APPLE, M. (1992) 'The text and cultural politics', *Educational Researcher*, **21**, 7, pp. 4–11, 19.

ARIAS, M. and CASANOVA, U. (eds) (1993) *Bilingual Education: Politics, Practice, Research*, Chicago: University of Chicago Press.

BANKS, J. (1993) 'The canon debate, knowledge construction, and multicultural education', *Educational Researcher*, **22**, 5, pp. 4–14.

BANKS, J. (1995) 'The historical reconstruction of knowledge about race: Implications for transformative teaching', *Educational Researcher*, **24**, 2, pp. 15–25.

BARTOLOMÉ, L. (1994) 'Beyond the methods fetish: Toward a humanizing pedagogy', *Harvard Educational Review*, **64**, pp. 173–94.

BEANE, J. (1991) 'Sorting out the self-esteem controversy', *Educational Leadership* (September), pp. 25–30.

BEMPECHAT, J. (1992) *Fostering High Achievement in African American Children: Home, School, and Public Policy Influences*, New York: ERIC Clearinghouse on Urban Education, Institute for Urban and Minority Education, Teachers College, Columbia University.

BENNETT, C. (1995) 'Research on racial issues in American higher education', in BANKS, J. and BANKS, C. (eds) *Handbook of Research on Multicultural Education*, New York: Macmillan, pp. 663–82.

BIGLER, E. and COLLINS, J. (1995) *Dangerous Discourses: The Politics of Multicultural Literature in Community and Classroom*, Albany: National Research Center on Literature Teaching and Learning, University at Albany, Report Series 7.4.

BOATENG, F. (1990) 'Combating deculturalization of the African-American child in the public school system: A multicultural approach', in LOMOTEY, K. (ed.) *Going to School: the African-American Experience*, Albany: State University of New York Press, pp. 73–84.

CORBETT, D. and WILSON, B. (1995) 'Make a difference with, not for, students: A plea to researchers and reformers', *Educational Researcher*, **24**, 5, pp. 12–7.

CORSON, D. (1993) *Language, Minority Education and Gender: Linking Social Justice and Power*, Clevedon, England: Multilingual Matters.

CUMMINS, J. (1994) 'From coercive to collaborative relations of power in the teaching of literacy', in FERDMAN, B., WEBER, R-M. and RAMÍREZ, A. (eds) *Literacy across Languages and Cultures*, Albany: State University of New York Press, pp. 295–331.

CUMMINS, J. (1996) *Negotiating Identities: Education for Empowerment in a Diverse Society*, Ontario, CA: California Association for Bilingual Education.

DONALDSON, K. (1996) *Through Students' Eyes*, New York: Bergin and Garvey.

ERICKSON, F. (1990) 'Culture, politics, and educational practice', *Educational Foundations*, **4**, 2, pp. 21–45.

FARRELL, E., PEGUERO, G., LINDSEY, R. and WHITE, R. (1988) 'Giving voice to high school students: Pressure and boredom, ya know what I'm sayin'?', *American Educational Research Journal*, **25**, pp. 489–502.

FINE, M. (1991) *Framing Dropouts: Notes on the Politics of an Urban High School*, Albany: State University of New York Press.

FORD, D. (1996) *Reversing Underachievement among Gifted Black Students: Promising Practices and Programs*, New York: Teachers College Press.

FORDHAM, S. and OGBU, J. (1986) 'Black students' school success: Coping with the "burden of acting white"', *Urban Review*, **18**, 3, pp. 176–206.

FRAU-RAMOS, M. and NIETO, S. (1993) '"I was an outsider": Dropping out among Puerto Rican youths in Holyoke, Massachusetts', in RIVERA, R. and NIETO, S. (eds) *The Education of Latino Students in Massachusetts: Issues, Research, and Policy Implications*, Boston: Gastón Institute for Latino Public Policy and Development, pp. 147–69.

FREIRE, P. (1970) *Pedagogy of the Oppressed*, New York: Seabury Press.

FREIRE, P. (1985) *The Politics of Education: Culture, Power, and Liberation*, New York: Bergin and Garvey.

GÁNDARA, P. (1995) *Over the Ivy Walls: The Educational Mobility of Low-income Chicanos*, Albany: State University of New York Press.

GARCÍA, E. (1994) *Understanding and Meeting the Challenge of Student Cultural Diversity*, Boston: Houghton Mifflin Company.

GARCÍA, E. (1995) 'Educating Mexican American students: Past treatment and recent developments in theory, research, policy, and practice', in BANKS, J. and BANKS, C. (eds) *Handbook of Research on Multicultural Education*, New York: Macmillan, pp. 372–87.

GIBSON, M. (1995) 'Perspectives on acculturation and school performance', *Focus on Diversity*, **5**, 3, pp. 8–10.

GILLBORN, D. (1995) *Racism and Antiracism in Real Schools*, Buckingham: Open University Press.

GOODLAD, J. (1984) *A Place Called School*, New York: McGraw-Hill.

GREENE, M. (1986) 'In search of a critical pedagogy', *Harvard Educational Review*, **56**, pp. 427–41.

HEATH, S. (1983) *Ways with Words*, New York: Cambridge University Press.

HIDALGO, N. (1991) '"Free time, school is like a free time": Social relations in city high school classes', Unpublished doctoral dissertation, Harvard University.

hooks, b. (1994) *Teaching to Transgress: Education as the Practice of Freedom*, New York: Routledge.

IRVINE, J. (1990) *Black Students and School Failure: Policies, Practices, and Prescriptions*, Westport, CT: Greenwood Press.

IRVINE, J. and FOSTER, M. (eds) (1996) *Growing Up African American in Catholic Schools*, New York: Teachers College Press.

JERVIS, K. (1996) '"How come there are no brothers on that list?": Hearing the hard questions all children ask', *Harvard Educational Review*, **66**, pp. 546–76.

KAHNE, J. (1996) 'The politics of self-esteem', *American Educational Research Journal*, **33**, pp. 3–22.

KNAPP, M., SHIELDS, P. and TURNBULL, B. (1995) 'Academic challenge in high-poverty classrooms', *Phi Delta Kappan*, **76**, pp. 770–6.

KOHL, H. (1993) 'The myth of "Rosa Parks, the tired"', *Multicultural education*, **1**, 2, pp. 6–10.

KOHL, H. (1994) *'I Won't Learn from You' and Other Thoughts on Creative Maladjustment*, New York: The New Press.

KOHN, A. (1994) 'The truth about self-esteem', *Phi Delta Kappan*, **76**, pp. 272–83.

LADSON-BILLINGS, G. (1994) *The Dreamkeepers: Successful Teachers of African–American Children*, San Francisco, CA: Jossey-Bass.

LEE, V., WINFIELD, L. and WILSON, T. (1991) 'Academic behaviors among high-achieving African-American students', *Education and Urban Society*, **24**, pp. 65–86.

LOMOTEY, K. (1990) *Going to School: The African-American Experience*, Albany: State University of New York Press.

MCLAREN, P. (1995) 'White terror and oppositional agency: Towards a critical multiculturalism', in SLEETER, C. and MCLAREN, P. (eds) *Multicultural Education, Critical Pedagogy, and the Politics of Difference*, Albany: State University of New York Press, pp. 33–70.

NATIONAL COMMISSION ON SECONDARY EDUCATION FOR HISPANICS (1984) *'Make Something Happen': Hispanics and Urban School Reform* (2 Vols.), Washington, DC: Hispanic Policy Development Project.

NEW, C. (1996) 'Teacher thinking and perceptions of African-American male achievement in the classroom', in RÍOS, F. (ed.) *Teaching Thinking in Cultural Contexts*, Albany: State University of New York Press, pp. 85–103.

NIETO, S. (1992) *Affirming Diversity: The Sociopolitical Context of Multicultural Education*, White Plains, NY: Longman.

NIETO, S. (1993) 'Creating possibilities: Educating Latino students in Massachusetts', in RIVERA, R. and NIETO, S. (eds) *The Education of Latino Students in Massachusetts: Issues, Research, and Policy Implications*, Boston: Gastón Institute for Latino Public Policy and Development, pp. 243–61.

NIETO, S. (1994) 'Lessons from students on creating a chance to dream', *Harvard Educational Review*, **64**, pp. 392–426.

NIETO, S. (1995) 'A history of the education of Puerto Rican students in US mainland schools: 'Losers', 'outsiders', or 'leaders'?', in BANKS, J. and BANKS, C. (eds) *Handbook of Research on Multicultural Education*, New York: Macmillan, pp. 388–411.

NIETO, S. (1996) *Affirming Diversity: The Sociopolitical Context of Multicultural Education*, (2nd edn.), White Plains, NY: Longman.

OGBU, J. (1994) 'Racial stratification and education in the United States: Why inequality persists', *Teachers College Record*, **96**, pp. 264–98.

OLSEN, L. (1988) *Crossing the Schoolhouse Border: Immigrant Students and the California Public Schools*, San Francisco: California Tomorrow.

PALLAS, A., NATRIELLO, G. and MCDILL, E. (1989) 'The changing nature of the disadvantaged population: Current dimensions and future trends', *Educational Researcher*, **18**, 5, 4, pp. 16–22.

PATCHEN, M. (1982) *Black-White Contact in Schools: Its Social and Academic Effects*, West Lafayette, IN: Purdue University Press.

PHELAN, P., DAVIDSON, A. and CAO, H. (1992) 'Speaking up: Students' perspectives on school', *Phi Delta Kappan*, **73**, pp. 695–704.

POLLARD, D. (1989) 'A profile of underclass achievers', *Journal of Negro Education*, **58**, pp. 297–308.

POPLIN, M. and WEERES, J. (1992) *Voices from the Inside: A Report on Schooling from Inside the Classroom*, Claremont, CA: Claremont Graduate School, Institute for Education in Transformation.

REYES, M. (1992) 'Challenging venerable assumptions: Literacy instruction for linguistically different students', *Harvard Educational Review*, **62**, pp. 427–46.

RIVERA, R. and NIETO, S. (1993) *The Education of Latino Students in Massachusetts: Issues, Research, and Policy Implications*, Boston: Gastón Institute for Latino Community Development and Public Policy.

SADKER, M. and SADKER, D. (1994) *Failing at Fairness: How America's Schools Cheat Girls*, New York: Charles Scribner's Sons.

SHOR, I. (1992) *Empowering Education: Critical Teaching for Social Change*, Chicago: University of Chicago Press.

SLEETER, C. (1994) 'White racism', *Multicultural Education*, **1**, 4, pp. 5–8, 39.

SLEETER, C. and GRANT, C. (1991) 'Mapping terrains of power: Student cultural knowledge vs. classroom knowledge', in SLEETER, C. (ed.) *Empowerment through Multicultural Education*, Albany: State University of New York Press, pp. 49–67.

SLEETER, C. and McLAREN, P. (eds) (1995) *Multicultural Education, Critical Pedagogy, and the Politics of Difference*, Albany: State University of New York Press.

SMITH, D., GILMORE, P., GOODMAN, S. and McDERMOTT, R. (1993) 'Failure's failure', in JACOB, E. and JORDAN, C. (eds) *Minority Education: Anthropological Perspectives*, Norwood, NJ: Ablex, pp. 209–31.

SOO HOO, S. (1993) 'Students as partners in research and restructuring schools', *Educational Forum*, **57**, pp. 386–93.

STEELE, C. (1992) 'Race and the schooling of black Americans', *The Atlantic Monthly*, April, pp. 68–78.

STEINBERG, L., BLINDE, P. and CHAN, K. (1984) 'Dropping out among language minority youth', *Review of Educational Research*, **54**, pp. 113–32.

TATUM, B. (1992) 'Talking about race, learning about racism: The application of racial identity development theory in the classroom', *Harvard Educational Review*, **62**, pp. 1–24.

TAYLOR, A. (1991) 'Social competence and the early school transition: Risk and protective factors for African-American children', *Education and Urban Society*, **24**, 1, pp. 15–26.

TREISMAN, U. (1992) 'Studying students studying calculus: A look at the lives of minority mathematics students in college', *The College Mathematics Journal*, **23**, 5, pp. 362–72.

UPSHUR, C. and DARDER, A. (1993) 'What do Latino children need to succeed in school? A study of four Boston public schools', in RIVERA, R. and NIETO, S. (eds) *The Education of Latino Students in Massachusetts: Issues, Research, and Policy Implications*, Boston: Gastón Institute for Latino Public Policy and Development, pp. 127–46.

VALENCIA, R. (1991) 'The plight of Chicano students: An overview of schooling conditions and outcomes', in VALENCIA, R. (ed.) *Chicano School Failure and Success: Research and Policy Agendas for the 1990s*, London: Falmer Press, pp. 3–26.

WALSH, C. (1991) *Pedagogy and the Struggle for Voice: Issues of Language, Power, and Schooling for Puerto Ricans*, New York: Bergin and Garvey.

WEINBERG, M. (1977) *A Chance to Learn: A History of Race and Education in the United States*, Cambridge: Cambridge University Press.

ZANGER, V. (1993) 'Academic costs of social marginalization: An analysis of Latino students' perceptions at a Boston high school', in RIVERA, R. and NIETO, S. (eds) *The Education of Latino Students in Massachusetts: Issues, Research, and Policy Implications*, Boston: Gastón Institute for Latino Public Policy and Development, pp. 170–90.

ZENTELLA, A. (1992) 'Individual differences in growing up bilingual', in SARAVIA-SHORE, M. and ARVIZU, S. (eds) *Cross-cultural Literacy: Ethnographies of Communication in Multiethnic Classrooms*, New York: Garland, pp. 211–25.

9   Critical Multiculturalism in Science and Technology Education

Derek Hodson

In 1993 I wrote an article in which I attempted to reconcile the demands of cultural pluralism and antiracism via a series of curriculum proposals grouped into three broad, but overlapping and interacting categories: 'Science Education in a Multicultural Setting', 'Antiracist Science Education' and 'Taking a Global View' (Figure 9.1) (Hodson, 1993a). Embedded within this framework are three different perceptions of science. First, science as perceived by the students: *their* understanding of scientific concepts, *their* explanations for phenomena and events, *their* knowledge of scientific procedures. Second, science as perceived by the community of scientists and expressed in the science curriculum as particular conceptual and procedural knowledge. Third, alternatives to the traditional view of the nature of science and scientific inquiry that reflect different philosophical and sociological perspectives on the purposes and procedures of scientific practice.

In responding to this article, Harvey Williams (1994) levels three charges against me. First, he says, my approach does violence to science; second, it patronizes ethnic and cultural minorities; third, it 'clash(es) with the accepted goals and values of education in a western democratic society'. In addition, Good and Demastes (1995) state that I am 'not taking science seriously' and Loving (1995) asserts that (i) I am a relativist (anything can count as science under my proposals, she says) and

---

I   Science Education in a Multicultural Setting
 • Issues of language
 • Drawing on the knowledge, beliefs and experiences of all children
 • Adopting appropriate teaching and learning styles

II Antiracist Science Education
 • Reviewing curriculum materials
 • Establishing more democratic procedures
 • Countering scientific racism

III Taking a Global View
 • Drawing on material from a wide range of cultures and countries
 • The multicultural history and contemporary practice of science
 • Science as culturally determined practice
 • Changing conventional views about the nature of science
 • Issues of freedom, equality and justice

Figure 9.1:   Some guidelines for the development of multicultural science education

(ii) I am promoting a 'jar of jelly beans' view of a multiethnic society. Loving, of course, approves the standard US 'melting pot' notion.

In a brief response to Williams' criticisms (Hodson, 1994a), I argued that my curriculum proposals are rooted very firmly in the pursuit of critical thinking and sociopolitical action by students on matters that relate to scientific, technological and environmental issues. If this approach clashes with existing goals and values, I am guilty — though not, I believe, for the reasons that Williams presents. Moreover, far from marginalizing minority groups, as Williams alleges, my proposals are designed primarily to empower them. This chapter attempts to elaborate that defence and to meet other criticisms of the article by articulating some of the theoretical under-pinnings of the original recommendations. Its principal, and interrelated concerns are the *personalization* of learning, the facilitating of *border crossings*, the *demythologizing* of science, and the *politicization* of science education.

The Personalization of Learning

Personalization of learning means taking account of the knowledge, experience, needs, interests and aspirations of each learner, regardless of their sociocultural background, and acknowledging that cultural factors outside the immediate environment of the school play an important role in the development of students' scientific concepts and, therefore, in the ways they respond to curriculum experiences.

During the past 20 years, extensive research into children's alternative conceptions in science has led to the development and widespread adoption of constructivist approaches to teaching and learning science (Bell, 1993; Driver et al., 1994). In essence, there are four main steps in this approach:

- identify students' ideas and views;
- create opportunities for students to explore their ideas and test their robustness in explaining phenomena, accounting for events and making predictions;
- provide stimuli for students to develop, modify and, where necessary, change their ideas and views;
- support their attempts to rethink and reconstruct their ideas and views.

Appleton (1993), Biddulph and Osborne (1984), Driver (1989), and Harlen (1992) present models for teaching and learning science that incorporate variations on and extensions to these four main steps.

Posner et al. (1982) argue that new learning is brought about when learners are dissatisfied with their current beliefs/understanding and have ready access to a new or better idea. To be acceptable, they argue, the new idea must meet certain conditions.

- it must be *intelligible* (understandable) — that is, the learner must understand what it means and how it can and should be used;

- it must be *plausible* (reasonable) — that is, it should be consistent with and reconcilable with other aspects of the student's understanding;
- it must be *fruitful* — that is, it should have the capacity to provide something of value to the learner by solving significant problems, suggesting new explanatory possibilities, and so on.

Dissatisfaction with an existing idea may reside in its failure to predict correctly or to control events beyond its previous restricted context — that is, it is no longer fruitful in the new situations which the learner has to confront. It may also be located in recognition that more vigorous alternatives meet the conditions of intelligibility and plausibility more satisfactorily than existing ideas. Hewson and Thorley (1989) describe the conceptual change approach to teaching and learning science as a matter of changing the status of rival conceptions with respect to the three conditions of intelligibility, plausibility and fruitfulness. Put simply, the teacher's task is to lower the status of the existing idea and raise the status of the new one.

One of the limitations of this conceptual change view of learning is that it ignores the persistence with which students cling to their existing views despite overwhelming evidence against them and despite powerful arguments in favour of the teacher's proffered alternative. It ignores, also, children's ready tolerance of inconsistencies among their ideas. For example, young children attempting to explain floating and sinking will quite happily shift from explanations based on weight to those based on size or texture, depending on the particular context. If children don't expect consistency among explanations, then inconsistency between existing views and 'official' views is not an incentive for change.

A second limitation is its treatment of conceptual change as an entirely rational process in which learners simply make a choice between rival conceptions or competing theories on the basis of compelling empirical evidence and/or theoretical argument. By contrast, Kuhn (1970) has argued that scientific revolutions (major theoretical revisions) cannot always be explained in entirely rational terms. Because it isn't possible to perform critical experiments capable of furnishing theory-independent data, it follows that there are no purely logical criteria (in the familiar usage of the term) for establishing the superiority of one theory over another. In other words, theories are empirically under-determined. Empirical adequacy is not enough in itself to establish validity. Moreover, in practice, empirical *in*adequacy is frequently ignored by individual scientists fighting passionately for a well-loved theory, and is often considered subordinate to the 'context of discovery' by the community-appointed validators (Knorr-Cetina, 1983). Additional factors that may play a part in decision-making include:

- elegance and simplicity (the aesthetics of science)
- similarity and consistency with other theories
- intellectual fashion, in the sense of compatibility with trends in other disciplines
- social and economic considerations
- cultural considerations

- the status of the researchers
- the views of 'significant others' — influential and powerful scientists, journal editors, publishers, and so on
- the priorities of research funding agencies

In other words, knowledge is negotiated within the community of scientists by a complex interplay of theoretical argument, experiment and personal opinion, underpinned by a complex of personal feelings and attitudes rooted in social, economic, political, moral and ethical considerations. If the community of scientists changes its views for all kinds of 'non-rational' reasons, why should it be any different for individual learners? A learner's goals, aspirations, feelings, experiences, values and attitudes will play a part. So too, will the learner's other knowledge (both scientific and non-scientific), intellectual tools, linguistic competence, and overarching epistemological and metaphysical beliefs. The greatest influence of all, however, may be the sociocultural location of the learner and his/her sense of identity — principally, class, gender and ethnic identity.

Hence, 'non-rational' factors that might influence an individual learner's acceptance or rejection of a new idea in a science class include: interest; perception of relevance; self-interest; feelings of anxiety, uncertainty, satisfaction, confidence and pride; aesthetic, political, economic and moral-ethical concerns. Put simply, how students feel about the ideas being presented to them, for whatever reasons, influences their learning. Feelings of wonder, delight, amusement, interest, disinterest, boredom and disgust will clearly impact in different ways on a learning task — sometimes favourably, sometimes unfavourably. Bloom (1992), for example, shows how emotions, values and aesthetics can influence not only students' willingness or reluctance to engage in a learning task, but also the kinds of meanings that they construct.

The first limitation of constructivist approaches can be overcome by regarding scientific understanding as the development of a *personal framework of understanding*, within which seemingly contradictory ideas can co-exist. The second limitation can be met by affording a much more prominent role to the affective and social dimensions of learning. Both of these matters are dealt with later in the chapter.

A third objection to the conventional rhetoric of constructivism — though an objection of a fundamentally different kind — is the charge of neglecting and trivializing scientific understanding. In a vigorous and highly publicized attack on the constructivist base of the New Zealand science curriculum, Michael Matthews (1993a, 1993b, 1995) described constructivism as a 'loony doctrine' which is leading the country into an educational and scientific abyss. At the heart of his criticism is a concern that constructivist approaches imply that students who construct their own understanding of the world are also building *scientific* understanding. Anything is allowed to count as science, he says, because the criteria of scientific truth are disregarded in favour of 'ensuring equity for all students, ensuring students communicate, challenging sensitively the ideas of students and providing resources' (Matthews, 1993b).

In one sense Matthews is quite right to be critical of (some) constructivists. Learning science is not simply a matter of 'making sense of the world' in whatever terms and for whatever reasons satisfy the learner, as Biddulph and Osborne's (1984) famous constructivist slogan seems to imply. It involves introduction into the world of concepts, ideas, understandings and theories that scientists have developed and accumulated (that is, *what* the scientific community knows). Scientific knowledge is more than personal belief reinforced by personally-gathered observational confirmation. It is an attempt to explain and account for the real nature of the physical universe (science has realist goals), regardless of whether it 'makes sense' in the everyday meaning of that expression. Indeed, much scientific knowledge flies in the face of commonsense, and the physics of Galileo, Newton or Einstein compares unfavourably with Aristotelian views if commonsense is to be the arbiter.

Scientific knowledge is that which has been subjected to, and has survived, critical scrutiny by members of the community of scientists, using whatever methods and criteria have been deemed appropriate to ensure the necessary degree of validity and reliability. Thus, a crucial part of science education involves understanding the particular rationality that scientists employ in generating and validating knowledge claims. What that rationality is, and how it is influenced by social, economic, political, moral and ethical factors, is a matter of some contention, and is discussed at length elsewhere (Hodson, 1993b). Suffice it to say that learning about the nature of science is not just a matter of learning how to conduct a 'fair test' by systematically controlling variables in order to satisfy oneself about a particular belief. It involves introduction into the established techniques, strategies, standards and criteria of science (that is, *how* the scientific community knows). It involves critical appreciation of the nature of scientific evidence, understanding of the role and status of scientific knowledge (including the crucial distinction between instrumentalist models and realist theories), and recognition of the social location, and hence cultural dependence of the scientific enterprise.

It is enculturation into these distinctively scientific ways of knowing, acting and communicating that constitute one of the principal goals of science and technology education. However, this goal of enculturation does not mean, as Matthews seems to imply, that the drive to personalize learning has to be abandoned. Nor does it mean that students have to give up other beliefs and values they may currently hold. Enculturation without assimilation is possible. Science education as enculturation can be reconciled with the notion of personalization through a reconsideration of the nature of scientific understanding and the elaboration of the idea of a personal framework of understanding.

Personal Frameworks of Understanding

Because of the variety of purposes that motivate theory building and model building in science, the precise meaning attached to a concept depends on the specific role that it has within a particular knowledge structure. Thus, a complex and sophisticated scientific theory or conceptual model may have several layers of meaning, some of which only become apparent through continued use in practical contexts. Different scientists conduct their activities at different levels of sophistication and, therefore, utilize different aspects of meaning. These, in turn, differ from those meanings commonly used by laypersons. Why, then, would we expect all students to have the same understanding? It is more reasonable to expect each student to have a unique conceptual profile, compounded of a variety of meanings accumulated for different purposes.

A number of writers have described meaning as comprising a central core of denotative meaning and a wide-ranging periphery of connotative aspects (see Sutton, 1992 for an extended discussion). Thus, our understanding of a term such as water, for example, comprises denotative elements — covalent molecule (formula H_2O) with inter-molecular hydrogen bonding, H-O-H bond angle = 104.9°, BP = 100C — together with all the other (often non-scientific) associations it has for us: runny, wet and cold, used for making tea, swimming in, and washing the car. Often, this framework of associations and connotations will include attitudinal and emotional elements. 'Water' may conjure up happy memories of windsurfing or distressing ones of nearly drowning; 'force' may trigger feelings of anxiety, fear or anger; 'spider' may trigger feelings of revulsion. For any individual, conceptual understanding is the current array of denotative *and* connotative aspects. It will necessarily vary from individual to individual; it will change over time in response to experience; and it will be strongly influenced by the sociocultural contexts in which the individual moves.

It has been traditional in science education to ignore personal, idiosyncratic and emotional connotations, even to attempt to suppress or eliminate them. Hence the use of specialized scientific terms and the insistence on a formalized linguistic code. While the increased explanatory power of specialized terms such as 'photosynthesis' is a sufficient case for their use, it is often the case that jargonization increases difficulty and decreases interest. It may even alienate some children from science. In my view, we should be encouraging rather than discouraging the connotative aspects of understanding, and their sub-cultural variations. It is likely that these other, personalized aspects of meaning, with their everyday associations, can provide the key anchoring points for new learning, and so render it more meaningful.

The notion of science education as enculturation requires that students acquire meanings that are similar to or coincident with those accepted by the scientific community, or the school curriculum versions of them. Thus, in teaching science, it is the teacher's task to assist students in modifying and developing their personal framework of understanding to incorporate the desired scientific aspects of meaning and an appreciation of when their use is appropriate. However, taking on new meaning should not necessarily entail relinquishing the old. 'Approved scientific meanings' can exist alongside a wide range of personal, idiosyncratic meanings and associations. Scientific understanding that cucumbers and tomatoes are fruit, for example, does not preclude the commonsense understanding that they are located in the vegetable section of the grocery store. What is important is recognizing when particular meanings are appropriate and being able to use them properly within the appropriate discourse. A central goal of science education is to show students when their own needs and purposes are well-served by scientific knowledge and scientific ways of proceeding, and when they are better served by other ways of knowing and acting. It is important, therefore, that teachers impress upon students that the aim of science education is not to eradicate commonsense ways of understanding by imposing *the* scientific way as the one true and universally valid mode of explanation. Rather, it is to assist each learner to incorporate further aspects of meaning, additional connotations and new relationships into their personal framework of understanding, and to know when and how to deploy scientific understanding.

Sociocultural Factors in Learning Science

Clearly, students will have a strong emotional commitment to ideas that are well-established and have been used successfully by them in contexts they regard as personally and/or socially important. Indeed, some ideas are so much a part of the student's everyday life that they are used automatically and unconsciously. Changing them is not easy, especially when they continue to be used by their peers and within family groups, and are promoted by religious teachings or the practices of other sociocultural groups to which the student belongs. Some views are like 'possessions': they have become so much a part of the student's view of self and sense of identity, held in the face of otherwise substantial changes, that if ever they were abandoned it would only be with the greatest reluctance and an acute sense of loss and discomfort (Abelson, 1986). Moreover, accepting views that are in opposition to views accepted and extensively used within other groups to which the student belongs, or wishes to belong, may be so emotionally stressful that it becomes virtually impossible. What is being argued here is that Posner et al.'s (1982) conditions for conceptual change need to incorporate an additional element: that students feel *comfortable* with the new idea, in the sense that it meets their emotional needs and is 'culturally safe'. In other words, one's social and cultural identity — comprising gender, ethnicity, religion and politics — impact very considerably on learning.

As Cobern (1993) argues, different cultural environments produce different 'worldviews' (sets of beliefs, held consciously or unconsciously, about the nature of reality and how one gains knowledge about it) that predispose people to feel, think and act in particular ways (see May's discussion of habitus in this volume). As a consequence, there are likely to be very significant cross-cultural differences in the way people conceptualize and interact with the natural world and significant differences, therefore, in the ways they respond to western science and its distinctive conventions for conceptualizing and investigating the natural world. Jegede (1995) has discussed in some detail the problems that arise for African students and their science teachers as a consequence of the incompatibility of the African worldview and the worldview implicit in western science, and Ogawa (1996) has described how Japanese science teachers struggle with similar problems. These problems are not, however, confined to the teaching of science in non-western countries. In a class comprising students from varied sub-cultural backgrounds there are clearly complex problems in ensuring that all students are 'comfortable' with the ideas being presented through the curriculum, 'comfortable' with the way they are presented, and 'comfortable' with the underlying worldview and 'ideological pivots' (Smolicz and Nunan, 1975) implicit in school science.

When teachers make the assumption that learning science is an entirely rational activity, and that an appraisal of the empirical evidence in favour of an idea will result in its ready acceptance, they fail to account satisfactorily for why some students who seem to have the requisite prior conceptual knowledge, and the intellectual capability to appraise the evidence, fail to engage in cognitive restructuring. They also tacitly accept the obverse: that when students decline to incorporate a particular idea into their personal framework of understanding it is because they don't understand the scientific evidence that supports it. As a consequence, they may misdirect their teaching efforts and, in doing so, may reinforce the student's reluctance to accept it. By contrast, the view that learning in science should be regarded as the development of a personal framework of understanding, within which multiple meanings (some contradictory) can co-exist, acknowledges the realities of scientific practice and the realities of ordinary daily life. Because it acknowledges that personal meaning includes an array of highly personal experiential and affective elements, much of which is culturally specific, it also recognizes the significance of these same factors in bringing about conceptual change and development.

Border Crossings

Within a particular society, each identifiable social group or sub-group has its distinctive patterns of beliefs, expectations and values that determine or define how its members act, judge, make decisions, approach and solve problems. In the words of Day et al. (1985), 'cognitive abilities are socially transmitted, socially constrained, socially nurtured, and socially encouraged'. Moreover, as Bakhtin (1981, 1986) points out, we also communicate regularly in a range of social languages and employ a variety of speech genres that are the characteristic modes of expression of particular sub-groups in society. Speech genres — which include military commands, everyday greetings, dinner table conversations, verbal exchanges concerned with buying and selling goods and services, cross examination of witnesses by courtroom lawyers, intimate talk between close friends or lovers, urgent communications between colleagues engaged in a specialized task, mother–infant talk, and so on — are not formalized languages, but they are distinctive and have clear purpose and socially agreed meaning. Each of us uses speech embedded in these social languages and speech genres to convey meaning quickly and reliably. Moreover, because speech is socioculturally constituted, each genre carries with it the common assumptions, interpretations and values of the group whose genre or social language it is.

Every individual is a member of a number of social groupings, some of which are long-term associations, others of which are merely temporary. Effective participation in these social groups is, of course, dependent on possession of the appropriate cultural knowledge — that is, the shared understandings, beliefs and language, codes of behaviour, values and expectations of the group. Thus, each person's profile of cultural knowledge is unique, reflecting their particular constellation of group memberships. Just as each student's personal framework of understanding is unique, so also is each student's complex of social group membership and their perceptions of what that membership entails and requires. When students, each with a distinctive personal framework of understanding, are presented with a particular learning task set within a distinctive educational context (involving a particular class or learning group), a unique learning context is created for each individual. Appreciation of the uniqueness of personal learning contexts helps to explain why some students learn successfully, while others of apparently equal ability do not, even in seemingly very similar circumstances. It helps to explain why particular students may learn on some occasions, but not on others, despite circumstances that to others may seem identical.

While the cognitive nature of the learning task and the scientific context in which it is located are both crucial factors influencing learning in science, they are bound together by an acting person who is uniquely located both socially and historically. Moreover, in most school learning situations, that 'acting person' is engaged in social interactions with others who are also uniquely located, and these interactions are themselves part of the construction of the learner's social identity. In short, learning is a complex, uncertain and socioculturally located activity. Its complexity can only be appreciated, and appropriate steps taken to facilitate better learning, by adopting a model of teaching and learning that recognizes the uniqueness of the individual learner, includes the sociocultural contexts in which the individual is located, and takes account of the complex nature of the interactions between the individual and the other elements in the learning context (the teacher, other students, learning materials, and so on).

The way in which an individual perceives these interacting elements, and feels about their influences, become a significant factor in determining learning behaviour, contributing to what Shapiro (1992) calls a 'personal orientation to science learning'. Among the many elements contributing to this personal orientation to science learning are: the student's views of school, science, and the activities associated with learning science; relationships with peers, teachers and family; learning preferences and other aspects of metacognitive awareness; self-image, aspirations and values. Some elements are wide-ranging and stable over time; they govern the student's overall attitude and commitment to learning science. Others are topic-specific, even lesson-specific, and influence short-term decision-making about learning behaviour.

For school-age students, the major social groupings of the family, the peer group and the school create distinctive 'social worlds' which may or may not have common cultural knowledge. Phelan et al. (1991) suggest that points of similarity and difference between these three social worlds lead to four types of transition into the culture of the school, a transition that is crucial to students' prospects of using the education system to further their life chances and career prospects. Their conclusions are that:

- congruent worlds facilitate smooth transitions;
- different worlds require transitions to be managed;
- diverse worlds lead to hazardous transitions;
- highly discordant worlds result in transitions being resisted or proving impossible.

In the first case, the sociocultural characteristics of the groups are not identical, but there is sufficient common ground to make transitions relatively unproblematic. In the second case, there are some differences that require students to make adjustments and reorientations as they move between groups. 'Border crossings' — to use Giroux's (1992) term — can be made, but they are not always easy and may, in Phelan et al.'s words, have significant 'personal and psychic costs' (cf. May, this volume). In the third situation, the real or perceived differences are such that transitions require more extensive adjustment and reorientation. Successful entry into the culture of the school may even require rejection of the values and aspirations of the other two worlds. It is in this kind of situation, say Phelan et al. (1991), that we often find adolescents teetering between school success and failure, involvement and disengagement, commitment and apathy (cf. Nieto, this volume). In the final scenario, the values, beliefs and expectations of the three social worlds are so discordant that boundary crossing is usually resisted. For those few who try, the emotional stress is such that they quickly give up. It is here that Bourdieu's notions of *habitus* (all the sociocultural experiences and influences that shape us as unique individuals) and *cultural capital* are useful. According to Bourdieu, some habitus are recognized as cultural capital by the school and are reinforced through academic success, others are not (see May, 1994, this volume).

For science students there is an additional border to cross: transition into the culture of science, or the particular school version of it. School science has its own set of beliefs, values and codes of behaviour — its 'ground rules' as Edwards and Mercer (1987) call them. It has its distinctive linguistic code. Costa (1995) describes the ways in which different students effect (or not) this transition. She describes the various patterns in the relationships between students' social worlds and their success in school science in terms of five broad categories of student. These five student 'types' experience the same science curriculum in very different ways, their experiences being positive or negative to the extent that the values, beliefs and expectations of their family and peer groups are consistent with those of the science classroom.

1   *'Potential Scientists'* — where the worlds of family and friends are congruent with the worlds of school and science, and the transition into the culture of school science is smooth and unproblematic. These students have educational aspirations and career plans in which science has a prominent role.
2   *'Other Smart Kids'* — where the worlds of family and friends are congruent with school, but not with science. These students can manage the transition into the culture of school science without too much difficulty. While science is not personally interesting to them, they can make instrumental use of it in pursuit of educational purposes.
3   *'I Don't Know Students'* — where the worlds of family and friends are inconsistent with both school and science. Transition into the culture of school science is hazardous, though possible at some personal cost. Often, these students find a way of meeting the demands of the system and obtaining reasonable grades without ever really understanding the material.

4 *'Outsiders'* — where the worlds of family and friends are discordant with both school and science. These students tend to be disillusioned with or alienated from school, in general, so that transition into the culture of school science is virtually impossible. They neither know about nor care about science.

5 *'Inside Outsiders'* — where the worlds of family and friends are irreconcilable with the world of school but potentially compatible with the world of science. Although these students have a natural interest in the physical world, transition into the culture of school science is prevented through lack of support both inside and outside school, and by their distrust of schools and teachers.

As teachers struggle to provide a science curriculum suitable for an increasingly diverse school population, it is important to know how some students negotiate boundaries successfully while others are impeded by them. It is likely that students of different ethnic groups will perceive boundaries differently and use different adaptation strategies as they move or attempt to move between social settings (Aikenhead, 1996a, b). Similarly, girls may perceive boundaries differently from the way boys perceive them and, therefore, may adopt different strategies for effecting transition. Moreover, for any one individual, patterns are not necessarily stable over time, and may be profoundly affected by changes in classroom or school climate, family circumstances and peer group friendships (Fensham, 1997). In Costa's (1995) California-based study, all students in the 'Inside Outsider' category were African-Americans. Just as significant is the observation that most of those for whom transition into the world of school science is smooth and unproblematic were from white middle-class family groups. It is also the case that transitions were generally smoother for boys than for girls.

Enculturation without Assimilation

Clearly, science teachers need to be more cognizant of the ways in which transition into the culture of school science can be eased for those students who currently experience difficulties, or who quit in the face of excessive emotional stress. Phelan et al. (1991) describe some of the strategies that students might be encouraged to adopt, many of which involve fostering new interests and new friendships. Pomeroy (1994) concentrates on changes that science teachers can effect, including provision of career support, adoption of culturally sensitive pedagogy, promotion of science language skills, and epistemological studies. Of paramount importance is the need to create school structures and curriculum experiences that facilitate border crossing and don't require students to give up or suppress important features of their lives outside the science classroom in order to gain access to science. This entails the creation of a school culture that values differences, ensures that all students feel a sense of belonging and self-worth, centralizes the ideal of social justice, and places a high value on teachers who can, themselves, move freely and comfortably between different social settings (May, 1994). It also requires a curriculum that shows students how science impacts on the lives of *all* students, on the lives of their friends and families, and on the environment, both locally and globally.

Jegede (1995) has developed the notion of *collateral learning* to describe how individuals can hold and develop western scientific thinking alongside traditional African knowledge and understanding. Regarding each individual as being in possession of a unique personal framework of understanding (as argued earlier) allows for Jegede's description of four categories of collateral learning (*parallel, simultaneous, dependent* and *secured*), located on a continuum, to be extended to all students in all classrooms. In my view there are two essential prerequisites to successful secured collateral learning: epistemological understanding (incorporating the demythologization of science essential to other aspects of border crossing to be discussed below) and metacognitive awareness.

In moving from commonsense understanding to scientific understanding, we don't just change the 'content' of our understanding, we significantly change its character. Science is more than a collection of context-specific or purpose-built explanations. Rather, it is a set of interrelated concepts and conceptual structures from which generalizable and universalist knowledge is constructed (Matthews, 1994).[1] Students who have not learned that scientific theory is coherent and consistent, and who do not understand the relationship between hypothesis and evidence, and among theory, observation and experiment, are rooted in a 'methodology of superficiality' (Gil-Perez and Carracosa-Alis, 1985) that cannot lead beyond commonsense knowledge. What is needed to effect the transition to more sophisticated conceptual understanding, without the attendant risk of assimilation into a 'culture of certainty' (Bencze and Hodson, 1998), is more sophisticated understanding of the nature of science. In particular, this involves understanding theories as complex structures rather than simple statements, viewing experiments as central to both theory testing and theory building, exploring the ways in which the community of scientists generates, validates and communicates new knowledge, and examining the role and status of that knowledge, and, crucially, when its use is appropriate and inappropriate. But students will not come to know about and understand these philosophical issues unaided. They must be taught — though whether this is best achieved by explicit teaching located in the history, philosophy and sociology of science, or by more indirect means, is an issue that is outside the scope of this chapter.

The capacity to reflect on one's own understanding of these matters and to understand and control one's own learning are further elements in the struggle against assimilation. However, the capacity to engage in critical reflection, and the attitudinal commitment that drives it, also have to be taught.

The constructivist teaching and learning strategies referred to earlier not only put great value on identifying and dignifying children's own ideas, many of which are culturally determined, they also give students a significant measure of responsibility for their own learning and make extensive use of student-controlled discussion as a way of developing ideas and reaching consensus. This pedagogy is, itself, a cultural artefact that may serve to advantage some students and disadvantage others.

Children from some cultural groups may be less comfortable than others in this situation and may find it more difficult to meet teacher expectations. Some parents may fail to support, or may actively oppose, the introduction of learning styles that encourage their children to adopt a critical and questioning stance. Durojaiye comments on this problem from an African perspective.

> Whilst the school encourages talking, the exchange of ideas, questioning and curiosity, the home may put a premium on being seen but not heard as a hallmark of good behaviour. The child's school experience often belongs to an entirely different world from his [sic] home experience. (1980, p. 11)

Girls brought up within Islamic tradition may experience difficulty in challenging what they perceive as the proper authority of an adult male teacher — a problem in many British and Canadian schools. Similar problems may exist for Polynesian immigrants into New Zealand.

> Many have learned from their parents that the teacher, like the priest or pastor, holds valuable knowledge and as such is to be respected, not questioned by mere students. Indeed, to ask a question can be a sign of lack of attention and disrespect. . . . The teacher represents the adult and 'know-all' passing on knowledge to the students, while the children remain passive and very much dependent on the teacher. . . . To teach the children to be critical thinkers and to ask questions in an inquiry approach is certainly opposing the conforming aspects of the culture. (Moli, 1991, pp. 41, 107)

While these kinds of distinctions seem to verge on stereotyping and may, therefore, be considered potentially racist in themselves, there does seem to be some validity in the claim that there are culturally determined preferences in learning style. In New Zealand, for example, radical educators have used this notion to articulate a set of guidelines for a preferred Maori pedagogy based on a *whānau* (extended family) structure (Jones et al., 1990; May, 1994, 1995, 1998; McKinley et al., 1992). The wide age range present within each classroom enables teachers to employ a form of peer tutoring based on the traditional *tuakana–teina* (elder–younger relatives) relationship. Cooperative learning is expected, and recognition of group efforts and achievements replaces the western practice of rewarding only individual accomplishment. The strong oral tradition of Maori culture is reflected in the extensive use of story-telling and song. There is a clear need for the development of other ethnically preferred teaching and learning initiatives, to be used as and when appropriate, to provide better access to significant knowledge and, thereby, to enhance social mobility.

Demythologizing Science

Despite a major effort in recent years to direct the attention of teachers and curriculum developers to the importance of considerations in the history, philosophy and sociology of science,[2] many school science curricula continue to promote deficient or distorted views of science. Apart from concern that a significant aspect of human-kind's cultural achievement should be so poorly understood by students, there are very clear indications that these distortions and falsehoods serve to exclude many girls and members of ethnic minorities from crossing the border into the culture of science.

In this regard, I have directed attention over the years to the eradication of a cluster of nine myths about science and science education that I believe are transmitted, either consciously or unconsciously, by teachers and curriculum materials.[3]

1. Observation provides direct and reliable access to secure knowledge
2. Science starts with observation
3. Science proceeds via induction
4. Experiments are decisive
5. Science comprises discrete, generic processes
6. Scientific inquiry is a simple, algorithmic procedure
7. Science is a value-free activity
8. The so-called 'scientific attitudes' are essential to the effective practice of science
9. All scientists possess these attitudes

In the context of critical multiculturalism, myth 7 should, perhaps, be afforded some priority and, in a sense, might be considered as subsuming the others.

Whereas it was once common for the school curriculum to present scientific discovery as the inevitable outcome of the 'correct' application of a rigorous, object-ive, disinterested, value-free and all-powerful scientific method, many contempor-ary science curricula are now beginning to recognize that science and technology (like art, music, literature and politics) are human endeavours that influence, and are influenced by the sociocultural context in which they are located. As Young (1987) states, 'Science is practice. There is no other science than the science that gets done'. What we do — that is, the questions we ask, the kind of problems we perceive and try to solve, and so on — depends on who we are and where we are. Science and technology are driven by the needs, interests, values and aspirations of the society that sustains them. So we might ask whether different societies would define and organize science differently and so produce different science. How much could be changed (aims, values, methods, criteria of validity, content, and so on) and it still be science?

The ways in which social and cultural influences determine the kind of science developed can be highlighted by consideration of contemporary 'alternative' or pseudosciences. Why, for example, is acupuncture dismissed by western scientists, despite its widespread and successful use in the East? The work of Wilhelm Reich, Immanuel Velikovsky and Erich von Daniken might make an interesting study. So too, the history of the notion of continental drift, now the basis of plate tectonics, but once dismissed as fanciful. The ways in which social and cultural influences can lead to distortion and misuse of science for political goals can be highlighted by studies of phrenology and its role in underpinning the unjust social system of nineteenth century England (Hodson and Prophet, 1986), and the Soviet suppression of Mendelian genetics in favour of Lamarckism during the 1950s. In similar vein, articles by Arnold (1990, 1992) reveal the extent to which some German archaeologists collaborated with the Nazi regime in promoting the claim that the Germanic culture of Northern Europe had been responsible for virtually every major achievement of western civilization, and that the Greeks were really Germans who had migrated South during Neolithic times to avoid a natural catastrophe.

From here it is but a short step to consideration of scientific racism: the misuse of the notion of 'race' to perpetuate stereotyping, legitimize discrimination and institutionalize injustice (Hodson, 1993a; Hodson and Dennick, 1994; cf. Rattansi, this volume). Suitable examples for presentation to students are the nineteenth-century misuse of the Darwinian principle of natural selection to argue that white Europeans are superior to Africans in evolutionary terms, thereby justifying colonization (Fryer, 1984; Gould, 1981); misinformation about sickle cell anaemia to exclude African–Americans from active flying duties in the US airforce and to prevent them achieving flight status with some commercial airlines (SSCR, 1985, 1987); and the continuing misrepresentation of research by psychologists such as Eysenck and Jensen to claim the intellectual superiority of 'Caucasians' (itself a racialized and racist designation).

On this latter subject, Brush (1989) provides powerful food for thought in his description of the way racial prejudice fuelled the development of the Stanford-Binet IQ test, still widely used as an objective measure of intellectual capacity, and the basis of the Scholastic Aptitude tests (SATs). Since SAT scores are used to control entry to selective colleges, and hence to positions of power and privilege in US society, science is seen to play a key role in sustaining institutional racism in American society. The history of sickle cell anaemia research provides another striking example of racially-driven scientific priorities. For decades, the disease (which primarily affects those of African descent) was ignored by US scientists. When it did gain a measure of attention, funding was directed to the 'elitist aspects of the biochemistry of the sickling process' rather than to screening and counselling programmes (Michaelson, 1987).

Challenging the other eight myths can be taken together as challenging or questioning conventional views of scientific rationality: asking questions such as whether science is characterized principally by its area of concern, its concepts and theories, its methods of inquiry, or its criteria for judging the validity of knowledge claims. Other questions include: 'What are the relationships among observation, theory and experiment?' 'What is the role and what is the status of scientific knowledge?' 'What are the underlying values of science' — what Smolicz and Nunan (1975) call its 'ideological pivots'? 'Could any of these things be different without the activity ceasing to be science?' 'What might African science, Maori science or Feminist science be like?' 'Do these terms mean anything?' Finally, 'If science could be different, *should* it be different?' 'Would these changes make it more accessible to students of ethnic minority cultures?' 'Would these changes have beneficial effects on the environment or the social fabric?' By confronting these kinds of questions, students come to recognize that science is not the simple straightforward business that is part of its public image. Thus, they are empowered by the curriculum to challenge and, possibly, to change it (see below).

It is these suggestions that so enraged Williams, Loving, Good and Demastes, as described earlier, and led them to accuse advocates of this approach of relativism as 'not taking science seriously'. There are two responses here. First, different ways of knowing yield different answers to the same question and, more often, ask different questions. In Pomeroy's (1996) words, 'they are not equal; they are different, and their value is that they provide alternative ways of understanding phenomena. One does not use a hammer to fasten a bolt; the appropriateness of the tool lies in the use to which it is put; equality has nothing to do with it'. Second, asking questions about what is distinctive about science and scientific understanding is an essential part of the epistemological understanding necessary for moving freely across borders between sub-cultures (see below). To say that scientific knowledge arises in a particular culture (the western scientific community) is not to discredit it or to say that it has no currency at all outside that social context, or that it may not (on occasions) be close to a true account of the world. Exposing students from non-western cultures to the ideas of science or to any other ideas that are from cultures other than their own, providing it is done sensitively, is not to do them a disservice. Quite the contrary; it is a key aspect of their education. Nor is there anything morally repugnant in asserting that traditional knowledge and everyday understanding often fail to stand up to rigorous scientific scrutiny. As Siegel (1997) points out, western science is 'biased' in the sense that it makes epistemological presuppositions that are cultural artefacts, and are not shared by some non-western cultures, but the bias is only a pernicious one when science is presented as absolute truth or as the *only* way of knowing. Consideration of traditional knowledge within the science curriculum is not a threat to science, nor is the presentation of scientific knowledge necessarily a threat to traditional knowledge. Within an individual's personal framework of understanding they can co-exist and can be separately accessed as and when appropriate. The key is a careful consideration of issues located in the history, philosophy and sociology of science.

Another all-too-prevalent myth is that science is exclusively European or North American (i.e., white-ethnocentred). This myth can be readily dispelled through historical studies (Hodson and Dennick, 1994). Studies in the history of medicine, astronomy and technology — particularly rich in Islamic, Indian and Chinese exemplars — help to promote awareness that current scientific ideas are not derived solely from post-Renaissance western societies. As Dennick remarks:

> Throughout European history since the Renaissance there has been a tendency to disparage and down grade the discoveries and achievements of other cultures and historians have been very prone to give credit where it is not due. (1992, p. 81)

Dennick cites Needham's (1954, 1969) assertion that the inventions he regards as the three most important of the millennium (papermaking and printing, gunpowder, and the navigational compass) were each used in China several hundred years before their alleged discovery by westerners and points out that many of the discoveries of Islamic scientists are ignored, or presented as solely European in origin. Indeed, Sardar suggests that the western world systematically plagiarized the work of Muslim scientists:

> Piracy was so common that as early as the twelfth century a decree was issued in Seville forbidding the sale of scientific writings to Christians because the latter translated the writings and published them under another name. (1989, p. 10)

A similar fate befell much of Indian science (Kumar and Kenealy, 1992; Machwe, 1979). In addition, the agricultural theory and practice of the pre-Columbian societies of the Americas were subsumed within European science without any acknowledgement (Weatherford, 1988). Even more serious in the context of critical multicultural/antiracist education is the systematic trivialization, distortion and suppression of African cultural history — a key element, of course, in the racist ideology that formerly legitimized slavery and colonial exploitation and still serves to deny a sense of cultural identity to those of African descent. Dennick (1992) points out that, despite the spectacular achievements of the civilizations of Ethiopia, Benin and Zimbabwe, for example, the myth is still propagated that significant African history began with the imperialist invasions. Moreover, the great civilization of Egypt is often portrayed as Semitic, rather than African.

When members of particular communities do not see themselves or their experiences, interests and aspirations included in curriculum representations of science, and when the view of science and the culture of science education are incompatible with their beliefs, values and traditions, it is not surprising that they are dissuaded from seeking admission. By demythologizing science, we can create an image of science and a culture of science education that is more welcoming and accessible to children from ethnic minority cultures. For too long, too many science teachers have taught a lie: that science is culturally neutral and value-free. It isn't. What is needed, and needed urgently, is a curriculum that reveals the values and sectional interests that have underpinned science in the past and do so at present, asks critical questions about the values and interests that should underpin science in future, and explores ways in which alternative voices can be heard and their views acted upon. Through such a curriculum, all students learn that scientific and techno-logical knowledge and expertise constitute a powerful resource that is accessible to, and can be used by all sociocultural groups to create a better world for themselves.

Of course, media images also play a significant role here in determining stu-dents' enthusiasm (or lack of it) for science and science education. Television, newspapers, comics, movies, advertising and museum exhibits provide fragments of knowledge (some valid, some fanciful, some entirely fictional), play a part in build-ing students' perceptions of who has a place in science, and convey attitudinal and emotional messages about science and technology — about use of animals, hazards to human health, environmental degradation, and so on. While media images are outside the control of science teachers, all should actively and critically address them and, where necessary, intervene with alternative views. They are just as much a target for critical attention as the science curriculum.

Aspects of Language

The language of science and scientific communication is strongly implicated in myth-making. Textbooks often present science solely from the perspective and within the assumptions of the current paradigm, thereby distorting chronology and disguising the revolutionary nature and social dependence and impact of major scientific advances. The distinctive style of scientific communication used in the research paper is designed to persuade readers to accept conclusions rather than to describe what actually happened day-by-day during a research inquiry. In that sense, says Medawar (1967), it is a fraud. It certainly helps to sustain the myth that the path of science is swift and certain.

The language of school science is often more complex than other language that students encounter; it is depersonalized through excessive nominalization (replacement of active verbs by abstract nouns) and an almost exclusive reliance on the passive voice. In short, it is emotionally detached, humourless, remote from real life, and uninviting. Emphasizing the formal language of science to the exclusion of everyday ways of speaking and writing, and insisting too early in a child's science education on careful and precise language, may help promote an ideology of authority concerning science and lead students to believe that scientific knowledge is fixed and certain (Lemke, 1987). By contrast, more familiar vocabulary and language forms help students to see the relationship between science and the real world and to appreciate how scientific knowledge derives from and complements everyday, commonsense knowledge.

Classroom language is often highly directive. Teachers can (and usually do) decide what will and will not be talked about, who has the right to speak and for how long, what is the 'correct' way to speak and to behave while speaking and listening, and what counts as legitimate knowledge, satisfactory evidence and proper argument. Furthermore, by choosing the language of expression, teachers decide in favour of a particular way of thinking and, therefore, in favour of the interests and values that underpin it. Taken together, the rules about the conduct of lessons, the conventions concerning who can speak and what can be spoken about (including what can be challenged), and the particular form of school talk and science talk, impose a set of conventions and restrictions that can be so formidable that many children are prevented from gaining access to science education.

> It is not surprising that those who succeed in science tend to be like those who define the 'appropriate' way to talk science: male rather than female, white rather than black, middle- and upper-middle class, native English speakers, standard dialect speakers, committed to the values of North-European middle-class culture (emotional control, orderliness, rationalism, achievement, punctuality, social hierarchy, etc.). (Lemke, 1990, p. 138)

Given the sociocultural location of language, and its accompanying sociopolitical cargo of meaning, important questions of authority, culture and power are raised. Whose view of reality is being promoted? Whose voices are heard? And why? In most classrooms there is a conscious or unconscious reflection of middle-class values and aspirations that serves to promote opportunity for middle-class children and to exclude children of ethnic minorities and low socio-economic status, who quickly learn that their voices and cultures are not valued. When the speech genres and interpretive frameworks of some children (in particular, those of ethnic minority cultures and low socio-economic status) are disregarded or specifically rejected as inferior, school science becomes implicated in a continuing suppression of opportunity and perpetuation of privilege. As O'Loughlin says:

> To the extent that schooling negates the subjective, socioculturally constituted voices that students develop from their lived experience, therefore, and the extent that teachers insist that dialogue can only occur on their terms, schooling becomes an instrument of power that serves to perpetuate the social class and racial inequalities that are already inherent in society. (1992, p. 816)

To ignore these matters, and to act as if power relationships do not impregnate classroom events is to ensure the perpetuation of the political status quo and the continued exclusion of significant numbers of students from a satisfactory science and technology education. To recognize the sociopolitical context of the classroom and to acknowledge the ways in which values and culturally determined meanings permeate all aspects of the language used in classrooms is to take the first step in facilitating border crossings and rebuilding society along more socially just lines. Moje (1995) has shown how some teachers utilize a language of belonging ('*You* are a scientist', '*We* believe that . . .', and so on) to foster student participation and cooperation and to promote a sense of belonging within the classroom that extends to a sense of belonging within the scientific community. It is important to recognize that if particular forms of language and language use can influence the thinking and attitudes of students in these positive ways, they can also act to exclude or alienate students, or contribute to their feelings of frustration and inadequacy. Adopting appropriate forms of language is just as much a part of curriculum decision-making as choosing wisely from among theories of learning.

The notion of a personal framework of understanding can now be expanded to include knowledge of, and ability to use properly, a range of social languages and speech genres. It is important that students recognize the sociocultural location of different speech genres and modes of discourse, including their own familiar everyday social language. Equally important is that they learn how and when to use other modes of discourse, and learn not to be intimidated or manipulated by the power inherent in those with which they have, as yet, little familiarity. This is a crucial aspect of the *politicization* of science education, the ultimate goal of which is to ensure that students are enabled to use a range of powerful discourses, especially the discourse of science and technology, to effect social change.

Politicizing Science Education

Politicization of science education can be achieved by the provision of opportunities for confronting a wide range of socio-economic issues that have a scientific,

Level 1   Appreciating the societal impact of scientific and technological change, and recognizing that science and technology are, to some extent, culturally determined.

Level 2   Recognizing that decisions about scientific and technological development are taken in pursuit of particular interests, and that benefits accruing to some may be at the expense of others. Recognizing that scientific and technological development is inextricably linked with the distribution of wealth and power.

Level 3   Developing one's own views and establishing one's own underlying value positions.

Level 4   Preparing for and taking action.

Figure 9.2:   Levels of sophistication for an issues-based curriculum

technological or environmental dimension. By grounding curriculum content in socially and personally relevant contexts, an issues-based approach can provide the motivation that is absent from current abstract, decontextualized approaches and can form a base for students to construct understanding that is personally relevant, meaningful and important. A mix of local and global issues focusing on aspects of the seven priority areas identified by the Bangalore Conference on *Science and Technology and Future Human Needs* (Tendencia, 1987) might constitute a reasonable starting point for curriculum building: Food and Agriculture; Energy Resources; Land, Water and Mineral Resources; Industry and Technology; The Environment; Information Transfer; Ethics, and Social Responsibility.

I have argued elsewhere (Hodson, 1994b) that we should regard an issues-based approach aimed at achieving critical scientific and technological literacy as having four levels of sophistication (Figure 9.2).

At the simplest level, case studies of the societal impact of inventions such as the steam engine, the printing press, or the computer can be used to bring about an awareness that science and technology are powerful forces that shape the lives of people and other species, and impact significantly on the environment as a whole. They can also be used to show that scientific and technological development are both culturally dependent and culturally transforming. In other words, science is a product of its time and place and can sometimes change quite radically the ways in which people think and act. For example, the science of Galileo, Newton, Darwin and Einstein changed our perception of humanity's place in the universe and pre-cipitated enormous changes in the way people address issues in politics, economics and history. 'Level One awareness' also includes recognition that the benefits of scientific and technological innovations are often accompanied by problems: hazards to human health, challenging and sometimes disconcerting social changes, environ-mental degradation and major moral-ethical dilemmas.

Much of science and environmental education, while recognizing these adverse features of development, is currently pitched at the level where decision-making in science and technology is seen simply as a matter of reaching consensus or effecting a compromise. At the second level of sophistication, students learn to recognize that scientific and technological decisions are taken in pursuit of particular interests and are justified by particular values. As a consequence, the advantages and disadvantages of scientific and technological developments often impact differentially on society. It is here that there are likely to be major differences between the cultural pluralist and critical multiculturalist approaches to science education. While the former might simply note the different ways in which developments affect people in other parts of the world, people who happen to be of different cultural and ethnic backgrounds, the latter assumes that ethnicity (and, incidentally, gender and social class as well) is central to definition of the issue and is an essential concept in understanding and thinking about it.

For example, a cultural diversity approach might deal with the symptoms of 'Third World' poverty (malnutrition and famine, inadequate sanitation, and diseases such as rickets, tuberculosis and cholera) but neglect to include a sociopolitical and historical analysis of its cause. At best, it would treat the issue of poverty simplistic-ally, as a consequence of climatic harshness and overpopulation. By contrast, the approach advocated in this chapter would recognize the role played by western governments and business interests in controlling the production and distribution of resources (cf. McLaren and Torres, this volume). Historical studies can be employed to illustrate that scientific advances have often been driven by European colonialist expansion — the need for better navigation giving rise to theoretical and instru-mental advances in astronomy, for example — and, since the mid-twentieth century, by military and commercial interests. Case studies can be used to achieve a level of critical scientific literacy that recognizes how science and technology serve the rich and the powerful in ways that are often prejudicial to the interests and well-being of the poor and powerless, sometimes giving rise to further inequalities and injustices. Such studies help students to see that material benefits in the West (North) are often achieved at the expense of those living in the 'Third World' (South). When case studies focusing on the infringement of Aboriginal land rights and the destruction of the Amazonian rainforest in the pursuit of short-term financial gain and economic growth are included, students quickly recognize that critical consideration of scientific and technological development is inextricably linked with questions about the dis-tribution of wealth and power. Moreover, they can be sensitized to the notion that problems of environmental degradation are rooted in societal practices and in the values and interests that sustain and legitimate them.

Level three is concerned primarily with supporting students in their attempts to formulate their own opinions on important issues and to establish their own value positions, rather than with promoting the 'official' or textbook view. It focuses much more overtly on values clarification, developing strong feelings about issues, and actively thinking about what it means to act wisely, justly and 'rightly' in different social, political and environmental contexts. This phase has much in com-mon with the goals of Peace Education (Hicks, 1988). It begins with the fostering of self-esteem and personal well-being in each individual, and extends to:

- respect for the rights of others
- mutual trust
- the pursuit of justice

- cooperative decision-making
- creative resolution of conflict between individuals, within and between communities, throughout the world

It culminates in a commitment to the belief that alternative voices can and should be heard, in order that decisions in science and technology reflect wisdom and justice, rather than powerful sectional interests (Maxwell, 1984). Levels two and three, taken together, shift questions of environmental improvement from the technical domain into the sociopolitical domain. The solution to environmental problems does not lie in a quick 'technical fix', but in sociopolitical action deriving from a re-orientation of societal values.

The final (fourth) level of sophistication in this issues-based approach is helping students to prepare for and take responsible action:

> . . . responsible action denotes those behaviours engaged in for the purpose of achieving and/or maintaining a dynamic equilibrium between quality of life and quality of environment. (Hines and Hungerford, 1984, p. 10)

As Curtin (1991) says, it is important to distinguish caring *about* and caring *for*. It is almost always much easier to proclaim that one cares about an issue than to do something about it. A politicized ethic of care (caring *for*) entails becoming actively involved in a local manifestation of a particular problem, exploring the complex sociopolitical contexts in which the problem is located, and attempting to resolve it. Preparing students for action necessarily means ensuring that they gain a clear understanding of how decisions are made within local, regional and national government, and within industry and commerce. Without knowledge of where and with whom power of decision-making is located, and awareness of the mechanisms by which decisions are reached, intervention is not possible. Of course, the likelihood of students becoming active citizens will be enhanced by encouraging them to take action *now*, and by providing opportunities for them to do so. Suitable action might include conducting surveys, making public statements and writing letters, organizing petitions and consumer boycotts of environmentally unsafe products, publishing newsletters, working on environmental clean-up projects, assuming responsibility for environmental enhancement of the school grounds, and so on.

At level 1 of an issues-based approach, students can be made aware of the societal and environmental impact of science and technology and alerted to the existence of alternative practices. At level 2, they can be sensitized to the sociopolitical nature of scientific and technological practice. At level 3, they may become committed to the fight to establish more socially just and environmentally sustainable practices. But only by proceeding to level 4 can we ensure that students acquire the knowledge and skills to intervene effectively in the decision-making processes and ensure that alternative voices, and their underlying interests and values, are brought to bear on policy decisions. A similar argument, leading to a curriculum proposal based on a five-phase 'responsibility spiral', is presented by Waks:

> By moving through the phases of the spiral, learners of all ages can be guided in forming their convictions and commitments, their life-style choices and values, as these bear upon the technology-dominated issues facing our society. As they move through these phases, on issue after issue, confronting and thinking through science and technology-dominated issues of increasing complexity, learners can make progress toward mature social responsibility. (1992, p. 13)

The link between politicization and personalization becomes apparent when we look at what is likely to translate environmental concern into environmental action: namely, ownership and empowerment. Those who act are those who have a deep personal understanding of the issues (and their human and environmental implications) and feel a personal investment in addressing and solving the problems. Those who act are those who feel personally empowered to effect change, who feel that they can make a difference, and know how to do so.

Changing Values and Taking Action

What I am arguing here is that education for critical scientific literacy is inextricably linked with education for political literacy and with the ideology of education as social reconstruction (cf. Kalantzis and Cope; Moodley, this volume). The kind of social reconstruction envisaged includes, of course, the confrontation and elimination of racism, sexism, classism, and other forms of discrimination, scapegoating and injustice.

In this approach it is not enough to view environmental problems merely as matters of careless industrialization and inexpert management of natural resources, because this ignores the underlying causes of the problems — the values underpinning industrialization and the exploitation of natural resources — and sees their solution as a technical problem, for which we need a technical solution. In that sense, the approach *de*politicizes the issues, thereby removing them from the 'realm of possibility' within which ordinary people perceive themselves as capable of intervention. As a consequence, dealing with environmental problems is left to 'experts' and officials, and ordinary citizens are disempowered.

Education for empowerment entails recognizing that the environment is not just a 'given', but a social construct. It is a social construct in two senses:

1   We act upon and change the natural environment, and so construct and reconstruct it through our social actions.
2   We perceive it in a way that is dependent on the prevailing sociocultural framework. Thus, our concept of 'environment' itself is a social construct, and so could be different. Indeed, many indigenous peoples do perceive it in significantly different ways (Knudtson and Suzuki, 1992).

By encouraging students to recognize the ways in which the environment is socially constructed we can challenge the notion that environmental problems are 'natural' and inevitable. If 'environment' is a social construct, environmental problems are social problems, caused by societal practices and structures, and justified by society's current values. It follows that solving environmental problems means addressing and changing the social conditions that give rise to them and the values that sustain them.

A crucial part of this kind of politicized science education is rejection of the notion of technological determinism — the idea that the pace and direction of technological change are inevitable and irresistible. We *can* control technology or, rather, we can control the controllers of technology. We can, and should promote the notion of technological choice, whereby citizens decide for themselves the kind of technology they will and will not use. Just as the people of New Zealand rejected nuclear weapons protection on moral/ethical grounds, so we should reject certain technologies for moral/ethical reasons, or for environmental reasons, or for reasons of social justice. Economics and personal comfort should not be the only criteria!

Education *in* and *through* the environment can play a substantial role in assisting the re-ordering of values and the development of new ones. Gough (1989), for example, describes how the kind of experiences advocated by the Earth Education movement can be utilized in re-orienting students' environmental understanding. Another striking example is the *Science Aotearoa* project[4] in New Zealand, which aims to give all students the opportunity to experience the forest, mountains and seashore through the historical consciousness of the indigenous Maori. By learning to be sensitive to the spirituality of the caves, the volcanoes and the trees — rather than seeing them merely as products of erosion, the outcome of geothermal activity and as resources for making paper or furniture — children can recover what many indigenous peoples around the world have never lost: a sense of unity between humanity and the environment. Movies and video can be a useful substitute, or powerful adjunct to outdoor experience. Addressing alternative values rooted in ecofeminism and/or the perspectives of indigenous peoples lays the groundwork for a serious consideration of alternative or more environmentally sustainable and appropriate technology. Budgett-Meakin (1992) has characterized this as technology which is sensitive to local social, cultural and economic circumstances, capitalizes on local skills, ingenuity and materials, makes sparing and responsible use of non-renewable resources, and is controlled by the community, thereby resulting in increased self-respect and self-reliance. Although it is a concept more familiar to us in connection with 'Third World' situations, 'appropriate technology' applies just as much to the industrialized world.

Adopting appropriate technology entails rejecting technologies that violate our moral-ethical principles, exploit and disadvantage minority groups, or have adverse environmental impact. The goal is a *humanized* technology: a technology more in harmony with people and with nature; a technology that is energy and materials conserving; a technology based on renewable resources and recycling; a technology predicated on durability rather than in-built obsolescence and deterioration. Science curricula usually promote the view that energy production based on oil and coal consumption, or hydro schemes and nuclear power, are the only viable alternatives, dismissing the use of wind, solar, tidal and biomass energy production as 'cranky' or hopelessly futuristic. Whose interests are being served by failing to make students

aware of alternatives — thus, avoiding the likelihood of any demand for such alternatives? Certainly not those of the wider community, or of the planet as a whole.

Inevitably, there are those who seek to maintain science education's current
preoccupation with abstract, theoretical knowledge and with pre-professional preparation, and some who regard the reformulation of science education in terms of
more overtly political goals as undesirable. Restriction of an issues-based curriculum
to the level of scientific and technological considerations (level 1, above) is seen by
many as 'politically safe', because of its supposed 'neutral' stance. It is my contention
that it is *not* neutral. Indeed, it implicitly supports current social practices, institutions and values. Insofar as it fails to address underlying sociopolitical and economic
issues, excludes consideration of social alternatives, sustains a 'technocratic' approach
to the confrontation of problems, and fails to equip students with the capacity to
intervene, the so-called 'neutral' approach actually reinforces the societal values that
created the problems in the first place. As such, it has to be regarded as education for
social reproduction and, more emotively, education *against* the environment and
against minorities. A critical multicultural science education provides a key means by
which these processes can be identified, contested, and changed.

Notes

1 The extent to which the universalist claims of science are justified is discussed, briefly,
later in the chapter. A more extensive discussion is provided by Hodson (1993b).
2 Matthews (1992) has documented the extraordinary rise of interest among science educators in the history and philosophy of science during the late 1980s and early 1990s.
3 I am not claiming that all nine myths are promoted by all science curricula. Rather, that
most curricula promote one or more of them and that, across the range of curricular
provision, all nine are in evidence.
4 'Aotearoa' is the Maori name for New Zealand. An account of the origin and development of the project can be found in Jesson (1990).

References

ABELSON, R. (1986) 'Beliefs are like possessions', *Journal for the Theory of Social Behavior*, **16**,
pp. 223–50.
AIKENHEAD, G. (1996a) 'Science education: Border crossing into the subculture of science',
Studies in Science Education, **27**, pp. 1–52.
AIKENHEAD, G. (1996b) 'Towards a First Nations cross-cultural science and technology cur-
riculum for economic development, environmental responsibility, and cultural survival',
Paper presented at the 8th IOSTE Symposium, Edmonton, Canada.
APPLETON, K. (1993) 'Using theory to guide practice: Teaching science from a constructivist
perspective', *School Science & Mathematics*, **93**, pp. 269–74.
ARNOLD, B. (1990) 'The past as propaganda: Totalitarian archaeology in Nazi Germany',
Antiquity, **64**, pp. 464–78.
ARNOLD, B. (1992) 'The past as propaganda', *Archaeology*, **45**, pp. 30–7.

BAKHTIN, M. (1981) *The Dialogic Imagination: Four Essays*, HOLQUIST, M. (ed.) Austin, TX: University of Texas Press.

BAKHTIN, M. (1986) *Speech Genres and Other Late Essays*, EMERSON, C. and HOLQUIST, M. (eds) Austin, TX: University of Texas Press.

BELL, B. (1993) *Children's Science: Constructivism and Learning in Science*, Geelong: Deakin University Press.

BENCZE, L. and HODSON, D. (1998) 'Coping with uncertainty in elementary school science: A case study in collaborative action research', *Teachers and Teaching: Theory and Practice*, **4**, pp. 77–94.

BIDDULPH, F. and OSBORNE, R. (1984) *Making Sense of Our World: An Interactive Teaching Approach*, Hamilton, New Zealand: University of Waikato.

BLOOM, J. (1992) 'Contexts of meaning and conceptual integration: How children understand and learn', in DUSCHL, R. and HAMILTON, R. (eds) *Philosophy of Science, Cognitive Psychology, and Educational Theory and Practice*, Albany: State University of New York Press, pp. 177–94.

BRUSH, S. (1989) 'History of science and science education', *Interchange*, **20**, pp. 60–70.

BUDGETT-MEAKIN, C. (1992) *Making the Future Work. Appropriate Technology: A Teacher's Guide*, London: Longman.

COBERN, W. (1993) 'Contextual constructivism: The impact of culture on the learning and teaching of science', in TOBIN, K. (ed.) *The Practice of Constructivism in Science Education*, Hillsdale, NJ: Lawrence Erlbaum, pp. 51–69.

COSTA, V. (1995) 'When science is "another world": Relationships between worlds of family, friends, school, and science', *Science Education*, **79**, pp. 313–33.

CURTIN, D. (1991) 'Toward an ecological ethic of care', *Hypatia*, **6**, pp. 60–74.

DAY, J., FRENCH, L. and HALL, L. (1985) 'Social influences on cognitive development', in FORREST-PRESSLEY, D., MACKINNON, G. and WALLER, T. (eds) *Metacognition, Cognition, and Human Performance. Vol 1: Theoretical Perspectives*, New York: Academic Press, pp. 33–56.

DENNICK, R. (1992) 'Analysing multicultural and antiracist education', *School Science Review*, **73**, pp. 79–88.

DRIVER, R. (1989) 'Changing conceptions', in ADEY, P., BLISS, J., HEAD, J. and SHAYER, M. (eds) *Adolescent Development and School Science*, Lewes, England: Falmer Press, pp. 79–99.

DRIVER, R., ASOKO, H., LEACH, J., MORTIMER, E. and SCOTT, P. (1994) 'Constructing scientific knowledge in the classroom', *Educational Researcher*, **23**, pp. 5–12.

DUROJAIYE, M. (1980) *The Contribution of African Universities to the Reform of Education*, Paris: UNESCO.

EDWARDS, D. and MERCER, N. (1987) *Common Knowledge: The Development of Understanding in the Classroom*, London: Methuen.

FENSHAM, P. (1997) 'Science education and sub-cultural border crossing', in HODSON, D. (ed.) *Science and Technology Education and Ethnicity: An Aotearoa/New Zealand Perspective*, Wellington: Royal Society of New Zealand, pp. 88–96.

FRYER, P. (1984) *Staying Power: The History of Black People in Britain*, London: Pluto Press.

GIL-PEREZ, D. and CARRACOSA-ALIS, J. (1985) 'Science learning as a conceptual and methodological change', *European Journal of Science Education*, **7**, pp. 231–6.

GIROUX, H. (1992) *Border Crossings: Cultural Workers and the Politics of Education*, New York: Routledge.

GOOD, R. and DEMASTES, S. (1995) 'The diminished role of nature in postmodern views of science and science education', in FINLEY, F., ALLCHIN, D., RHEES, D. and FIFIELD, S.

(eds) *Proceedings of the Third International History, Philosophy and Science Teaching Conference, Vol. 1*, Minneapolis: University of Minnesota, pp. 480–7.

GOUGH, N. (1989) 'From epistemology to ecopolitics: Renewing a paradigm for curriculum', *Journal of Curriculum Studies*, **21**, pp. 225–41.

GOULD, S. (1981) *The Mismeasure of Man*, Harmondsworth, England: Penguin.

HARLEN, W. (1992) *The Teaching of Science*, London: David Fulton.

HEWSON, P. and THORLEY, N. (1989) 'The conditions of conceptual change in the classroom', *International Journal of Science Education*, **11**, pp. 541–3.

HICKS, D. (1988) *Education for Peace: Issues, Principles and Practice*, London: Routledge.

HINES, J. and HUNGERFORD, H. (1984) 'Environmental educational research related to environmental action skills', Monograph in Environmental Education and Environmental Studies Series. Columbus, OH: Ohio State University.

HODSON, D. (1993a) 'In search of a rationale for multicultural science education', *Science Education*, **77**, pp. 685–711.

HODSON, D. (1993b) 'Teaching and learning about science: Considerations in the philosophy and sociology of science', in EDWARDS, D., SCANLON, E. and WEST, D. (eds) *Teaching, Learning and Assessment in Science Education*, London: Paul Chapman/Open University, pp. 5–32.

HODSON, D. (1994a) 'Response to Williams' comment', *Science Education*, **78**, pp. 521–5.

HODSON, D. (1994b) 'Seeking directions for change: The personalisation and politicisation of science education', *Curriculum Studies*, **2**, pp. 71–98.

HODSON, D. and DENNICK, R. (1994) 'Antiracist education: A special role for the history of science and technology', *School Science & Mathematics*, **94**, pp. 255–62.

HODSON, D. and PROPHET, B. (1986) 'A bumpy start to science education', *New Scientist*, **1521**, pp. 25–8.

JEGEDE, O. (1995) 'Collateral learning and the eco-cultural paradigm in science and mathematics education in Africa', *Studies in Science Education*, **25**, pp. 97–137.

JESSON, J. (1990) 'Science Aotearoa: Its origin and development', Unpublished MA thesis, University of Auckland.

JONES, A., McCULLOCH, G., MARSHALL, J., SMITH, G. and SMITH, L. (1990) *Myths and Realities: Schooling in New Zealand*, Palmerston North: Dunmore Press.

KNORR-CETINA, K. (1983) 'The ethnographic study of scientific work', in KNORR-CETINA, K. and MULKAY, M. (eds) *Science Observed*, London: Sage, pp. 115–40.

KNUDTSON, P. and SUZUKI, D. (1992) *Wisdom of the Elders*, Toronto: Stoddart.

KUHN, T. (1970) *The Structure of Scientific Revolutions*, Chicago: University of Chicago Press.

KUMAR, A. and KENEALY, P. (1992) 'An issue of cultural diversity in science', in HILLS, S. (ed.) *The History and Philosophy of Science in Science Education, Vol II*, Kingston: Queen's University, pp. 1–15.

LEMKE, J. (1987) 'Social semiotics and science education', *American Journal of Semiotics*, **5**, pp. 217–32.

LEMKE, J. (1990) *Talking Science: Language, Learning and Values*, Norwood, NJ: Ablex.

LOVING, C. (1995) 'Comment on "multiculturalism, universalism, and science education"', *Science Education*, **79**, pp. 341–8.

MACHWE, P. (1979) *Hinduism: Its Contribution to Science and Civilization*, New Delhi: Vikas Publishing House.

MATTHEWS, M. (1992) 'History, philosophy and science teaching: The present rapprochement', *Science and Education*, **1**, pp. 11–47.

MATTHEWS, M. (1993a) 'Constructivism in New Zealand science education', Paper presented at the University of Auckland, New Zealand.

MATTHEWS, M. (1993b) 'Curriculum reform degrades science', *New Zealand Herald*, August 26.

MATTHEWS, M. (1994) *Science Teaching: The Role of History and Philosophy of Science*, New York: Routledge.

MATTHEWS, M. (1995) *Challenging New Zealand Science Education*, Palmerston North, New Zealand: Dunmore Press.

MAXWELL, N. (1984) *From Knowledge to Wisdom*, Oxford: Basil Blackwell.

MAY, S. (1994) *Making Multicultural Education Work*, Clevedon, England: Multilingual Matters.

MAY, S. (1995) 'Deconstructing traditional discourses of schooling: An example of school reform', *Language and Education*, **9**, pp. 1–29.

MAY, S. (1998) 'Language and education rights for indigenous peoples: Maori in Aotearoa/New Zealand', *Language, Culture and Curriculum*, **11**, 3.

MEDAWAR, P. (1967) 'Is the scientific paper a fraud?', *The Listener*, 12 Sept, pp. 377–8.

McKINLEY, E., WAITI, P. and BELL, B. (1992) 'Language, culture and science education', *International Journal of Science Education*, **14**, pp. 579–95.

MICHAELSON, M. (1987) 'Sickle cell anaemia: An "interesting pathology"', in GILL, D. and LEVIDOW, L. (eds) *Antiracist Science Teaching*, London: Free Association Press, pp. 59–75.

MOJE, E. (1995) 'Talking about science: An interpretation of the effects of teacher talk in a high school science classroom', *Journal of Research in Science Teaching*, **32**, pp. 349–71.

MOLI, S. (1991) *Science Student Teachers' Views of Teaching and Learning: A Samoan Case Study*, Hamilton, NZ: University of Waikato.

NEEDHAM, J. (1954) *Science and Civilization in China* (7 vols), Cambridge: Cambridge University Press.

NEEDHAM, J. (1969) *The Grand Titration: Science and Society in East and West*, London: Allen and Unwin.

OGAWA, M. (1996) 'The Japanese view of science in their elementary science education program', Paper presented at the 8th IOSTE Symposium, Edmonton, Canada.

O'LOUGHLIN, M. (1992) 'Rethinking science education: Beyond Piagetian constructivism toward a sociocultural model of teaching and learning', *Journal of Research in Science Teaching*, **29**, pp. 791–820.

PHELAN, P., DAVIDSON, A. and CAO, H. (1991) 'Students' multiple worlds: Negotiating the boundaries of family, peer, and school cultures', *Anthropology and Education Quarterly*, **22**, pp. 224–50.

POMEROY, D. (1994) 'Science education and cultural diversity: Mapping the field', *Studies in Science Education*, **24**, pp. 49–73.

POMEROY, D. (1996) 'Science educators as cultural workers: Philosophical implications', Paper presented at the 8th IOSTE Symposium, Edmonton, Canada.

POSNER, G., STRIKE, K., HEWSON, P. and GERTZOG, W. (1982) 'Accommodation of a scientific conception: Toward a theory of conceptual change', *Science Education*, **66**, pp. 211–27.

SARDAR, Z. (1989) *Explorations in Islamic Science*. London: Mansell.

SHAPIRO, B. (1992) 'A life of science learning: An approach to the study of personal, social and cultural features in the initiation to school science', in HILLS, G. (ed.) *History and Philosophy of Science in Science Education, Vol II*, Kingston: Queen's University, pp. 429–47.

SIEGEL, H. (1997) 'Science education: Multicultural and universal', Paper presented at History and Philosophy of Science and Science Teaching Conference, Calgary, Canada.

SMOLICZ, J. and NUNAN, E. (1975) 'The philosophical and sociological foundations of science education: The demythologizing of school science', *Studies in Science Education*, **2**, pp. 101–43.

SSCR (1985) *Science Education for a Multicultural Society*, Leicester, England: SSCR/Leicestershire Education Authority.

SSCR (1987) *Better Science: Working for a Multicultural Society. Curriculum Guide No. 7*, London: Heinemann/ASE.

SUTTON, C. (1992) *Words, Science and Learning*, Buckingham: Open University Press.

TENDENCIA, C. (ed.) (1987) *Science and Technology Education Towards Informed Citizenship*, Proceedings of the fifth ACASE-Asian symposium. Penang, Malaysia: RECSAM.

WAKS, L. (1992) 'The responsibility spiral: A curriculum framework for STS education', *Theory into Practice*, **31**, pp. 13–9.

WEATHERFORD, J. (1988) *Indian Givers: What the Native Americans Gave to the World*. New York: Crown.

WILLIAMS, H. (1994) 'A critique of Hodson's "In search of a rationale for multicultural science education"', *Science Education*, **78**, pp. 515–9.

YOUNG, R. (1987) 'Racist society, racist science', in GILL, D. and LEVIDOW, L. (eds) *Antiracist Science Teaching*, London: Free Association Press, pp. 16–42.

10   Multicultural Education: Transforming the Mainstream

Mary Kalantzis and Bill Cope

Multicultural education, to this point, has primarily been conceived as the project of improving the educational and social opportunities of cultural and linguistic 'minorities'. And very properly so. Although being of a cultural and linguistic 'minority' does not predestine a child to educational failure or lack of social mobility, it is undoubtedly the case that the educational prospects of particular cultural and linguistic groups are adversely affected under particular circumstances (Kalantzis and Cope, 1988). A view of multicultural education as something that exclusively addresses 'minorities', either as groups inequitably excluded from social access or as a positive presence, however, has its own limitations and difficulties. This chapter analyses the major educational paradigms for the way they frame the issue of diversity. The historical move from educational theories and practices whose project was assimilation, to philosophies and practices of pluralism which regard 'minority' students as their exclusive concern, we will argue, has created as many new problems as it has solved old ones. From this experience, it is now time to move on to new visions of multicultural education, visions which have the potential to transform pedagogy for all students, and to reconstitute mainstream social and educational practices in the interests of all.

   To start this exploration, we need to reconsider the most basic terms of the debate. Unsatisfactory conceptual constructs often creep into one's terms of reference, and these colour the whole of one's analysis. Taking one of the most fundamental of these key terms, the presence of a majority implied in the concept 'minority' accepts the aggregating pretensions of groups that would like to think of themselves as a majority. In the United States, for example, the majority is variously conceived of as 'white', if one accepts the category 'race' as it is used in the US census, or, in a more popular parlance, 'WASP'. But how is it that the latest immigrant from eastern Europe is, by fiat of being classed 'white', automatically in the same category as descendants of the Pilgrim Fathers? If the business of culture or 'race' is one of ancestry, then the biggest ethnic group in the United States is people of English ancestry. But at just 14 per cent of the population, it would be hard to call Americans of English background an ethnic majority. And if the Amish of Pennsylvania and lapsed Episcopalian gays are both 'WASP', this does not have much use as a cultural category either. In Australia, to take another example, the majority is frequently referred to as Anglo-Celtic, both by government agencies as they deal with diversity, and in popular discourse. But again, this is an absurd aggregation of groups that have traditionally defined their identity against the other's imperial predilections: the Irish, the Scots and the Welsh against the English, for example, not to mention the vehement traditions of regional and class, cultural and linguistic differentiation even within England. The idea of Anglo-Celt, historically and culturally, is no more meaningful than Palestineo-Israeli or Turko-Greek.

Similarly, the concept of 'race' does not describe a physiological or phenotypical reality that has any social significance beyond the construction historically put upon it by racist discourse (cf. McLaren and Torres; Rattansi, this volume). In the United States, for example, 'race' in the case of black–white relations is more accurately a marker of the legacy of slavery than of any inherent way humans might tend to react to different skin colours. 'Race', in other words, describes a social relation rather than something of biological significance. How is it that many 'Whites' (the 'majority') can comfortably call themselves unhyphenated Americans whilst 'Blacks' are at best hyphenated African-Americans, a 'minority' despite the fact that most are descendants of people who first came to the Americas centuries ago? Similarly, the categories 'Hispanic-American' and 'Asian-American' are not really about 'race', but markers of certain historical and social relations (cf. May, this volume).

So the category 'majority', as the other of 'minority', is a fiction. This is not to say that there is not a dominant — a group that imagines itself to be a majority bound by 'race' and culture, and imagines itself thus in order to justify its social position. This imagining projects itself historically, back into narratives of the past and forward into various futures. It also projects itself across social realms into powerful positions of cultural symbolism, politics and socio-economic power. It is this dominant that generates categories like 'white' and 'WASP' and 'Anglo-Celt', and along with them the complementary categorization 'minorities'. These are its own cultural categories, invented to suit its own imagination of what is culturally, linguistically and 'racially' appropriate to its own dominance.

A multicultural education that accepts these categories, that accepts its brief to be for 'minorities' exclusively, brings with it two kinds of limitations. First, it limits its charter to those groups that the dominant has already constructed as 'minorities', possibly in need of some sort of remedial help to improve their social access, or in need of cultural affirmation. In reality, however, the majority imagined by the dominant is much more fractured than this, both culturally and socio-economically. A large number of those the dominant conceives to be members of its own apparent majority do not understand themselves to be majority/dominant, at least not unequivocally so or so all the time. The 'problem' of cultural and linguistic diversity, in other words, is a much bigger one than the dominant culture would like to have us believe.

Cultural diversity, moreover, is becoming increasingly pertinent for every member of society, including those most comfortably at home in the dominant culture, untroubled because they imagine themselves to be the cultural majority. Multicultural education is just as much an issue for them as any other member of society. Maybe it is even more important for the children of the dominant culture, given the unfortunate combination of their ideologically self-inflicted relative isolation from issues of diversity, and, in a longer-term social sense, the fact that there is probably a greater than average likelihood for them than for their 'minority' peers that they will end up in positions of power and social responsibility. Diversity is one of the fundamental issues of our times, for all people. Who would have predicted at the beginning of the 1980s that the Cold War would end, not in nuclear holocaust, but with the ethnic implosion of the Soviet Union? In the United States, some conservative commentators have even gone so far as to say that, now the Cold War has ended, multiculturalism replaces Marxism as the fundamental threat to the social fabric (Cope and Kalantzis, 1998; cf. May, this volume). In every country of the world, cultural and linguistic diversity is emerging as one of the great political issues for the next century.

Nor is it likely that the tide of diversity will turn. We live in a time of both increasing globalization and increasing localization. Rather ironically, these are two sides of the one epochal coin. Human movement on a massive scale will be a defining feature of the next century, movement on a scale even greater than the great migrations of the nineteenth and twentieth centuries: skills migrants, temporary workers, refugees, illegals, family reunions. This itself is a phenomenon of the increasing globalization of the labour market, in which national borders present less and less of a barrier to movement. And, contrary to the hopes of the proponents of the melting pot, this human movement produces increasing diversity at a local level. The sheer scale of movement, in fact, will mean that melting pot theories will be less true to empirical reality than they ever were. This is a globalization that simultaneously means localization.

Global markets, global capital, global communications and global culture play on local diversity as much as they erase it. This is a globalization that not only universalizes certain fundamental anthropological forms such as the commodity and the market, but also, seemingly contradictorily, juxtaposes particularistic differences: the imported feel of a product bought locally, the distant ownership of a local firm, the affectedly exotic tourist destination that is now so close, the senses of cultural specificity that constitute some of the allure of the products of the global culture industry.

This is a globalization that means localization, a globalization that relentlessly brings about the increasing interrelation of differences. These two divergent trends reduce the relevance of that intermediate political entity, the nation–state, and its cultural imaginings in the form of nationalism. Nations and nationalisms were traditionally marked by a singular ethnic descriptor or a single set of cultural affinities. But the narrative of nation is no longer working as well as it once did. All this will surely add up to a new world order, to recycle a term which must give us more cause for scepticism, even trepidation, than it does confidence in the future. Needless to say, as we students and teachers go on living our lives in a social institution so fundamentally important as the school, we will need to come to grips with these issues.

So this is the first major reason why we need to move beyond the sort of multicultural education which has an exclusive interest in the welfare of 'minorities': the issue is just much bigger and much more fundamental than the construction 'minority' would have us believe. But there is a second reason, too. An exclusive concern for the schooling of 'minorities', formulated under the rubric of pluralism, does not necessarily mean that this sort of multicultural education does the best thing even for the students that it conventionally regards as its own constituency. In particular, it accepts the minority/majority distinction in such a way that it is unable to *reconstruct* the mainstream or dominant culture.

The project of multicultural education is more than a 'live and let live' pluralism which satisfies itself with affirming diversity. Cultures do not exist in isolation. They make themselves in social relation. They define themselves by the differences that lie beyond their own boundaries. It follows that, just as much as the category 'minority' is the creature of a broader social context, so it is possible for 'minorities' to seize the initiative in a world in which diversity is a critical issue, and seize it in such a way that the 'majority' has to reconceive itself — as diverse, as a group which has to negotiate cultural boundaries and relations rather than impose its self-image on others. Unless multicultural education considers itself to be a mainstream issue, an issue that has the potential to transform the mainstream in positive ways, the inequitable relation of different cultural and linguistic groups will remain unchanged.

In the light of this broad understanding of the scope and potential of multicultural education, this chapter is a critique of pluralist multicultural education and an outline of an alternative approach. From this point, it proceeds in two steps. First, it discusses three strategies for dealing with diversity in schools: assimilation; pluralist multiculturalism; and, out of an emergent critique of the latter, the possibility of an equitable, critical multiculturalism in which cultural difference is effectively employed as a resource for securing social access. Second, the chapter considers the sort of pedagogy that most comfortably accompanies each of these educational strategies: traditional curriculum, progressivist curriculum and an explicit pedagogy for social inclusion and access.

Managing Cultural Diversity: Three Models

In the history of education since the foundation of modern, mass institutionalized schooling, two main models seem to have emerged for dealing with cultural and linguistic diversity: assimilation and cultural pluralism. Out of a critique of the last model, arguably, there is the possibility of another — a critical multicultural education that is oriented to social access without prejudice to difference.

Assimilation

The curriculum of modern, mass education has always addressed the issue of cultural diversity. Theorist of nationalism Ernest Gellner argues, in fact, that one of the central functions of institutionalized schooling in the rise of the modern nation-state was to erase diversity — to remove a critical part of socialization into the public arena in order to establish standard forms of official state languages and homogeneous senses of identity to inculcate loyalty to the State (Gellner, 1983; see also May, 1999).

The task of school in assimilating diversity, it seemed in the halcyon years of nationalism, was relatively straightforward. This was the advice of the New South Wales Department of Education in 1951, at the height of Australia's post-war mass immigration programme:

> The fact that the New Australian Child is eager to master the language and, indeed, is forced to do so if he wishes to take his place amongst Australian children, makes the teacher's task much easier. It has been found that children with little or no command of English appreciate being given an 'adjustment period' of a fortnight or so during which they can observe their new class and 'get the feel' of the new conditions without being unduly worried by formal classwork. The adjustment process is helped by seating the migrant beside a sympathetic Australian child. (New South Wales Department of Education, 1951)

The term 'New Australian' and the ease with which it was expected immigrants would 'adjust' sum up well the glib cultural assumptions upon which assimilation was based. Underlying this seeming benign neglect, however, was a conscious social project; a project the same in essence as the 'melting pot' theories that complemented mass immigration policies in the United States. Assimilation to the dominant culture had both economic and cultural aspects. The economic aspect was supposed to entail the successful incorporation of the children of immigrants and indigenous peoples into the project of industrial society. Schools had the generic role of giving students appropriate skills, sorting them into the social hierarchy via the mechanism of 'ability', and teaching them discipline and respect. In Australia, for example, the cultural aspect of assimilation was founded on an expectation that all children would end up with singularly 'Anglo' affinities, identifying themselves with the British Monarch as head of state, the Westminster system of parliament, the English Common Law, and speaking English without a trace of the accent of another language. There are, of course, striking international parallels to the Australian policy of assimilation. Each nation-state has its own particular narrative of nation, but with the same overall intent in relation to the mission of the nation-state (cf. May, this volume).

But assimilation was never the simple matter that the policy makers tried to make it seem. Assimilation did not work as well as their rhetoric implied it should. More and more the evidence pointed to the less than happy reality that 'minority' students were educationally disadvantaged. At the same time, it became clear that cultural and linguistic diversity were things that simply could not be erased. On the contrary, they became an unavoidable part of the *public* environment. Linguistic and cultural heritage remained a cornerstone of the domestic life of both the immigrants and the indigenous peoples of the New World. 'Ethnic' organizations and lobby groups were emerging and, in countries where significant numbers of 'minorities' had the vote, possibly even beginning to constitute an important electoral pressure group.

Of course, one of the reasons why assimilation didn't work was that its proponents were never entirely serious about it. The name of the game, at least in part, was a structural racism designed to keep difference the way it was, rather than that more honest project of socio-economic assimilation that would have attempted to provide equitable access for all immigrants and, in the New World, for indigenous peoples as well. Nevertheless, no matter how cynically one views the verbiage of assimilation, it became clear that even the rhetoric was transparently not working anywhere in the world by the early 1970s.

Multiculturalism as a Superficial Pluralism

One of the responses to this changing situation was the emergence of philosophies of cultural pluralism, often under the rubric of 'multiculturalism'. In Australia, the transition from the assimilationist model to a multicultural model of educational and social policy occurred between the mid-1960s and the mid-1970s, influenced variously by the development of multiculturalism as an official policy in Canada (cf. Moodley, this volume) and the Civil Rights movement in the United States (cf. Sleeter and Montecinos, this volume). One of the key committees recommending multicultural education policies in Australia said that schools 'should encourage the development and maintenance of the student's self-esteem and personal identity while at the same time offering the opportunity for the student to understand and appreciate alternative lifestyles and cultural patterns other than his or her own'. The task of assisting in the maintenance of the child's home language, for example, was no less than 'the deliberate preservation and encouragement of ethnic identity' (Committee on Multicultural Education, 1979). This represents a striking official reversal of the rhetoric of assimilation.

In reality, and notwithstanding the radical language of cultural pluralism, this multiculturalism in the Australian case represented a cost-cutting measure for the government and a retreat from the principles of the welfare state. It reflected an international move to restore the logic of the market against the intervening state. The trend was established to distance migrant services from the general welfare framework with its 'assimilative' intent. Now, 'ethnic-specific services' were to be provided more and more by the communities themselves through quasi-professional self-help agencies. So called 'ethnic schools', for example, were given a $30 government grant per student per year to support them to teach languages other than English outside normal school hours. This was extremely cheap, to say the least. It involved highly committed, poorly paid and sometimes poorly trained teachers in a semi-voluntary capacity. And it meant that mainstream day schools did not have to worry too much about servicing the language needs of their students. In these mainstream schools, multiculturalism came to mean celebratory festivities and studying colourful lifestyles, thereby conveniently displacing the issue of life chances (Kalantzis and Cope, 1984; Kalantzis et al., 1984–5). Behind this was a pluralist variant of the cultural deficit model. If only 'their' cultures were affirmed instead of negated, so the argument seemed to go, all would be well; 'ethnic disadvantage' would be reduced.

At the same time, to continue with the Australian example, Aboriginal policy shifted from assimilation to self-management and later to self-determination, again paralleling developments in Canadian and US policies (cf. Moodley, this volume). In the spirit of devolving responsibility from the state to communities, this involved the imposition of a philosophy of self-help and cultural autonomy upon Aboriginal 'homelands' that were of marginal value to non-Aboriginals. Loud official proclamations of a newfound pluralism were not accompanied by the resources that were needed for genuinely independent development. And they came with some far from traditional expectations about what good self-management or viable self-determination looked like. In schools, exhortations to teach Aboriginal cultures and languages were not matched with the resources needed simply to document the hundreds of languages near extinction, let alone translate these from cultures that were oral into written, schooled curricula; cultures upon which institutionalized schooling had historically been a colonial imposition.

This brief discussion of the development of pluralist multicultural education policy in Australia aims to illustrate some of its practical limitations. The details of empirical historical experience may differ from country to country, but, broadly speaking, the fundamental issues that emerge remain the same. The move to a pluralist version of multiculturalism as state policy, in other words, can also conveniently entail the structural marginalization of the issues of diversity through ethnic-specific servicing. It does not mean that education authorities have to rethink the way mainstream public institutions or school curricula operate. It can construct the 'ethnic' or traditional 'other' as exotic in order to marginalize it, or, returning to the Greek roots of the word exotic as connoting the outside, in order to keep that other out. This kind of multiculturalism didn't even have to provide access to the goods of the dominant culture, which was at least the promise, if not the reality, of assimilation. Indeed, pushing the critique beyond the well-meaning hopes of the enthusiasts of pluralism, it may well have even exacerbated a social fragmentation in which difference is not just colourful and worthy of celebration, but is simultaneously a marker and maker of inequitable social division. Any problems there might be, according to this sort of pluralism, are matters of cultural dissonance, not social injustice. If only the attitudinal principles of tolerance were accepted and communities were given a chance to look after themselves in their own way, it seemed, we would arrive at multiculturalism. Whilst mouthing good intentions about pluralism, however, this sort of multiculturalism can end up doing nothing either to change the mainstream or to improve the access of those historically denied its power and privileges. It need not change the identity of the dominant culture in such a way that there can be genuine negotiation with 'minorities' about matters social or symbolic or economic. It need not change education in such a way that issues of diversity are on the agenda for all students. It need not change education so that diversity might become a positive resource for access rather than a cultural deficit to be remedied by affirmation of difference alone.

After Superficial Pluralism

Historically, the critique of pluralist multicultural education arose in Australia from two sources, and there are important strategic lessons in this for the way educational change comes about. The first was from an alliance of intellectuals, lobbyists and critical policy makers. Having reached the promised discursive land of pluralism without having realized its material promise, this alliance set to work on a new agenda which would work. In a deliberate revision of earlier policies, the 1987 report of the National Advisory and Coordinating Committee on Multicultural Education argued for an *equitable* multiculturalism which not only concerned itself with ethnic identity but simultaneously with strengthening students' life chances (National Advisory and Coordinating Committee on Multicultural Education, 1987). The National Policy on Languages maintained that careful management of Australia's diverse language resources, including Aboriginal languages, would produce complementary benefits: enrichment, economic opportunities, external relations and equality (Lo Bianco, 1987). And in 1989, the high-profile Office of Multicultural Affairs in the Prime Minister's Department announced that multiculturalism made economic sense: it was an essential for Australia's economic well-being (Office of Multicultural Affairs, 1989). This new rhetoric was an unholy but pragmatic alliance of the discourse of social justice and the discourse of economic rationalism (see Clyne, 1997; May, 1997). Multiculturalism was simultaneously a project of social equity and, even in the crudest of economic terms, in everybody's self-interest.

The second source for a critique of pluralism was teacher practice. In schools, teachers were faced with very practical everyday needs that were not met by pluralist multiculturalism. In response, they found themselves agents in what we have already termed a self-corrective phase. They found themselves, by dint of necessity, moving towards a multiculturalism oriented to social equity and the practical needs of all students. In a study of this phenomenon, we found teachers cynical about 'the stuff on festivals' that seemed to sum up the tokenism and bad faith of the pluralist version of multiculturalism. This was, moreover, a multiculturalism that produced stereotypes which had as much potential to feed into racism as to alleviate it (cf. Carrim and Soudien; Moodley, this volume). 'Cultural identity in terms of what people wear and eat doesn't mean anything; it's not hitting the mark'. According to another teacher, 'culture is more subtle and dynamic' than this. It's not a matter of preservation of a distanced 'their culture', but a dialogue, a dynamic process of negotiation (Kalantzis et al. 1990; cf. May, this volume).

The rest of this chapter will concern itself with the pedagogical models that fit with these three overall social and educational programmes for managing diversity. By the time we get to discussing the third, emergent model, the chapter will be presenting a vision for education in a society in which every citizen has multilayered allegiances: local or ethnic, national, and global; in which people's economic and cultural orientations are unavoidably international; and in which equitable access is guaranteed to social and educational institutions. Diversity, in this vision, would not be a problem for 'minorities', but a core issue for all public institutions. Multicultural education would be a path to equitable access. Cultural difference would be used as a resource. And a new epistemology of culture would inform all our human transactions.

Pedagogies for Cultural Difference

To these three approaches to education for cultural and linguistic diversity correspond three very different types of pedagogy that have emerged or that are emergent in education systems in many western countries. The assimilationist approach to cultural and linguistic diversity was complemented by a traditional transmission pedagogy. Pluralist multiculturalism was realized in education by the medium of progressivist pedagogy. And, beside the attempts to reconstruct multiculturalism so that it goes beyond the limitations of pluralism, there are emerging the elements of what we want to characterize as an explicit pedagogy for inclusion and access. At this point, our account moves from history to theory, although these modes of argumentation are not so distinct. The pedagogies not only represent historically evolved and chronologically successive paradigms, linked to educational movements. They have also defined their own agendas theoretically against each other, and continue to do so. The dialogue and the social experimentation go on. All three pedagogies are still alive and well. In this sense, historical questions are also theoretical questions for us. Diachrony translates itself into synchrony. History is far from bunk.

*The Traditional Curriculum of a Classical Canon and
Its Assimilationist Mission*

The historical origins of traditional curriculum stretch back to the beginnings of modernity. Rather ironically, its traditionalism was always much more an ideological affectation than it was a practical reality. Substantively, traditional curriculum in its founding moments harked back to the classics of ancient Greece and Rome, thereby constructing the foundations for a western Canon that lived on through the 'Great Books' of western literature and the 'Great Men' of history. In its form, however, in the way it was packaged as pedagogy, this classicism was quintessentially modern. Symbolic of this modernity was the textbook form. Arguably an invention of the sixteenth century French scholar, Petrus Ramus, the first textbooks were obsessed with the classical European past — teaching, for example, the rhetoric, dialectic, grammar, logic and mathematics of ancient Greece and Rome. The real novelty of the textbook form, however, was that rhetoric, dialectic and so on were to be learnt, not through the practice of rhetoric or dialectic as had been the case in classical times, but through ingesting formalized, written accounts which dissected their elements and reconstituted them as rationalizing taxonomies (Ong, 1983). The modern aspect of the Ramus text was not its substantive reference but its epistemology of scientific rationalism and its subsequent pedagogy in which fixed, formal knowledge was to be absorbed passively by students.

In the nineteenth century, traditional curriculum was to become the founding pedagogy of mass, institutionalized schooling. Drawing on Enlightenment principles epitomized by the Ramus texts, its view of knowledge was that there were fixed facts and constant social 'truths' in the world, capable of formal, systematic and definitive representation in the text. These were epistemic inventions drawn from the peculiar cultural imaginings of modernity. A consequence of this epistemology was a pedagogy of transmission. 'Facts' and 'truths' were things that students were to assimilate on the teacher's instruction. This epistemological framework translated down as far as the details of the classroom. Typically, in Cuban's (1984) summation, teacher talk in traditional curriculum exceeded student talk during instruction; the teacher interacted with the whole class rather than with groups; the use of classroom time was determined by the teacher; and chairs and desks were arranged in rows facing the blackboard.

To give a couple of examples of how this pedagogy was realized, language teaching involved memorizing spelling; exercising traditional grammar; and then testing 'correct', formal knowledge of 'standard' English in examinations. The author of a nineteenth century grammar school reader, a text that counted 'proper' pronunciation as one of its main goals, counselled:

> if children are required to utter correct sounds forcibly at the age when the organs of speech are most tractable, the habit of uttering words distinctively, and of pronouncing them correctly, will soon be formed. The voice should be early and frequently exercised upon the elementary sounds of the language . . . and classes of words containing sounds liable to perversion or suppression should be forcibly and accurately pronounced. . . . If the learner habitually mispronounce words, if he pervert or suppress important sounds — as *prudunt* for *prudent*, or *boundin* for *bounding* — his attention should be directed to the table of words containing sounds similar to those mispronounced, and the voice should be exercised upon it until the defect is remedied. (Swan, 1844, pp. 3–5)

There are a number of profound cultural assumptions here about the inadequacy or inappropriateness of languages or dialects other than an English pronounced in a certain sort of way; '. . . until the defect is remedied'. This is where cultural and linguistic assimilation came into its own. Nor was this just a curriculum that was assimilative in its prejudiced disdain for accents and cultures other than that of a white middle-class. Traditional curriculum was not primarily concerned with its immediate referents. More importantly, as Graff argues, it was an instrument to inculcate 'punctuality, respect, discipline, subordination'. It was a medium 'for tutelage in values and morality'. The social purpose of this sort of schooling was to create 'a controllable, docile and respectful workforce, willing and able to follow orders' (1987, p. 262). Or, to take another archetypical example of how scientific rationalism overlaid the ideology of classicism, 'foreign' languages such as Latin or even the prestigious modern European languages, were taught formally and for their own sake — the formality being 'traditional' grammar, that quintessentially modern, scientific invention; and the formality also being in the interests of 'discipline' before knowledge of the subject matter.

However exclusionary in practice, traditional curriculum had pretences to universality. All students were supposedly being given the facts and truths of the world, including the cultural and linguistic contents of the canon and of 'standard' English, so that they could become successful people. But these were false pretences. Having presented a curriculum comfortably within the cultural and linguistic horizons of some students, but outside the horizons of others, traditional curriculum disingenuously accounted for different outcomes in terms of another of its characteristic educational inventions, 'ability', and within one of its own cultural and epistemological frames, individualism. When students failed — and maybe even it was because they were wantonly resisting the call to assimilate the contents of the cultural narrative of curriculum (cf. Nieto, this volume) — they were counselled by reference to their individual 'ability'. The rhetoric of assimilation, in other words, was a lie. The imperative to assimilate, by no accident, was also the criterion for excluding a social group on the grounds of their ostensible individual failure.

As diachrony meets synchrony, so we must be ready to move out of the past tense and into the present to bring a discussion of traditional curriculum up to date. Cuban (1984) argues, in fact, that the pedagogy used in schools in the United States has changed remarkably little in the past century. Added to this, we live at the moment of a powerful re-emergence of public advocacy for traditional curriculum. This is a moment of 'back to basics', or what might be called classical revivalism. Certainly ideas of what is classical have shifted somewhat, away from the languages and societies of ancient Greece and Rome, although it seems that 'our' western roots are still central. But the epistemological notions of 'fact' and 'truth' at the root of traditional curriculum and the idea that there is a canon, are firmly back on the agenda. In the United States, this is the basis of the best-selling work of Bloom, D'Souza and Hirsch for the attacks on multiculturalism by the provocateurs in the debate about 'political correctness' (Cope and Kalantzis, 1998; cf. May, this volume). Not only are we being called upon to salvage, or rather reinvent, a canon of 'western Culture' from the ravages of multiculturalism, feminism and all manner of post-Cold War social evils, but we are also being asked to buy the assumptions of traditional curriculum about the nature of knowledge, the status of truth and the role of the teacher in relation to the student.

Progressivism and Pluralism

Progressivism has a long history, too, though not so long as the traditional curriculum of a classical canon, which has been with us since the first moments of modernity. Progressivism lives in our present, whilst stretching almost a century back into our past. John Dewey in the United States and Maria Montessori in Italy were two of its first and most brilliant exponents. Its founding principles were that students should be active learners; that they should learn by doing; that education should be through practical experience rather than having to absorb facts; that the process of learning was more important than the content; that learning had to be meaningful rather than formal; and that the most effective learning was relevant to the individual rather than institutionally imposed. Over the twentieth century, however, there have been significant developments internal to the progressivist paradigm, even though the founding principles remain intact. The broad tenor of this shift can be summed up as a move from ideological modernism to ideological postmodernism.

Within the history of progressivism, one aspect of this shift is the evolution of a pluralist view of cultural and linguistic diversity out of what was in the first instance an assimilationist view.

Unlike its predecessors, Dewey's pedagogy was ideologically modern. His committed social modernism — a confidence in the culture of industrial modernity and the possibility of progress — led into a pedagogy which celebrated universal processes in a world where the only inviolable fact was change itself. Gone were fixed facts and formal truths. Science was experience; technology was action; social progress was through participation. So the real content of education was the *process* of learning and the only relevant facts were creatures of activity. For example, language learning, according to Dewey, should never be formal and always for a purpose. It should be 'done in a *related* way, as the outgrowth of the child's social desire to recount his experiences and get in return the experiences of others' (1956, pp. 55–6). Dewey applauded the fact that some schools were installing printing presses so that the children themselves could print some of the pamphlets, posters, or other papers the school needed. They were motivated to do this, not just because they found setting the type enjoyable and interesting, but because there was a good reason to be producing the copy for print. But still, there was a singular cultural end to this teaching — the 'correct' acquisition of the standard English which seemed to be required for practical purposes in an industrial social setting. 'Type setting is an excellent method of drilling in spelling, punctuation, paragraphing and grammar, for the fact that the copy is going to be printed furnishes a motive for eliminating mistakes which exercises written by a pupil for his teacher never provides' (Dewey and Dewey, 1915, pp. 84–5).

Dewey's conception of language made no concession to the fact that students' experiences of language outside school might be very different, be they native speakers of languages other than English or speakers of a non-standard dialect. So universalist, modernist ends remained in this sort of progressivism; ends that were in the last analysis not so different from those of traditional curriculum. In this respect, the modernist phase of progressivism was just as assimilative of cultural and linguistic difference as had been traditional curriculum. 'There is in a country like our own a variety of races [sic], religious affiliations, economic divisions. Inside of the modern city, in spite of its nominal political unity, there are probably more communities, more differing customs, traditions, aspirations, and forms of government or control than existed in an entire continent in an earlier epoch'. As a positive counterbalance to this, there was 'the assimilative force of the American public school'. Only through public schooling, Dewey argued, 'can the centrifugal forces set up by the juxtaposition of different groups within one and the same political unit be counteracted' (see also May, this volume).

The curriculum itself was a critical instrument in creating a new cultural singularity. 'Common subject matter accustoms all to a unity of outlook upon a broader horizon than is visible to the members of any group while it is isolated' (Dewey, 1966, pp. 21–2). The Howland School, a Chicago public school in a 'foreign district', staged a large festival play: a pageant illustrating the story of Columbus to which 'a few tableaux were added about some of the most striking events in pioneer history, arranged to bring out the fact that this country is a democracy'. The whole school took part. The pageant had 'value as a unifying influence in a foreign community', and, indeed, a value to the nation 'greater than the daily flag salute or patriotic poem'. This, Dewey notes approvingly, was an approach to teaching history far removed from the 'dry Gradgrind facts of a routine textbook type' (Dewey and Dewey, 1915, pp. 129–31). In the end, however, the cultural homilies about Columbus and pioneering and patriotism were not so different from those of traditional curriculum.

Even if the cultural assumptions in this sort of progressivism were still assimilative, there were certainly new pedagogical modes at work in the curriculum of modernism and experience. Motivated student activity was a central pedagogical tool, for example. Behind these new pedagogical modes were cultural assumptions that would eventually take progressivism beyond assimilation. As the century wore on, another, pluralist variant of progressivism emerged. To use two increasingly common descriptors, this new form of progressivism is now often called 'postmodern', a cultural phenomenon linked to the intellectual movement, 'poststructuralism' (cf. Rattansi, this volume).

In stark contrast to the universalistic pretensions of modernism, the key term of postmodernism is difference. No longer are there any overall social meanings in the world, no master narratives such as the western Canon. There are just contingent readings, intertextualities, intersubjectivities. As there is 'no privileged place for western culture,' say Aronowitz and Giroux (1988), it is the task of schools 'to legitimate subaltern discourses as equal'. Language, 'a system of signs structured in the infinite play of difference', positions readers and listeners as well as writers and speakers according to 'race', class and gender. Thus schools have to make space for invariably different student 'voices'.

Dewey's fundamental assumptions live on in the postmodern variant of progressivism — in the centrality of student activity, relevance and motivation. In fact, it is almost possible to argue that in postmodernism they are taken to their logical conclusion. Ellsworth goes even further down the path of difference in her critique of Aronowitz and Giroux, finding vestiges of universalizing, rational discourse in their notion of critical pedagogy (cf. McLaren and Torres, this volume). Such a discourse, she argues, is culturally loaded and works on the assumption that other discourses are inferior. In an even more radical stance than theirs, she speaks of her experience of facilitating rather than teaching, and of the classroom as a space where students can articulate viewpoints that can be never more than partial, never more than representative of different interests and viewpoints (Ellsworth, 1989). Again, there are fundamental epistemological questions at stake here, and these invariably have pedagogical consequences.

Despite the tags 'postmodern' or 'poststructuralist', the shift within progressivist pedagogy is not so new at all. Descending from the dizzying heights of fashionable theory, pedagogues have been trying out similar ideas in schools for a long time. Progressivism's turn to difference has been evolutionary rather than sudden. To take the example of language teaching and learning, the universalist pretensions of 'standard' English have been under fire for some time. One side of the attack has come from linguists such as Labov, who argue that non-'standard' dialects do certain things much more effectively than the white middle-class dialect that, out of pure prejudice, is called 'standard'. 'Black English Vernacular' communicates about death, for example, with less circumlocution and certainly less evasively than middle-class English. What it does, such as regulate the street life of young males, it does with flair and effect (Labov, 1972). Schools, as a consequence, fail speakers of dialects such as this simply because they do not speak the teachers' dialect. Teachers and curricula combine to make a peremptory judgement on the value of cultural and linguistic difference.

The other side of the attack on notions of 'standard' English has come from the language pedagogues who line up behind the banners of 'whole language' and 'process writing'. Again, the principles underlying their pedagogies are fundamentally the same as those articulated by Dewey, yet they also develop these principles in a philosophical and social direction remarkably like that labelled 'postmodern' in high theory. Starting with a critique of traditional curriculum, one of the gurus of the 'whole language' movement, Ken Goodman (1986), insists that text has to remain functional and purposeful for students to learn effectively. No more parsing or drilling or myopic correction of the things deemed incorrect. He uses as an analogy the way children learn oral language — a developing process in the meaningful interplay of adults' and children's oral texts. As, in Goodman's view, written and oral languages have all the same basic characteristics, children should learn how to use written language through schooling in a way directly analogous to the 'natural' way young children learn oral language. Immersion, or lots of doing reading and writing and doing it for a reason that fits in with the child's own interests, experience and intentions, it seems, is the best way to learn. A whole language curriculum, as a consequence, will draw on 'authentic resources' instead of textbooks; on student experience and communicative intentions rather than formal language facts to be ingested. It will focus, not on language in the abstract, but on the meaning the child wants to communicate.

In a similar vein, one of the inventors of 'process writing', Donald Murray, argues that students should as a matter of basic principle be allowed to find their own subject. 'It is not the job of the teacher to legislate the student's truth. It is the responsibility of the student to explore his own world with his own language, to discover his own meaning. The teacher supports but does not direct this expedition to the student's own truth' (1982, p. 129). Murray's colleague, Donald Graves (1983), speaks of the role of student motivation in learning, the power of student ownership of their own texts, and the importance of allowing free expression to student 'voice' (cf. Hodson, this volume).

In some senses, this is not so unlike Dewey's progressivism. In another sense, however, the reverence for difference that informs the work of these language pedagogues is founded on a more radical cultural relativism and individualism than Dewey's. The basis for effective and meaningful learning is each child's life experience. As far as whole language is concerned, there are no disadvantaged students, says Goodman. There are just different students. So schools must 'reject negative, elitist, racist views of linguistic purity that would limit children to arbitrary "proper" language' (Goodman, 1986, p. 25). At the root of this pedagogy is an individualism that easily knits with a kind of cultural relativism in which individual difference can be traced back to cultural difference — 'culture' in the broadest sense including gender, ethnicity, and socio-economic factors. Dewey had certainly been no relativist, either when it came to cultural diversity, or, more fundamentally, about knowledge.

Issues for a Pedagogy after Superficial Pluralism

Despite having cultural diversity as one of its central concerns, a pedagogy of process, a pedagogy of pluralism, a pedagogy whose most fundamental epistemological principle is irreducible difference, does not necessarily serve the needs of its diverse subjects, be they cast as 'minority' or 'majority' actors.

First, despite pretences to cultural openness, even the most advanced progressivisms are profoundly culture–bound. Cultural relativism itself is a cultural prerogative unique to white liberalism. It also reflects what is by now prevailing conventional wisdom about the status of knowledge and the anxieties of postmodernity, a conventional wisdom rarely in accord with the epistemological and pedagogical expectations of many of its more socially marginal subjects (see also May, this volume). What, for example, is the cultural relation of a multiculturalism that values all differences as relative, to immigrant cultures that revere clerical and textual authority and that expect teachers to be authority figures who transmit fixed knowledges? In all honesty, just how multicultural can this sort of relativism afford to be? Delpit highlights this kind of cultural disjunction at the level of classroom discourse. What appears to be an open, child-centred, democratic pedagogy, is, she argues, a culture-laden imposition. Progressivism's apparent anti-authoritarianism is a cultural hoax. It is a cultural product of white liberalism, a liberalism whose discourse operates with the semblance of calm reasonableness but which, underneath, is based on cultural imperatives that, in their effect and when correctly read, are as authoritarian as any.

For example, in contrast to the culture of black Americans, liberal discourse uses veiled rather than explicit commands. Under the cloak of child-centredness it is another discourse of adult authority. 'Would you like to do this next, Betty?' White children know that this means they are expected to do something. To black children, the white liberal teacher who operates in this discourse appears to have no authority, and the class reacts accordingly. The problem for black students is misreading the cues from the point of view of a discourse that expresses authority by other means (Delpit, 1988). In a quite different way, the pretence to cultural neutrality of progressivism serves the dominant culture poorly too, insofar as it precludes its inhabitants from seeing their own discourses, such as liberalism and individualism, as deeply 'ethnic' rather than neutrally open (cf. May, this volume). It thus reduces the possibility of there ever being insightful and productive dialogue across and between cultures and discourses.

Second, as a consequence of its culture-bound character, progressivism favours certain children 'naturally' over others. In the case of 'naturalistic' literacy pedagogies for example, children from print-immersed environments are favoured, in practice if not in principle, over those for whom the nature and point of literacy are more distant from their commonsense, domestic experience. More broadly, a process or inquiry pedagogy which is premised on the notion that knowledge is a function of the critical ego, does not accord with many other cultural views of the source of knowledge. So, who succeeds in a curriculum with these sorts of cultural presuppositions? Is it an accident that a pedagogy founded on individual motivation works best for students from domestic cultures with child-centred approaches to socialization?

Despite its democratic rhetoric, an 'open', 'naturalistic' progressivism frequently only leads to a mismatch of teaching and learning styles that disadvantages students whose cultures are more distant from the culture of progressivist schooling. And, again, 'naturalistic' pedagogies do not even serve the dominant culture terribly well. For example, the 'natural' assumptions of schooled literacy — that scientific reports speak empirical facts separated from human interests (see Hodson, this volume), or that narrative is the unique voice of the creative individual — are in fact culturally specific ways of using language that come with their own ideological blinkers and conceits. What comes 'naturally' to successful white, middle-class student writers, in other words, could become a more powerful form of knowledge if it were 'denaturalized', if it were put under a multicultural scrutiny — a scrutiny, for example, of cultures where cultural agendas are more explicit and discourses are more obviously socially received rather than 'natural' or universal.

Third, educational philosophies of difference are at best quiescent and at worst complicit in reproducing inequitable forms of social division (see also McLaren and Torres, this volume). The differences in the world are neither relative nor innocent. Labov's reverence for what he calls Black English Vernacular may well have made a valuable contribution to the proper revision of long-standing educational prejudices based on notions of cultural deficit. But it is simply patronizing to say that the differences in the world are relative when one discourse can earn you a significant income as a linguistics professor and the other discourse is more likely to be one element in a social process that leaves you dependent on a meagre social security benefit. It may be unfair or unjust that the discourses correlate with monetary valuations on people's heads, but so long as they do, educators cannot uncritically rejoice in diversity. In schools, one of the consequences of this kind of relativism is curriculum diversification in the name of 'needs', 'interests', 'choice' and 'relevance'. So, alongside subject English in some Australian secondary schools (still Shakespeare and all that 'irrelevant' stuff), we find alternative courses: 'Communication Skills', relevant to filling out forms, going for a job, reading the newspaper. Adolescents, with a keen nose for euphemisms, call the latter course 'Veggie English' (Kalantzis et al., 1990).

The danger of diversifying curriculum in the interests of 'relevance' is to create a new streaming in a pseudo-democratic garb. Students who would have failed in a comprehensive, traditional curriculum now pass in what everyone except the most enthusiastic progressivists know to be 'Micky Mouse' courses. To give another example, 'multicultural studies' and 'ethnic studies' courses are to be found primarily in schools with many students from non-English speaking backgrounds. The content of curriculum is drawn from the community, from local experience, and from the cultural backgrounds of students. All too easily, and in the name of cultural self-esteem, this can end in a celebratory multiculturalism of spaghetti and polka; a multiculturalism that trivializes culture and is more concerned with the affirmation of difference than with what students need in linguistic-cognitive terms if they are to gain some degree of broader social access (May, 1994). Meanwhile, in other schools, students of the dominant culture (just as unhelpfully) continue to learn the old master narratives of 'development', 'progress' and 'western Civilization'. Again, pluralist multiculturalism, focusing as it does on 'minority' students, leaves curriculum for 'successful' students unchanged, a quite unsatisfactory state of affairs given the processes of globalization and localization that mark our epoch; processes that make cultural diversity a critical issue in everybody's lives.

Fourth, under progressivism, teachers are installed as professionals. Instead of being mouthpieces for received, universalistic syllabuses and textbooks, their charter is to negotiate a school-based curriculum sensitive to the cultural differences of their students. Rather ironically, however, this often means that teaching is reduced to management: teacher as negotiator, teacher as facilitator. In one piece of research, we observed classroom interaction in order to analyse the linguistic and cognitive contents of teacher–student discourse. We found that in classrooms where the teacher was most concerned not to impose a point of view, in order to encourage group work and independent student activity, teacher talk was almost exclusively managerial — 'organize yourselves this way'; 'you take this role in the discussion/work' — and thus, ironically, more authoritarian than in another more traditional classroom where the teacher was primarily concerned to transmit content (Kalantzis et al., 1989).

There is also the ironical turn in the progressivist disdain for the textbook. Certainly, textbooks have typically been based on transmission pedagogy, casting students in a passive relation to knowledge. With traditional textbooks, however, there was some element of student and parent access to the shape of curriculum. At any point in the course there was a sense of where you had come from and where you were going, a progressivism that has nominally abandoned textbooks, however, often resorts to photocopying from the same old books. But now, the photocopies represent the worst fiat of arbitrary authority — daily, *ad hoc*, teacher imposed. Students even lose a sense of the direction of the curriculum and the minimal access and control they had with traditional textbooks: to go back over work or to go ahead. This is a curriculum, moreover, that all too often ends up fragmented, eclectic, and inefficient, as teachers, far from having the time or the energy to be more sensitive to diversity, have to reinvent the same pedagogical wheel, based on the same commonsenses about school subjects and learning, from classroom to classroom, school to school.

As educators, we have been forced to ask ourselves the question, how is it that a paradigm which purported to do so much could achieve so little? We may be able to discount the accusations of the 'back to basics' people that educational standards are falling as unwarranted and politically motivated hysteria. But, rather tragically, and no matter how unsatisfactory we know the results of traditional curriculum to have been for students from cultures other than the dominant one, we can only return the Scottish 'not proven' verdict on the question of whether any tangible overall educational and social benefits have come out of the revolution in pedagogy and the revolution in social policy that came with progressivism, multiculturalism and their more superficial ideologies of pluralism.

In the light of this experience, what would be the most likely shape of a pedagogy after pluralism, a pedagogy after progressivism? Following are four principles for such a pedagogy, a response to the four elements in the critique of progressivism. In one sense, these principles set out to distance a postprogressivist pedagogy clearly, both from the traditional curriculum of a classical canon, and from progressivist curriculum in either its modernist or postmodernist guises. But in another sense, it is not an 'after' pedagogy. It lives neither after traditional curriculum nor after progressivist pedagogy. Rather, it lives within and between the paradigms, in the insights that emerge in the vibrant debate, and out of practical contingency. Indeed, these principles should be seen, not as the basis for a new theory, but as a commonsense for good teaching, an account of what good teachers have always done in spite of, or even to spite, the paradigms that prevailed at the time.

First, whereas traditional curriculum has a quite explicitly singular cultural message in relation to which students are either to assimilate or fail, and whereas pluralist progressivism is founded on principles of difference, openness and anti-authoritarianism which are in fact, deceptively, as culture-laden as any, a postprogressivist pedagogy would define *positively* the cultural stakes in education. Curriculum is a dialogue between student discourses and the culture of schooling. To take the latter element in this dialogue first, schooling is a critical site for social mobility, and part of this process is successful induction into the culture of schooling, such as schooled literacy (reading and writing) and the linguistic and cognitive capacities that come with it. These are educational tools for social access. And central to these tools, given our epoch, must be multiculturalism itself.

This is not a multiculturalism that, in the fashion of pluralism, pretends to cultural agnosticism. This is not a multiculturalism of irreducible difference. Rather, this is a multiculturalism that is a core social and educational value; a positive, value-laden response to diversity; an evolving, negotiated and renegotiated set of common principles. A dialogue of centre and margins in which centre is able to move beyond the repressive tolerance of allowing difference its own exotic and thus marginal spaces. Indeed, it allows for the possibility that, in the negotiation process, the centre will itself need to shift. Curriculum in a reconstituted culture of schooling does, in other words, have the potential to provide all students with tools for social access. But to achieve this, the culture of schooling will itself have to have shifted significantly, enshrining developing senses of multiculturalism as a core value (May, 1994).

Now to take the other element in the dialogue, student discourses. Student differences need not predestine students to failure (the cultural deficit model with its programme of assimilation). Nor need they be left, inequitably, simply as the colourful and exotic, to be celebrated, to be tolerated, to be respected, cultures to live and let live (pluralist multiculturalism). Instead, cultural diversity can be marshalled as a resource for access. Speakers of Black English Vernacular, for example (or

'Ebonics' in more recent parlance), have a unique resource for unpacking the way 'standard' English works, and its limitations. Learning the devices of this English, however, does not mean that speakers of Black English Vernacular will have to assimilate. Indeed, their cultural perspective might be a demonstrable advantage. Their perspective has the potential to give them insights into how 'standard' English works, how it gets some social jobs done but not others. This sort of dialogue might also give the inhabitants of the dominant discourse valuable critical insights into language and culture, insights not achievable within the commonsense of the culture and discourses familiar to them. This dialogue might even become the basis for cultural crossovers, transgressions and the kind of rule bending that are the basis of cultural creativity. It might produce new realms of reference and expression both for Black English Vernacular and white, middle-class English. In this case, the 'ethnic' would no longer be synonymous with the exotic. The ordinary would be seen to be ethnic so that the exotic can be seen to be ordinary.

Second, whereas traditional curriculum is explicit about its singularity and its universal cultural mission (thereby establishing predictable patterns of 'failure'), and pluralist progressivism expounds an inexplicit 'naturalism' which ends up favouring certain groups of students over others, a postprogressivist pedagogy will attempt to be explicit but without prejudice to diversity. If social access is one of the objectives of education, then those for whom the cultures and discourses of power do not come 'naturally' need to have the ways and means of these cultures and discourses spelt out explicitly. And if we admit there is something positive to be learnt by inhabitants of the dominant culture and discourse from a transcultural dialogue with those on the margins, the same principles of explicitness apply. Against the assumptions of the progressivists, the culture of schooling is a decidedly *un*natural thing. Cazden (1988) discusses the peculiarity of the discourse of schooling, with its exophoric references that speak of the outside world without being the outside world. To take the example of literacy, the analogy drawn by the progressivists between the way oral and written languages are learnt is far from the truth. Not only is mastery of written language learnt in a totally different site — the institution of schooling — but children learning literacy at school have the resource of oral language, and with it the ability to generalize about language. Grammar, conceived not as the disciplinary formalism of traditional grammar but in its broadest sense as a metalanguage, is one instance of uniquely schoolish exophoric reference. It is a resource for school learning, a way of being explicit about language rather than relying on immersion and 'doing' alone.

These are all arguments why students whose backgrounds are more marginal to the discourses of power particularly need explicit curriculum. They are also arguments why even those students from dominant cultures and discourses are taught more efficiently with an explicit pedagogy in an institution whose resources are limited and becoming more and more stretched. *Explicitness about the culture of schooling, however, does not have to mean assimilation* (cf. Hodson's views on science, this volume). Curriculum, rather, should be a process of lending consciousness, lending language and lending culture for purposes outside the child's domestic or commonsense purview. This is a lending and borrowing which needs to go both ways, between cultures that are in positions of relative social power and those that are not. Precisely because different cultures and languages are denaturalized in the process of making their methods and intentions explicit, there can be no assumption that they need be used for any more than contingent, strategic, culturally located ends. Effective negotiation of life possibilities in a multicultural context involves a constant process of shunting backwards and forwards, across and between cultures and levels of necessarily multilayered identity.

Third, postprogressivist curriculum would neither use a singular pedagogy for all students (as does traditional curriculum) nor would it diversify curriculum simply in order to affirm difference (pluralist progressivism). Rather, all students would be educated for cultural and linguistic diversity, and insofar as curriculum has the goal of providing students with tools for social access, variant, specialist pedagogies would be required for this common end. English as a Second Language or bilingual education have the potential to be such specialist pedagogies, even though, in many moments of their practice, they do not stretch beyond the limitations of pluralism. But what is this common end? Vygotsky and Luria's historical psychology of language provides important insights into the peculiar linguistic and cognitive features of industrialized social settings. In contrast to cultures that think and speak through strings of empirical association, industrialized cultures think through generalizing concepts linked into theoretical frames of mind (Luria, 1976; Vygotsky, 1962, 1978). We are no longer even capable of remembering the extraordinarily long strings of people's names that made up people's understandings of kinship structures in agricultural or gathering and hunting societies. To make sense of industrial social worlds, and to operate effectively in them, we have to know instead the relation of generalized and generalizing institutions — schooling, the law, the workplace (see also Gellner, 1983). Not only would it be unhelpful to our understanding of these institutions to learn the names of all the individuals that one might encounter or need; it would impossible. At the deepest of levels, herein lie the linguistic and cognitive bases of social access to the culture of modernity. And an element integral to these core, cognitive capacities in the era of the globalization and localization is a linguistic and cognitive capacity to deal effectively with difference itself — to understand 'culture' as a concept in the Vygotskian sense, and one that is central for dealing with diversity in a way that is productive for all parties to the dialogue. This is the cognitive basis for reading the broadest possible repertoire of discourses in a multicultural context.

Fourth, against the unashamed authoritarianism of traditional curriculum and the feigned anti-authoritarianism of progressivist curriculum, a postprogressivist pedagogy would need to specify the nature of the asymmetrical relationship of teacher and student. Curriculum and teachers should stand in an authoritative rather than an authoritarian position in relation to students — authoritative insofar as they represent expert knowledges about pedagogy and the substantive discipline areas, yet not authoritarian insofar as this negates the transcultural dialogue that is effective pedagogy; a pedagogy that is able to marshal differences as a resource for access without prejudice to the integrity of those differences. Fundamental to the pedagogical architecture of such a programme is curriculum explicitness at two levels; two types of curriculum scaffolding. The first, micro level is a pedagogical explicitness in the recursive patterns that make up learning experiences and through which knowledge is made. This level of explicitness appeared, albeit with a whole series of unsatisfactory pedagogical assumptions, within the chapters of traditional textbooks: the chapter head, followed by the authorial text, factually oriented questions and activities, followed by tests. But pedagogy is hardly explicit at all in progressivist curriculum. It is left to the hidden hand of the photocopier and teacher as manager/manipulator of student 'experience'.

The second, macro level is what Bruner (1977) calls the fundamental structure of the subject — where to start, how to develop understandings, where ideally students should end up in an academic discipline, and to what metacognitive ends. In the age of contingent intertextualities and student-based curriculum, it is possible to lose sight of these fundamental objectives. These need not be traditional 'academic' or 'disciplinary' objectives revived. Indeed, in the face of cultural diversity, and in view of progressivism's proper critique of traditional, universalizing, homogenizing, 'factual' notions of the nature of knowledge, the fundamental nature of school knowledge needs to be put under scrutiny and redeveloped. Teachers need to become experts again, true professionals deserving proper respect both for their expertise in areas of substantive content and as pedagogues. One example of this approach in the area of literacy is the 'multiliteracies' approach that is described in the next section of this chapter.

This is to speak in the most general pedagogical terms, to talk of the broad sweep of pedagogical developments. Indeed, this discussion may well seem a far cry from the normal concerns of multicultural education. But this is precisely the point. Thinking through the issues as they affect so called 'minorities' leads us to rethink whole paradigms. In any event, if cultural diversity is now on the agenda for all of us in some very fundamental ways, pedagogy in general needs rethinking. It was difference, after all, that was one of the essential reasons for the establishment of mass, institutionalized schooling, with its programme of assimilation into the homogenizing project of the nation-state. It was difference that was a central concern in the later developments within progressivism. So it is hardly surprising that difference, once again, should be a fundamental motive force in education.

Transforming the Mainstream: A Case Study in Literacy Pedagogy

So far, this chapter has spoken in very general terms about different approaches to education for cultural and linguistic diversity. We will now briefly illustrate our case with the example of the Multiliteracies Project: an attempt to create a framework for literacy pedagogy in which the issue of diversity is at the very heart of both curriculum form and curriculum content.

In the latest write-up of the project, we explain how we coined the word 'Multiliteracies' to describe two important arguments we might have with the emerging cultural and institutional and global order (New London Group, 1996).

The first is about the growing significance of cultural and linguistic diversity. The news on our television screens scream this message at us every day. And, in more constructive terms, we have to negotiate differences every day, in our local communities and in our increasingly globally interconnected working and community lives. As a consequence, something paradoxical is happening to English. At the same time as it is becoming a *lingua mundi*, a world language, and a *lingua franca*, a common language of global commerce, media and politics, English is also breaking into multiple and increasingly differentiated English*es*, marked by accent, national origin, subcultural style and professional or technical communities. Increasingly, the name of the game in English is crossing linguistic boundaries. Gone are the days when learning a single, standard version of the language was sufficient. Migration, multiculturalism and global economic integration daily intensify this process of change. The globalization of communications and labour markets makes language diversity an ever more critical local issue.

The second major shift encompassed in the concept of Multiliteracies is the influence of new communications technologies. Meaning is made in ways that are increasingly multimodal. Today, written-linguistic modes of meaning interface with visual, audio, gestural and spatial patterns of meaning. This is particularly the case with desktop publishing and the electronic 'hypermedia', where meanings are made in the relationship of text to images, icons, page layouts, screen formats, sound effects and spatial representations of the world. In fact, there is a striking convergence of the 'multi' of multimedia and the 'multi' of local and global multiculturalism. On the one hand, the relation of visual and other modes of meaning to text have been part of the increasing globalization of English, and much meaning is carried in the visual and other supports (such as icons, images, audio and diagrammatic representations of space or structure) as well as the text itself. On the other hand, the increasing power of these communications technologies brings the subtleties of diversity ever closer to home.

These developments have the potential to transform both the substance and pedagogy of literacy teaching in English, and in the other languages of the world. No longer do the old pedagogies of a formal, standard, written national language have the use they once did. Instead, the Multiliteracies argument suggests an open-ended and flexible functional grammar which assists language learners to describe language differences (cultural, subcultural, regional/national, technical, context specific, and so on) and the multimodal channels of meaning now so important to communication.

Similarly, dramatic changes are occurring in the domains of citizenship, working life and community life which will have an inevitable effect on the way literacy is taught. The languages needed to make meaning are radically changing in three realms of our existence: our working lives, our public lives, and our private lives.

First, in our working lives, we are living through a period of dramatic global economic change. New business and management theories and practices are emerging across the 'developed' world. These theories and practices stress competition and markets centred around change, flexibility, quality, and distinctive niches — not the mass products of the 'old' capitalism. The changing nature of work has been variously called 'post-Fordism' and 'fast capitalism' (cf. McLaren and Torres, this volume). Post-Fordism replaces the old hierarchical command structures epitomized in Henry Ford's development of mass production techniques and represented in caricature by Charlie Chaplin in *Modern Times*. Instead, with the development of post-Fordism or fast capitalism, more and more work organizations are opting for 'flattened hierarchy'. Commitment, responsibility and motivation are won by developing a 'workplace culture' where the members of an organization identify with its 'vision' and 'mission' and 'corporate values'. The old vertical chains of command are replaced by the horizontal relationships of 'teamwork'. A division of labour into its minutest, deskilled components is replaced by 'multiskilled' all-round workers who are flexible enough to be able to do complex and integrated work (Cope and Kalantzis, 1997).

With a new worklife comes a new language. A good deal of this change is the result of new technologies, such as the iconographic, text and screen-based modes of interacting with automated machinery. 'User-friendly' interfaces operate with more subtle levels of cultural embeddedness than interfaces based on abstract commands. But much of the change is also the result of the new social relationships of work. Whereas the old 'Fordist' organization depended upon clear, precise and formal systems of command such as written memos and the supervisor's orders, effective teamwork depends to a much greater extent on informal, oral and interpersonal discourse. This informality also translates into hybrid and interpersonally sensitive informal written forms, such as EMail. These are just a few examples of revolutionary changes in technology and the nature of organizations that have produced a new language of work. These are all reasons why a literacy pedagogy has to change if it is to be relevant to the new demands of working life.

But fast capitalism is also a nightmare (see also McLaren and Torres, this volume). Corporate cultures and their discourses of familiarity are more subtly and more rigorously exclusive than the most nasty — honestly nasty — of hierarchies. Replication of corporate culture demands assimilation to mainstream norms that only really works if one already speaks the language of the mainstream. If one is not comfortably a part of the culture and discourses of the mainstream, it is even harder to get into networks that operate informally than it was to enter into the old discourses of formality. This is a crucial factor in producing the phenomenon of the 'glass ceiling', the point at which employment and promotion opportunities come to an abrupt stop. And fast capitalism, notwithstanding its discourse of collaboration, corporate culture and shared values, is also a vicious world driven by the barely restrained market. As we remake our literacy pedagogy to be more relevant to a new world of work, we need to be aware of the danger that our words might become co-opted by economically and market driven discourses, no matter how contemporary and 'postcapitalist' these may appear. It may well be that market directed theories and practices, even though they sound humane, will never authentically include a vision of meaningful success for all students.

In responding to the radical changes in working life that are currently underway, we need to tread a careful path in which students have the opportunity to develop skills for access to new forms of work through learning the new language of work.

But at the same time, as teachers, our role is not simply to be technocrats. Our job is not to produce docile, compliant workers. Students need to develop the skills to speak up, to negotiate and to be able to engage critically with the conditions of their working lives.

Indeed, the twin goals of access and critical engagement need not be incompatible. We might, for example, take fast capitalism at the best of its word and be relevant to that word, yet at the same time we could push that word in the direction of utopian possibility. In the realm of work, we will call that possibility 'productive diversity' (Cope and Kalantzis, 1997). The diversity of communities and workforces and the multiplicity of discourses can be harnessed as a productive asset. Cross-cultural communication and the negotiated dialogue of different languages and discourses can be a basis for worker creativity, for the formation of locally sensitive and globally extensive networks which closely relate an organization to its clients or suppliers, and structures of motivation in which people feel that their different backgrounds and experiences are genuinely valued.

Just as work is changing, so is the realm of public life. This is a second major site of social transformation. Over the past two decades, the century-long trend towards an expanding, interventionist, welfare state has been reversed. The domain of citizenship, and the power and importance of public spaces, are diminishing. Economic rationalism, privatization, deregulation and the transformation of public institutions such as schools and universities so that they operate according to market logic — these changes are part of a global shift.

This shift coincides with the end of the Cold War. Until the 1980s, the global geopolitical dynamic of the twentieth century had taken the form of an argument between communism and capitalism. This turned out to be an argument about the role of the State in society, in which the interventionist welfare state was capitalism's compromise position. The argument was won and lost when the communist block was unable to match the escalating cost of the capitalist world's fortifications. The end of the Cold War represents an epochal turning point. Indicative of a new world order is a liberalism that eschews the State. In just a decade or two, this liberalism has prevailed almost without exception globally. Those of us who work either in state-funded or privately funded education know what this liberalism looks like. Market logic has become a much bigger part of our lives.

Meanwhile, in some parts of the world, once strong centralizing and homogenizing states have all but collapsed. Everywhere, states are diminished in their roles and responsibilities. This has left space for a new politics of difference. In worst case scenarios — in Sarajevo, Colombo, Kabul, Belfast, Beirut — the absence of a working, arbitrating State has left governance in the hands of gangs, bands, paramilitary organizations and ethnonationalist political factions. In best case scenarios, the politics of culture and identity have taken on a new significance. Negotiating these differences is now a life and death matter. Now, the perennial struggle for access to wealth, power and symbols of recognition is increasingly articulated through the discourse of identity and recognition (Kalantzis, 1998).

Schooling in general and literacy teaching in particular were central parts of the old order. The expanding, interventionary states of the nineteenth and twentieth centuries used schooling as a way of standardizing national languages. In the Old World, this meant imposing national standards over dialect differences. In the New World, it meant assimilating immigrants and indigenous peoples to the standardized 'proper' language of the colonizer (Kalantzis and Cope, 1993).

Just as global geopolitics have shifted, so schools have to service linguistic and cultural diversity. Their fundamental role has changed. The meaning of literacy pedagogy has changed. Local diversity and global connectedness not only mean that there can be no standard; they mean that the most important skill students need to learn is to *negotiate* dialect, register and semiotic differences, code switching, interlanguages and hybrid cross-cultural discourses. Indeed, this is the only hope for averting the catastrophic conflicts about identities and spaces that now seem ever ready to flare up.

The decline of the old, monocultural, nationalistic 'civic', has left a space vacated that needs to be filled again. We propose this space is claimed by a civic pluralism. Instead of states that require one cultural and linguistic standard, we need states that arbitrate differences. Access to wealth, power and symbols must be possible no matter what one's identity markers — such as language, dialect and register — happen to be. This is the basis for a cohesive sociality, a new civility in which differences are used as a productive resource and in which differences are the norm. It is the basis for the postnationalist sense of common purpose that is now essential to a peaceful and productive global order (Kalantzis, 1998; May, 1999).

To this end, cultural and linguistic diversity is a classroom resource just as powerfully as it is a social resource in the formation of new civic spaces and new notions of citizenship. This is not just so that educators can provide a better 'service' to 'minorities'. Rather, such a pedagogical orientation will produce benefits for all. For example, there will be a cognitive benefit to all children in a pedagogy of linguistic and cultural pluralism, including for 'mainstream' children. When learners juxtapose different languages, discourses, styles and approaches, they gain substantively in meta cognitive and meta linguistic abilities and in their abilities to critically reflect on complex systems and their interactions.

And in a third major realm, in our private lives, equally momentous changes are taking place. We live in an environment where subcultural differences — differences of identity and affiliation — are becoming more and more significant. Ethnicity, gender, generation, and sexual orientation are just a few of the markers of these differences. To those who yearn for 'standards', this appears as evidence of distressing fragmentation of the social fabric.

Indeed, in one sense it is just this, an historical shift where singular national cultures have less hold than they once did. For example, one of the ironies of less regulated, multi-channel media systems is that they undermine the concept of collective audience and common culture. They promote the opposite: an increasing range of accessible subcultural options and the growing divergence of specialist and subcultural discourses. This spells the definitive end of 'the public' — that homo-geneous imagined community of modern democratic nation states (Gellner, 1983). Accordingly, the challenge is to make space available so that different lifeworlds can flourish, spaces where local and specific meanings can be made. The new multimedia and hypermedia channels can and sometimes do provide subcultural identities the opportunity to find their own voices. These technologies have the potential to enable greater autonomy for different lifeworlds.

Yet, the more diverse and vibrant these lifeworlds become and the greater the range of the differences, the less clearly bounded the different lifeworlds appear to be. The word 'community' is often used to describe the differences that are now so critical — the 'Italian-American' community, the 'gay community', the 'business community', and so on — as if each of these communities had neat boundaries. And as people are simultaneously the members of multiple lifeworlds, so their identities have multiple layers, each layer in complex relation to the others. No person is a member of a singular community. Rather, they are members of multiple and overlapping communities — communities of work, of interest and affiliation, of ethnicity, of sexual identity, and so on.

Language, discourse and register differences are markers of lifeworld differences. As lifeworlds become more divergent and their boundaries become more blurred, the central fact of language becomes the multiplicity of meanings and their continual intersection. Just as there are multiple layers to everyone's identity, there are multiple discourses of identity and multiple discourses of recognition to be negotiated. We have to be proficient as we negotiate these many lifeworlds — the many lifeworlds each of us inhabit, and the many lifeworlds we encounter in our everyday lives. This creates a new challenge for literacy pedagogy.

Schools have always played a critical role in determining students' life opportunities. Schools regulate access to orders of discourse, to symbolic capital. They provide access to the world of work; they shape citizenries; they provide a supplement to the discourses and activities of communities and private lifeworlds. As these three major realms of social activity have shifted, so the roles and responsibilities of schools must shift.

Institutionalized schooling traditionally performed the function of disciplining and skilling people for regimented industrial workplaces, assisting in the making of the 'melting pot' of homogeneous national citizenries, and smoothing over inherited differences between lifeworlds. This is what Dewey called the assimilatory function of schooling, the function of making homogeneity out of differences.

Now, the function of classrooms and learning is in some senses the reverse. Every classroom will inevitably reconfigure the relationships of local and global difference that are now so critical. To be relevant, learning processes need to recruit, rather than attempt to ignore and erase, the different subjectivities students bring to learning. Curriculum now needs to mesh with different subjectivities, and their attendant languages, discourses and registers, and use these as a resource for learning. This is the necessary basis for a pedagogy which opens possibilities for greater access. The danger of glib and tokenistic pluralism is that it sees differences to be immutable and leaves them fragmentary. Insofar as differences are now a core, mainstream issue, the core or the mainstream has changed.

Given this, the starting point for the Multiliteracies notion is an investigation of how texts are historically and socially located and produced, how they are 'designed' artefacts. Two key aspects of the Multiliteracies notion of 'Design' distinguish it from the approach to the question of teaching language conventions taken by many earlier traditions of literacy pedagogy: *variability* and *agency*. Traditional grammar teaching, for example, taught to a single social-linguistic end: the official, standard or high forms of the national language. The issue of language variability was barely part of the teaching process. And always closely linked to this issue of variability is the issue of agency or subjectivity. The language experiences students brought to learning traditional grammars, for instance, were irrelevant; the aim was to induct students into the standard written form through a pedagogy of transmission. School was about the reproduction of received cultural and linguistic forms.

The Design notion takes the opposite tack on both of these fronts: the starting point is language variation — the different accents, registers and dialects that serve different ends in different social contexts and for different social groups. And the key issue of language use is agency and subjectivity — the way in which every act of language draws on disparate language resources and remakes the world into a form that it has never quite taken before. The reality of language is not simply the reproduction of regularized patterns and conventions. It is also a matter of inter-textuality, hybridity, and language as the basis of cultural change. In this sense, language is both an already Designed resource and the ground of Designs for social futures.

And just as the Design notion starts with a very different set of assumptions about meaning, so, as a consequence, it also ends up with a very different notion of culture. Instead of a focus on stability and regularity, the focus is on change and transformation. Individuals have at their disposal a complex range of representational resources, never of one culture, but of the many cultures in their lived experience, the many layers of their identity and the many dimensions of their being. The breadth, complexity and richness of the available meaning-making resources are such that representation is never simply a matter of reproduction. Rather, it is a matter of transformation, of reconstruing meaning in a way which always adds something to the range of available representational resources (cf. May; Rattansi, this volume).

Which leads us into the question of appropriate pedagogy in a context where diversity is a central concern in the mainstream of educational endeavour. To what extent are we talking about a universal learner in a world that is inherently diverse? There is, indeed, a paradoxical universal, and that is that the crucial grounding for all learning must be the heterogeneity of learners, their situatedness in various lifeworlds.

As a practical, pedagogical response, The New London Group proposes that good teaching needs to have four angles on learning: Situated Practice, Overt Instruction, Critical Framing and Transformed Practice. There is nothing terribly surprising in each of these four angles; each is well represented in the history of educational theory and in teachers' contemporary pedagogical practices. The Multiliteracies Project aims to supplement — not critique or negate — the various existing literacy teaching practices. Our argument is that all four need to be part of the learning process, though not necessarily in any particular fixed sequence or as neatly separate bits.

Situated Practice involves immersion in experience and the utilization of Available Designs, including those from the students' lifeworlds, and simulations of the relationships to be found in workplaces and public spaces. *Overt Instruction* involves systematic, analytical, and conscious understanding. In the case of Multiliteracies, this requires the introduction of explicit metalanguages which describe and interpret the Design elements of meaning. *Critical Framing* involves interpreting the social and cultural context of particular Designs of meaning. This involves the students standing back from the meanings they are studying and viewing them critically in relation to their social and cultural context. What do they do, why do they do it, and for whom? *Transformed Practice* entails transfer in meaning-making practice, which puts a transformed meaning to work in other contexts or cultural sites.

Cultural and linguistic diversity are central to all four of these pedagogical orientations. The inevitability of heterogeneous lifeworlds is highlighted by Situated Practice. The discussion of patterns of meaning that work in different social and cultural contexts sees a kind of contrastive linguistics replace the grammar of standard language forms (Overt Instruction). One can then analyse why these patterns of meaning work and in whose interests (Critical Framing). And finally, the learner can make or change their own world, even in the smallest of meaning-interventions (Transformed Practice).

A Pedagogy for Cultural Difference and Social Access

Starting with a proposition about the inadequacy of a pedagogy of pluralism that conceives 'minorities' as its primary concern, this chapter has argued that the processes of globalization and localization that make diversity a central fact of our times, also demand that we rethink pedagogy in some fundamental ways. As we rethink pedagogy in the light of diversity, it becomes increasingly obvious that a reconstituted multicultural education is centrally important for *all* students and implicates pedagogy in a more generalized sense. If we accept that the dialogue of core and margins has the potential to transform the core, so too in education, the process of rethinking multicultural education so that it addresses itself to all students, has the potential to transform, not only our educational paradigms, but the social and cultural epistemologies that underlie them.

The schema in Tables 10.1 and 10.2 summarizes our argument about how a critical, postpluralist, postprogressivist multicultural education can reconstitute the mainstream.

Table 10.1: *General principles of approaches to education*

General Principles			
Issue	**Paradigm**		
	Traditional curriculum; cultural assimilation.	*Progressivist curriculum; cultural pluralist variant of multiculturalism.*	*A critical, post-progressivist curriculum and a multiculturalism oriented to social equity.*
The social and cultural project of education in a context of cultural and linguistic diversity	Assimilation to the dominant culture: skills — industrial; affinities — singularly 'Anglo'.	Cultural pluralism; celebration of differences.	Core culture transformed by multilayered allegiances; a society international in economic and cultural orientation; equitable access to non-racist social institutions.
Structural effects	Rhetorical and structural exclusion of diversity.	Structural marginalization of diversity; differentiation of curriculum; ethnic-specific servicing. The mainstream (curriculum, public institutions etc.) remains essentially unchanged.	Transformation of mainstream structures — curriculum, public institutions — in response to cultural and linguistic diversity; structural openness to cultural and linguistic diversity.
Social/cultural effects	Didn't actually assimilate, perhaps was never intended to; less acceptable given changing politics.	No significant need to rethink the way curriculum/public institutions operate; marginalizing the exotic; a variation of the 'cultural deficit' model — affirm difference.	Diversity as a core issue for curriculum and public institutions; education for equitable access; new epistemology for a new sort of liberal democratic society; cultural difference as a resource for social access.

Table 10.2: Pedagogical strategies

Issue	Pedagogy		
	Paradigm		
	Traditional curriculum; cultural assimilation.	Progressivist curriculum; cultural pluralist variant of multiculturalism.	A critical, post-progressivist curriculum and a multiculturalism oriented to social equity.
Focus of curriculum	Singular, universalist, monolithic curriculum, aimed at all students in an undifferentiated way.	Multicultural education aimed at students from minority cultural/linguistic groups.	Education for social access and cultural and linguistic pluralism — for all students; variant pedagogies but singular ends.
Structure of curriculum	Comprehensive.	Diversified.	Reconstituted core curriculum plus openness to diversity.
Syllabus source	Centralized education authorities; teachers as transmitters of received, official, singular knowledge and values.	School-based curriculum; teachers as facilitators; contents of curriculum based in community, students, local experience, cultural backgrounds of students; rhetoric of choice, relevance, needs.	Core linguistic-cognitive requirements for access; epistemological and social skills to live with cultural and linguistic diversity; cultural and linguistic difference as a resource for social access.
Cultural/social agenda	Benevolent transmission; social discipline; inflexible standards; pass/fail according to 'ability'.	Self-esteem; cultural maintenance; relativism according to 'needs' and 'relevance'.	Esteem through enhancing life chances; definite contents to skills and socially powerful knowledge; antiracism.
Epistemology	Monocultural, monological.	Cultural relativism.	Multiculturalism as a critical dialogue; renegotiated common social principles.
Pedagogical modes	Rote learning.	Inquiry learning; 'naturalism'.	Authoritative contents; openness to diversity; active learning and developing essential structures of knowledge.
Media	The textbook.	Community, experience.	Exemplary curriculum materials and professional development.
Teaching/learning styles	Relationship of teaching and learning styles not regarded as an issue.	Despite rhetoric of openness, frequent mismatch of the culture of schooling and student cultures.	Need to negotiate teaching/learning styles to maintain a productive dialogue between the teachers/curriculum and students.
Assessment	Knowledge/ability is fixed and quantifiable.	No universal knowledge — just meanings to individuals according to their peculiar experiences.	Comparability instead of 'standards'; measurement impacts productively back on curriculum and not the fate of individual students.

References

ARONOWITZ, S. and GIROUX, H. (1988) *Postmodern Education: Politics, Culture and Social Criticism*, Minneapolis: University of Minnesota Press.

BRUNER, J. (1977) *The Process of Education*, Cambridge, MA: Harvard University Press.

CAZDEN, C. (1988) *Classroom Discourse: The Language of Teaching and Learning*, Portsmouth, NH: Heinemann.

CLYNE, M. (1997) 'Managing language diversity and second language programmes in Australia', *Current Issues in Language and Society*, 4, pp. 94–119.

COMMITTEE ON MULTICULTURAL EDUCATION (1979) *Education for a Multicultural Society*, Canberra: Commonwealth Schools Commission.

COPE, B. and KALANTZIS, M. (1997) *Productive Diversity*, Sydney: Pluto Press.

COPE, B. and KALANTZIS, M. (1998) 'White noise: The attack on "political correctness" and the struggle for the western canon', *Interchange*, forthcoming.

CUBAN, L. (1984) *How Teachers Taught: Constancy and Change in American Classrooms, 1890–1980*, New York: Longman.

DELPIT, L. (1988) 'The silenced dialogue: Power and pedagogy in educating other people's children', *Harvard Educational Review*, 58, pp. 280–98.

DEWEY, J. (1956) *The School and Society*, Chicago: University of Chicago Press (Original, 1900).

DEWEY, J. (1966) *Democracy and Education*, New York: The Free Press (Original, 1916).

DEWEY, J. and DEWEY, E. (1915) *Schools of Tomorrow*, New York: E.P. Dutton.

ELLSWORTH, E. (1989) 'Why doesn't this feel empowering? Working through the repressive myths of critical pedagogy', *Harvard Educational Review*, 59, pp. 297–324.

GELLNER, E. (1983) *Nations and Nationalism*, London: Basil Blackwell.

GOODMAN, K. (1986) *What's Whole in Whole Language?*, Portsmouth, NH: Heinemann.

GRAFF, H. (1987) *The Legacies of Literacy: Continuities and Contradictions in Western Culture and Society*, Bloomington: Indiana University Press.

GRAVES, D. (1983) *Writing: Teachers and Children at Work*, Exeter, NH: Heinemann Educational Books.

KALANTZIS, M. (1998) 'Multicultural citizenship', in HUDSON, W. (ed.) *Rethinking Australian Citizenship*, Melbourne: Cambridge University Press, forthcoming.

KALANTZIS, M. and COPE, B. (1984) 'Multiculturalism and education policy', in BOTTOMLEY, G. and DE LEPERVANCHE, M. (eds) *Class, Gender and Ethnicity in Australia*, Sydney: Allen and Unwin, pp. 82–97.

KALANTZIS, M. and COPE, B. (1988) 'Why we need multicultural education: A review of the "ethnic disadvantage" debate', *Journal of Intercultural Studies*, 9, pp. 39–57.

KALANTZIS, M. and COPE, B. (1993) 'Histories of pedagogy, cultures of schooling', in COPE, B. and KALANTZIS, M. (eds) *The Powers of Literacy*, London: Falmer Press, pp. 38–62.

KALANTZIS, M., COPE, B. and HUGHES, C. (1984–5) 'Pluralism and social reform: A review of multiculturalism in Australian education', *Thesis Eleven*, 10/11, November–March.

KALANTZIS, M., COPE, B. and NOBLE, G. (1989) *The Economics of Multicultural Education*, Canberra: Office of Multicultural Affairs, Department of the Prime Minister and Cabinet.

KALANTZIS, M., COPE, B., NOBLE, G. and POYNTING, S. (1990) *Cultures of Schooling: Pedagogies for Cultural Difference and Social Access*, London: Falmer Press.

LABOV, W. (1972) *Language in the Inner City: Studies in the Black English Vernacular*, Philadelphia: University of Pennsylvania Press.

LO BIANCO, J. (1987) *National Policy on Language*, Canberra: Commonwealth Department of Education, Australian Government Publishing Service.

LURIA, A. (1976) *Cognitive Development: Its Cultural and Social Foundations*, Cambridge, MA: Harvard University Press.

MAY, S. (1994) *Making Multicultural Education Work*, Clevedon, England: Multilingual Matters.

MAY, S. (1997) 'Just how safe is Australia's multilingual language policy? A reply to Clyne', *Current Issues in Language and Society*, **4**, pp. 144–7.

MAY, S. (1999) *Language, Education and Minority Rights*, London: Longman, forthcoming.

MURRAY, D. (1982) *Learning by Teaching: Selected Articles on Writing and Teaching*, Montclair, NJ: Boynton/Cook.

NATIONAL ADVISORY AND COORDINATING COMMITTEE ON MULTICULTURAL EDUCATION (1987) *Education in and for a Multicultural Society: Issues and Strategies for Policy Making*, Canberra: NACCME.

NEW LONDON GROUP (1996) 'A pedagogy of multiliteracies: Designing social futures', *Harvard Educational Review*, **66**, pp. 60–92.

NEW SOUTH WALES DEPARTMENT OF EDUCATION (1951) *The Education Gazette*, September.

OFFICE OF MULTICULTURAL AFFAIRS (1989) *National Agenda for a Multicultural Australia: Sharing Our Future*, Canberra: Australian Government Publishing Service.

ONG, W. (1983) *Ramus, Method and the Decay of Dialogue*, Cambridge MA: Harvard University Press.

SWAN, W. (1844) *The Grammar School Reader*, Philadelphia: Thomas, Cowperthwait and Co.

VYGOTSKY, L. (1962) *Thought and Language*, Cambridge, MA: MIT Press.

VYGOTSKY, L. (1978) *Mind in Society: The Development of Higher Psychological Processes*, Cambridge, MA: Harvard University Press.

Notes on Contributors

Nazir Carrim is a Lecturer in the Department of Education at the University of the Witwatersrand in Johannesburg, South Africa where he teaches the sociology of education. He has written extensively on racism and antiracism within the South African educational context, and has published in a range of international journals including *Compare*, *Curriculum Studies*, and *International Studies in Sociology of Education*. His current interests include human rights education, 'race', class, gender and sexual orientation in education and social theory in general.

Bruce Carrington is a Senior Lecturer in Education at the University of Newcastle upon Tyne, UK. He has a long-standing interest in issues relating to 'race', ethnicity and education and has published extensively in this area, including *'Race' and the Primary School: Theory into practice* (with Geoffrey Short, NFER/Nelson, 1989); and *Education, Racism and Reform* (with Barry Troyna, Routledge, 1990). In addition to his ongoing empirical work with Geoffrey Short into children's and young people's constructions of national identity, he has recently completed a comparative study of antiracist and multicultural education in Canada and the United Kingdom with Alastair Bonnett.

Bill Cope is a former First Assistant Secretary in the Department of the Prime Minister and Cabinet, and Director of the Office of Multicultural Affairs, in Canberra, Australia. Before that, he was Research Manager and then Director of the Centre for Workplace Communication and Culture in Sydney, Australia, a position to which he returned at the end of 1996. His most recent book, *Productive Diversity* (with Mary Kalantzis, Pluto Press, 1997), examines the organizational imperatives of multiculturalism in the context of global economic integration and local diversity.

Derek Hodson is Professor of Science Education at the Ontario Institute for Studies in Education, Toronto, Canada — an appointment he has held since 1991. Prior to this, he spent six years teaching science education and curriculum studies at the University of Auckland, New Zealand. He has also had eight years experience in pre-service science teacher education at the University of Manchester and ten years experience teaching science in secondary schools in England, Scotland and Wales. He has wide research interests and has published extensively in science education journals. His most recent book is *Teaching and Learning Science: Towards a personalized approach* (Open University Press, 1998).

Mary Kalantzis is Dean of the Faculty of Education, Language and Community Services at Royal Melbourne Institute of Technology, Australia. Formerly, she was Director of the Institute of Interdisciplinary Studies at James Cook University of North Queensland. Until 1997, she was a part time Commissioner of the Human Rights and Equal Opportunity Commission and Chair of the Queensland Ethnic Affairs Ministerial Advisory Committee, whose role is to advise the Queensland Premier on all matters relating to multiculturalism. Her publications include co-authorship of: *Mistaken Identity: Multiculturalism and the demise of nationalism in Australia* (with Stephen Castles, Bill Cope and Michael Morrissey, Pluto Press, 1988/1990/1992); *Minority Languages and Dominant Culture* (with Bill Cope and Diana Slade, Falmer Press, 1989); *Cultures of Schooling: Pedagogies for cultural difference and social access* (with Bill Cope, Greg Noble and Scott Poynting, Falmer Press, 1990); and *The Powers of Literacy* (with Bill Cope, Falmer Press and University of Pittsburgh Press, 1993).

Stephen May is a Lecturer in the Sociology Department, University of Bristol, UK. Prior to this, he was a secondary school teacher in multiethnic schools and, subsequently, a teacher educator in New Zealand. He has written widely on multi-cultural and antiracist education and, more recently, on the wider interconnec-tions between language, education, minority rights, and the organization of modern nation-states. He also has research interests in social theory (particularly, the work of Bourdieu), nationalism and ethnicity, sociolinguistics and language policy, indigenous education, and bilingualism and bilingual education. His recent major publications include *Making Multicultural Education Work* (Multilingual Matters, 1994); *The Shaping of Ethnonational Identities* (edited with Steve Fenton, Macmillan, 1999, forthcoming); and *Language, Education and Minority Rights* (Longman, 1999, forthcoming).

Peter McLaren is Professor at the Graduate School of Education and Information Studies, University of California, Los Angeles. He is a faculty advisor for the Chicano Studies Research Institute, UCLA, an associate of the Paulo Freire Institute, Sao Paulo, and serves on the Board of Directors for the Latino Museum of History, Art, and Culture in downtown Los Angeles. He is the author of numerous books in-cluding *Schooling as a Ritual Performance*, 2nd ed., (Routledge, 1993), *Critical Pedagogy and Predatory Culture* (Routledge, 1995), *Revolutionary Multiculturalism* (Westview Press, 1997), *Life in Schools*, 3rd ed. (Longman, 1997) and *Counternarratives* (with Henry Giroux, Colin Lankshear, and Mike Peters, Routledge, 1997). A leading exponent of critical pedagogy, he lectures worldwide.

Carmen Montecinos is an Associate Professor in the Department of Educational Psychology and Foundations at the University of Northern Iowa. Her research interests include multicultural teacher education in the United States, with particular attention to groups that are under-represented in the profession. She is currently working on an edited book on multicultural education in Latin America.

Kogila Moodley is Professor of Sociology in the Department of Educational Studies and holds the David Lam Chair in Multicultural Education at the University of British Columbia, Canada. Born and raised in the Indian community in Durban, she graduated from the University of Natal with a BA, received her MA from Michigan State University and PhD from the University of British Columbia. Among her academic awards have been fellowships from Deutscher Akademischer Austauschdienst (DAAD) and the Australian National University. Apart from her co-authored books on South Africa, her publications include some fifty articles in books and scholarly journals, as well as *Race Relations and Multicultural Education* (University of British Columbia, 1984), and *Beyond Multicultural Education* (Detselig, 1993). She serves on the Board of the International Sociological Association's Research Committee on Ethnic, Minority and Race Relations, and the editorial board of *Ethnic and Racial Studies*.

Sonia Nieto is Professor of Education in the Cultural Diversity and Curriculum Reform Program, School of Education, University of Massachusetts in Amherst, USA. Before moving to Massachusetts, she taught in the Bronx in the first bilingual school in north eastern USA and was also a college professor in the Puerto Rican Studies Department at Brooklyn College. Her research interests include multicultural and bilingual education, the education of Latinos and the role of parents, curriculum reform, and Puerto Rican children's literature. She has published extensively in these areas and her recent major publications include *The Education of Latinos in Massachusetts* (edited with Ralph Rivera, Gaston Institute, 1994); and *Affirming Diversity*, 2nd. ed., (Longman, 1996). In 1991 she received the Outstanding Accomplishment in Higher Education Award from the Hispanic Caucus of the American Association of Higher Education.

Ali Rattansi is Reader in Sociology and Director of Communications Policy Studies at City University, London. He has written widely on social and cultural theory, issues of racism, ethnicity and identity and the cultural politics of education. His books include *Marx and the Division of Labour* (Macmillan, 1982); *Postmodernism and Society* (edited with Roy Boyne, Macmillan, 1990); *Racism and Antiracism* (edited with Peter Braham and Richard Skellington, Sage, 1992); *'Race', Culture and Difference* (edited with James Donald, Sage, 1992); and *Racism, Modernity, Identity* (edited with Sallie Westwood, Polity Press, 1994).

Geoffrey Short is a Senior Lecturer in Education at the University of Hertfordshire, UK. He has a long-standing interest in multicultural and antiracist education, areas in which he has published widely. In recent years he has turned his attention to the role of the school in combatting anti-Semitism. He has written a number of articles on the development of children's understanding of Jewish culture and identity and has published widely in the area of Holocaust education. In 1996, he was commissioned by the Council of Europe to compile a report on the teaching of the Holocaust in a number of European countries.

Christine Sleeter is a Professor in the Center for Collaborative Education and Professional Studies at California State University, Monterey Bay. Previously, she was a Professor of Teacher Education at the University of Wisconsin-Parkside. She has written widely on multicultural education and teacher education, and she consults nationally and internationally in these areas. Her major publications include *Turning on Learning* (with Carl Grant, Merrill Pub. Co, 1989); *Keepers of the American Dream* (Falmer Press, 1992); *Developing Multicultural Teacher Education Curricula* (edited with Joe Larkin, SUNY Press, 1995); *Multicultural Education and Critical Pedagogy* (edited with Peter McLaren, SUNY Press, 1995); and *Multicultural Education as Social Activism* (SUNY Press, 1996). In 1994 she was awarded the US National Association for Multicultural Education Research Award.

Crain Soudien teaches the sociology of education in the School of Education at the University of Cape Town, Western Cape, South Africa, where he has been lecturing for ten years. He has a PhD in Sociology of Education and Comparative Education from SUNY, Buffalo, USA. His research interests are 'race', class and gender in education and public history, and he has published widely in these areas in international journals such as *Interchange*, *Equity and Excellence*, and *'Race', Ethnicity and Education*.

Rodolfo Torres is Professor of Public Policy and Chicano Studies, California State University, Long Beach, and Visiting Professor of Educational Policy, University of California, Irvine. His research centres on the political economy and policy dimensions of racialized social relations, and the sociological debates around post-Fordism and 'postindustrial' change as they relate to schooling and the hardening of class inequalities. His most recent publications include articles in *Socialist Review*, *New Political Science*, and *Journal of Black Studies*. He has recently edited *The Latino Studies Reader: Culture, economy, and society* (with Antonia Darder, Blackwell, 1998) and *New American Destinies: A reader in contemporary Asian and Latino immigration* (with Darrell Hamamoto, Routledge, 1997).

Index